A-Z BOURNEMOUTH

CONTENTS

REFERENCE

A Road	A35
B Road	B3064
Dual Carriageway	
One-way Street Traffic flow on A Roads is indicated by a heavy line on the driver's left.	→
Large Scale Pages Only	⇒
Restricted Access	
Pedestrianized Road	
Track	
Footpath	
Residential Walkway	
Railway	Level Crossing / Station / Tunnel
Built-up Area	

Local Authority Boundary	
New Forest Boundary	
Postcode Boundary	

Map Continuation	10 — Large Scale Town Centre — 4
Car Park Selected	P
Church or Chapel	†
Fire Station	■
Hospital	H
House Numbers A & B Roads only	83 96
Information Centre	i
National Grid Reference	⁴10
Police Station	▲
Post Office	★
Toilet	▽
With facilities for the Disabled	♿
Educational Establishment	
Hospital or Hospice	
Industrial Building	
Leisure or Recreational Facility	
Place of Interest	
Public Building	
Shopping Centre or Market	
Other Selected Buildings	

SCALE

Map Pages 6-73 1:15,840 4 inches to 1 mile	Map Pages 4-5 1:7,920 8 inches to 1 mile
0 ¼ ½ Mile	0 ⅛ ¼ Mile
0 250 500 750 Metres	0 100 200 300 Metres
6.31 cm to 1 km 10.16 cm to 1 mile	12.63 cm to 1 km 20.32 cm to 1 mile

Geographers' A-Z Map Company Ltd.

Head Office:
Fairfield Road, Borough Green, Sevenoaks, Kent, TN15 8PP
Telephone 01732 781000 (General Enquiries & Trade Sales)

Showrooms:
44 Gray's Inn Road, London, WC1X 8HX
Telephone 020 7440 9500 (Retail Sales)
www.a-zmaps.co.uk

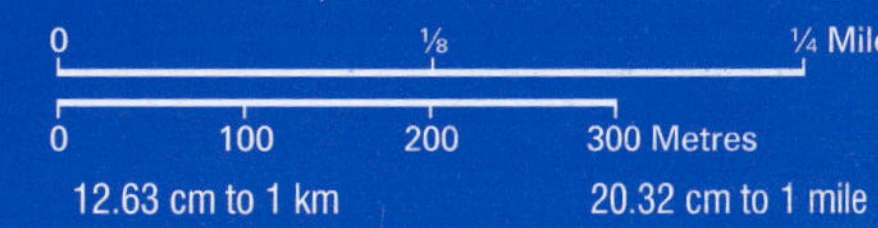

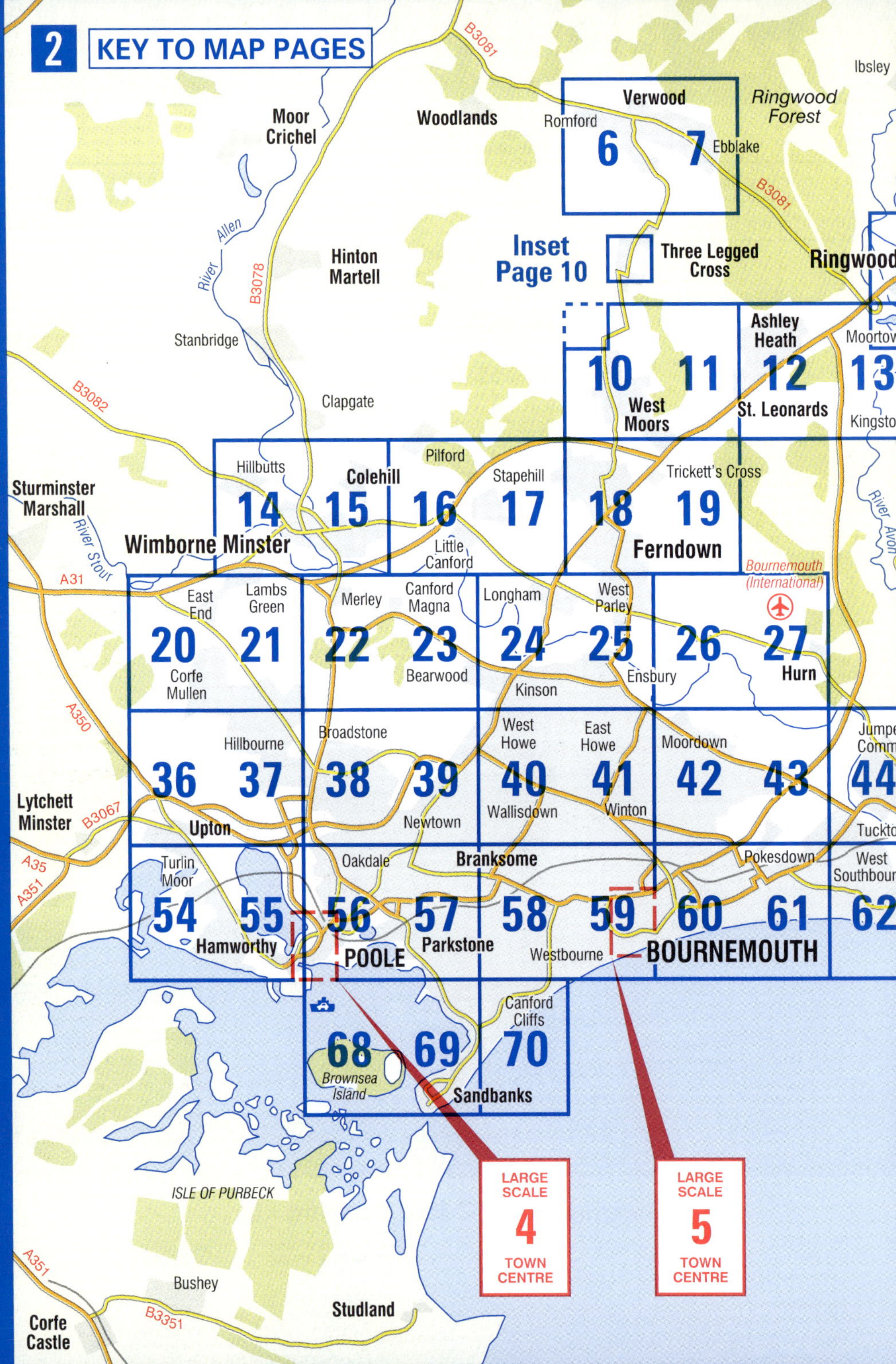

2 KEY TO MAP PAGES
Ibsley
B3081
Moor Crichel
Woodlands
Romford
Verwood
6
7
Ebblake
Ringwood Forest
B3081
River Allen
B3078
Hinton Martell
Inset Page 10
Three Legged Cross
Ringwood
Stanbridge
B3082
Clapgate
10
West Moors
11
Ashley Heath
12
St. Leonards
13
Moortown
Kingston
River Avon
Sturminster Marshall
River Stout
Hillbutts
Colehill
Pilford
Stapehill
Trickett's Cross
14
15
16
17
18
19
Wimborne Minster
Little Canford
Ferndown
Bournemouth (International)
A31
East End
Lambs Green
Merley
Canford Magna
Longham
West Parley
20
21
22
23
24
25
26
27
Corfe Mullen
Bearwood
Kinson
Ensbury
Hurn
A350
Lytchett Minster
B3067
Hillbourne
Broadstone
West Howe
East Howe
Moordown
Jumper Commo
36
37
38
39
40
41
42
43
44
Upton
Newtown
Wallisdown
Winton
Tuckton
A35
A351
Turlin Moor
Oakdale
Branksome
Pokesdown
West Southbourn
54
55
56
57
58
59
60
61
62
Hamworthy
POOLE
Parkstone
Westbourne
BOURNEMOUTH
A351
Canford Cliffs
68
69
70
Brownsea Island
Sandbanks
ISLE OF PURBECK
LARGE SCALE
4
TOWN CENTRE
LARGE SCALE
5
TOWN CENTRE
B3351
Bushey
Studland
Corfe Castle

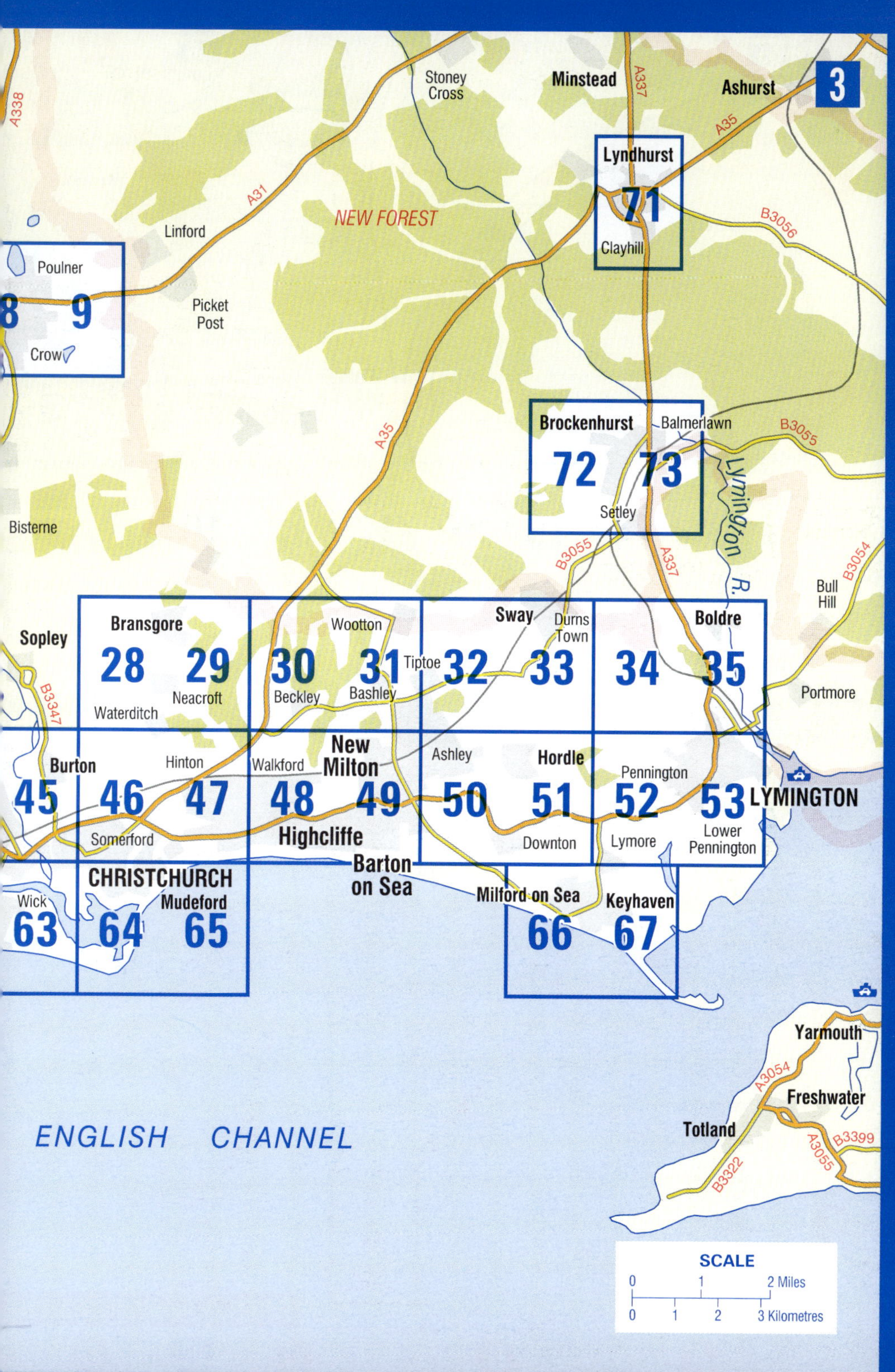

3
A338
Poulner
8
9
Crow
Linford
A31
Picket
Post
Stoney
Cross
NEW FOREST
Minstead
A337
Ashurst
A35
Lyndhurst
71
Clayhill
B3056
Bisterne
A35
Brockenhurst
72
Balmerlawn
73
Setley
B3055
Lymington R.
B3055
A337
B3054
Bull
Hill
Sopley
B3347
Bransgore
28
29
Neacroft
Waterditch
Wootton
30
Beckley
31
Bashley
Tiptoe
Sway
32
Durns
Town
33
Boldre
34
35
Portmore
Burton
45
Hinton
46
Somerford
47
Walkford
New
Milton
48
Highcliffe
49
Ashley
50
Hordle
51
Downton
Pennington
52
Lymore
53
Lower
Pennington
LYMINGTON
Barton
on Sea
Wick
63
CHRISTCHURCH
64
Mudeford
65
Milford on Sea
66
Keyhaven
67
ENGLISH   CHANNEL
Yarmouth
A3054
Freshwater
Totland
B3322
A3055
B3399
SCALE
0   1   2 Miles
0   1   2   3 Kilometres

4
55
A
STERTE CT.
401
PROMENADE
Sterte
STERTE WEST RD.
B
VIEW RD.
STERTE
ESPLANADE RD.
Poole High Sch.
C
Football & Greyhound Stadium
Pav.
56
Longfleet RD.
D
HECKFORD RD.
CANFORD RD.
HECKFORD RD.
SHAFTESBURY RD.
1
HOLES
A350
HOLES BAY
Holes Bay
BAY ROAD
BH15
Works
77
B3093
WIMBORNE
44
DENMARK LANE
ELIZABETH RD.
ADELAIDE RD.
CRANES RD.
DENMARK RD.
43
Centenary Hall
A350
HIGH ST. NTH.
ELLE ABETH RD.
2
BACK WATER CHANNEL
Offices
DENMARK
234
KEEL HO.
Subway
THE GEORGE ROUNDABOUT
PARKSTONE ROAD
TOWNGATE HOUSE
Wks.
091
Mill
Warehouse
POOLE STATION
SERPENTINE RD.
2
VANGUARD RD.
TOWNGATE BRIDGE
243
VOYAGER HOUSE
SELDOWN LANE
Lib. ST.
HIGH STREET
DOLPHIN CENTRE
Arts Centre
Sub.
3
Timber Yard
Depot
Builder's Yard
67
ROAD
59
Hunger Hill
Winchester Pl.
Falkland SQ.
TOWNGATE SHOP. CEN.
Poole Sports Centre
Bus Station
Works
SLIP WAY
QUAY
B3068
STREET
ROAD
NORTH ST.
KINGLAND CRES.
KINGLAND RD.
PITWINES
Supermarket
Bus Depot
56
WHITTLES
BUTTS ST.
WEST
Works
NIGHTINGALE LA.
LANE
CHAPEL LA.
POST OFFICE
HIGH ST.
LAGLAND ST.
Superstore
CLOSE
55
Boatbuilding Yard
MARSTON RD.
TWY. Works
MALTHOUSE
HAY
GLOBE LA.
THE BROMBYS
NEWFOUNDLAND
CLOSE
BRIDGE
Quay West Marina
Westover Ho.
BALSTON TER.
68
25
Mkt.
CLOSE
MARKET
Old Town M.
STREET
Ballards PAS.
EMERSON CL.
PITWINES
EMERSON RD.
NIDDLETON
West Quay
Works
Patrick Ho.
A350
25
NEW
Buffalo Mews
DEAR HILL
Old Town
South Rd Combined Sch.
GREEN ROAD
Newfoundland Drive RBT.
4
WILKINS WY.
WEST QUAY RD.
Sunseeker Ho.
A'BYNS GUILDHALL CT.
Hall
CARTER'S H. LA.
WESTONS LA.
Nelson CT.
Club
EMERSON
WHATLEIGH
GREEN CL.
Play. Grd.
Waterloo Wharf
BAY HOG LANE
LEVEL'S
Guildhall Mus.
BOWLING GRN ALLEY
OLD ORCHARD
Grenville CT.
SOUTH ROAD
Rodney CT.
GRACE DARLING HO.
VALLIS CL.
GREEN GS.
LANDER CT.
Boat Yard
POPLAR CL.
MARKET ST.
NEW ST.
PROSPEROUS ST.
EAST STREET
Lagland CT.
S. PERRY QUAY
Playgrd.
VALLIS RD.
DEE WAY
BARBERS PILES
JAMES ST.
ST. JAMES CL.
ST. GEORGE'S ALMHOUSES
CASTLE ST.
Old Orchard
SKINNER ST.
Daniel GDS.
Playgrd.
PERRY GARDENS
BAITER
STANLEY ROAD
BALLARD ROAD
GREEN GS.
LABRADOR DR.
5
WEST ST.
WEST ST.
THAMES STREET
CHURCH
THAMES MALL
CINNAMON
NEW STREET
Mus.
OLD ORCHARD SHOP. CEN.
THE SEED WAREHOUSE
DRAKE CT.
Drake R.
TAYLOR'S BLDGS.
Gray's Yard
EAST QUAY
FISHERMANS RD.
EAST QUAY
BALLARD ROAD
GREEN GS.
Barbers Gate
SARUM ST.
GRAND PARADE
THE STRAND
BALL LA.
BENT'S ALL.
CASTLE ST.
QUAY POINT
Poole Pottery
Fishermans Quay
Old Lifeboat House
Bridge Ho. Lifeboat Ho.
Barbers Wharf
ST. CLEMENTS LA.
Yeatmans Mus.
Old Mill
PARADISE ST.
HOSER LA.
KEY LA.
CANUTE HO.
Q U A
Aquarium
THE KIOSKS
THE QUAY
Breakwater
LITTLE CHANNEL
Boat Building Yard
Depot
FERRY ROAD
Ballast Quay
The Bulwarks
Brownsea Island Ferry (Foot) May-Sept.
Wareham Ferry (Foot)
6
NEW QUAY ROAD
Ship Building & Repair Yard
The Bulwarks
NEW HARBOUR ROAD
LUCAS RD.
Depots
090
Freightliner Terminal
PORT OF POOLE
A
Customs Sheds
401
New Quay
B
POOLE TOWN CENTRE
C
68
D
Ferry Passenger Terminal

408
409
092
091
E
F
59
G
H
5
BOURNEMOUTH TOWN CENTRE
MEYRICK PARK GOLF COURSE
Cricket Ground
Pav.
1
Club House
Pavilion
Leighton Lodge
Nursing Home
Meyrick Park Lodge
Meyrick Park Mansions
PARKVIEW
Bowl. Grn.
Pav.
Ten. Cts.
Bowl. Grn.
Putting Grn.
BRADLEY RD.
CENTRAL DRIVE
CENTRAL DRIVE
BRAIDLEY ROAD
WYCHWOOD DR.
WYCHWOOD CL.
WYCHWOOD GRANGE
MERLEWOOD CL.
SILCHESTER CL.
ST. VALERIE RD.
CAVENDISH ROAD
Copper Beeches
THE DEANS
DEAN PARK RD.
BOURNE PINES
PORTLAND PL.
FAIRTHORN CT.
ROAD
BODORGAN ROAD
BRAIDLEY ROAD
WIMBORNE A347 ROAD
DEAN PARK
ROAD
Horseshoe Court
Horseshoe Common
2
WESSEX A338 WAY
WESSEX A338 WAY
The Bourne
BRANKSOME WOOD RD.
Subs.
Sub.
Horseshoe Common
DEAN PARK CRES.
Horseshoe Common Roundabout
MADEIRA ROAD
OLD CHRISTCHURCH ROAD
Council Offices
War Mem. Vic.
Hall
ST. STEPHEN'S
DURRANT RD.
ST. STEPHEN'S CT.
TRYSTWORTHY
AMIRA CT.
SUNBURY CT.
BRAMPTON CT.
Town Hall
Churchill Hall
Offices
Subs.
RICHMOND GDNS.
FERNHILL FLATS
FERN BANK
RICHMOND HILL DR.
MOUNT HEATHERBANK
RICHMOND HOUSE
EITH
RICHMOND GDNS.
VENLAM PL.
GRANVILLE PL.
DALKEITH LA.
DALKEITH STEPS
BURLINGTON ARCADE
CHRISTCHURCH
OLD CHRIST. CHURCH LA.
FIR VALE RD.
3
GLEN FERN RD.
ST. PETER'S COURT
ST. PETER'S CRES.
ALEXANDRA LODGE
PARSONAGE RD.
BH2
BH1
MAJORCA MANSIONS
SUFFOLK RD.
CRESCENT ROAD
BRADBURNE ROAD
BOURNE AVENUE
Central Gardens
War Meml.
Hampshire Ct.
Hampshire Ho.
Bourne Ct.
ALBERT ROAD
YELVERTON ROAD
RICHMOND HILL
LODGE RD.
OLD CHRISTCHURCH RD.
Quadrant Arcade Shop. Cen.
ST. PETER'S ROAD
ELLERSLIE CHAMBERS
4
BATH HILL COURT
59
NORWICH
SPICER CT.
NORWICH CT.
ANGLIA CT.
PARK GATE M.
NORWICH RD.
THE AVENUE
AVENUE LA.
THE TRIANGLE
BRANKSOME BUILDINGS
COMMERCIAL ROAD
ORCHARD WALK
ORCHARD ST.
THE AVENUE SHOPPING CENTRE
COMMERCIAL ROAD
THE SQUARE
Sub.
EDMONDSHAM HOUSE
H.P.O.
Post Office
CRITERION ARCADE
THE ARCADE
ST. PETER'S WLK.
CHRISTCHURCH ROAD
GERVIS
EXETER RD.
60
UPPER HINTON
WESTOVER ROAD
ST. PAUL'S ROAD
BH1
POOLE HILL
COMMERCIAL ROAD
POOLE HILL PL.
ST. MICHAEL'S PL.
MANGINS PL.
ST. MICHAEL'S
PURBECK
TREGONWELL
TERRACE ROAD
ORCHARD ROAD
UPPER TERRACE RD.
Vistarama
Lower Gardens
THE EXETER
The Bourne
Cinemas
5
Y.M.C.A.
Bandstand
Bath Hill Rdbt.
Lower Gardens
WEST CLIFF COTTS.
SOUTH VW.
MICLS. PL.
ST. MICHAEL'S LANE
BEECHWOOD CT.
CARLTON MT.
KNIGHTSBRIDGE CT.
CRANBORNE ROAD
EXETER ROAD
EXETER CRESCENT
SANDRINGHAM COURT
EXETER GRANGE
EXETER PARK ROAD
CAPELLA CT.
STAUNTON
EXETER PK. MANSIONS
The Pavilion
IMAX Cinema
EAST CLIFF
PROMENADE
HAHNEMANN ROAD
HAHNEMANN RD.
West Cliff Mews
ARNEWOOD CT.
TOLLARD CT.
AVON HO.
TOWER CT.
FAIR LEA
The Winter Gardens
Bournemouth International Centre
Bournemouth International Cen. Rdbt.
B3066
WEST CLIFF RD.
PRIORY ROAD
EXETER ROAD
BATH ROAD
B3066
KERLEY RD.
BEACON ROAD
SOUTH CLIFF RD.
Oceanarium
Pier Approach
UNDERCLIFF
DURLEY RD. S.
DURLEY
WEST CLIFF GARDENS
West Cliff
West Cliff
WEST CLIFF PROMENADE
WEST CLIFF ZIG-ZAG
WEST CLIFF LIFT
Beacon Steps
PROMENADE
UNDERCLIFF
6
POOLE BAY
Bournemouth Pier
Pier Theatre
Landing Stage
E
F
59
G
H
408
409

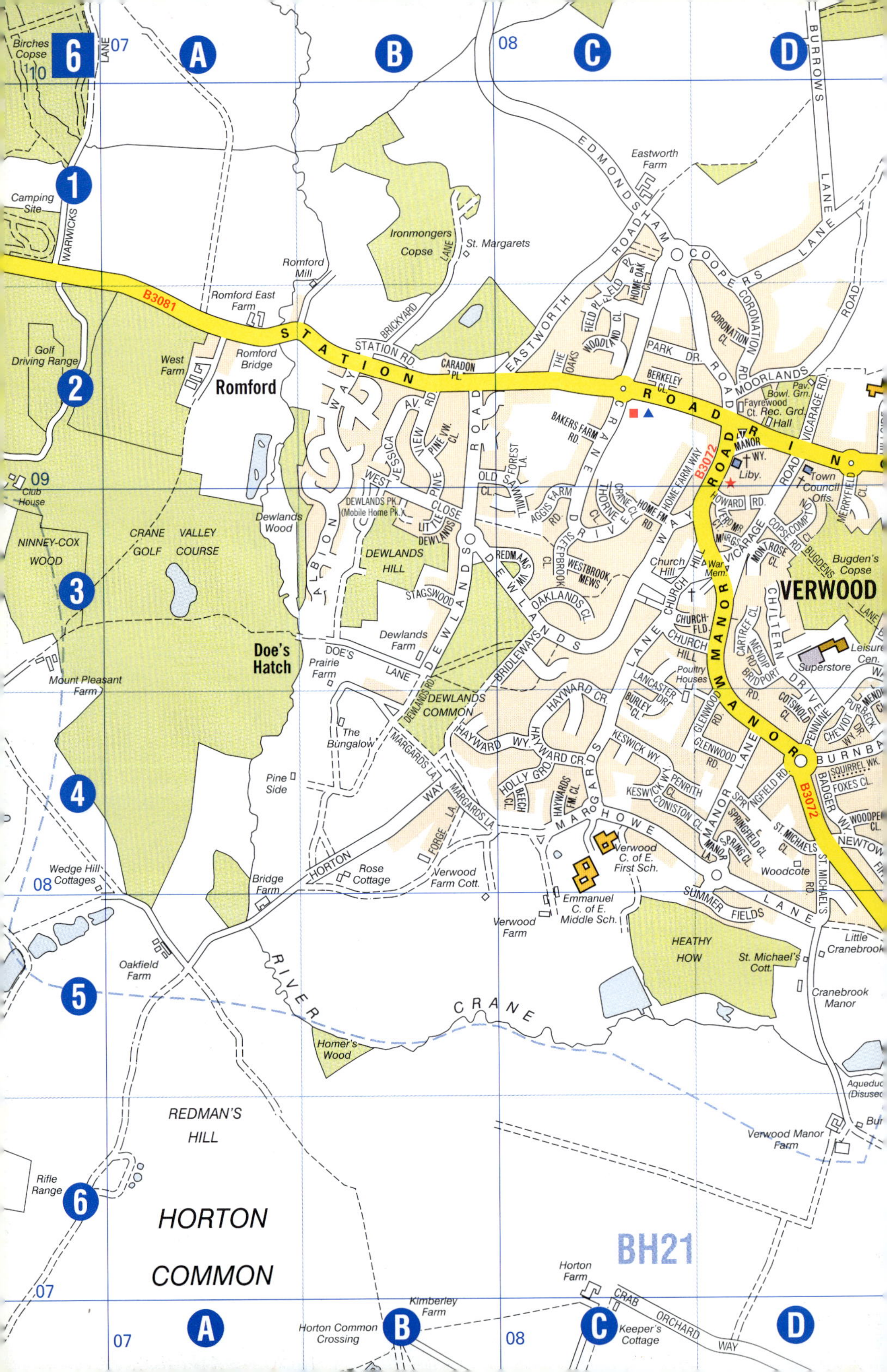

Birches Copse
LANE 07
110
A
B
08
C
D
BURROWS LANE
6
Camping Site
1
WARWICKS
EDMONDSHAM ROAD
Eastworth Farm
COOPERS
Romford Mill
Ironmongers Copse
St. Margarets
LANE
B3081
STATION
Romford East Farm
BRICKYARD
CARADON PL.
STATION RD.
EASTWORTH
THE OAKS
HOME OAK
WOODLAND CL.
FIELD PLACE FIELD
PARK DR.
CORONATION RD.
CL.
CORONATION
MOORLANDS
VICARAGE RD.
Golf Driving Range
West Farm
Romford Bridge
2
Romford
BERKELEY
ROAD
Pav. Grn.
Bowl. Grn.
Fayrewood Ct. Rec. Grd.
Hall
WAY
STATION RD.
AV.
ROAD
CRANE
BAKERS FARM RD.
HOME FM.
HOME FARM WAY
R
B3072
MANOR
WY.
Liby.
Town Council Offs.
MERRYFIELD
PINE VW. CL.
WEST VIEW RD.
JESSICA
PINE
OLD SAWMILL
S. FOREST LA.
AGGIS FARM RD.
THORNE CL.
CRANE CL.
HOWARD RD.
VERD MR.
VICARAGE RD.
MON. ROSE CL.
COPSE RD.
BUGDENS CL.
NO. COMP. CL.
09
Club House
Dewlands Wood
CLOSE
LITTLE DEWLANDS
CL.
REDMANS VW.
STEEPBROOK
DRIVE
Church Hill
CHURCH HILL
HOME
MNR. GDS.
MNR.
NR.
Bugden's Copse
NINNEY-COX WOOD
CRANE VALLEY GOLF COURSE
DEWLANDS PK. (Mobile Home Pk.)
DEWLANDS HILL
ALBION
STAGSWOOD
DEWLANDS
DEWLANDS VW.
OAKLANDS CL.
Westbrook Mews
War Mem.
CHURCH HILL
VERWOOD
LANE
LEISURE CEN.
Superstore
3
DOE'S LANE
Dewlands Farm
Doe's Hatch
DOE'S LANE
Prairie Farm
BRIDLEWAYS
CHURCH-FLD.
CHURCH HILL
Poultry Houses
CARTREF CL.
MENDIP
BRIDPORT
COTSWOLD CL.
PENNINE
PURBECK
CHEVIOT WY. DR.
WY.
BURNBA
Mount Pleasant Farm
The Bungalow
DEWLANDS COMMON
HAYWARD CR.
HAYWARD WY.
HAYWARD CR.
KESWICK WY.
LANCASTER DR.
BURLEY CL.
GLENWOOD RD.
GLENWOOD LANE
MANOR
SPRINGFIELD RD.
B3072
SQUIRREL WK.
BADGER
FOXES CL.
WOODPE CL.
Woodcote
Little Cranebrook
4
Pine Side
MARGARDS LA.
WAY
MARGARDS LA.
FORGE LA.
HOLLY GRO.
BEECH CL.
HAYWARDS FM. CL.
KESWICK WY.
PENRITH CL.
CONISTON CL.
SPRINGFIELD CL.
SPRING CL.
ST. MICHAELS CL.
NEWTOWN
Wedge Hill Cottages
08
Bridge Farm
HORTON
Rose Cottage
Verwood Farm Cott.
MARGARDS
HOWE LA.
MANOR LA.
Verwood C. of E. First Sch.
SUMMER FIELDS
LANE
ST. MICHAEL'S RD.
Cranebrook Manor
Oakfield Farm
RIVER
Verwood Farm
Emmanuel C. of E. Middle Sch.
HEATHY HOW
St. Michael's Cott.
5
Homer's Wood
CRANE
Aqueduct (Disused)
REDMAN'S HILL
Verwood Manor Farm
Bur
Rifle Range
6
HORTON
COMMON
BH21
Horton Farm
07
A
07
Kimberley Farm
B
08
CRAB ORCHARD WAY
C
Keeper's Cottage
D
Horton Common Crossing

09
E
F
MOUNT ARARAT
4 10
G
H
Fire Tower 11
7
10
1
BOVERIDGE
HEATH
Bailey's Plantation
Stephen's Castle
2
WILD CHURCH
BOTTOM
HAMPSHIRE
DORSET
Hillside First School
Forest Lodge
Moorside Cottage
09
ROAD
SCHOOL
ST. STEPHEN'S LANE
STARLIGHT WY.
STRATHMORE DRIVE
SHERWOOD DR.
NOON GDS.
NOON HILL DR.
NOON HILL RD.
Noon Cott.
NOON HILL
EAST DORSET
NEW FOREST
3
BH31
NEWTOWN
HEATHLANDS CL.
CRESCENT RD.
SHARD CL.
WOOD HILL
RAYMOND CL.
FOXHILLS HILL
Noon Hill Farm
WOOD
ACORN WAY
OAKS MEAD
SHIRES MEADOW
Hainault Farm
VERWOOD IND. EST.
B3081
Depot
HAINAULT DR.
HAINAULT DR.
ROAD
BLACK HILL
Black Hill Works
Works
ASPEN
SOUTHERNHAY
RD.
THE
ENS LA
SANDY LANE
NEWTON
ROAD
Works
LANE
ROAD
CHASE
HUNTERS CL.
OWLS
THE LEA
MEADOW GRO.
LOMBARDY CL.
DRIVE
LAVENDER CL.
THE FORESTSIDE
4
VERNE RD.
STANLEY CL.
PADDOCK GRO.
ORCHARD ORCH.
PINE WK.
FAIRWOOD
BARBERRY WY.
BELMONT
THE GROVE
THE KINGFISHERS
ROAD
MEADOW
CT.
BLUE-BERRY DR.
LABURNUM CL.
MAGNOLIA CL.
ROSBY CL.
Playing Field
RINGWOOD
BITTERNE WY.
SW.
NIGHTINGALE CL.
CLAYLAKE DR.
BLACKTHORN WY.
WHITEBEAM WY.
MONEYFLY
AVENUE RD.
BLACK MOOR
FOREST
08
THOMAS LOCKYER CL.
OTTER
THE CURLEW
OWLS
MEADOW
WOODLINKEN
Enterprise Park
Ebblake
HILLMEADOW
LANE
ROAD
DRIVE
WOODLINKEN WY.
ACACIA CL.
WISTERIA DR.
ROAD
THE FORELLE CEN.
RINGWOOD
N RD.
LAKE
MONMOUTH RD.
BURN CL.
INTGOOM
CLOSE
Cemetery
Parkland CL.
Ebblake Bridge
5
ROAD
Potterne Hill
BINGHAM DR.
BINGHAM CL.
MONMOUTH CL.
BROOK
ROWAN DR.
THE
BRUNEL CL.
BLACK MOOR
ROAD
EBBLAKE INDUSTRIAL ESTATE
Ebblake Ho.
B3081
Oakleigh
HAZELWOOD DRIVE
RIVER
Industrial Estate
BESSEMER CL.
Ebblake Stream
ROAD
POTTERNE
Potterne Park Poultry House
Playing Field
POTTERNE
Potterne Farm
CRANE
POTTERNE WOOD
6
Potterne Poultry Farm
WAY
Poultry Houses
Poultry Houses
Rock Vale
B3072
VERWOOD
English Farm
MOORS VALLEY
COUNTRY PARK
RINGWOOD FOREST
ster's Wood
Cottage Farm
E
F
4 10
G
H
11
07

8 14
07
Withybed Copse
A
Meadow Lake
Vincent's Lake
B
Ford Cottage
415
Runnymede Lake
C
LANE
SNAIL'S LANE
WOOLMER LANE
D
Linbr
North
BLASHFORD
A338
ROAD
Woolmer Farm
Sand & Gravel Works
Dockens Water
Upper Hurst Farm
HEADLANDS BUSINESS PARK
Headlands Adventure Centre
Hurst Pond
Boat House
Kingfisher Lodge
Wash Pit
WATER SIDE
NORTH
NORTH POULNER RD.
SEYMOUR
MORANT RD.
FAIRLIE
KINGFISHER
RIVER AVON
1
Lifeland Copse
Gouldings Farm
Kingfisher Lake
WANSTEAD CL.
2
UP MEAD
Hurst Old Farm
HURST
SALISBURY RD.
Linbrook Court
NORTHFIELD LA.
HIGHFIELD
BROADSHARD
HAMPTON DR.
MEADOW
MEADOW WY.
RD.
LUMBY DR. CARAVAN PK.
CAVENDISH
06
LIN Brook
SALISBURY RD.
SML. WT.
FARM CL.
HIGHFIELD AV.
BROADSHARD CL.
MEADOW CL.
RD.
MEADOW RD.
CORNER MOBILE H PK.
HAMPSHIRE DORSET
3
A338
GRAVEL LA.
POUND CL.
REGENCY PLACE
HIGHFIELD AV.
HIGHFIELD DR.
MIDDLETON RD.
GEORGIAN CT.
Avonlea Prep. Sch.
OAK LA.
BEECHCROFT
GIPSY LA.
FIELDWAY
SALISBURY TGR.
MANOR CT.
Sub.
POUND ORCHARD
KESTREL COURT
LILAC CL.
WINSTON
WESSEX RD.
A31
MANOR GS.
HAMPTON RD.
PARSONAGE
BISHOPS
MANOR RD.
QUEENS
WAY
KEPPEL CL.
SPITTLEFIELD
4
A31
Little Gs.
MANSFIELD ROAD
LINDEN CT.
LINDEN GS.
THE SWEEP
HAMPTON PL.
TRAM.
Play Area
Pav.
Bowl Grn.
Ten. Cts.
Pav.
Mt. PLEASANT
Ringwood School
GREEN LA.
BISHOPS CT.
CADOGAN RD.
Hall
STALLARDS LA.
THE FURLONG
FURLONG
THE FURLONG SHOPPING CEN.
P
Elmsdown
Sports Ground
Playing Field
Ringwood Rec. Cen.
MANOR RD.
CLOUGH'S LA.
REDWOOD CL.
POPLAR CRES.
WESTBURY
Offs.
STAR LA.
CENTRE PL.
MEETING HO.
MON-MOUTH CT.
CARVERS IND. EST.
CARVERS LA.
Playing Field
EAST VIEW
POPLAR
HILTOM
PINE TREES RD.
Daniel's Ct.
MARKET
SHOP. CEN.
NORTHBRLD LA.
PEDLR'S WK.
SOUTHAMPTON RD.
COLLINS LA.
KINGSFIELD RD.
GUY'S CL.
ADDISON
WESTBURY CL.
DICKSON HIGH
The Silver Jubilee Gs.
STREET
STRIDES LA.
New Ct.
Indly
WHITE LION COURTYARD
LYNE'S LA.
HIGH ST.
CHRISTCHURCH RD.
MIDDLE LA.
SCHOOL LA.
TOP LA.
Ringwood C. of E. Inf. Sch.
CLARKS CL.
COLLEGE
Cemetery
Ringwood County Jun. Sch.
Pav.
JOYCE TOWN
DICKSON GDS.
CONISTON CL.
GARDINER CL.
WEST
THE BRIDGES
STUBBINGS MEADOW (CARAVAN PK.)
LOEWEY'S LA.
KING'S ARMS LA.
KINGSBURY'S LA.
Friday Cross
KINGS ARMS RW
GOOSEBERRY LA.
EBENEZER LA.
Comm. Cen.
W. BARROWS LA.
Nursery
QUOMP
HIGHTOWN
Ringwood Trad. Est.
Victoria Gds.
EUSTON GR.
WATERLOO CL.
CHARING CL.
HIGHTOWN
RD.
BROOKS CL.
HIGHTOWN TRADING EST.
Ashley Cottages
05
A31
Avon Dairy
BICKERLEY TER.
BICKERLEY
Bickerley Grn.
Lib.
ENYON RD.
Quaker Ct.
WOODSTOCK RD.
Androse Gds.
CASTLEMAN
Victoria
WATERLOO WY.
EMBANKMENT WAY
PULLMAN WAY
ARCH
Endeavour Park
OVERWOOD ROAD
LANE
King Stream
OLD MILL FLATS
RIVERSIDE
Bickerley Common
Mill Stream
COW STONE LA.
DUCK ISLAND LA.
SOUTHFIELD
NEW ST.
Ringwood Trad. Est.
CROW ARCH LA. INDUSTRIAL ESTATE
The H
5
HURN RD.
WESTOVER
Westover Farm
NEW FOREST EAST DORSET
Hall
SOUTHFIELD MS.
PARKSIDE
Millstream
Depot
13
WARREN CL.
WARREN LA.
LANE
Decoy Pond
MILLSTREAM TRADING ESTATE
STAG BUSINESS PARK
Peewitts
WILLOW DR.
B3347
Moortown
MOORLAND GATE
Moortown House
6
CHASE
WARREN DR.
CLOSE
Wind Pump
04
14
A
13
B
Golf Range
Millstream
SHIRES CL.
MEADOW-LANDS
415
C
MOORTOWN RD.
LONG LA.
D

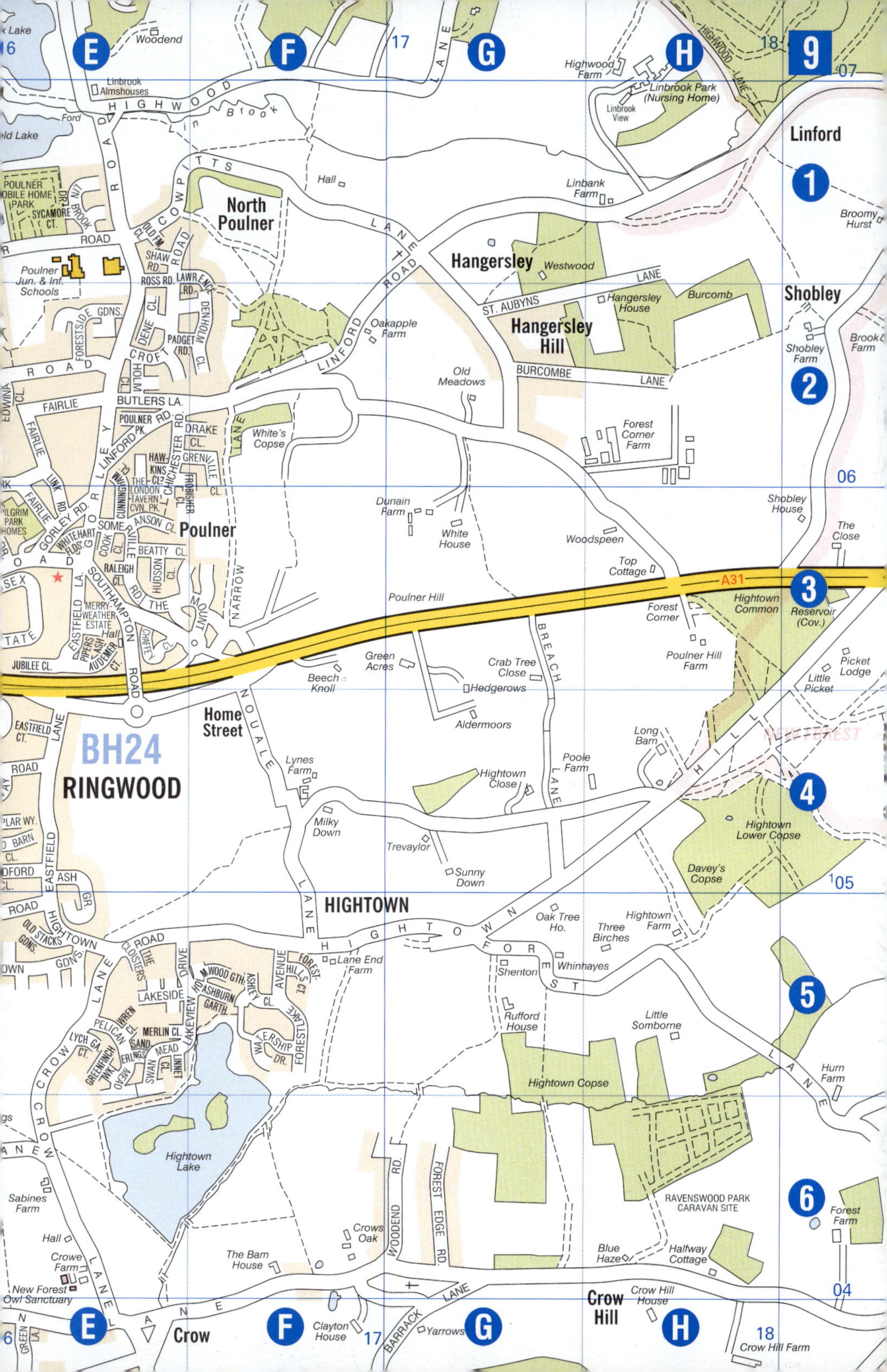
E
F
17
G
H
18
9
07
Woodend
Highwood Farm
Linbrook Park (Nursing Home)
Linbrook View
Linford
Linbrook Almshouses
HIGHWOOD ROAD
Lin Brook
COWPITTS
Ford
Old Lake
Broomy Hurst
POULNER MOBILE HOME PARK
SYCAMORE CT.
Hall
Linbank Farm
Shobley
1
NORTH POULNER
NIT BROOK
OLD FM CL.
SHAW RD.
ROSS RD.
LAWRENCE RD.
DENHOLM CL.
Hangersley
Westwood
LANE
Shobley Farm
Brook Farm
2
Poulner Jun. & Inf. Schools
FORESTSIDE GDNS.
DENE CL.
CROFT HOLM
PADGET RD.
LINFORD ROAD
Oakapple Farm
Hangersley House
ST. AUBYNS
Hangersley Hill
Burcomb
LANE
06
EDWINA CL.
FAIRLIE
FAIRLIE
BUTLERS LA.
POULNER RD.
POULNER PK.
DRAKE CL.
HAWKINS CL.
GRENVILLE CL.
FROBISHER CL.
White's Copse
BURCOMBE
LANE
FAIRLIE LINK
LINFORD RD.
GORLEY RD.
CUNNINGHAM
THE LONDON TAVERN CVN. PK.
CHICHESTER RD.
Old Meadows
Forest Corner Farm
Shobley House
PILGRIM PARK HOMES
WHITEHART FLDS.
COOK CL.
SOMERVILLE CL.
ANSON CL.
Poulner
Dunain Farm
Woodspeen
The Close
ESSEX
MERRYWEATHER ESTATE
EASTFIELD LA.
PIPERS ASH
BEATTY CL.
HUDSON CL.
RALEIGH CL.
White House
Top Cottage
A31
3
Reservoir (Cov.)
JUBILEE CL.
AUDEMER CT.
CHAFFEY CL.
SOUTHAMPTON ROAD
THE MOUNT
NARROW
Poulner Hill
Forest Corner
Hightown Common
Poulner Hill Farm
Picket Lodge
Little Picket
EASTFIELD CT.
Green Acres
BREACH LANE
Beech Knoll
Hedgerows
Crab Tree Close
Long Barn
NEW FOREST
EASTFIELD ROAD
NOUALE LANE
Home Street
Aldermoors
Poole Farm
4
BH24 RINGWOOD
Lynes Farm
Hightown Close
Hightown Lower Copse
POPLAR WY.
BARN CL.
BEDFORD CL.
ASH GR.
HIGHTOWN GDNS.
Milky Down
Trevaylor
Davey's Copse
05
OLD STACKS GDNS.
THE CLOISTERS
ROAD
HOLMWOOD GTH.
ASHBURN GARTH
AVENUE
FOREST HILLS CT.
Sunny Down
HIGHTOWN
Oak Tree Ho.
Three Birches
Hightown Farm
5
LAKESIDE
WREN CL.
MERLIN CL.
LAKEVIEW DRIVE
ASHLEY CL.
FORESTLAKE AVENUE
HIGHTOWN
FOREST
Lane End Farm
Shenton
Whinhayes
PELICAN
GREENFINCH
SAND.
SWAN MEAD
LINNET CL.
WATERSHIP DR.
Rufford House
Little Somborne
Hurn Farm
LYCH GA. CT.
MERLINGS
Hightown Copse
CROW LANE
CROW
Hightown Lake
RAVENSWOOD PARK CARAVAN SITE
6
Forest Farm
Sabines Farm
Crows Oak
WOODEND RD.
FOREST EDGE RD.
Blue Haze
Halfway Cottage
Hall
Crowe Farm
The Barn House
New Forest Owl Sanctuary
GREEN LA.
CROW LANE
Crow
Clayton House
17
BARRACK LANE
Yarrows
Crow Hill House
Crow Hill
Crow Hill Farm
E
F
G
H
18
04

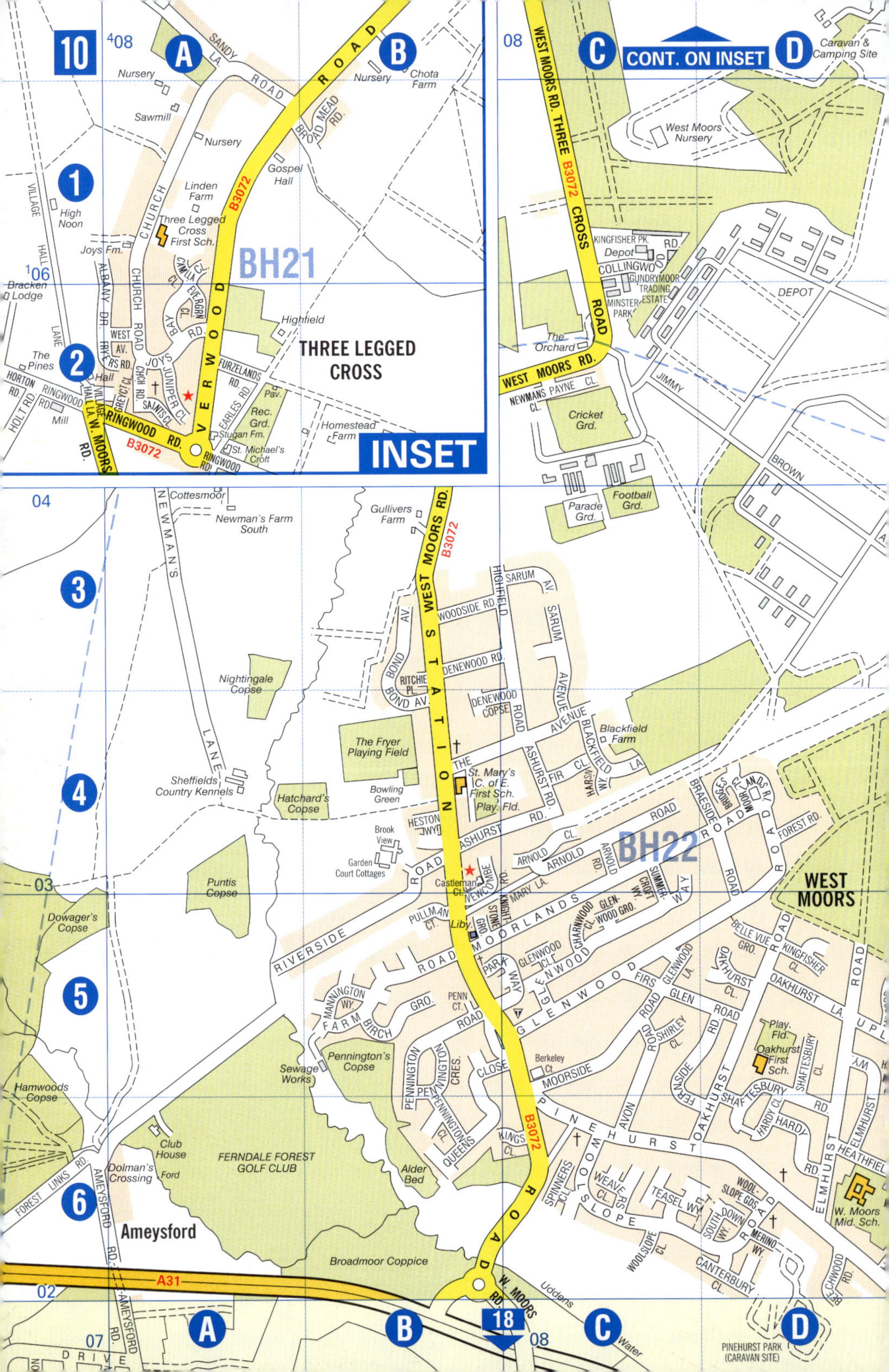

10
408
A
SANDY LA.
B
08
WEST MOORS RD. THREE
C
CONT. ON INSET
D
Caravan & Camping Site
Nursery
BROAD MEAD RD.
Nursery
Chota Farm
West Moors Nursery
Sawmill
ROAD
Nursery
ROAD
B3072
CROSS
Linden Farm
Gospel Hall
Kingfisher Pk.
RD.
1
High Noon
Three Legged Cross First Sch.
BH21
Depot
COLLINGWOOD
GUNDRYMOOR TRADING ESTATE
DEPOT
Joys Fm.
MINSTER PARK
106
Bracken Lodge
CHURCH ROAD
VERWOOD
Highfield
The Orchard
ROAD
The Pines
2
WEST AV.
FRYERS RD.
CAMILLA CL.
EVERGREEN CL.
BAY RD.
JUNIPER CL.
Highfield
THREE LEGGED CROSS
WEST MOORS RD.
JIMMY
HORTON RD.
RINGWOOD RD.
HOLT RD.
Hall
JOYS
FURZELANDS RD.
EARLES RD.
NEWMANS
PAYNE CL.
Cricket Grd.
Mill
SAINTS CL.
CHCH RD.
GREYS CL.
VILLAGE HALL LA. W. MOORS
RINGWOOD RD.
B3072
Pav.
Rec. Grd.
Homestead Farm
INSET
BROWN
RD.
Stugan Fm.
St. Michael's Croft
RINGWOOD RD.
Parade Grd.
Football Grd.
04
Cottesmoor
Gullivers Farm
WEST MOORS RD.
Newman's Farm South
B3072
SARUM AV.
3
NEWMANS
HIGHFIELD
WOODSIDE RD.
SARUM
LANE
Nightingale Copse
BOND AV.
DENEWOOD RD.
AVENUE
Blackfield Farm
RITCHIE PL.
BOND AV.
DENEWOOD COPSE
AVENUE
ASHURST RD.
BLACKFIELD
Blackfield LA.
HASS WY.
The Fryer Playing Field
STATION
ROAD
FIR CL.
4
Sheffields Country Kennels
Hatchard's Copse
Bowling Green
St. Mary's C. of E. First Sch. Play. Fld.
BRAESIDE RD.
HOOM CL.
FOREST RD.
BH22
Brook View
HESTON WYD.
ARNOLD
ARNOLD CL.
ROAD
Puntis Copse
Garden Court Cottages
ASHURST
ARNOLD RD.
SUMMER CROFT WY.
WAY
WEST MOORS
03
Dowager's Copse
Castleman Ct.
NEWCOMBE
MARY LA.
GLENWOOD CL.
CHARNWOOD CL.
GLENWOOD GRO.
ROAD
BELLE VUE GRO.
KINGFISHER CL.
ROAD
Liby.
MOORLANDS
5
RIVERSIDE
PULLMAN CT.
STONE
KNIGHT
GLENWOOD
OAKHURST CL.
OAKHURST LA.
UPL
MANNINGTON WY.
ROAD
PARK WAY
GLENWOOD FIRS
GLEN LA.
Play. Fld.
BIRCH GRO.
PENN CT.
ROAD
GLENWOOD RD.
SHIRLEY CL.
FERNSIDE RD.
Oakhurst First Sch.
SHAFTESBURY CL.
FARM
Pennington's Copse
ROAD
GLEN RD.
HEATHFIEL
Hamwoods Copse
Sewage Works
PENNINGTON GRO.
Berkeley Ct
MOORSIDE
AVON
HARDY CL.
HARDY RD.
WOOL- SLOPE GDNS.
ELMHURST
Club House
PENNINGTON CRES.
CLOSE
SHAFTESBURY RD.
WOOL- SLOPE RD.
Dolman's Crossing
Ford
PENNINGTONS CL.
QUEENS
KINGS CL.
SPINNERS CL.
WEAVERS CL.
TEASEL WY.
MERINO WY.
W. Moors Mid. Sch.
6
FOREST LINKS RD.
FERNDALE FOREST GOLF CLUB
Alder Bed
B3072
WOOLSLOPE
SOUTH DOWN WY.
WOOLSLOPE CL.
CANTERBURY CL.
Ameysford
AMEYSFORD RD.
Broadmoor Coppice
ROAD
PINEHURST
SPINNERS CL.
A31
02
07
DRIVE
A
AMEYSFORD RD.
B
W. MOORS RD.
18
W. MOORS RD.
Uddens
C
Water
D
PINEHURST PARK (CARAVAN SITE)
08

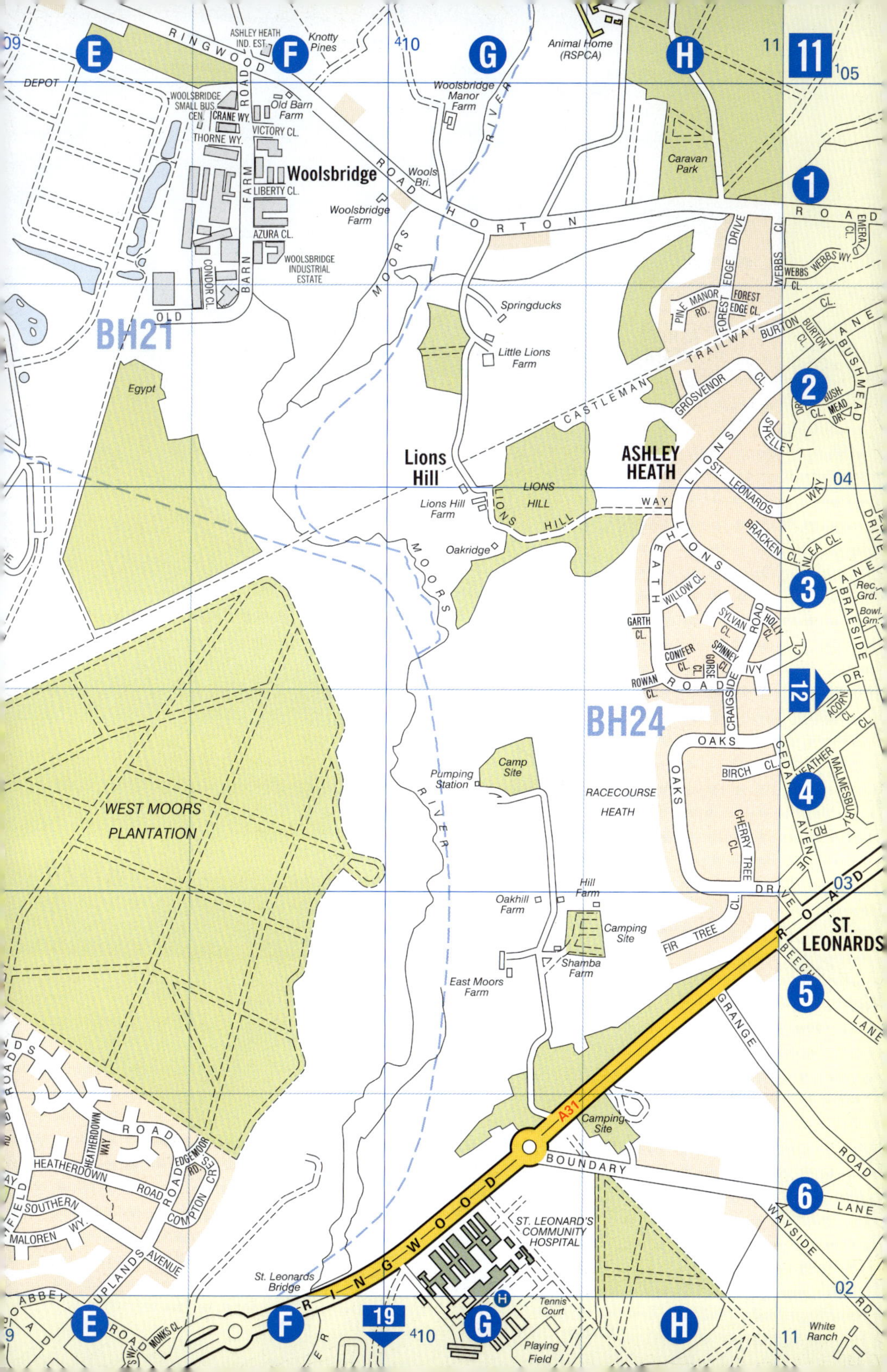

E
RINGWOOD
ASHLEY HEATH IND. EST.
F
Knotty Pines
410
G
Animal Home (RSPCA)
H
11
11
105
DEPOT
09
WOOLSBRIDGE SMALL BUS. CEN.
CRANE WY.
Old Barn Farm
Woolsbridge Manor Farm
RIVER
1
THORNE WY.
VICTORY CL.
Woolsbridge
Wools Bri.
Caravan Park
ROAD
EMERALD CL.
Woolsbridge
LIBERTY CL.
Woolsbridge Farm
HORTON
WEBBS WY.
AZURA CL.
WEBBS CL.
WOOLSBRIDGE INDUSTRIAL ESTATE
MOORS
PINE MANOR RD.
FOREST EDGE DRIVE
FOREST EDGE CL.
BARN FARM
CONDOR CL.
Springducks
BURTON CL.
BURTON
LANE
BUSHMEAD
OLD
Little Lions Farm
CASTLEMAN
TRAILWAY
2
BUSH CL.
MEAD DR.
BH21
Egypt
GROSVENOR CL.
SHELLEY
DRAY
LEA CL.
WAY
04
Lions Hill
ASHLEY HEATH
ST. LEONARDS
LIONS
WAY
BRACKEN CL.
3
LANE
Lions Hill Farm
LIONS HILL
HILL
WAY
HEATH
WILLOW CL.
HOLLY CL.
BRAESIDE
Rec. Grd.
Oakridge
LIONS HILL
ROAD
IVY CL.
Bowl. Grn.
GARTH CL.
SYLVAN CL.
CONIFER CL.
SPINNEY CL.
GORSE CL.
IVY
12
ACORN CL.
DR.
ROWAN CL.
CRAIGSIDE
BH24
OAKS
CEDAR
HEATHER
MALMESBURY RD.
Pumping Station
Camp Site
OAKS
BIRCH CL.
4
WEST MOORS PLANTATION
RIVER
RACECOURSE HEATH
CHERRY TREE CL.
AVENUE
03
D
Oakhill Farm
Hill Farm
DRIVE
ST. LEONARDS
Camping Site
FIR TREE CL.
FIR TREE
GRANGE
BEECH
Shamba Farm
5
East Moors Farm
A31
LANE
ROADS
HEATHERDOWN WAY
ROAD
Camping Site
BOUNDARY
WAYSIDE
6
HEATHERDOWN
EDGEMOOR RD.
COMPTON CRES.
FIELD
SOUTHERN WAY
MALOREN WY.
A31
ST. LEONARD'S COMMUNITY HOSPITAL
LANE
02
ABBEY
UPLANDS AVENUE
MONKS CL.
St. Leonards Bridge
FRINGWOOD
E
F
19
410
G
Tennis Court
H
11
ROAD
9
Playing Field
White Ranch

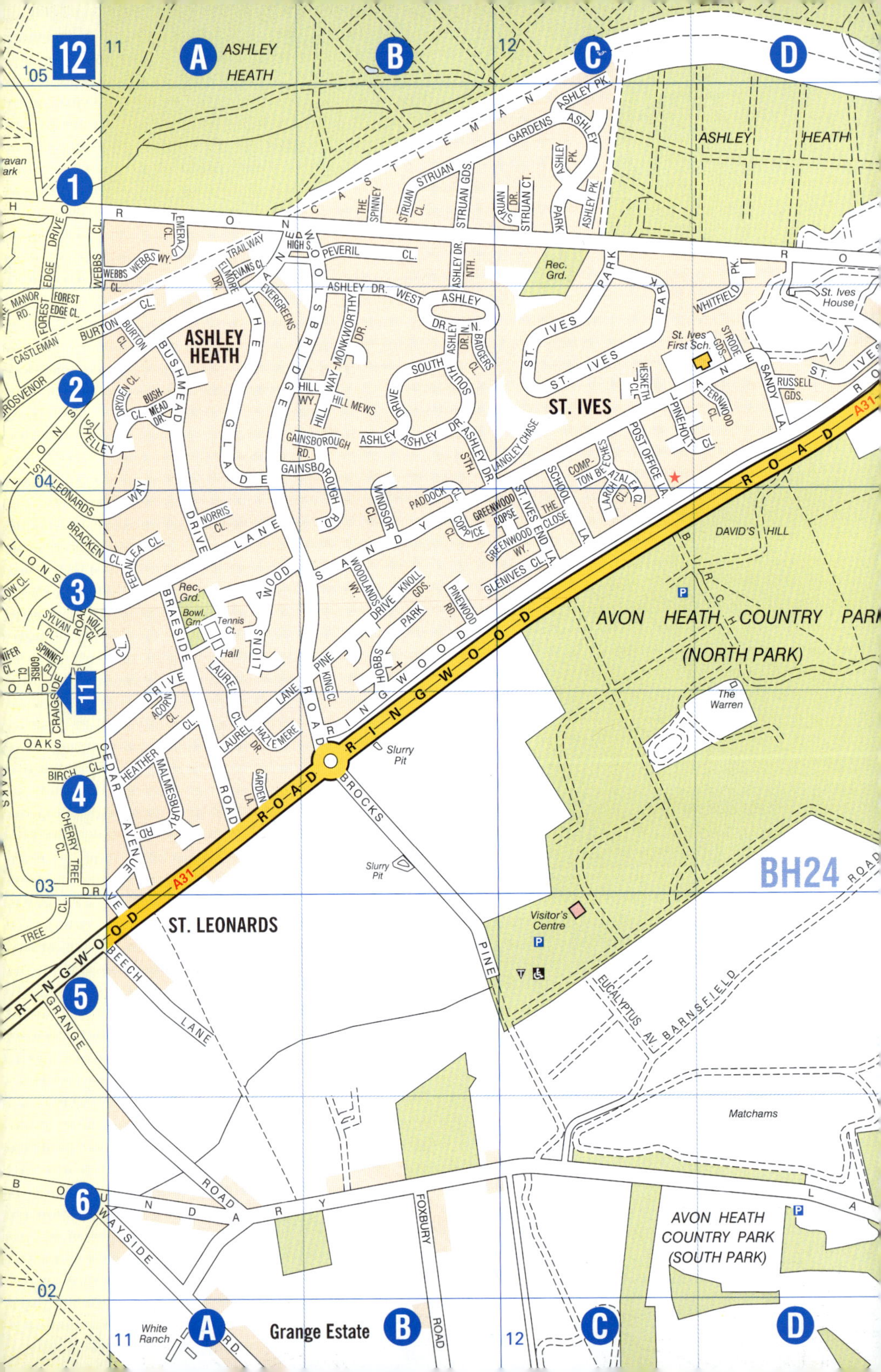

12
11
105
A
ASHLEY HEATH
B
12
C
ASHLEY PK.
D
ASHLEY HEATH
1
Caravan Park
THE SPINNEY
STRUAN
STRUAN CL.
STRUAN GDS.
STRUAN DR.
STRUAN CT.
GARDENS
ASHLEY PK.
ASHLEY PK.
ASHLEY PARK
ASHLEY PK.
Rec. Grd.
ST. IVES PARK
WHITFIELD PK.
St. Ives House
St. Ives First Sch.
STRODE GDS.
RUSSELL GDS.
SANDY LA.
ST. IVES ROAD
H
FOREST EDGE DRIVE
WEBBS CL.
WEBBS WY.
EMERALD DR.
TRAILWAY
HIGH S.
PEVERIL CL.
ELMORE DR.
EVANS CL.
EVERGREENS
THE GLADE
WOOLSBRIDGE
ASHLEY DR. WEST
MONKWORTHY DR.
ASHLEY DR. N.
ASHLEY DR. NTH.
ASHLEY DR. N.
BADGERS CL.
ASHLEY
ST. IVES
A31
Manor Rd.
Forest Edge Cl.
BURTON CL.
BURTON CL.
DRYDEN CL.
BUSH-MEAD DR.
BUSHMEAD DR.
2
ASHLEY HEATH
SHELLEY WAY
HILL WY.
HILL MEWS
GAINSBOROUGH RD.
GAINSBOROUGH RD.
ASHLEY DRIVE SOUTH
SOUTH ASHLEY DR.
ASHLEY DR. STH.
LANGLEY CHASE
HESKETH CL.
FERNWOOD CL.
PINEHOLT CL.
POST OFFICE LA.
GROSVENOR
04
ST. LEONARDS
BRACKEN CL.
FERNLEA CL.
NORRIS CL.
WINDSOR CL.
PADDOCK CL.
COPPICE CL.
GREENWOOD COPSE
ST. IVES SCHOOL
THE CLOSE
COMPTON BEECHES
LARCH CL.
AZALEA CL.
DAVID'S HILL
LIONS LANE
SANDY WOOD
WOODLANDS WY.
DRIVE
KNOLL GDS.
PINEWOOD PARK
PINEWOOD RD.
GREENWOOD WY.
GREENWOOD END LA.
GLENIVES CL.
AVON HEATH COUNTRY PARK
(NORTH PARK)
3
LOW CL.
SYLVAN CL.
SPINNEY CL.
GORSE CL.
HOLLY CL.
ROAD
Rec. Grd.
BRAESIDE
Bowl. Grn.
Tennis Ct.
Hall
PINE LANE
HOBBS
KING CL.
RINGWOOD
The Warren
11
CRAIGSIDE
OAKS
OAKS
DRIVE
ACORN CL.
LAUREL CL.
LAUREL CL.
HALE MERE
CEDAR AVENUE
HEATHER
MALMESBURY RD.
GARDEN LA.
ROAD
Slurry Pit
BROCKS
BH24
4
BIRCH CL.
CHERRY TREE CL.
03
TREE CL.
CHERRY TREE DR.
A31
Slurry Pit
Visitor's Centre
ST. LEONARDS
PINE
5
BEECH LANE
GRANGE
RINGWOOD ROAD
EUCALYPTUS AV.
BARNSFIELD
Matchams
B
BOUNDARY
WAYSIDE
6
ROAD
FOXBURY ROAD
AVON HEATH COUNTRY PARK
(SOUTH PARK)
02
11
White Ranch
A
Grange Estate
B
12
C
D

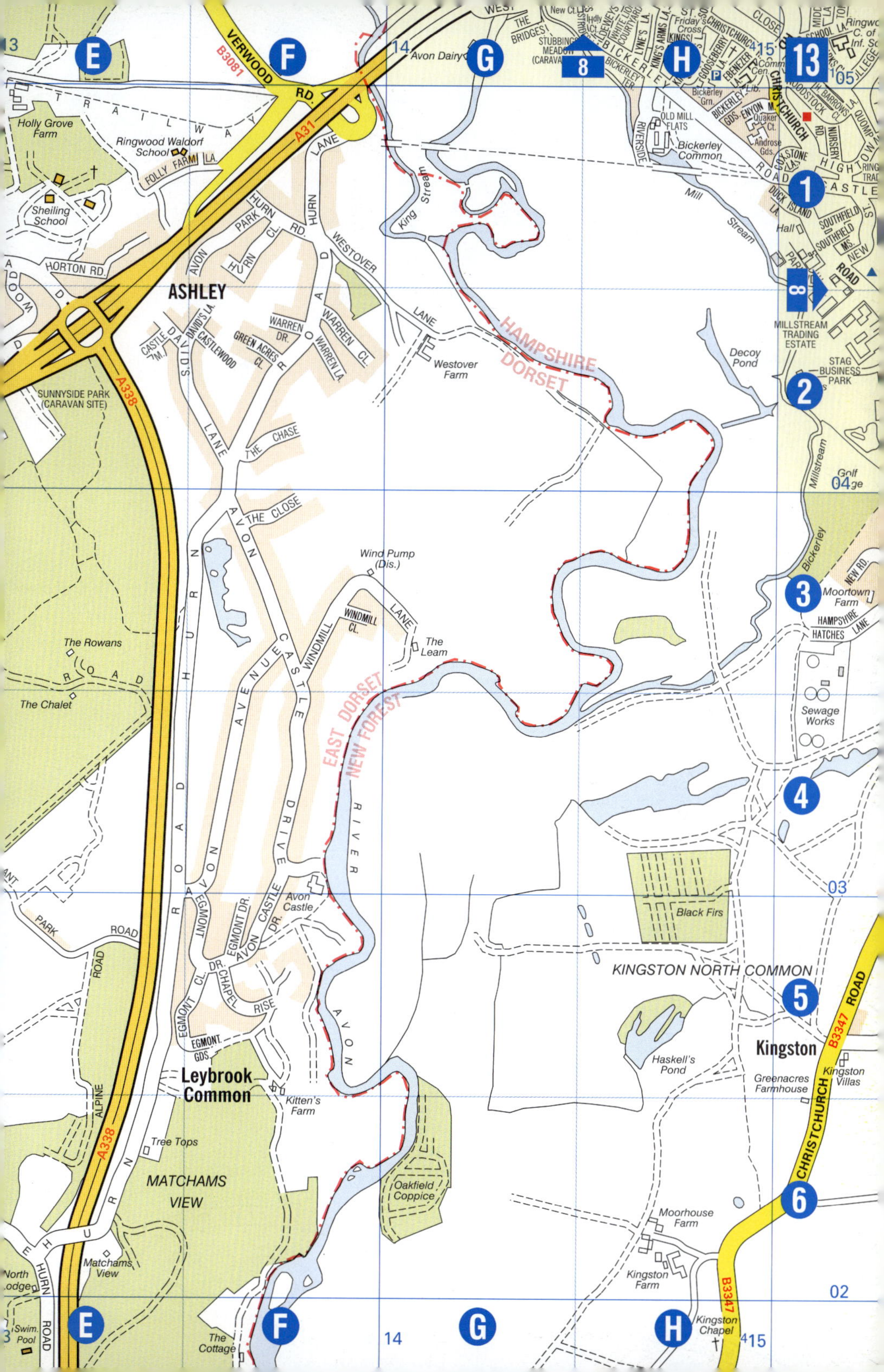

E
VERWOOD
B3081
RD.
F
A31
14
Avon Dairy
G
THE BRIDGES
STUBBING MEADOW (CARAVAN)
New Ct. Lts.
8
WEST
Hdly.
DENEWS
WHITE
COURTYARD
BICKERLEY
LYNE'S LA.
KING'S ARMS LA.
KING'S LA.
Friday's Cross
ST. CHRISTCHURCH
CLOSE
MIDC
SCHOOL LA.
Ringwood
C. of Inf. Sc.
415
13
05
H
GOOSEBERRY LA.
Comm. Cen.
EBENEZER LA.
Lib.
BICKERLEY GDS.
ENYON
Quaker Ct.
Androse Gds.
RINGW
TRAI
HIGH ST.
CASTLE
Holly Grove Farm
TRAILWAY
Ringwood Waldorf School
FOLLY FARM LA.
King Stream
RIVERSIDE
OLD MILL FLATS
Bickerley Common
Bickerley Grn.
Old Mill
Quaker Ct.
1
COXSTONE LA.
DUCK ISLAND
Hall
SOUTHFIELD
SOUTHFIELD MS.
NEW
ROAD
HORTON RD.
AVON
HURN PARK CL.
HURN RD.
HURN LANE
WESTOVER RD.
WESTOVER LANE
Sheiling School
ASHLEY
CASTLE DAVID'S FM.
DAVID'S LA.
CASTLEWOOD
GREEN ACRES CL.
WARREN DR.
WARREN LA.
WARREN CL.
Westover Farm
HAMPSHIRE
DORSET
Mill Stream
8
MILLSTREAM TRADING ESTATE
Decoy Pond
STAG BUSINESS PARK
2
A338
SUNNYSIDE PARK (CARAVAN SITE)
LANE
Millstream
Golf Course
04
THE CHASE
AVON
THE CLOSE
HURN
AVENUE
Wind Pump (Dis.)
Bickerley
NEW RD.
Moortown Farm
3
HAMPSHIRE
HATCHES LANE
The Rowans
ROAD
R O A D
CASTLE
WINDMILL CL.
WINDMILL LANE
The Leam
Sewage Works
The Chalet
DRIVE
EAST DORSET
NEW FOREST
RIVER
4
03
PARK
ROAD
EGMONT DR.
EGMONT DR.
CASTLE DR.
AVON CASTLE
AVON CASTLE
Avon Castle
Black Firs
KINGSTON NORTH COMMON
KINGSTON VILLAS
A338
ALPINE
EGMONT CL.
CHAPEL RISE
EGMONT GDS.
AVON
5
B3347
Kingston
Haskell's Pond
Greenacres Farmhouse
Kingston Villas
Leybrook Common
Kitten's Farm
Tree Tops
CHRISTCHURCH
ROAD
MATCHAMS VIEW
Oakfield Coppice
Moorhouse Farm
6
North Lodge
Matchams View
HURN
Swim. Pool
E
The Cottage
F
14
G
H
Kingston Farm
Kingston Chapel
B3347
415
02

Marsh Copse
02
14
99
A
B
400
C
D
Biddle's Copse
Camping Site
Caravan Park
Wilksworth Farm
Tennis Courts
1
RIVER
CATLEY COPSE
Tadden
Chilbridge
Hound Hill
ALLEN
2
BLANDFORD
B3082
Daffodil Copse
Hill Butts House
Pound Farm
Pound Farm
Bickham Farm
Bickham Copse
The Row
Entrance
East Copse Lodge
01
Pamphill Dairy
Hall
Elm Grove
Bonhams
Hillbutts
Stone
STREET
Pumping Station
Long Close Farm
Stone Lane Industrial Est.
Knobcrook
Walford Mill Craft Cen.
3
P
Pamphill Farm
Hart's Copse
Queen Elizabeth's School
ROAD
Stone Farm
THE
STONE
FARMERS
CON.
DRY'S
WALFORD GDS.
KNOB. SHEPPDS.
FLD.
CROOK
WEST
Manor House
Pamphill Green
Pamphill
Grove Wood
Sports Ground
Pamphill C. of E. First School
Queen Elizabeth's Leisure Centre
Playing Field
THE BROADS
Stone Park
CULVER HAYES PL.
CULVERHAYES
CL.
BLIND LA.
CEMETERY
Cemetery
Redcotts
Hall
Wimborne First Sch.
SCHOOL LA.
BOROUGH
CHAPEL LA.
LANE
Manor Cottage
Little Pamphill
VINE
HILL
Farrs House
Stone Park House
ST. MARGARET'S
HILL
St. Margaret's Almshouses
ST. MARGARET'S CL.
NETHERWOOD
VICTORIA
VICTORIA HOSP.
CUTHBURY GDS.
Rec. Grd.
Ten. Cts.
REDCOTTS RD.
Bowl. Grn.
Play Fld.
B3078
T.H.
West-field
Hall
Moray Ct.
Kingsmead
Bartley Ct.
HOLLY
4
Firs Farm
Walnut Farm
COWGROVE
Roman Road (course of)
LANE
B3082 RD.
Westfield Cl.
Ten. Cts.
Depot
VICTORIA RD.
CUTHBURY CL.
Trumpeters Ct.
Kings-mead Ct.
WEST
ROW
CHURCH
COOK ROW
100
Higher Dairy
Court House
Lower Dairy Cottage
Eye Bridge
RIVER
Founder Hole
OLD CUTHBURY CL.
OLD RD.
KING STREET
Pye Corner
P
BEAUFORT MS.
Queen Elizabeth C
Cowgrove
Roman Road (course of)
Julian's Bridge
JULIAN'S
ROAD
STREET
THE
LEAZE
Dean's C
Fish
5
Netherwood Mead
Eye Mead
STREET
STOUR
6
MILL
B3078
EAST DORSET
WIMBORNE
POOLE
A31
MINSTER
Merley Hall Farm
BY-PASS
WILLETT
ROAD
99
99
A
MILL
STREET
Springfield
Sewage Works
ROAD
B
21
400
C
WILLETT
ASH...
D
Lake Farm

01
E
Furzehill
F
02
G
H
03
15
02
East Dorset District Council Offices
B3078
...worth ...ages
1
Long Lane Farm
PILFORD
Eastc...
Dogdean Farm
Iona
Owen Wood
Merry Field Hill
COLEHILL
LONNEN WOOD CL.
LONNEN
SANDY
Dumpton School
Cricket Ground
Pav.
Colehill Farm
FOUR WELLS RD.
WALLOW MA...
Sunday's Barn
Research & Development Farm
Deans Grove Farm
MERRIFIELD
NEW MERRI-FIELD
GLYNVILLE CT.
GLYNVILLE LE.
GLYNVILLE ROAD
RD.
Long How
BH21
Walford Farm
Deans Grove
Vicarage
MARSH FIELD
ROTARY
Howell Ho.
PARK HOMER RD.
WESTON RD.
HYSLOP CL.
RD.
PAGET CL.
ROAD
01
The Haven
Stone Firs
Tumulus
Barrow Firs
St. Michael's C. of E. Mid. Sch.
War Mem.
KYRCHIL
MIDDLEHILL
PARK HOMER
PARK HOMER RD.
DRIVE
OLIVERS
Hillside
GREENHILL CL.
GREENHILL
GREEN. HILL A.
KYRCHIL WY.
NORTHLEIGH
Beaucroft Sch.
3
BOUNDARY DR.
Cricket Grd.
WIMBORNE
WHITEWAYS
North Leigh House
VINERIES
VINERIES
VINERIESZ
HAYESWO...
RD.
GIDDYLAKE
LACY CL.
CHERITON WY.
Woodland House
COLBORNE AV.
COLBORNE
16
Walford
MILTON RD.
SHAKESPEARE RD.
WALFORD CL.
BURT'S CL.
NELSON CL.
CHAUCER
VENATOR PL.
GIDDYLAKE
BYRON RD.
COURT ENAY DR.
ONSLOW GDS.
HILL
HIGHLAND RD.
BEAUCROFT RD.
TOWER LA.
BEAUCROFT ROAD
QUINCE LA.
ROAD
FAIRFIELD CL.
LEIGH LANE
Little Orchard
CHURCHMOOR RD.
HAYESWO...
...ay. Fld.
Allenbourn Mid. Sch.
RIVER CL.
ELIZABETH RD.
GLENDALE CL.
BADBURY
BEAUFORT DR.
LACY VW.
MARLBOROUGH PL.
MARLBOROUGH
HIGHLAND VW.
HIGHLAND VW.
CL.
WESLEY RD.
WESLEY R.
Tennis Cts.
Cottage Farm
4
Gulliver Ct.
Helic Ho.
MINSTER VW.
ONSLOW
POPLAR
ROYSTON DR.
ASH-DENE CL.
PINE TREE CL.
WESLEY AV.
HORNBEAM WY.
Little Orchard
Marlborough ALLEN CT.
GREENHAYES RI.
Rowlands
ROWLANDS HILL
CRANFIELD AV.
Grangewood Hall
BOURNE CT.
DENE CL.
OAK RD.
BIRCHDALE
GREENCLOSE LA.
LEIGH COMMON
LEIGH COMMON
comm Cen
Magistrates Ct.
YEW TREE CL.
ST. JOHN'S
FAIRFIELD
VILLAS
FAIRFIELD
CHENE RD.
WIMBORNE MINSTER
Old Manor Ho.
Old Manor Farm
Millbank Ho.
Pav
CUTHBURGA RD.
LEWENS
LEGG
RETREAT RD.
WELLAND RD.
Old Highways Mews
B3073
ROAD
Bytheway
HANHAM RD.
Cricket Grd.
LEWENS LANE
PARKWOOD RD.
HARLSTN. VS.
HILL
MDW. CT.
CRWL CT.
Brookside Farm
...erstore Ho.
CROWN MEAD
LEIGH RD.
East Brook
Sch.
GRENVILLE RD.
GRENVILLE
DAY'S CT.
BEECH CT.
PARMITER RD.
Leigh
5
EAST ST.
ROWLANDS HILL
RODWAY
LEIGH
AVENUE
STEVENSONS RD. WK.
RICHMOND CL.
DAY'S GDS.
GORDON RD.
BARNES RD.
BROOK
PARMITER DRIVE
BROOKSIDE ROAD
EAST STREAM CL.
SHAMROCK CT.
CRESCENT
CATHERINES RD.
ST. JOHN'S
JANE CL.
ST. STEVENS
CRESCENT
TAPPER CT.
LIVINGSTONE RD.
PARMITER WAY
Depot
River Allen
POOLE
B3073
STEVENSONS RD.
BROADWAY GDS.
ALLEN RD.
OSBO...
ETHEL...
NEW Flower Ct.
Saville Ct.
EDEN GRO.
STOUR
MARKET WY.
BOROUGH ROAD
CHRIST CT.
HARDY CT.
St. Johns
RIVERSIDE PK. INDUSTRIAL ESTATE
DAY'S CT.
CRESCENT
Pav
Playing Field
Works
Depot
Purification Works
TRINITY IND. EST.
Park Farm
River Allen
ROAD
OAKLEY HILL
STATION
CRITTEN ...
GRIFFIN...
Leigh Park
CHURCHILL ROAD
CRESCENT ROAD
Works
TRINITY IND. EST. Depot
Filter Beds
6
Canford Bridge
Works
EAST DORSET POOLE
BROOK PARK IND. EST.
WIMBORNE
MINSTER
BY-PASS
Dawson's Hole
A31
River Stour
99
E
F
22
02
G
H
03
MERLEY
ULLSWATER RD.
DERWENTWATER ...
WAY
...house RD.
Hatch Hole Weir

16
02 03 04
A Pilford B C BEDBOROUGH PLANTATION D
Brookside
PILFORD
Eastcote
WOOD VW.
LONNEN WOOD CL.
PILFORD RD.
PILFORD HEATH RD.
PILFORD HEATH ROAD
Bedborough
The New Wigwam
1
COLEHILL LITTLE LONNEN
Colehill Farm
LONNEN
SANDY LANE
SANDY CL.
HEATH CL.
CANNON HILL PLANTATION
DUDDENS DRIVE
COLEHILL
FOUR WELLS RD.
MALLARD
HERON
LAPWING RD.
HAWK CL.
CANNON HILL GDS.
A31
2
HASLOP RD.
WEST RD.
MARIANNE RD.
GLYNVILLE CT.
GLYNVILLE RD.
TOM GREEN
BRACKENHILL RD.
CANNON HILL RD.
CANNON HILL RD.
QUARRY RD.
QUARRY DR.
Cannon Hill
PAGET CL.
Lib.
Colehill Hall
First Sch.
Quarry Cl.
Howell Ho.
ROTARY CL.
PARK RD.
O.R RD.
Colehill First Sch.
MIDDLEHILL DR.
HARNESS CL.
HORSESHOE CL.
CANFORD VIEW
SITS CL.
COLT CL.
HUNTER DR.
WAY
Canford Bottom
BH21
Stapehill Farm
PARK HOMER RD.
STROUD CL.
MINDEN CL.
ROAD
FARRIERS CL.
BRIDLE
SADDLE CL.
HALTER RISE
WAY
PARK HOMER DRIVE
OLIVERS
ASHMEADS WY.
Hayeswood First Sch.
PLACE
CANFORD LANE
TROT CL.
COLT CL.
PORTERS CL.
SPUR
STIRRUP CL.
WILLOW DR.
3
OLIVERS
ASHMEADS CL.
SUNNY-BANK RD.
SUNNYBANK WY.
LAWNS
FREEMANS CL.
LAWNS CL.
FRYERS COPSE
15
HAYESWOOD RD.
CUTLERS
Playing Field
BNW DR.
SUNNY-BANK
JESS-OPP RD.
FREEMANS LA.
DALES CL.
DRIVE
Little Orchard
St. Catherines R.C. Prim! Sch.
Church Moor Copse
CUTLERS PL.
PLACE
FREEMANS
LAWNS RD.
BOTTOM
Stapehill Farm
Cottage Farm
CHURCHMOOR RD.
CUTLERS
CUTLERS PL.
CANFORD LANE
DALES
DRIVE
WIMBORNE
ABBEY GS.
Hall
4
CEDAR DR.
DRIVE
FOXCROFT
BRIAR WY.
DRIVE
STAPEHILL CRES.
WEST
B3073
WYELANDS AVENUE
FOX CL.
LAYMOOR LA.
The Bog
Laymoor Copse
FOXCROFT
HOUNDS WY.
Hayes
MARTINDALE AV.
MARTINDALE AV.
HENBEST CL.
B3073
LEIGH
B3073
ROAD
Bytheway
HAYES
HAYES CL.
HAYES
CEDAR CL.
FERNWAY
WIMBORNE
ROAD
HAM LANE
Sub.
Manor Farm
OLD
FOX LA.
HAM
Little Burle
Little Canford
5
Brookside Farm
WIMBORNE
THE ACORNS
SUMMERFIELD CL.
BY-PASS
MINSTER
STOUR CL.
Park Farm
A31
ROAD
EAST DORSET POOLE
Stour
Depot
6
WIMBORNE
Trunk Hole
Filter Beds
CANFORD MAGNA GOLF COURSE
Seymoor's Cliff
Stourbank Nurseries
99
Hatch Hole Weir
O'Gaunt's Chen
Beaufort House
Gisborough Hall
23
River Stour
A B Canford School C 04 D
03

Ameysford
The Birches
FERNDOWN 06
FOREST
17
05
E
F
G
H
07
02
Bedborough Farm
UDDENS PLANTATION
A31
LEESON DR.
LEESON DR.
DRIVE
Ameysford Road
KINGSWAY
1
PINE GLEN
JUNIPER CL.
REDWOOD
MAPLE
STONECHAT CL.
NUTHATCH CL.
Telford Road
Lancaster Rd.
Lindbergh Rd.
BUNTING
DUNLOCK CL.
SISKIN CL.
PINE AV.
HILLCREST AV.
Mitchell Rd.
FERNSIDE PK. INDUSTRIAL ESTATE
KESTREL CL.
HILLTOP RISE
AUTUMN CL.
PRUNUS CL.
ROAD
PINE CL.
Blunt's Farm
HAVILAND
WHITTLE RD.
HILLTOP CL.
HILLTOP
PRUNUS CL.
RYAN CL.
CURLEW CL.
LARKS
LARKS CL.
COPPICE AV.
ELFIN CL.
BEAUFORT'S
BRACKEN RD.
CLAYFORD AV.
WARREN WALK
COPPICE AV.
MEWS
WINWROOD WAY
JOHNSON ROAD
CLAYFORD
COPPICE AV.
COPPICE AV.
HILL VW. RD.
01
B
CEDAR
RED OAKS CL.
COPPICE AV.
LABURNUM CL.
EAST
HILLTOP
UDDENS
CEDAR TRADE PARK
PARK LANE
BARROW VW.
AVENUE
Ferndown Upper Sch.
STANF
CHURCH
MAI
CAISTER
Works
BRICKYARD
ROAD
Sports Grd.
3
GRO.
UDDENS TRADING ESTATE
OLD FORGE RD.
WEST WIMBORNE
ST. JAMES' RD.
CHERRY
CHESTNUT GRO.
DRIVE
WIMBORNE ROAD
FOREST
Ferndown Sports Centre
King George's Playing Field
18
STAPEHILL
Highway Farm
FOREST VIEW DRIVE
PADDOCK CL.
Playing Field
PEL
Burial Grd.
STAPEHILL LANE
St. Stephens Cottages
FOREST WY.
FOREST VIEW DR.
Ferndown Middle School
Cen.
4
Stapehill Abbey
BH22
Ferr First
Burrell's Copse
Works
KEEPERS LANE
STAPEHILL ROAD
Ferndown Forest
ROAD AWARD
ROAD
KEEPERS
Nursery
KEEPERS
Simon's Ground
100
Keeper's Hill Nursery
Great Barrow
Big Burles
POMPEY'S
BRABOUR
5
Pompey's Corner
GORGES DRIVE
GROVE
LONG
Little Moors Farm
The Roughs
Old Gravel Pits
LIFETON ROAD
BEECH FARM
HEATH FARM CLO.
PUB
SQUARE CL.
Crow Copse
LANE
DUNEDIN CL.
DUNEDIN DR.
HEATH WAY
HEATH AVE.
6
Big Copse
DUNEDIN GDNS.
ST. JUST CL.
A348
WOOD
LOCKSL
RINGWOOD ROAD
HAMPRESTON
LANE HAM
B3073
Captain's Row
CONEYGAR LANE
Greenacres Farm
ANGEL LA.
99
Hampreston C of E First Sch
Rectory
Dowden's Copse
Beacon Farm
POMPEY
24
E
F
06
G
H
07
05

Ameysford
18
02 07
A Broadmoor B 10 08 C D
Uddens Water
A31
WEST MOORS RD.
B3072
Tom's Coppice
PINEHURST PARK (CARAVAN SITE)
Cemetery
Thorny Ham
LEESON DRIVE
LEESON DR.
KINGSWAY
1
STONECHAT CL.
NUTHATCH CL.
SISKIN CL.
BUNTING
JUNIPER CL.
CEDAR WY.
REDWOOD DRIVE
PINEWOOD DRIVE
HAZEL DRIVE
MAPLE DR.
LARCH DR.
WILLOW WY.
WILLOW WY.
ROBINSWOOD DR.
AVENUE
BEAU FOYS A.
MARTINS ROAD
GLADELANDS MOBILE HOME PARK
Motel
Superstore
The Warren
WOODLAND WLK.
WOODLAND WLK.
HILLTOP RISE
LARKS RISE
LARKS DRIVE
PRUNUS CL.
PINE CL.
HILLCREST AV.
PINEWOOD WAY
PINE CL.
QUEENS ROAD
HEATHER DR.
HEATHER WY.
EVERGLADES CL.
HIGH TREES WLK.
LYNWOOD WLK.
MARTINS CL.
STENARTS WY.
MARTINS GARDEN WK.
BADGERS WK.
WOODSIDE ROAD
2
COPPICE AV.
COPPICE AV.
COPPICE AV.
COPPICE AV.
Warren
01
LABURNUM
WIMBORNE
DRUE
ELFIN DR.
THE LAURELS
CLIVEDEN ROAD
RYAN CL.
RYAN GDS.
QUEENSWOOD DR.
PINE WOOD GDS.
EAST
WIMBORNE ROAD EAST
VICTORIA
WEST MOORS ROAD
B3072
WIMBORNE ROAD
MONKTON
MONKTON CL.
WHINCROFT CL.
WHINCROFT DRIVE
Wickham Ct.
EASTWOOD
AMBERWOOD ROAD
A348
TURBARY
AMEYS
PICKARD ROAD
FORD CL.
3
Ferndown Upper Sch. Sports Grd.
BEAUFOYS MEWS
THE BEAUFOYS
BEAU FOYS ROAD
Beaufoys Ct.
STANFIELD RD.
CHESTER ROAD
MILBOURNE ROAD
MAYFIELD CLOSE
Bramley Ct.
BRAMLEY
POMONA CL.
RUSSET WY.
VICTORIA ROAD
VICTORIA GARDENS
Diana Cl.
GLENDALE AV.
GREENWOOD AV.
WOODSIDE CL.
WOODSIDE AV.
PRINGLES
APPLE TREE GRO.
Broomfield Ct.
BH22
17
Ferndown Sports Cen.
King George's Playing Field
CHURCH ROAD
CHERRY GRO.
WESTWOOD
SOUTHWOOD
MAYFIELD AVENUE
PENROSE RD.
ALBERT ROAD
Consort Ho.
PRINCES RD.
Prince's Ct.
Oakham Grange
Victoria Ho.
Homelands Ho.
MANOR ROAD
FERNDOWN
PRINGLES DR.
ORCHARD CL.
LINKS ROAD
GOLF
4
Playing Field
Ferndown Middle School
Youth Cen.
Ferndown First School
PETER GRANT WAY
OLD SCHOOL CL.
MOUNTBATTEN DR.
ST. MARY'S RD.
ST. MARY'S RD.
ALBERT ROAD
Shelley Ct.
Milton Ct.
Byron Ct.
LIBRARY
St. Mary's WK.
Penny's WK.
Lib.
Comm. Day Cen.
FERNDOWN CEN.
FERNDOWN CEN.
CARROLL
AVENUE
ORCHARD AVENUE
CRAIGWOOD DR.
FERNDOWN GOLF COURSE
100
Great Barrow
AVENUE ROAD
BRABOURNE
LONGACRE
RINGWOOD ROAD
A348
SINNEYS LA.
Penny's Ct.
Lee Ct.
Dudsway Ct.
Delkeith Ct.
St. Mary's M.
FERNLEA CL.
FERNLEA AV.
CHANDER
NEW ROAD
A347
DUDSBURY AVENUE
DUDSBURY GDNS.
WOODACRE GDNS.
OLD PINES CL.
Grayson Ct.
CLOSE
GOLF LINKS RD.
Club House
5
THE GROVE
ST. GEORGES DRIVE
MORDEN ROAD
MELBURY CLO.
SHERBORNE DRI.
WINCOMBE DRIVE
DORSET AVENUE
STALBRIDGE DRI.
WINCOMBE CL.
AVENUE
Hotel
EVENING GLADE
6
Old Gravel Pits
DUNEDIN CL.
DUNEDIN GDS.
CLIFTON CT.
LINDSEY CT.
WOOD RINGWOOD ROAD
A348
GLENMOOR DRIVE
MONSAL AVE.
HEATH FARM CLO.
HEATH FARM WAY
SHERWOOD AVE.
HEATH FARM
DARLEY ROAD
MATLOCK ROAD
WOLLATON CR.
GLENMOOR ROAD
DORSET ROAD
DORSET AVENUE
ELLESFIELD
BERKLEY AVENUE
Parley First Sch.
Alexandria Ct.
NEW ROAD
A347
GORSELAND
GREENWAYS
Elysium Ct.
PINE END
SPANS WALK
BIRCH RD.
WENDY CR.
LONE PINE MOBILE HOMES PARK
DRAKES RD.
ALDRIDGE WY.
WORLEY CR.
ANNA LA.
PETER CL.
LONE PINE
ALDRIDGE DRI.
DANE DRIVE
GOLDEN
LONE PINE
99
KINGSWOOD
JUST CL.
LOCKSLEY ROAD
Red Roofs
LONE PINE WY.
Ralph's Barrow
A 07 B 25 08 C NEW RD. D

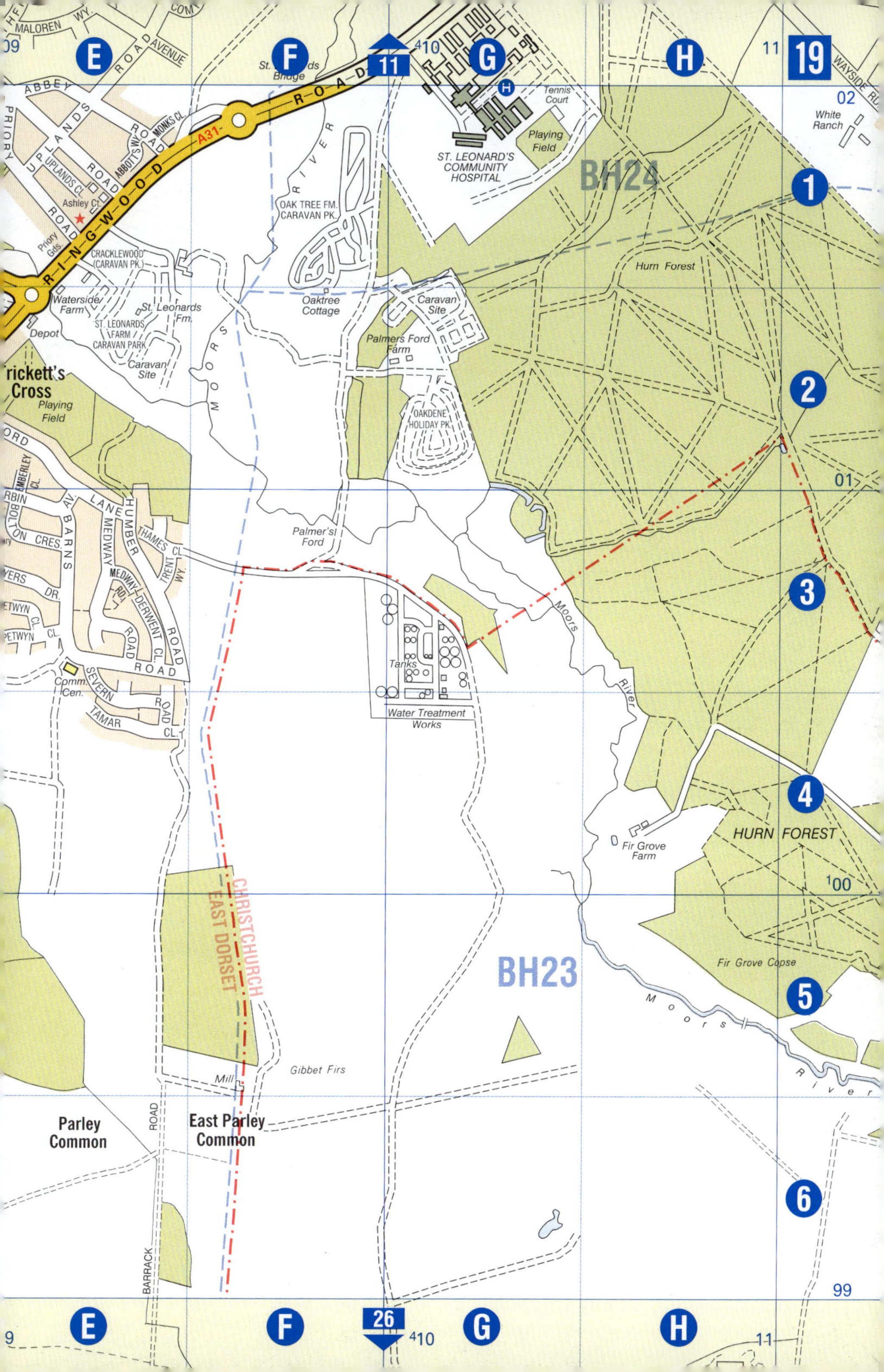

MALOREN WY.
ABBEY
PRIORY
E
F
St. Leonards Bridge
11
410
G
H
Tennis Court
11
19
WAYSIDE RD.
02
White Ranch
ROAD AVENUE
MONKS CL.
ABBOTTS WY.
ROAD
RINGWOOD ROAD
A31
RIVER
St. Leonard's Community Hospital
BH24
UPLANDS CL.
Ashley Ct.
Priory Gds.
ROAD
CRACKLEWOOD (CARAVAN PK.)
Oak Tree Fm. Caravan Pk.
Playing Field
Hurn Forest
1
Waterside Farm
St. Leonards Farm / Caravan Park
St. Leonards Fm.
Oaktree Cottage
Caravan Site
2
Depot
Caravan Site
MOORS
Palmers Ford Farm
01
rickett's Cross
Playing Field
OAKDENE HOLIDAY PK.
3
Moors River
EMBERLEY CL.
LANE BARNS
HUMBER
MEDWAY RD.
THAMES CL.
TRENT WY.
Palmer's Ford
BOLTON CRES.
ORBIN
MEDWAY
DERWENT CL.
ROAD
ERS DR.
ETWYN CL.
ETWYN CL.
ROAD ROAD
Tanks
4
HURN FOREST
Comm. Cen.
SEVERN
TAMAR
ROAD CL.
Water Treatment Works
Fir Grove Farm
100
Fir Grove Copse
CHRISTCHURCH EAST DORSET
BH23
5
Moors River
Mill
Gibbet Firs
River
Parley Common
ROAD
East Parley Common
6
BARRACK
9
E
F
26
410
G
H
99
11

20
97 98 99
A B C D
1 2 3 4 5 6
RIVER STOUR
Sewage Works
The Old Mill
Ford
Weir
Weir
Court House
Court Farm
Lower Russell's Copse
Higher Russell's Copse
A31 Caravan
Cha
S
Clay Pit
Brog Street
STREET
CANDY
MILL
A31
Bailey Gate
Mill House
Mill Farm
Mill Cottages
LANE
BLANDFORD
B3074
Glendon
BROG
AV.
RECTORY CL.
OLD RECTORY
BADBURY VW.
VIOLET FM. CL.
Training Area
Water Works
Water Works Cottages
BRICKYARD
RED
LANE
Old Court Copse
Himmon Copse
Draglens Hedgerow
Withy Bed
Sleight
SLEIGHT LANE
ROAD
Recreation Ground
Wimborne
MDW. FM. CL.
RIDGEWAY
Lockyer Middle Schoo
98
Big Payne
Hill View Farm
Kennel Copse
Clay Pit
Red Lane Copse
High Ditch Copse
Pardy's Copse
Meadow Farm
Cemetery
Woodside Farm
KNOLL LANE
Knoll Copse
Knoll Farm
PARDY'S
HAYWARDS
ROAD
Joiner's Copse
Newtown
NEWTOWN LA.
OLD
MARKET
ROAD
Henbury Plantation
Chalk Pit Copse
Mountain Clump
Knoll Clump
Castle Court Prep. Sch.
Padenca
Meadow View
BH21
Oakfields
ORCHARD LA.
Rectory
Georges
TOWERS
ORCHARD CL.
MS.
Lib.
P
97
Playing Field
Grant's Copse
LANE
CENTRAL CROFT
CL.
GEORGE RD.
AVENUE
SO
0 97
4
Home Farm
Atwell's Copse
BROADMOOR
BROOK
Brook Lane Farm
Wistoria Cott.
Blythe
BLANEY WY.
HENBURY RISE
Road
BROWNSEA AVE.
SOUTH LANDS
ALLEN HILL
Spur Copse
Home Farm
WATERLOO LANE
Poultry Houses
HAVEN RD.
Henbury View First Sch.
LAUREL CL.
HENBURY VIEW
BIRCH CL.
ERICA DR.
HENBURY CL.
WAREHAM
Florence Cottage
WYATTS
WYATTS CL.
STONY DOWN PLANTATION
Broom Copse
Little Manor Farm
CHAPEL
CHAPEL LANE
VIEWSIDE CL.
THORNTON CL.
MOORSIDE RD.
HANHAM ROAD
Rushcomt First Sc
Stony Down House
Riding School
Stony Down Farm
Cherrett's Clump
Saw Mill
Binley
RUSHALL
ROAD
GORSE RD.
HILLSIDE
CORFE VIEW
CORFE VW. RD.
QUEEN'S RD.
DENNIS RD.
EAST WAY
Hill View
HIGHMOOR
96
CORFE MULLEN
HECKFORD ROAD
HILLCREST RD.
TERENCE RD.
COURTNEY PL.
THE PDE.
ALBERT
BLACKSMITH CL.
Hartnell Ct.
HIGHMOOR RD.
VICTORIA
COLIN CLO
DALKEIT ROAD
36
kside Park
Kennels
Riding
FROUD WY.
RSIDE RD.
WAREHAM ROAD
IVOR
WOOD
CT.
A B 36 C D
97 98

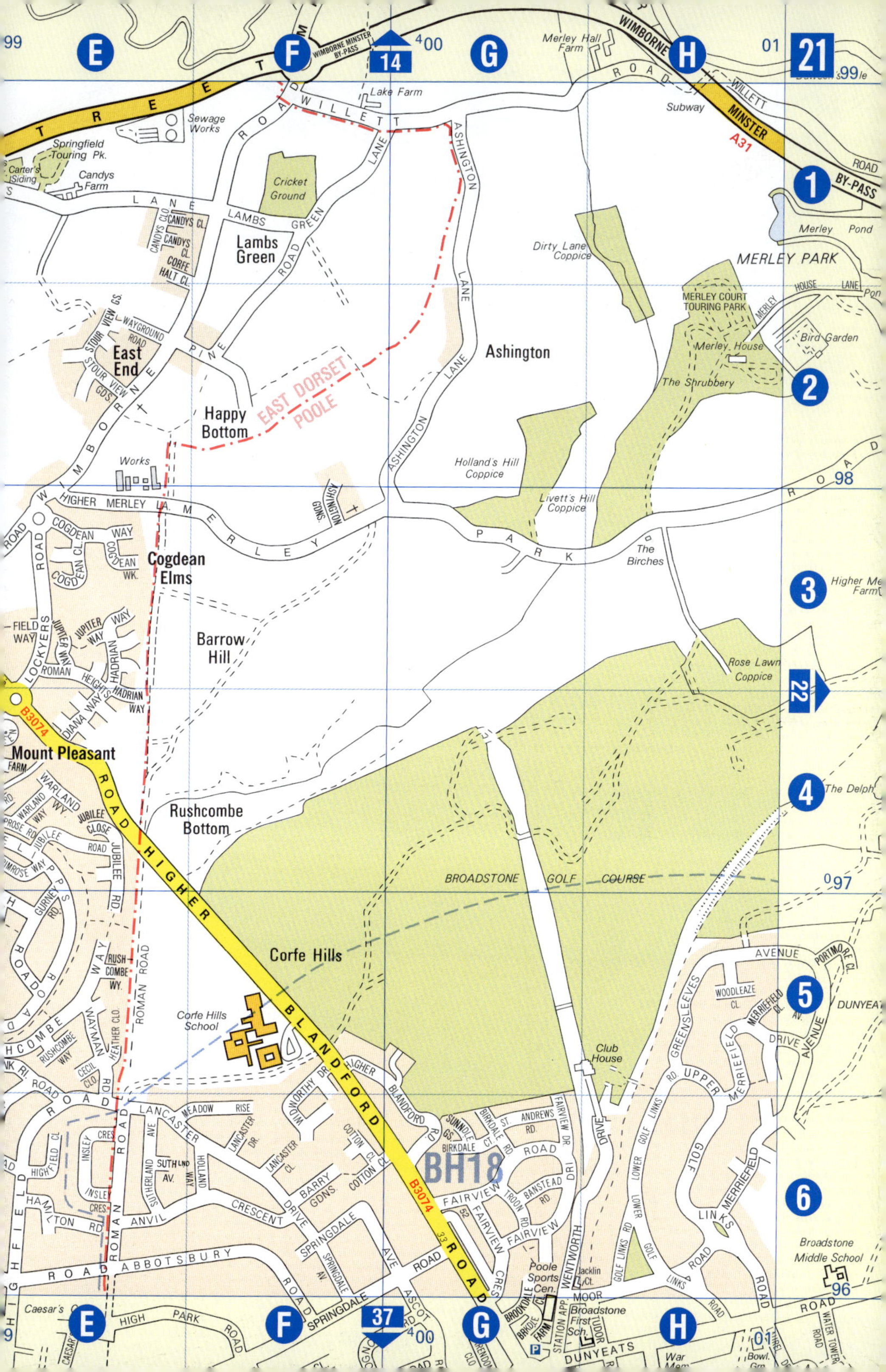
99
E
F
G
H
01
21
WIMBORNE
Merley Hall Farm
WIMBORNE MINSTER BY-PASS
14
400
Road
99 le
Dawson
STREET
Lake Farm
WILLETT
Subway
MINSTER
A31
BY-PASS
1
Springfield Touring Pk.
Sewage Works
Road
LANE
Merley Pond
Carter's Siding
Candys Farm
LAMBS
GREEN
Cricket Ground
ASHINGTON
MERLEY PARK
LANE
Candys Cl.
CANDYS CL.
CANDYS CL.
CORFE HALT CL.
Lambs Green
Road
Dirty Lane Coppice
MERLEY COURT TOURING PARK
HOUSE LANE
Pon
STOUR VIEW GS.
WAYGROUND
East End
PINE
Road
Ashington
Bird Garden
WIMBORNE
STOUR VIEW
STOUR VIEW GDS.
Happy Bottom
EAST DORSET
POOLE
ASHINGTON
Merley House
The Shrubbery
2
Road
ROAD
Works
ASHINGTON GDNS.
LANE
Holland's Hill Coppice
HIGHER MERLEY LA.
MERLEY
Livett's Hill Coppice
Higher Me Farm
COGDEAN
WAY
Cogdean Elms
PARK
The Birches
3
COGDEAN CL.
COGDEAN WK.
Rose Lawn Coppice
22
FIELD WAY
JUPITER WAY
Barrow Hill
LOCKYERS
JUPITER WAY
ROMAN
HADRIAN WAY
The Delph
DIANA WAY
HEIGHTS
HADRIAN WAY
4
B3074
Mount Pleasant
FARM
WARLAND
WARLAND WY.
JUBILEE
Rushcombe Bottom
ROAD
HIGHER
097
ROSE
JUBILEE CLOSE
JUBILEE ROAD
PRIMROSE WAY
GURNEY RD.
JUBILEE RD.
BROADSTONE GOLF COURSE
AVENUE
PORTMORE CL.
WAY
RUSH COMBE WY.
Corfe Hills
GREENSLEEVES RD.
WOODLEAZE CL.
MERRIEFIELD
DUNYEA
5
HCOMBE
RUSHCOMBE WAY
WAYMAN
ROMAN ROAD
Corfe Hills School
BLANDFORD
Club House
MERRIEFIELD CL. AV.
DRIVE
AVENUE
CECIL CLO.
HEATHER CLO.
HIGHER
UPPER
ROAD
WIDWORTHY DR.
BLANDFORD RD.
SUNNDLE GS.
BIRKDALE ST.
ANDREWS RD.
FAIRVIEW DR.
GOLF LINKS RD.
GOLF LINKS RD.
INSLEY CRES.
MEADOW
RISE
LANCASTER DR.
BIRKDALE
ROAD
DRIVE
MERRIEFIELD
INSLEY CRES.
HIGHFIELD CL.
LANCASTER AVE.
SUTHERLAND AV.
HOLLAND WAY
LANCASTER CL.
COTTON CL.
BIRKDALE
BH18
BANSTEAD RD.
TROON RD.
LOWER GOLF LINKS RD.
LOWER GOLF LINKS RD.
6
HAM TON CRES.
SUTHLND AV.
BARRY GDNS.
COTTON CL.
FAIRVIEW
Broadstone Middle School
HIGHFIELD ROAD
ROMAN ROAD
ANVIL
CRESCENT
DRIVE
SPRINGDALE
SPRINGDALE AV.
B3074
FAIRVIEW CRES.
WENTWORTH
DRIVE
GOLF LINKS ROAD
WATER TOWER
96
Caesar's
ABBOTSBURY
AVE.
ROAD
ROAD
Poole Sports Cen.
MOOR
Broadstone First Sch.
TUDOR RD.
TINSEL RD.
E
F
37
400
G
H
01
9
HIGH PARK ROAD
SPRINGDALE
ASCOT
CLENDON
DUNYEATS
Jacklin Ct.
STATION APP.
BROOKDALE FARM
BIRKDLE
War Mem
Bowl. Grn.
CAESAR'S
ROAD
Roman road

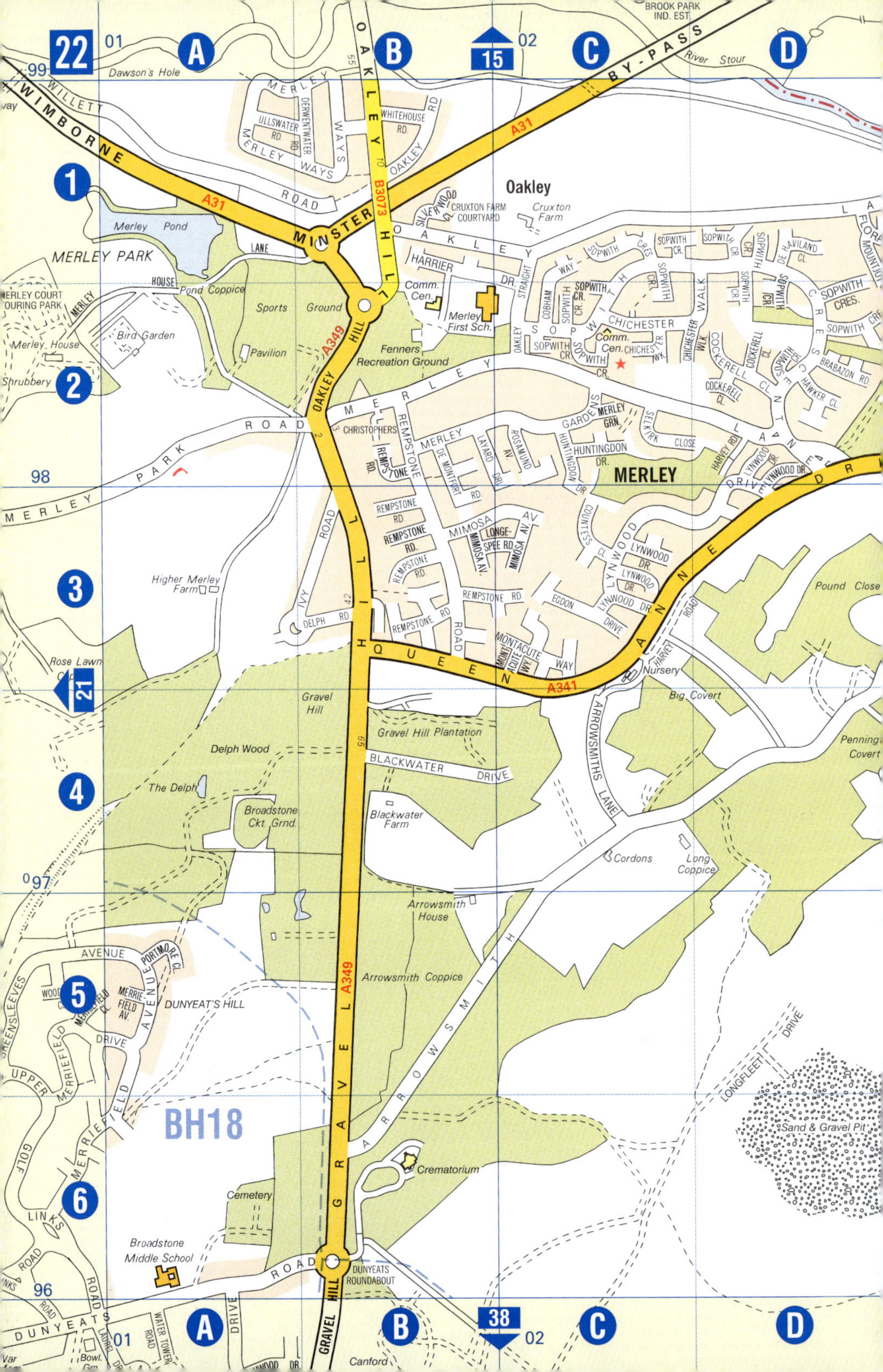

22
01
99
A
B
15
02
C
BROOK PARK IND. EST.
BY-PASS
River Stour
D
Dawson's Hole
WILLETT
WIMBORNE
WAY
MERLEY WAYS
DERWENTWATER RD.
ULLSWATER RD.
MERLEY WAYS
OAKLEY WAYS
TO OAKLEY
WHITEHOUSE RD.
OAKLEY RD.
A31
1
A31
Merley Pond
MERLEY PARK
HOUSE
MINSTER
LANE
ROAD
Pond Coppice
B3073
OAKLEY HILL
SILVERWOOD
Oakley
Cruxton Farm Courtyard
Cruxton Farm
SOPWITH
SOPWITH CRES.
SOPWITH CR.
SOPWITH CR.
HAVILAND CL.
LA FLOR
MOUNT
MERLEY COURT TOURING PARK
MERLEY HOUSE
Merley House
Bird Garden
Sports Ground
A349
OAKLEY HILL
HARRIER DR.
Comm. Cen.
Merley First Sch.
STRAIGHT
COBHAM
SOPWITH WAY
SOPWITH CR.
Comm. Cen.
CHICHESTER
CHICHESTER WALK
CHICHESTER WLK.
SOPWITH CR.
COCKERELL CL.
COCKERELL CL.
SOPWITH CR.
BRABAZON RD.
HAWKER CL.
SOPWITH CRES.
2
Shrubbery
Pavilion
Fenners Recreation Ground
CHRISTOPHERS
REMPSTONE RD.
MERLEY
DE MONTFORT
LAYARD DR.
ROSAMUND AV.
GARDENS
MERLEY GRN.
HUNTINGDON DR.
SELKIRK CLOSE
COCKERELL CL.
HARVEY RD.
LYNWOOD DR.
CHICHESTER CL.
98
MERLEY
MERLEY PARK
ROAD
REMPSTONE RD.
REMPSTONE RD.
MIMOSA
LONGE-SPEE RD.
MIMOSA AV.
MIMOSA AV.
COUNTESS CL.
MERLEY
LYNWOOD DR.
LYNWOOD DR.
LYNWOOD DR.
ROAD
DRIVE
LYNWOOD DR.
3
Higher Merley Farm
Rose Lawn
21
DELPH RD.
OAKLEY HILL
A349
REMPSTONE RD.
REMPSTONE RD.
EGDON
MONTACUTE WAY
MONTACUTE WY.
DRIVE
A341
Nursery
ARROWSMITHS LANE
Big Covert
Pound Close
QUEEN
ANNE
ROAD
Penning Covert
Gravel Hill
Delph Wood
Gravel Hill Plantation
BLACKWATER DRIVE
4
The Delph
Broadstone Ckt. Grnd.
Blackwater Farm
Cordons
Long Coppice
97
AVENUE
PORTMORE CL.
SHEENSLEEVES
WOOD CL.
MERRIEFIELD CL.
MERRIE FIELD AV.
MERRIEFIELD AVENUE
DUNYEAT'S HILL
A349
GRAVEL
Arrowsmith House
Arrowsmith Coppice
ARROWSMITH
LONGFLEET DRIVE
5
DRIVE
UPPER
GOLF
BH18
Sand & Gravel Pit
6
LINKS
LINKS ROAD
ROAD
Broadstone Middle School
Cemetery
ROAD
GRAVEL HILL
Crematorium
DUNYEATS ROUNDABOUT
96
DUNYEATS
01
WATER TOWER
Bowl. Grn.
WOOD DR.
A
DRIVE
GRAVEL HILL ROAD
Canford
B
38
02
C
D

Trunk Hole
E
F
16
04
G
Seymoor's Cliff
Stour
H
405
23
99
lampr
CANFORD MAGNA
GOLF COURSE
John O'Gaunt's Kitchen
Beaufort House
Canford School
Gisborough Hall
Tennis Courts
Park Cottages
River
1
Itch Hole
Weir
Playing Field
Open-air Theatre
CANFORD PARK
Playing Field
Canford School Golf Course (Private)
Club House
Manor F
MILL TER.
Playing Field
Manor R
CANFORD MAGNA
FARM
CEMY.
Canford Magna
Court House
Playing Field
Playing Field
EAST DORSET
POOLE
2
arden Coppice
Playing Field
Moortown Coppice
98
AVE
MAGNA
South Lodge
Moortown Drive
A341
Playing Field
Moortown Farm
Sports Club
Ten. Cts.
Driving Range
Knighton
3
Knighton House
BH21
Nurseries
GOLF COURSE
Knighton Farm
Knighton Lane
24
Brake Hills
Stoat's Hill
Withy Bed
Knighton
4
New Covert
A341
124
097
use Tip
Lane
R O A
WHEELER'S LA
121
Knighton Lodge
THE ORCHARD
Avenue
RUNNYMEDE
Runnymede Ave
D
WOOD
5
Bearwood Primary School
John
King John Av
King John Av
Runnymede Ave
Charter
Rd.
Tourney Rd
Avenue
Runnymede Av
AVENUE
BARONS RD.
King
Viscount Wlk.
Merton Grange
Wheelers
King John Av
King John Av
John
Avenue
King John Cl
King John Av
Dukes Dr.
Eastlands Farm
Ross Gns.
Viscount Wlk.
King John Av
Knights Road
Weldon
Spicer Lane
Ven
6
Viscount
Marquis Wk.
Wheelers
Way
BH11
Knights Lane
Eleanor Dr.
Knights Drive
High
Holly Green Rise
Viscount
Monks
King
Plantaganet Cres.
Richard Dr.
ANS Jou Cl.
Stephen
Fitzwilliam
Crusader Rd
Lane
Bearwood
King Richard Dr.
Lionheart Cl.
Courtenay Rd
Hull
High
Bearwood Playing Field
Crusader Rd
Road
Road
096
E
F
39
04
G
H
405

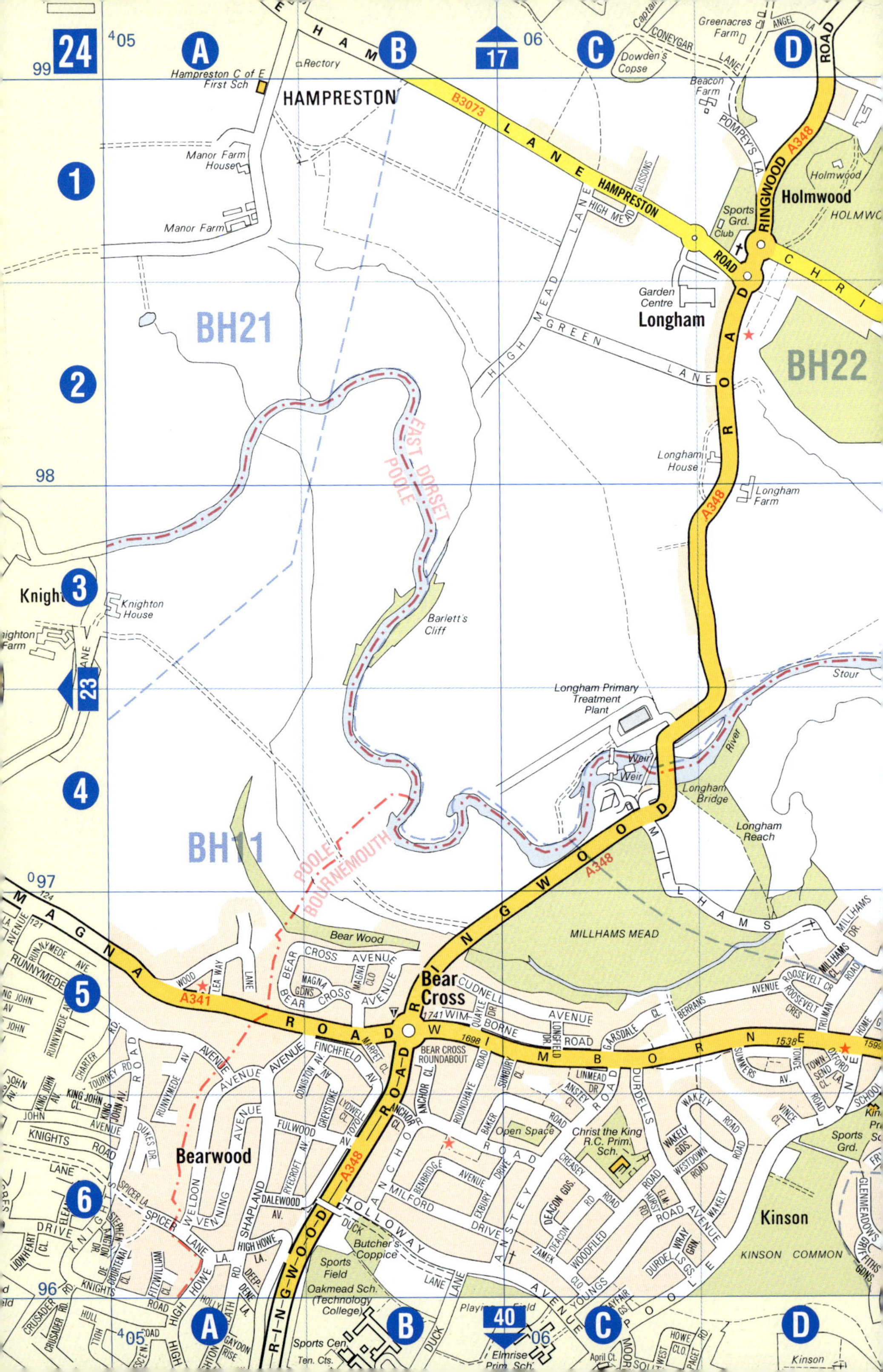

24
99
405
A
B
17
06
C
D
Capitai
CONEYGAR
Greenacres Farm
ANGEL LA
ROAD
Hampreston C of E First Sch
Rectory
Dowden's Copse
HAMPRESTON
B3073
Beacon Farm
RINGWOOD
A348
Holmwood
Holmwood
1
Manor Farm House
HAMPRESTON
LANE
POMPEY'S LA
HOLMWO
Sports Grd. Club
HIGH MEAD
Manor Farm
LANE
ROAD
BH21
Garden Centre
Longham
CHRI
D
HIGH GREEN LANE
BH22
2
98
Longham House
A348
Longham Farm
Stour
Knight
3
Knighton House
Barlett's Cliff
Longham Primary Treatment Plant
River
nighton Farm
23
LANE
Weir
Weir
Longham Bridge
4
Longham Reach
BH11
POOLE
EAST DORSET
BOURNEMOUTH
Longham Reach
RINGWOOD
A348
MILLHAMS
097
124
Bear Wood
MILLHAMS MEAD
MILLHAMS CL
MILLHAMS ROAD
MAGNA
121
AVENUE
BEAR CROSS AVENUE
ROOSEVELT CR
ROOSEVELT CRES
RUNNYMEDE AV
BEAR CROSS GDNS
MAGNA CLO
MAGNA AVENUE
Bear Cross
CUDNELL
AVENUE
GARSDALE CL
BERRANS
AVENUE
15.38
E
1598
5
A341
WOOD
LEA WAY
LANE
BEAR CROSS AVENUE
1741 WIM
QUAYLE DR
BORNE
DR
RINGWOOD
1698
ROAD
SUMMERS AV
TOWN
OXFORD
SEND CL
LANE
NG JOHN AV
RUNNYMEDE AVE
CHARTER
RD
TOURNEY RD
ROAD
RUNNYMEDE AV
AVENUE
FINCHFIELD
MARKET CL
ANCHOR CL
Bear Cross Roundabout
CUDNELL CLO
SHIBURY CL
LINMEAD DR
ANSTEY CL
DURDELLS
WAKELY GDNS
WESTDOWN ROAD
VINCE CL
Sports Grd
KING JOHN CL
JOHN AV
GREYSTONE
CONISTON AV
LYDWELL CL
A348
ANCHOR CL
ROUNDHAYE
BAKER ROAD
ROAD
ANSTEY
WAKELY
WAKELY ROAD
ELM ROAD
HURST ROAD
Pri
KNIGHTS ROAD
JOHN AVENUE
DUKES DR
FULWOOD AVENUE
Open Space
Christ the King R.C. Prim. Sch.
CREASEY RD
ELM ROAD
WRAY CL
ROAD
Kinson
6
SPICER LA
WELDON ROAD
VENNING AV
SHAPLAND AV
DALEWOOD AV.
HOLLOWAY
MILFORD
BENBRIDGE AVENUE
EXBURY DRIVE
DEACON GDS
DEACON RD
ZAMEK CL
WOODFILED CLO
DURDELLS GDNS
MAYFAIR
KINSON COMMON
GLENMEADOWS
Bearwood
LIONHEART CL
KNIG
DE
SPICER LANE
HIGH HOWE LA.
RD
HIGH HOWE LA.
DEEP
DENE LA.
DUCK
Butcher's Coppice
ANSTEY LANE
YOUNGS
POOLE
KINSON
96
405
A
RINGWOOD
FITZWILLIAM CL
HOLLY LA
GAYDON RISE
HEATH LA.
Sports Field
Oakmead Sch. (Technology College)
Sports Cen
Ten. Cts.
B
DUCK LANE
40
06
AVENUE
Playing Field
MOOR
C
HOWE CLO
PAGET RD
WEST CLO
Kinson
D
CRUSADER RD
HULL
TITH
ROAD
Elmrise Prim Sch
April Ct.

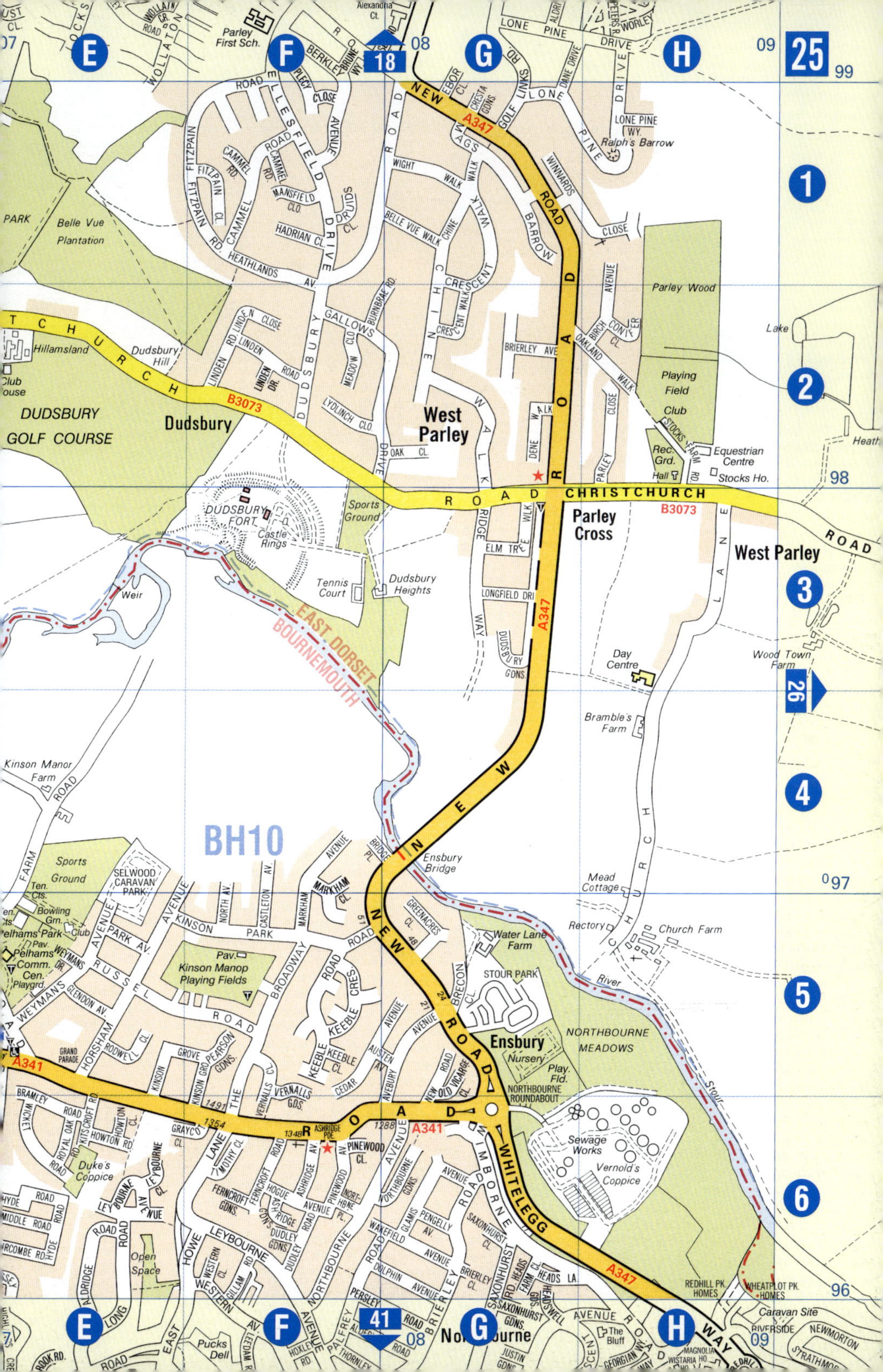

E 07
Alexandria Ct.
Parley First Sch.
F 18 08
Berkley
G 08
LONE PINE
DANE DRIVE
WORLEY
DRIVE
H 09
25 99
WOLLATON CR. ROAD
CL.
OCKS CL.
CLOSE
AVENUE
PLEY
DRIVE
A347
WAGS
EBOR CL.
CRESTA GDNS.
GOLF LINKS RD.
LONE PINE WY.
Ralph's Barrow
1
FITZPAIN ROAD
CAMMEL
ELLESFIELD ROAD
CAMMEL RD.
MANSFIELD CLO.
HADRIAN CL.
WIGHT WALK
BELLE VUE WALK
CHINE WALK
WALK
ROAD
BARROW
WINNARDS CLOSE
LINDEN RD.
NEW
AVENUE
BIRCH CL.
CONIFER CL.
Parley Wood
FITZPAIN
FITZPAIN CL.
FITZPAIN RD.
HEATHLANDS AV.
DRUIDS CL.
DUDSBURY
GALLOWS CLO.
BURNBRAE RD.
CRESCENT
CHRISTCHURCH CRES.
CRESCENT WALK
BRIERLEY AVE.
OAKLAND CL.
Playing Field Club
PARK
Belle Vue Plantation
LINDEN RD. LINDEN CLOSE
LINDEN ROAD
MEADOW CLO.
DENE WALK
STOCKS FARM RD.
Lake
2
TCHURCH
Hillamsland
Dudsbury Hill
B3073
DUDSBURY
LINDEN DR.
LYDLINCH CLO.
West Parley
PARLEY CLOSE
Rec. Grd.
Hall
Equestrian Centre
Stocks Ho.
Heath
Club House
DUDSBURY GOLF COURSE
Dudsbury
OAK CL.
ROAD
ROAD CHRISTCHURCH
B3073
West Parley
ROAD
98
DUDSBURY FORT
Castle Rings
Sports Ground
RIDGE WLK.
ELM TRE WLK.
Parley Cross
LANE
3
Weir
Tennis Court
Dudsbury Heights
EAST DORSET
BOURNEMOUTH
LONGFIELD DRI
WAY
A347
DUDSBURY GDNS.
Day Centre
Wood Town Farm
26
Kinson Manor Farm
ROAD
NEW
Bramble's Farm
4
BH10
Sports Ground
SELWOOD CARAVAN PARK
AVENUE
NORTH AV.
AVENUE
CASTLETON AV.
MARKHAM AV.
BRIDGE PL.
N
Ensbury Bridge
GREENACRES CL.
Mead Cottage
097
Ten. Cts.
Bowling Grn.
Club
Pelhams Park
Pav.
Weymans Comm. Cen.
Playgrd.
KINSON PARK
MARKHAM CL.
ROAD
NEW
48
Water Lane Farm
Rectory
Church Farm
CHURCH
River
5
WEYMANS AV.
GLENDON AV.
RUSSEL
PARK AV.
Pav.
Kinson Manor Playing Fields
BROADWAY
ROAD
KEEBLE CRES.
BRECON CL.
Stour Park
STOUR
NORTHBOURNE MEADOWS
A341
GRAND PARADE
HORSHAM
RODWELL CL.
GROVE
PEARSON GDNS.
AVENUE
KEEBLE CL.
KEEBLE CL.
AUSTEN AV.
AVENUE
ROAD
21
24
NEW ROAD
VICARGE CL.
OLD
Ensbury
Nursery
Play. Fld.
NORTHBOURNE ROUNDABOUT
Sewage Works
Vernold's Coppice
6
BRAMLEY
WICKET ROAD
ROYAL OAK
KITSCROFT RD.
HOWTON RD.
KINSON
THE
VERNALLS CL.
VERNALLS GDS.
1491
1354
1348
ASHRIDGE PDE.
PINEWOOD CL.
1288
A341
WHITELEGG
A347
REDHILL PK. HOMES
WHEATPLOT PK. HOMES
HYDE ROAD
MIDDLE ROAD
RCOMBE RD.
ALDRIDGE
LONG
EAST
Open Space
HOWE
LEYBOURNE
WESTERN
LEYBOURNE
BOURNE AVENUE
TIMOTHY CL.
GRAYCO
FERNCROFT GDNS.
ASHRIDGE GDNS.
PINEWOOD PL.
DUDLEY GDNS.
NORT. HBNE.
NORTHBOURNE
WAKEFIELD AVENUE
DOLPHIN AVENUE
PERSLEY AVENUE
GLAMIS AV.
PENGELLY AV.
SAXONHURST CL.
BRIERLEY CL.
SAXONHURST
HEADS RD.
HEADS LA.
HEDSWELL CL.
WHITELEGG WAY
E
Pucks Dell
F 41 08
Northbourne
G 09
H WAY
Caravan Site
RIVERSIDE
NEWMORTON
STRATHMO
BROOK RD.
JUSTIN GDNS.
GEORGIANA WAY
The Bluff
MAGNOLIA HO.
WISTARIA HO.
REDHILL

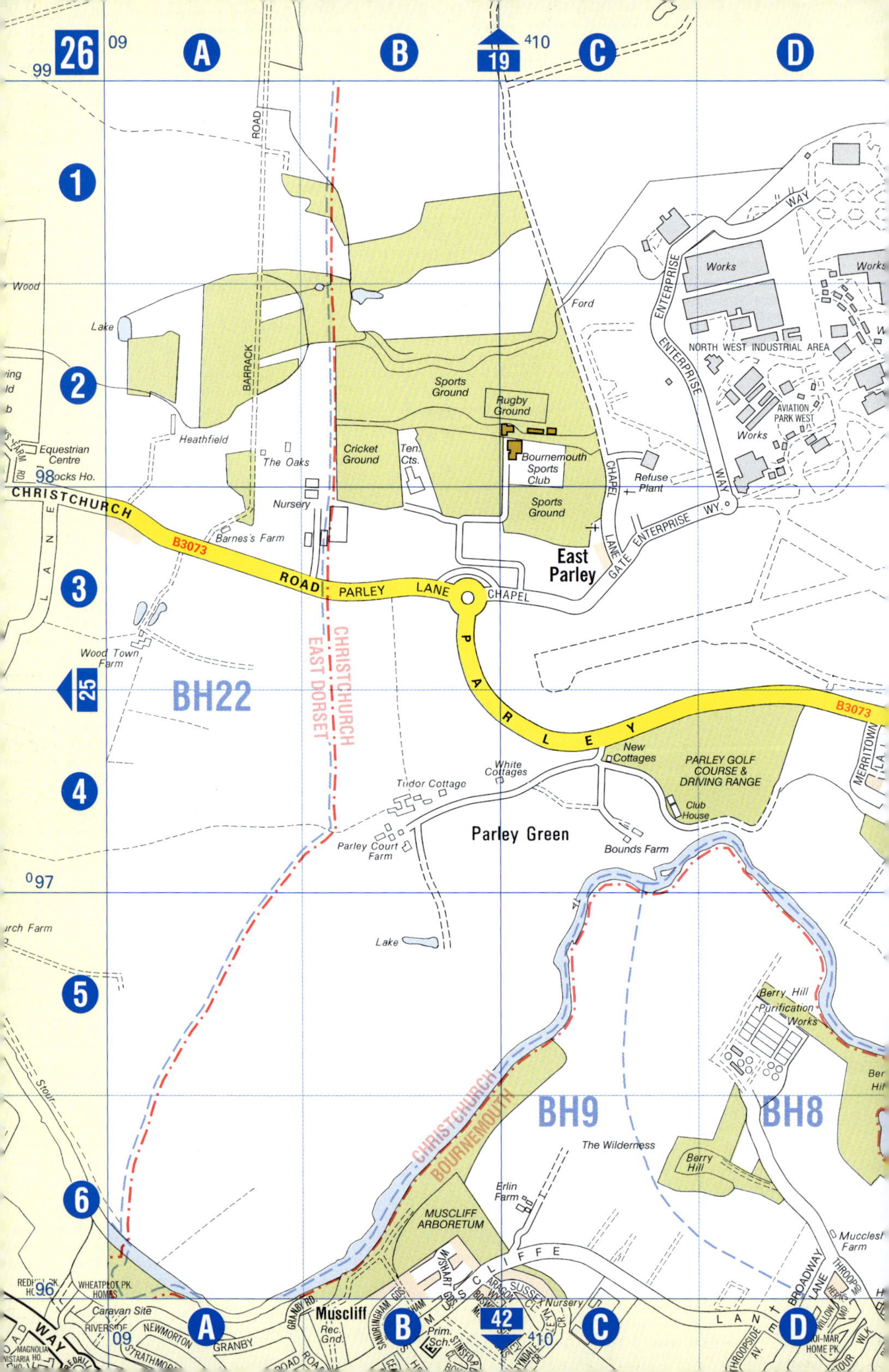

26
09
99
A
B
410
19
C
D
1
Wood
Lake
2
ing
d
b
Equestrian
Centre
ocks Ho.
98
CHRISTCHURCH
Heathfield
The Oaks
Nursery
Barnes's Farm
B3073
ROAD
PARLEY
LANE
CHAPEL
BARRACK
ROAD
Sports
Ground
Cricket
Ground
Ten.
Cts.
Rugby
Ground
Bournemouth
Sports
Club
Sports
Ground
East
Parley
CHAPEL LANE
GATE
ENTERPRISE
WY.
ENTERPRISE
WAY
ENTERPRISE
WAY
Ford
Refuse
Plant
Works
NORTH WEST INDUSTRIAL AREA
Works
Works
Works
AVIATION
PARK WEST
Wo
3
CHRISTCHURCH
EAST DORSET
25
BH22
Wood Town
Farm
Tudor Cottage
White
Cottages
Parley Court
Farm
Parley Green
New
Cottages
Club
House
Bounds Farm
PARLEY GOLF
COURSE &
DRIVING RANGE
B3073
MERRITOWN
LANE
4
97
0
Lake
5
Stour
Berry Hill
Purification
Works
Ber
Hil
6
CHRISTCHURCH
BOURNEMOUTH
BH9
BH8
The Wilderness
Berry
Hill
Erlin
Farm
Mucclesf
Farm
REDHILL PK.
HC.
WHEATPLOT PK.
HOMES
Caravan Site
RIVERSIDE
MAGNOLIA
WISTARIA HO.
REDHILL
WAY
ROAD
NEWMORTON
STRATHMOR
GRANBY
GRANBY RD.
ROAD
Muscliff
Muscliff
Rec.
Gnd.
SANDRINGHAM GDS.
HAM
STINSFO
Prim.
Sch.
B
42
410
MUSCLIFF
ARBORETUM
WYSHART
CLIFFE
WYSHART GDS.
ARAGON
BOSW
WAY
SUSSEX
CL.
TYNDALE
CL.
Nursery
CR.
C
ARAGON CL.
BROADWAY
LANE
THROOPSIDE
HERB.
THROOP
AV.
WILLOW
WD.
TUR
ROI-MAR
HOME PK.
D
96
09
0
A
B
C
D

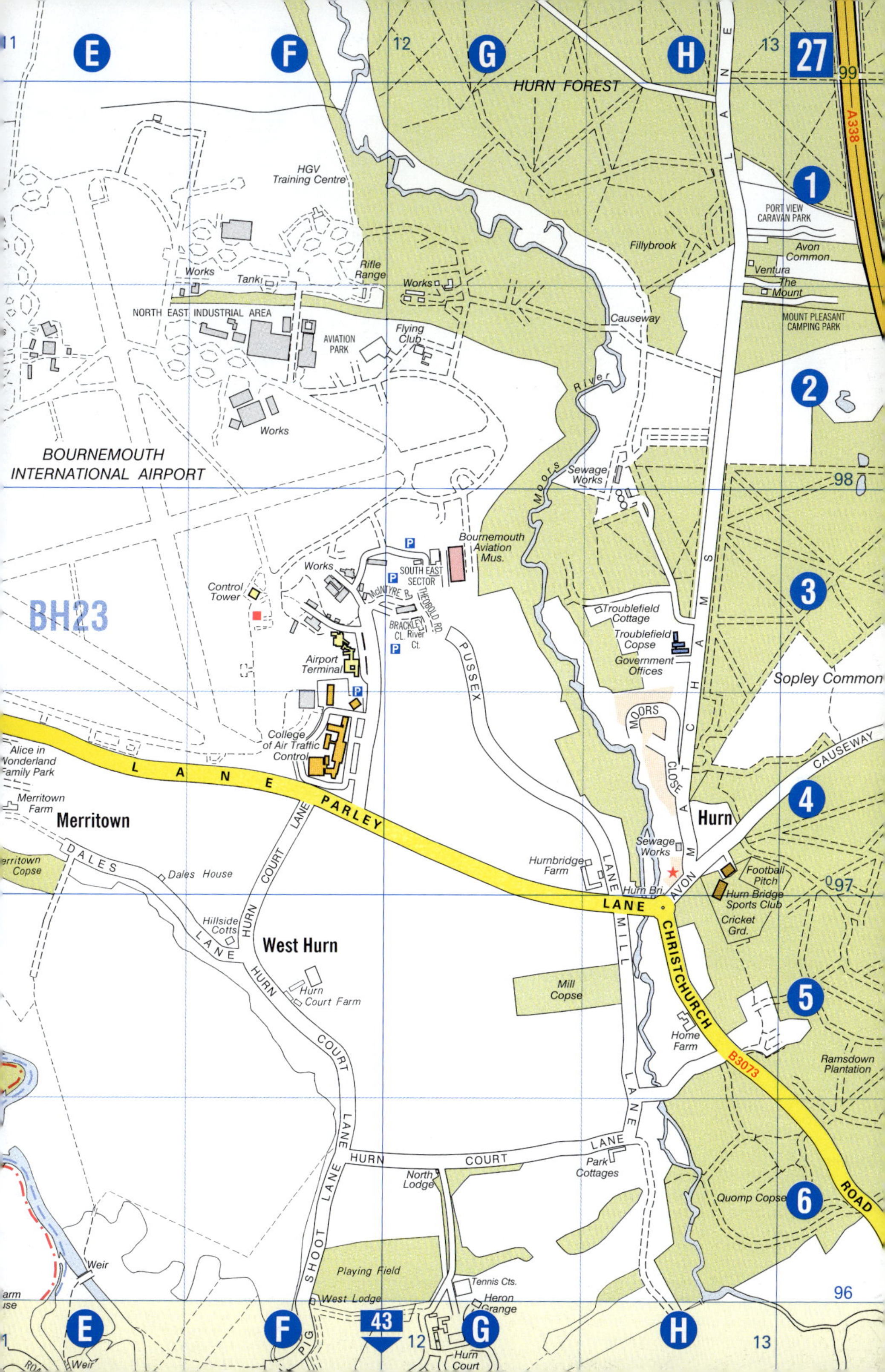
E
F
12
G
H
13
27
99
A338
HURN FOREST
1
PORT VIEW CARAVAN PARK
HGV Training Centre
Fillybrook
Avon Common
Ventura
The Mount
Works
Tank
Rifle Range
Works
Causeway
MOUNT PLEASANT CAMPING PARK
NORTH EAST INDUSTRIAL AREA
AVIATION PARK
Flying Club
River
2
Works
BOURNEMOUTH INTERNATIONAL AIRPORT
Moors
Sewage Works
98
BH23
Control Tower
Works
P
P
SOUTH EAST SECTOR
McINTYRE R.
Bournemouth Aviation Mus.
Troublefield Cottage
3
THEOBOLD RD.
BRACKLEY CL. River Ct.
Troublefield Copse
Government Offices
Sopley Common
P
Airport Terminal
P
PUSSEX
MOORS
CLOSE
CATCHAMS
College of Air Traffic Control
LANE PARLEY
Hurn
4
CAUSEWAY
Alice in Wonderland Family Park
Merritown Farm
Merritown
Hurnbridge Farm
LANE
Sewage Works
AVON
Football Pitch
DALES
Dales House
Hurn Bri.
Hurn Bridge Sports Club
097
Merritown Copse
MILL LANE
LANE
Cricket Grd.
Hillside Cotts
West Hurn
HURN LANE
LANE
5
Hurn Court Farm
CHRISTCHURCH
Mill Copse
Home Farm
B3073
Ramsdown Plantation
COURT LANE
North Lodge
LANE
Park Cottages
Quomp Copse
6
ROAD
SHOOT LANE
HURN COURT LANE
Weir
Playing Field
West Lodge
Tennis Cts.
Heron Grange
Weir
E
F
PIG
43
12
G
Hurn Court
H
13
96

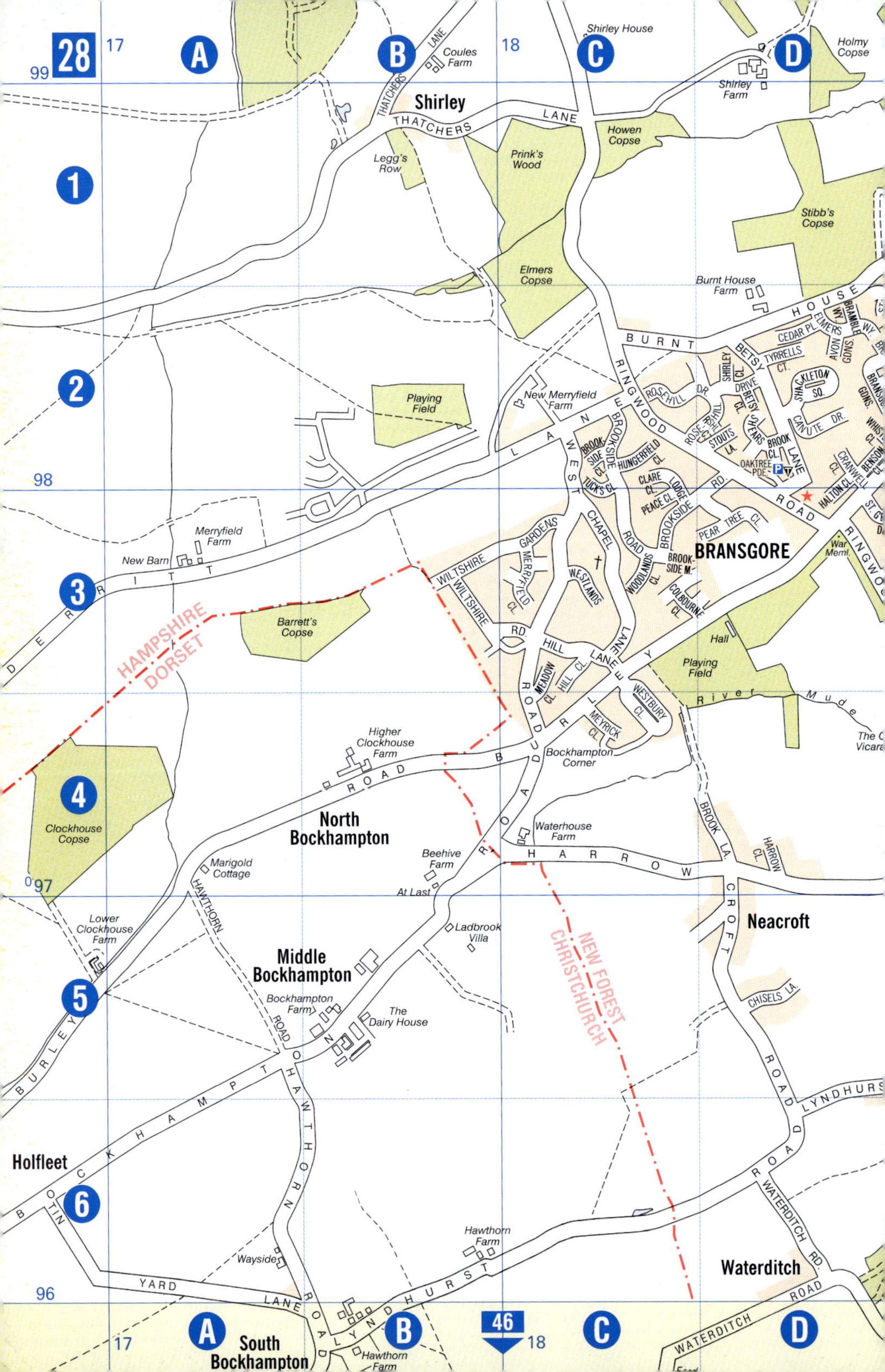

28
99
17
18
A
B
C
D
Shirley House
Holmy Copse
Coules Farm
Shirley
Shirley Farm
THATCHERS
THATCHERS LANE
LANE
Legg's Row
Prink's Wood
Howen Copse
Stibb's Copse
1
Elmers Copse
Burnt House Farm
BURNT HOUSE
ELMERS
WY
BRAMBLE
WY
BR
BRANSGORE
GDNS
WHIS
AVON
CEDAR PL.
TYRRELLS CT.
SNDG
Playing Field
New Merryfield Farm
RINGWOOD
SHIRLEY CL.
BETSY DRIVE
SHACKLETON SQ.
ROSEHILL DR.
BROOKSIDE CL.
ROSE HILL
BETSY SHEARS
BROOK CL.
2
LANE
WEST
HUNGERFIELD CL.
STOUTS LA.
CANUTE DR.
BROOK LANE
CRANWELL CL.
BENSON CL.
98
TUCK'S CL.
CLARE CL.
LODGE CL.
RD.
HALTON CL.
OAKTREE PDE.
P
PEACE CL.
BROOKSIDE
PEAR TREE CL.
ROAD
St. G
Merryfield Farm
GARDENS
CHAPEL
PEAR TREE CL.
RINGWOOD
New Barn
MERRYFIELD CL.
CHAPEL ROAD
WOODLANDS CL.
BRANSGORE
3
DERRITT LANE
HAMPSHIRE
DORSET
WILTSHIRE
WILTSHIRE RD.
WESTLANDS
BROOK-SIDE M.
COLBOURNE CL.
War Meml.
Barrett's Copse
HILL
MEADOW CL.
HILL CL.
LANE
Y
Hall
The Vicara
Higher Clockhouse Farm
ROAD
HILL
MEYRICK CL.
WESTBURY CL.
Playing Field
River Mude
4
ROAD
Bockhampton Corner
Clockhouse Copse
B
Waterhouse Farm
North Bockhampton
Beehive Farm
HARROW
BROOK LA.
HARROW CL.
Marigold Cottage
At Last
Neacroft
97
HAWTHORN
NEW FOREST
CHRISTCHURCH
CROFT
Lower Clockhouse Farm
Ladbrook Villa
5
BURLEY
Middle Bockhampton
CHISELS LA.
Bockhampton Farm
The Dairy House
ROAD
ROAD
Holfleet
6
BOTIN
BOCKHAMPTON
HAWTHORN
LANE
Hawthorn Farm
LYNDHURST
Waterditch
WATERDITCH RD.
96
Wayside
YARD LANE
LYNDHURST ROAD
WATERDITCH ROAD
17
A
South Bockhampton
B
46
18
C
D
Hawthorn Farm

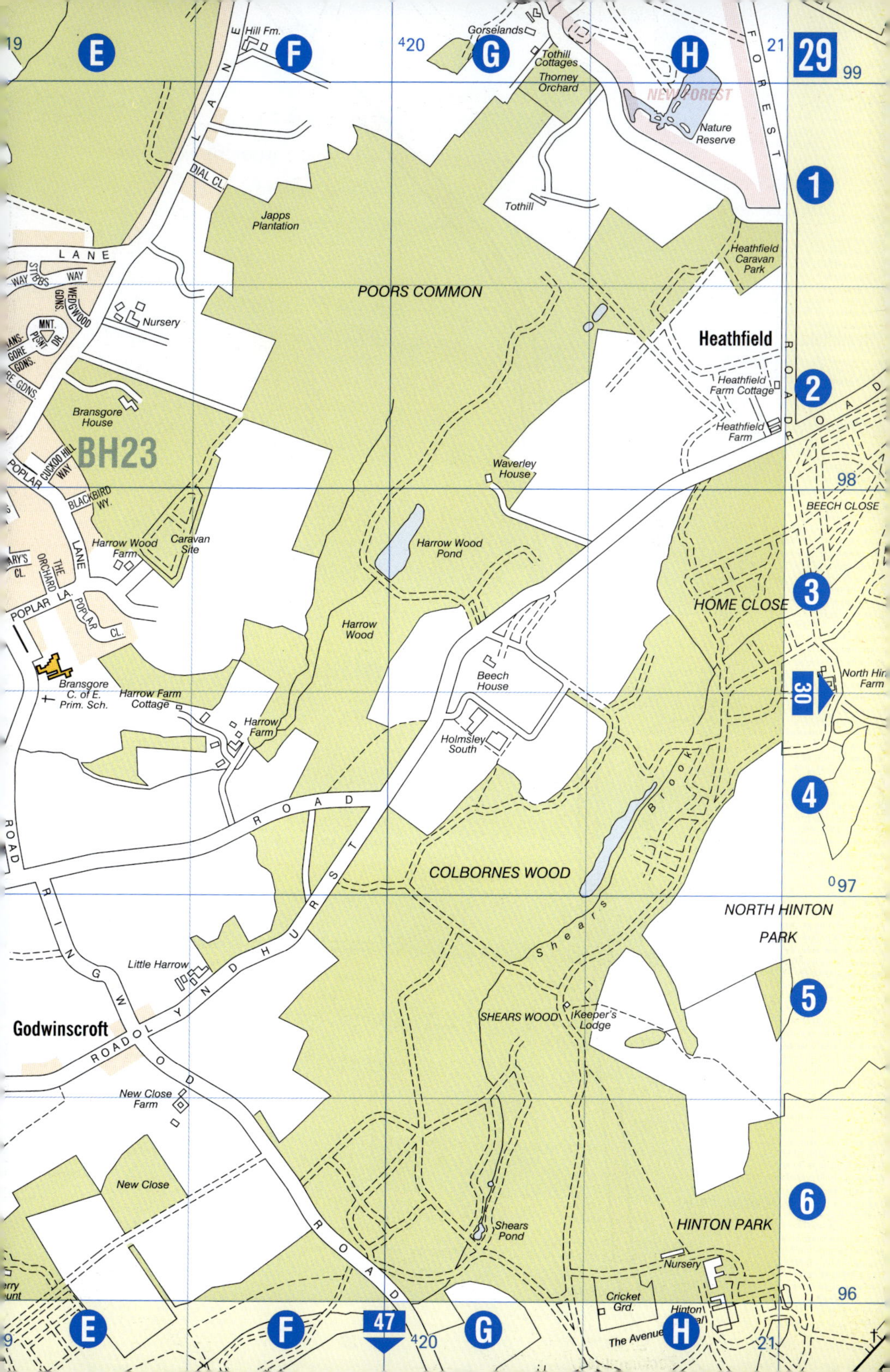

19
E
Hill Fm.
F
20
Gorselands
G
Tothill Cottages
Thorney Orchard
H
21
NEW FOREST
29
99
FOREST ROAD
Japps Plantation
POORS COMMON
Tothill
Nature Reserve
Heathfield Caravan Park
1
Heathfield
LANE
DIAL CL.
Nursery
WEDGWOOD GDNS.
WAY
WAY
STIBBS
MNT. PISH. DR.
TRANS-GORE GDNS.
GORE GDNS.
LANE
Heathfield Farm Cottage
2
Heathfield Farm
98
BEECH CLOSE
Bransgore House
BH23
POPLAR
CUCKOO HILL WAY
BLACKBIRD WY.
Waverley House
Harrow Wood Pond
HOME CLOSE
3
North Hinton Farm
LANE
POPLAR LA.
POPLAR CL.
THE ORCHARD
MARY'S CL.
Harrow Wood Farm
Caravan Site
Harrow Wood
Beech House
30
4
Bransgore C. of E. Prim. Sch.
Harrow Farm Cottage
Harrow Farm
Holmsley South
Brook
Shears
97
ROAD
ROAD
COLBORNES WOOD
NORTH HINTON PARK
RING WOOD
LYNDHURST
ROAD
Little Harrow
5
SHEARS WOOD
Keeper's Lodge
Godwinscroft
ROAD
New Close Farm
New Close
6
HINTON PARK
Nursery
Shears Pond
Cricket Grd.
erry unt
E
9
F
47
420
G
The Avenue
Hinton
H
21
96

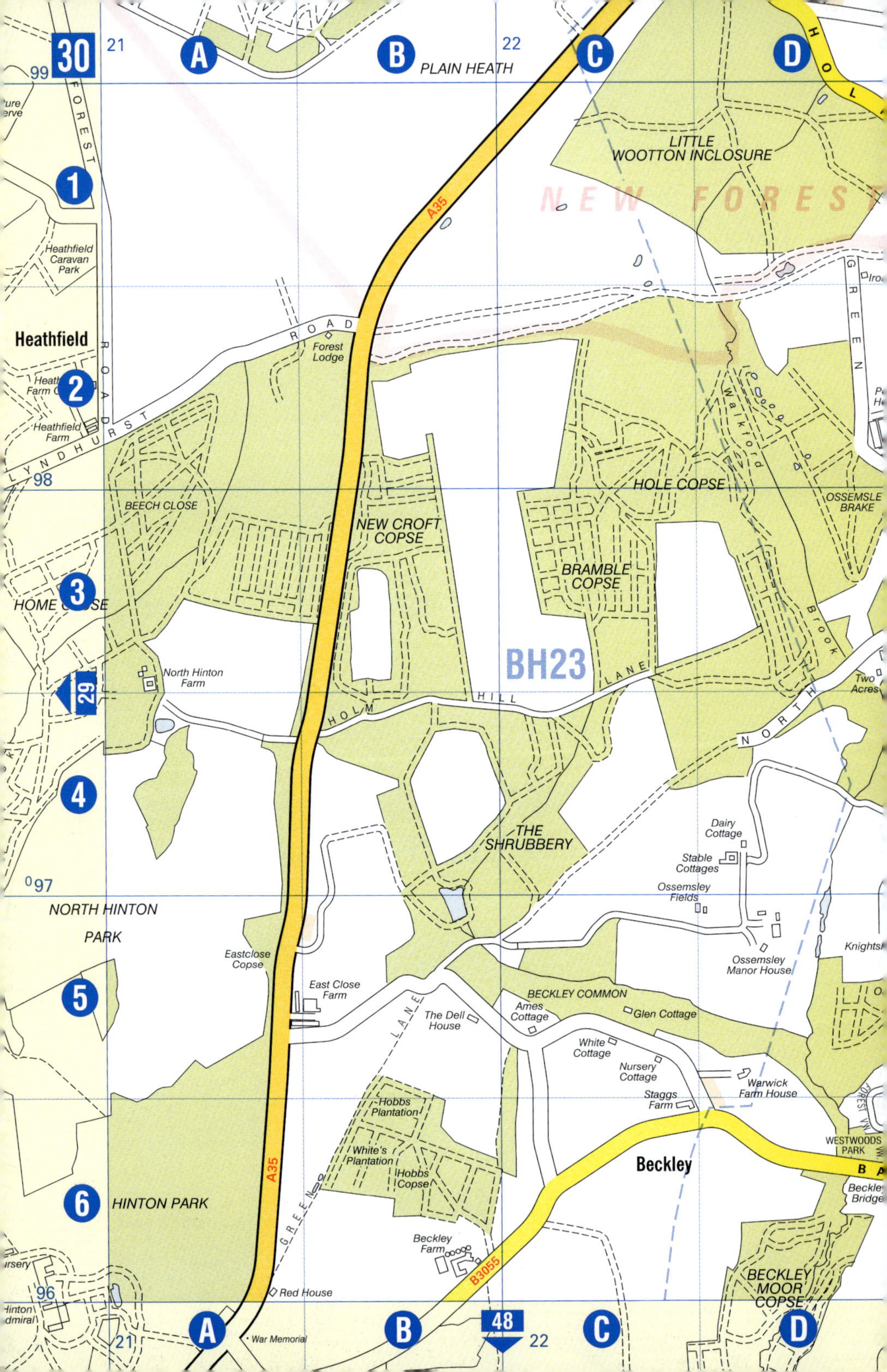

30
99 21
A
B 22
PLAIN HEATH
C
D
HOL
NEW FOREST
LITTLE
WOOTTON INCLOSURE
1
Heathfield
Caravan
Park
FOREST
A35
ROAD
Forest
Lodge
Walkford
GREEN
Iro
Heathfield
ROAD
LYNDHURST
Heath
Farm C
2
Heathfield
Farm
98
HOLE COPSE
OSSEMSLE
BRAKE
P
H
BEECH CLOSE
NEW CROFT
COPSE
BRAMBLE
COPSE
BH23
Brook
3
HOME CLOSE
NORTH
Two
Acres
North Hinton
Farm
29
HOLM
HILL
LANE
NORTH
4
THE
SHRUBBERY
Dairy
Cottage
Stable
Cottages
Ossemsley
Fields
Ossemsley
Manor House
Knights
0 97
NORTH HINTON
PARK
Eastclose
Copse
BECKLEY COMMON
Glen Cottage
WE
O
5
East Close
Farm
LANE
The Dell
House
Ames
Cottage
White
Cottage
Nursery
Cottage
Warwick
Farm House
FOREST V
WESTWOODS
PARK
Staggs
Farm
Hobbs
Plantation
Beckley
B
Beckl
Bridge
White's
Plantation
GREEN
6
HINTON PARK
A35
Hobbs
Copse
B3055
Beckley
Farm
BECKLEY
MOOR
COPSE
96
Hinton
dmiral
Red House
A
B
48
22
C
D
War Memorial
21

31
99
98
97
96
E F 24 G H 425
E F 49 G H 425
23 24 25
1
2
3
32
4
5
6
BROWNHILL RD.
Treetops
Rhinefield Farm
RHINEFIELD ROAD
WOOTTON FARM ROAD
WILVERLEY
SLEY DRIVE
B3058
Forest Mead
Wattons Farm
Manor Farm
Wooton Oaks
Valesmoor Farm
Pear Tree Cottage
Wootton Heath Farm
Wootton Heath
Wootton
Hinton Holms
BROCKENHURST ROAD
TIPTOE
Holly Cott.
Byways
Eastley
Nursery
Wootton Hall
ROAD
ROUGH
Forest Close
Grey Tops
orselands
Wild Acres
Dar
Cra
Arne Cor
Big Rough
Fir-Belt
Badgers Run
Oaklands
Willie's Holms
Scroy House
Scroy Farm
Forest Gdns.
THE LEG
Portnalls Farm
Ossemsley
Jones's Covert
Far Forest
ocksbridge Copse
LANE NORTH
DRIVE
OSSEMSLEY
SOUTH DRIVE
Squirrels
Blackstocks
Long Meadow
Arreton
Arreton Farm
Four Winds
BASHLEY
ROAD
COMMON
B3058
Ytene Way
Yew Tree Farm
Burley Villa Farm
Charfield
MARLPIT
Marlpit Farm
MARLPIT LANE
Ewerby Farm
Woodcutters
Depot
WOOTTON ROAD
ST. JOHNS RD.
BH25
Nursery
Nursery
Sawmill
ST. JOHNS
Bashley Park
Caravan Park
Caravan Park
Caravan Park
Bashley Park
BASHLEY DR.
BASHLEY DR.
Bashley
Sports Grd.
Hall
Pav.
Cricket Grd.
Nursery
Lynwood Farm
Bashley Copse
NEW LANE
SMITHY LANE
Oakmead
CROSS ROAD
B3055
ROAD
SWAY
FERNHILL LANE
B3058
MARK'S LA.
B3055
Har
CPS.
Gayfie
Re
LANE
DRIVE
OTTERS WK.
THE FALLOWS
CULLWOOD LA.
BROCKHILLS
ASHLEY DRIVE
Estate Farm
msley pse
Glendene Park
Bashley Cottages
ECHERRY TREE DRIVE
Bashley Manor Farm House
Bashley Wild Ground
Bashley Croft
Ferndene Farm
Great Wear Copse
STEM LANE
EEN LANE
VELVET DRIVE
HART CL.
PARK RD.
LAWN CL.
ANTLER
DARK
Ballard School
Ballard
Pond Copse
FOREST OAK DRIVE
HOLLANDS WOOD
THE LANES
SHEVES LA.
FERNHILL LINE
FERN FLDS.
HORNS
GAINSBOROUGH
BROOK
DERWENT RD.
SPINNEY WY.
DEERLEAP WY.
GOY PL.
THETCHERS RD.
GRAS MERE GDNS.
APPLESLADE WY.
KESWICK RD.
KESWICK CT.
WINTON WAY
AVENUE
The Fernmount Centre
FOREST SPINES
VIOLET LA.
PALMER PL.
LINFORD CL.
ARRS
LARKSHILL CL.
Kamptee Copse
Woodland
IXEN WLK.
Partridge
GN.
CULL LANE
CULL WOOD
WHATLEY WY.
CRES.
OSC CL.
AKESHILL CL.
MARSTON ROAD
MARSTON CL.
CHARLES CRES.
GORSEFIELD RD.
HILTON RD.
FERNDALE
AVENUE NORTH
RAMPTON CL.
SHLEY
WCHESTER RD.
MON LA.
BARR

32
99
P
4 25
A
BROADLEY INCLOSURE
B
26
Avon
C
Green Ashen Bank
D
Pump House
Inis
1
ELKHAMS GRAVE
NEW FOREST
Water
Greenslade
Boundway Hill
Broadley Farm
Boundway End
Forest Close
Stanley's Farm
Upper Mead End Farm
Chapel Farm
Boundway Farm
Oakfield
Lower Meadend Farm
MEAD END
2
Nursery
TIPTOE
98
Wootton Hall
Langham Lodge
Forest Farm
Holm Farm
Marley Mount Farm
Fir Tree Farm
Meadend House
Craiglea
Danelea
The Haven
Forest House
Homestead
Kennington Cottage
Oaklands
Broadley Farm
ROAD
ROUGH ROAD
WOOTTON
MARLEY
MOUNT
Sandlea
Broadley House
Barn Farm
Grey Tops
Tiptoe Prim. Sch.
Fairlight Cott.
Amberwood Farm
Littledown Farm
3
Depot
Gorselands
DANEHURST NEW RD.
Field Gate
Tiptoe Lodge Farm
CRABBSWOOD
Yewtree
Crabbswood Farm
JOHNS RD.
31
Wild Acres
Arnewood Common
Tiptoe
Kingswood
Sunnyside
Whiteoaks
VALEVIEW
WOOTTON
MIDDLE
Danehurst
Touchwood
Glenwood
BH25
Deemster Farm
Cago Cottage
LANE
4
Caravan Park
Blacklands Farm
Brockhills Farm
Sunnyholme
NORTHOVER LA.
Oak Farm
Ar Ma
Danes Stream Coppice
Danesford
Hall
ROAD
ARNEWOOD
BRIDGE
97
Bashley Park
Danestream Farm
Danewood
Inverurie
Meadow Farm
Swaylett
B3055
Dene Lodge
5
Rose Cottage
Hordle Dene
Arnewood Cottage
Oakfield Nusery
Tiptoe Farm
SWAY
HARS BADGERS CPS.
Gayfield
Stanley Holiday Centre
Miranda
WY
PARTRIDGE
DRIVE
Danes Stream
BROCKHILLS
Stanleys Farm
WOODLAND
VIXEN WLK.
GN.
WOOD
OTTERS WK.
Fairmeads Farm
Stanley's Copse
THE FALLOWS
CULL
CULLWOOD LA.
Stanley Park Country Club
Longacres
Hordle Grange Nursing Home
6
HOLLANDS
FERN
AKESHILL CL.
CHARLES CRES.
MARS ROAD
ASHLEY AVENUE
Vaggs Farm
96
MARSTON
GORSEFIELD RD.
HILTON RD.
OAKWOOD AVENUE
WINCHESTER RD.
ASHLEY COMMON ROAD
Vernalls Farm
Concord
4 25
A
HOLLY LA.
BURN GDS.
B
50
26
C
Rec. Grd.
D
2
ASHLEY
GDS. PE
SIL

27
E
Forest Lea
BRIGHTON
BULDOWNE WK.
F
28
JORDANS LA.
G
H
29
33
99
OAKENBROW
THE CLOSE
GILPIN PL.
RHINERS
GILPIN HAWTHORN DR.
KITCHERS CL.
HIGHFIELD GS.
DURRANT WAY
MANCHESTER TER.
OXFORD RD.
LITTLE BURN
HIGHFELD CL.
B3055
NEW FOREST
Widden Bottom
owen
Nettlehorns House
LANE
Makaira
NORMANDY CL.
ROAD
MIDDLE
STANFORD RISE
ANDERWOOD
CRUSE CL.
WIDDEN CL.
ROAD
DRIVE
BRIDGERS CL.
THORNS
SET
CENTENARY CL.
ST. JAMES RD.
ROAD
BACK LA.
Rec. Grd.
Pav.
Earthworks
1
Mead End Rise
SWAY
Marlings
HERON CL.
STATION ROAD
CHURCH
WESTBEAMS RD.
HYDE CL.
CRITTALL CL.
Durnstown
Durns Town
PITMORE
CHAPEL LA.
Little Purley Farm
Sunnydale
Horseshoe Cottage
2
Rushcroft Farm
Sway
St. Luke's C. of E. Prim. Sch.
DURNSTOWN
HILL
COOMBE
Long Orchard
ROWAN CL.
HOLLIES CL.
Sway Place
BIRCHY
Switchells
Manor Farm
98
JUBILEE CT.
ROAD
ROAD
SOUTH
OLD VICARAGE LA.
Tebourba Cottages
Playford Rise
Meadow End
Many Trees
Little Coombe
Stud Farm
Clayton Farm
Clayton
Cross Oaks
Woodpeckers
Sway House Cottage
Little Acre
3
MADEND
Avon Wood
Claywood
Sway Court
Cedar Cottage
Pauls Place
PAULS LANE
Field House
Many Trees
Kings Lane
Bunny
SO41
Valley Farm
BRIDGE
Scanlands
SWAY
Kings Farm
Nursery
ROAD
Arnewood Bridge
Greylands
34
Arnewood Manor Farm
ARNEWOOD
BARROWS LANE
Bridge View
Lower Mead
Stafford Cottage
Avon Lea
Flexford Farm
LANE
4
wood Farm
East Lodge
ROAD
B3055
LINNIES
Towers Farm
Downlands Farm
Swiss Cottage
Avon
The Wharie
Flexford Mill
97
AGARS
Little Arnewood House
Avon Water House
Arnewood Court
Arnewood Ct. Turkey Farm
Weir
Water
SWAY LANE
MILL
Flexford Ho.
Knight Bridge Ho.
South Sway
Arnewood Court Turkey Farm
FLEXFORD
Highlight Nurseries
Little Place
Hazelhurst Farm
Bridge Farm
Flexford Ho.
South Sway Farm
5
LANE
Overton Farm
Hazelhurst I
Shepherds Wilds
Sewage Works
South Sway Farm House
Gordleton Rise
Oak Bank Farm
Barrows Copse
6
White Cottage
Partridge Farm
LANE
South Barrows
Plough Close
Broadmead Cottages
STREET
Gordleton Mill
Agar's Nursery
Silverland
Nurseries
Cook's Farm
Weir
Downlands Farm
WOODCOCK LA.
E
Poultry Farm
F
Bell Farm
51
28
STREET
Linfoot's
SILVER
G
STREET
H
96
29
Flanders Farm
Nursery

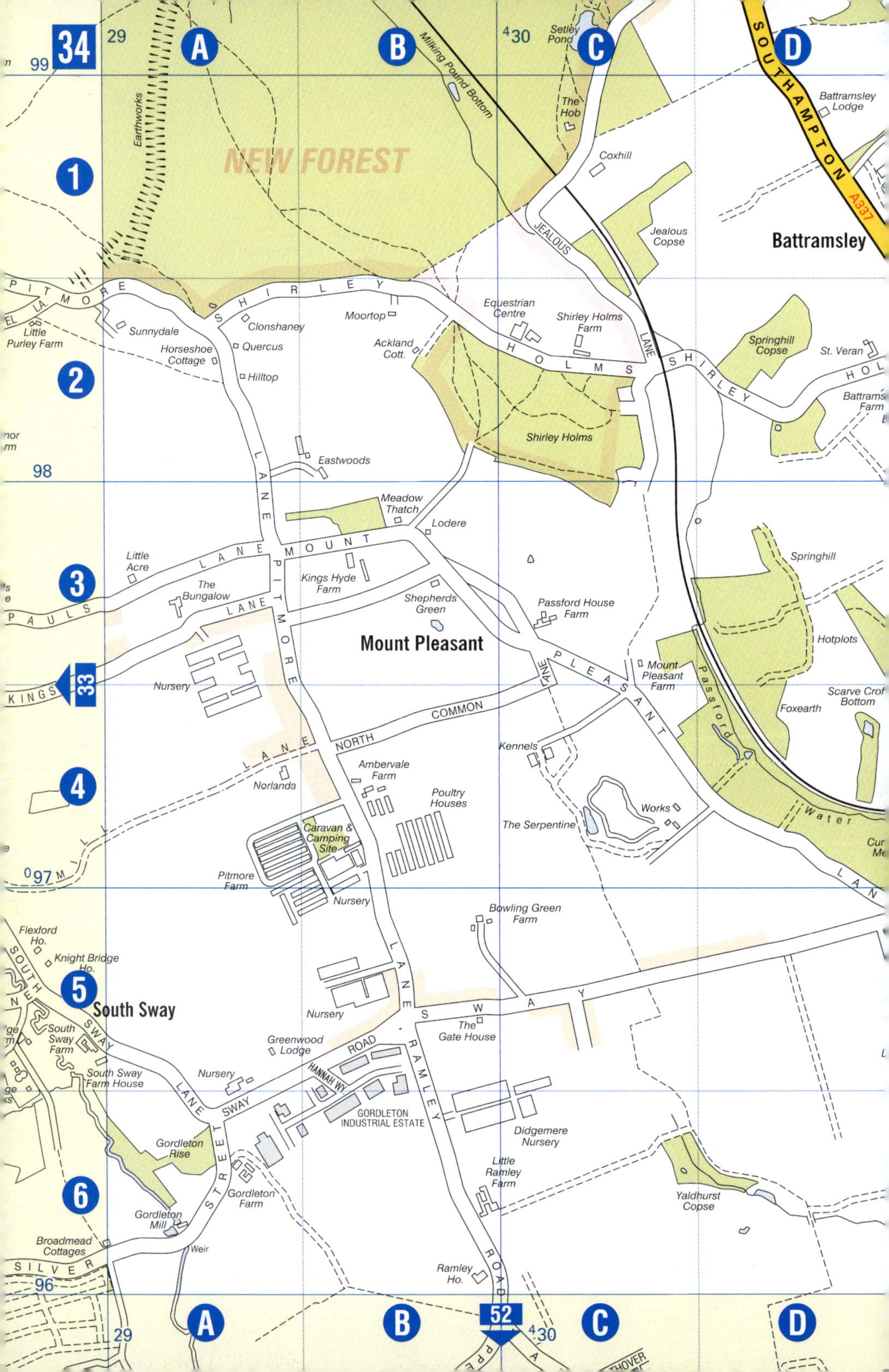
34
29
99
A
B
Milking Pound Bottom
30
Setley Pond
C
SOUTHAMPTON
A337
D
Battramsley Lodge
1
NEW FOREST
The Hob
Coxhill
Jealous Copse
Battramsley
JEALOUS
Equestrian Centre
Shirley Holms Farm
Springhill Copse
St. Veran
PITMORE LA.
SHIRLEY
Sunnydale
Clonshaney
Moortop
HOLMS
SHIRLEY
HOL
Little Purley Farm
Horseshoe Cottage
Quercus
Ackland Cott.
LANE
Battrams Farm
2
Hilltop
Shirley Holms
nor rm
Eastwoods
98
Meadow Thatch
Lodere
Springhill
Little Acre
MOUNT
Kings Hyde Farm
Passford House Farm
Springhill
The Bungalow
Shepherds Green
Mount Pleasant Farm
Hotplots
PAULS
LANE
PITMORE
Mount Pleasant
Passford
Scarve Crof Bottom
KINGS
33
Nursery
PLEASANT
Foxearth
LANE
COMMON
LANE
Kennels
3
LANE
NORTH
Ambervale Farm
Water
4
Norlands
Poultry Houses
The Serpentine
Works
Cur Me
97
M
Caravan & Camping Site
LAN
Pitmore Farm
Nursery
Bowling Green Farm
Flexford Ho.
Knight Bridge Ho.
LANE
SWAY
The Gate House
5
SOUTH
South Sway
SWAY
Nursery
S
W
A
Y
South Sway Farm
Greenwood Lodge
ROAD
RAMLEY
ge m
South Sway Farm House
Nursery
STREET
Hannah Wy.
Didgemere Nursery
ge
Gordleton Rise
SWAY
GORDLETON INDUSTRIAL ESTATE
Little Ramley Farm
6
Gordleton Farm
Yaldhurst Copse
Gordleton Mill
Broadmead Cottages
Weir
Ramley Ho.
ROAD
SILVER
96
A
29
B
52
30
C
A
PPE
THOVER
D

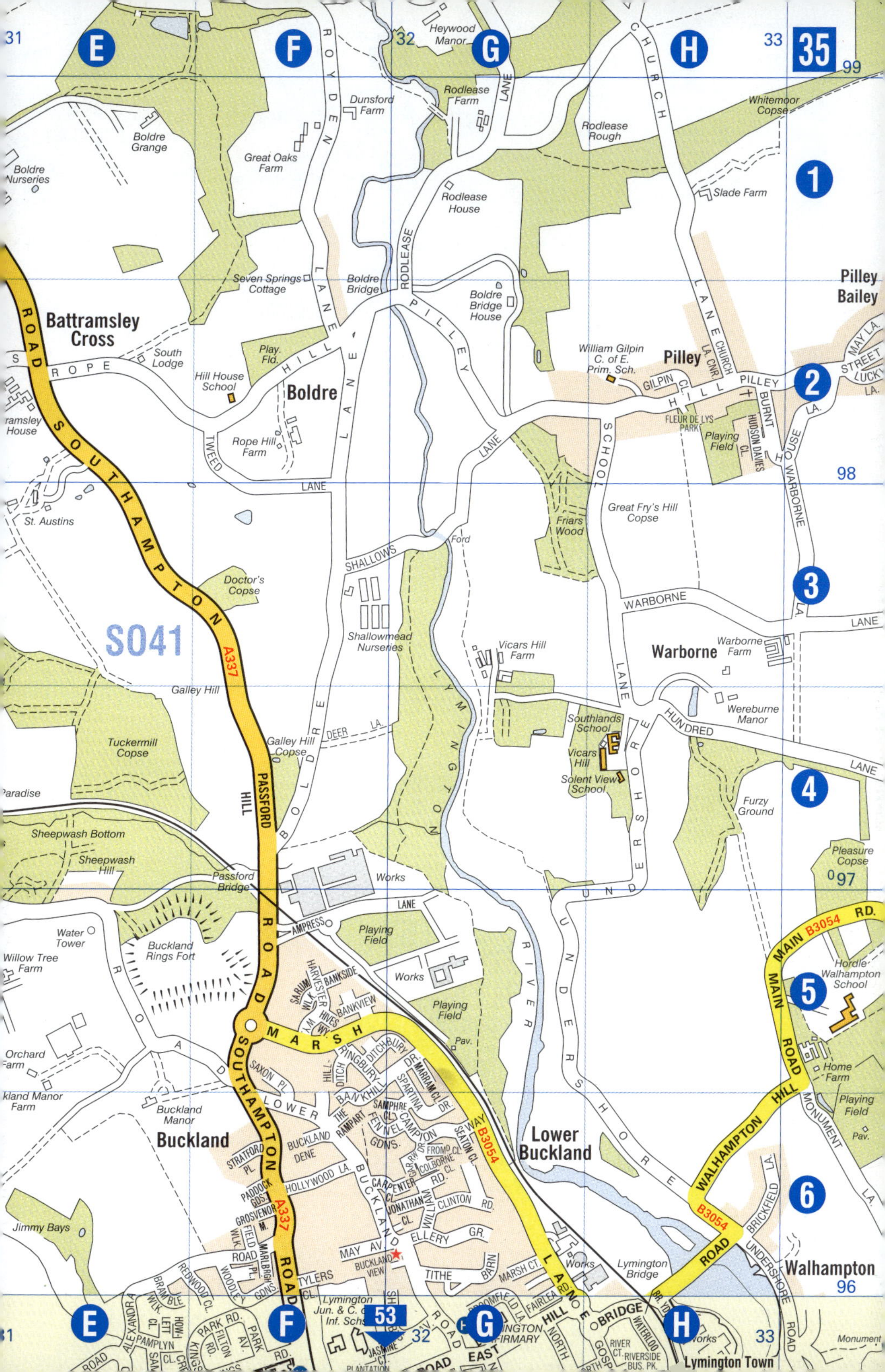

31
E
F
32
G
H
33
35
99
Heywood Manor
Dunsford Farm
Rodlease Farm
Boldre Grange
Boldre Nurseries
Great Oaks Farm
Rodlease House
Rodlease Rough
Whitemoor Copse
Slade Farm
1
Pilley Bailey
Seven Springs Cottage
Boldre Bridge
Boldre Bridge House
William Gilpin C. of E. Prim. Sch.
Pilley
MAY LA.
STREET
LUCKY LA.
Battramsley Cross
South Lodge
Play. Fld.
Hill House School
Boldre
GILPIN HILL
FLEUR DE LYS PARK
Playing Field
HUDSON DAVIES CL.
BURNT LA.
PILLEY
2
ramsley House
ROPE
Rope Hill Farm
TWEED
HILL LANE
SCHOOL LANE
LANE CHURCH
LA. CNR.
WARBORNE HOUSE
98
St. Austins
LANE
SHALLOWS
Ford
Friars Wood
Great Fry's Hill Copse
3
SO41
Doctor's Copse
Shallowmead Nurseries
Vicars Hill Farm
WARBORNE
Warborne Farm
Warborne
Galley Hill
DEER LA.
Southlands School
Vicars Hill
Solent View School
HUNDRED LANE
Wereburne Manor
Furzy Ground
4
Tuckermill Copse
Galley Hill Copse
BOLDRE ROAD
LYMINGTON
UNDERSHORE
Pleasure Copse
97
Paradise
Sheepwash Bottom
Sheepwash Hill
Passford Bridge
Works
RIVER
MAIN RD.
B3054
Hordle Walhampton School
5
Water Tower
Willow Tree Farm
Buckland Rings Fort
PASSFORD
AMPRESS
LANE
Playing Field
Works
Playing Field
Pav.
MAIN ROAD
WALHAMPTON HILL
Home Farm
MONUMENT LA.
Orchard Farm
kland Manor Farm
SOUTHAMPTON ROAD
MARSH
SARUM WLK.
HARVESTER WLK.
BANKSIDE
HIVES
BANKVIEW
DITCHBURY
RINGBURY
DITCH
Playing Field
Pav.
UNDERSHORE
6
Buckland Manor
Buckland
STRATFORD PL.
A337
Buckland Dene
SAXON PL.
LOWER
THE RAMPART
BANK HILL
FEN WEL GDNS.
DR.
MARRIAM CL.
SPARTINA DR.
SAMPHRE CL.
CAMPION CL.
WAY
SEATON CL.
FROMD CL.
COLBORNE CL.
B3054
Lower Buckland
Lymington Bridge
WALHAMPTON
B3054 ROAD
BRICKFIELD LA.
UNDERSHORE ROAD
Walhampton
96
Jimmy Bays
PADDOCK GDNS.
GROSVENOR M.
HOLLYWOOD LA.
CARPENTER CL.
JONATHAN CL.
WILLIAM CL.
CLINTON RD.
ELLERY GR.
MAY AV.
Buckland View
TYLERS CL.
TITHE BARN
BUCKLAND
MARSH CT.
Works
Monument
E
ALEXANDRA CL.
PAMPLYN CL.
HOW4 LEFT CL.
PARK RD.
KINGS
REDWOOD CL.
BRAMBLE WLK.
WOODLE
MARLBRGH PL.
ROAD
PARK AV.
FILTON CL.
F
53
SOUTHAMPTON ROAD
Lymington Jun. & C. Inf. Schs.
JASMINE CT.
PLANTATION
32
G
EAST
ROAD
ington Firmary
BROOMFIELD LA.
FAIRLEA RD.
HILL NORTH
GOSP
BRIDGE
RIVER CT.
RIVERSIDE BUS. PK.
WATERLOO
GOSP RTH
H
Works
Lymington Town
33
Monument

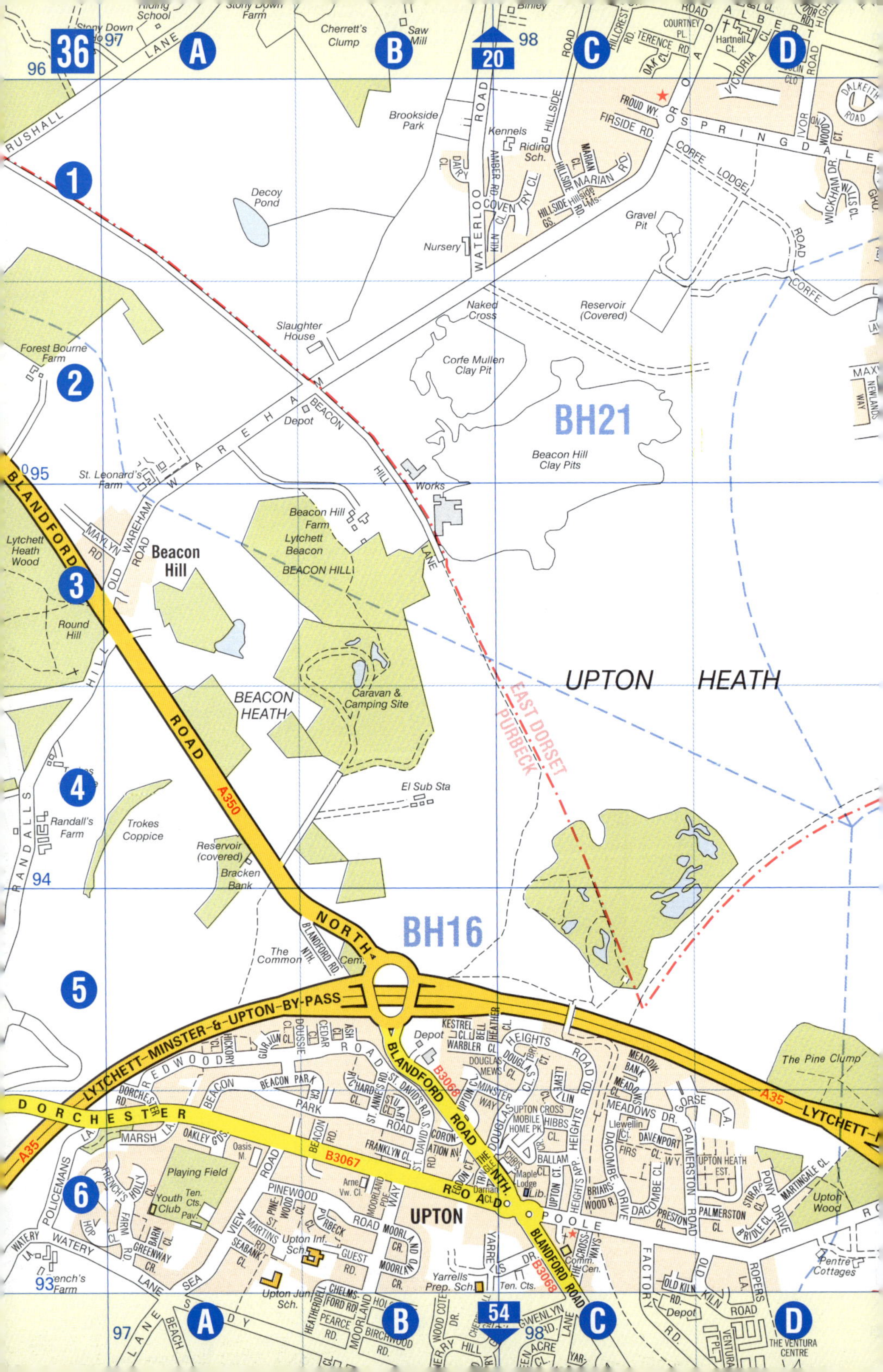
36
96 97 98
A B C D
1 2 3 4 5 6
20
54
RUSHALL
Stony Down
Riding School
Stony Down Farm
LANE
Cherrett's Clump
Saw Mill
Brookside Park
Binley
HILLCREST
COURTNEY PL.
TERENCE RD.
OAK CL.
ALBERT ROAD
HARTNELL CT.
VICTORIA
IVOR WOOD CT.
WICKHAM DR.
WILLS CL.
DALKEITH ROAD
DUBLIN CLO.
SPRINGDALE ROAD
FROUD WY.
FIRSIDE RD.
MARIAN RD.
CORFE LODGE ROAD
CORFE
Decoy Pond
WATERLOO ROAD
DAIRY CL.
AMBER RD.
COVENTRY CL.
Kennels
Riding Sch.
HILLSIDE
HILLSIDE GDS.
MARIAN MS.
HILLSIDE RD.
Nursery
Naked Cross
Gravel Pit
Reservoir (Covered)
MAX NEWLANDS WAY
Slaughter House
Corfe Mullen Clay Pit
BH21
Beacon Hill Clay Pits
Forest Bourne Farm
095
WAREHAM
Depot
BEACON
St. Leonard's Farm
Works
BLANDFORD
MAYLIN RD.
OLD WAREHAM ROAD
Beacon Hill
Beacon Hill Farm
Lytchett Beacon
BEACON HILL
HILL LANE
UPTON HEATH
Lytchett Heath Wood
Round Hill
ROAD
A350
BEACON HEATH
Caravan & Camping Site
EAST DORSET
PURBECK
RANDALLS HILL
Randall's Farm
Trokes Coppice
El Sub Sta
Reservoir (covered)
Bracken Bank
NORTH
094
BH16
The Common
Blandford Rd. Nth.
Cem.
The Pine Clump
LYTCHETT-MINSTER & UPTON-BY-PASS
KESTREL CL.
Depot
WARBLER CL.
BELL HEATHER CL.
HEIGHTS CT.
MEADOW BANK
MEADOWS CL.
A35
LYTCHETT
DORCHESTER ROAD
A35
REDWOOD RD.
HICKORY
GURJUN CL.
BOUSSIE CL.
CEDAR CL.
ASH CL.
ROAD
BLANDFORD ROAD
B3068
Douglas MEWS
MINSTER WAY
Douglas CL.
LIN CL.
HEIGHTS RD.
MEADOWS DR.
GORSE LA.
Dorchester La.
BEACON PARK
BEACON PARK
RICHARDS CL.
ST. ANNE'S RD.
ST. DAVID'S RD.
STUART ROAD
UPTON CROSS
HIBBS CL.
Llewellin CL.
FIRS CL.
DAVENPORT WY.
DACOMBE DRIVE
UPTON HEATH EST.
MARSH LA.
OAKLEY GDS.
Oasis M.
FRANKLYN CL.
ST. DAVID'S RD.
CORONATION AV.
MOBILE HOME PK.
BALLAM CL.
BRIARS WOOD R.
PALMERSTON CL.
STIRRUP CL.
MARTINGALE CL.
Upton Wood
FRENCH'S FARM RD.
HOLLY RD.
Playing Field
Ten. Cts.
Youth Club
Pav.
PINEWOOD RD.
BEACON RD.
B3067
MOORLAND WAY
Arne Vw. Cl.
CHRIST CH.
Maple Lodge
Lib.
HEIGHTS APP.
PRESTON CL.
PONY DRIVE
BRIDLE CL.
POLICEMANS LA.
HOP CL.
BARN CR.
GREENWAY CR.
VIEW RD.
PINE CL.
MARTINS RD.
PURBECK CL.
ROAD
MOORLAND CR.
GUEST RD.
POOLE ROAD
BLANDFORD ROAD
B3068
CROSS WY.
Comm. Cen.
OLD KILN RD. Depot
OLD KILN ROAD
ROPERS LA.
Pentre Cottages
WATERY LA.
WATERY LANE
French's Farm
93
SEABANK CL.
Upton Inf. Sch.
UPTON
MOORLAND CR.
Yarrells Prep. Sch.
Ten. Cts.
YARRELLS DR.
GWENLYN RD.
GREEN ACRE CL.
VENTURA
THE VENTURA CENTRE
97 98
LADY BEACH LANE
SEA LANE
HEATHERLEY RD.
CHELMSFORD RD.
PEARCE RD.
MOORLAND RD.
BIRCHWOOD RD.
HOLLY RD.
Upton Junr. Sch.
WOOD COTE DR.
CHERRY HILL GRN.
FERRY RD.

E
F
G
H
37
99
400
21
01
96
ABBOTSBURY
SPRINGDALE
FAIRVIEW
WENTWORTH
Poole Sports Cen.
GOLF LINKS RD.
GOLF
RD.
Broadstone School
WATER TOWER
ROMAN
ANVL
SPRINGDALE
ASCOT
HIGHER BLANDFORD
BROOKDALE
FARM
Broadstone First Sch.
STATION APP.
Macaulay
TUDOR
LAUREL
DRIVE
WESTROFT
Caesar's Camp
HIGH PARK ROAD
ROAD
BOGNOR
Berwyn
DUNYEATS
War Mem.
Bowl. Grn.
1
HIGHFIELD
WAY
CAESAR'S WAY
LEWESDON
DRI.
CHEAM
CLARENDON
Story Lib.
KIRKWAY
MACAULAY
BROADWAY
Cricket Ground
BROADSTONE
Drinmere
Springdale First Sch.
Rec Ground
WYNNE
CL.
WESTHEATH RD.
Playground
Beech Grove
GLADELANDS WY.
SILVERDALE CLOSE
BARTERS LANE
RIDGEWAY
Broadstone Recreation Ground
WHITC
GLADELANDS
ROMAN ROAD
BH18
The Clump
WEST WAY
GRANGE RD.
CHARBOROUGH ROAD
Plainfield Farm Rec. Grd.
2
THE CLOSE
CORFE WAY
WEST WY.
Southlands Ct.
HEYSHAM
SHARLANDS CL.
95
HADLEY WY.
CLARENDON ROAD
WEST WAY
SANDFORD WY.
YORK
WALLACE CL.
BENRIDGE CL.
BARN ROAD
MEDFORD RD.
BEACON
UPTON
LYTCHETT
BEECHWOOD CL.
HARRABY GREEN
BLANDFORD
FONTMELL
BEACON GDS.
CORFE WAY
SYDNEY RD.
LYTHAM ROAD
TWIN OAKS
Pocket Park
MEDFORD RD.
GREENHAYES
BEACON ROAD
MALLOW CL.
PINESPRINGS
BROADSTONE
MISSION LA.
MISSION RD.
RIBBLE CL.
LYTHAM RD.
ACORN DR.
TWIN OAKS
EDWINA DR.
STEEPLE
KINGCUP CL.
BRYONY
STONECROP CL.
SPINDLE
SORREL
NORTHBROOK
WITHAM
STOBOROUGH
PICKERING CL.
NORTHBROOK ROAD
YORK CL.
EDWINA DR.
CHETWODE WY.
ROAD
DOGWOOD
COWSLIP
SUNDEW
RD.
UPTON PTON RD.
WHITBY CRES.
SKIPTON CL.
Hillbourne
Hillbourne Mid. Sch.
Southbrook Farm
HASTINGS RD.
CLYDE RD.
CRESCEN
METHUEN
38
The Hermitage
DRIVE
AVENUE
KEIGHLEY
WHITBY
WETHERBY CLO.
Hillbourne First Sch.
ALLENBY CLO.
ALLENBY ROAD
CHAFFINCH CL.
GREEN FINCH CL.
CANNON CL.
COVENTRY CRESCENT
KITCHENER
MILNE
ROBERTS
The Parade
MARSHAL
BULLFINCH CL.
PRIMROSE
CANNON CL.
MEAD CL.
AVENUE
CAVAN
APSLEY
DENISON
4
HAWTHORN DR.
SPRUCE CL.
BUCK THORN CL.
SANDPIPER CL.
YORK ROAD
RUGBY RD.
GORT RD.
PLUMER ROAD
CAVAN
FRENCH CL.
UNDERWOOD
LAMBS CRES.
ROAD
LARCH CL.
ROWAN DR.
SYCAMORE CL.
CREEK
RUGBY
WAVELL
ROAD
MARSHAL CRESCENT
PLANTA
BEECHBANK
ROWAN
HONEYSUCKLE LA.
CLOVER DR.
SOPERS
Works
Sports Grd.
94
HYACINTH CL.
BLUEBELL LA.
TARN DRI.
BROADSTONE
AVENUE
MOOR
Sports Club
Play. Fld.
Ten. Cts.
Parkstone Grammar Sch. Playing Field
HOLLY HEDGE
GOLDFINCH
LINNET RD.
Creekmoor Ponds
SWALLOW CL.
PRIORS RD.
BORLEY
BALENA
BALENA CL.
BH17
Indoor Bowls Club
5
NUFFIELD INDUSTRIAL ESTATE
MEADOWSWEET
WOODPECKER
DRIVE
PETERSHAM
PINE TREE WLK.
BENMOOR ROAD
Albany Park
HATCH
BLACKBIRD CL.
NORTHMEAD DR.
SWIFT
Comm. Lib. Cen.
WIGHTJAR CL.
Tanglewood Lodge
PETERSHAM LANE
CABOT
A349
BROADSTONE
Works
LONGMEADOW
WOODPECKER
GREBE CL.
NUTHATCH CL.
OAKMEAD RD.
PI- GRIMS WY.
CABOT CL.
Warehouse
A349
Superstore
Fleets Bridge
FLEETS CORNER
Northmead Copse
MARTIN
NORTHMEAD
MILLSTREAM
LITTLEMEAD CL.
MILLFIELD DRIVE
STALBRIDGE ROAD
PORTER ROAD
A349
WATERLOO
UPTON
UPTON-BY-PASS
MILLFIELD
ROBERTS
HAZELBURY RD.
BURY RD.
PERGIN WAY
BOX CL.
KENNART RD.
NIDE
PORTER ROAD
WIMBORNE RD.
6
ROAD
BUSHELL
Upton Park Farm
UPTON COUNTRY PARK
A35
THE ALPHA CEN.
FLEETSBRI. BUS. CEN.
Creekmoor Bridge
WESSEX GATE RETAIL PARK
FLEETS WAY
BH15
93
FLEETWOOD
CHRISTOPHER
E
F
G
H
55
400
01
Upton House
Upton Park
WILLIS WAY
PURBECK POOLE
EAST DORSET POOLE
Roman Road (Course of)
B3074
205
153
32

38
96
DUNYEATS ROAD
Broadstone Middle School
A
ROAD
DUNYEAT ROUNDABOUT
B
22
C
D
CANFORD HEATH
1
Cricket Ground
BROADSTONE
Bowl. Grn.
WATER TOWER
LAUREL GS.
ASHWOOD DR.
ASHWOOD PARK
A349 GRAVEL HILL
Canford Heath Nature Reserve
DRIVE
LODGE HILL
Playground
Broadstone Recreation Ground
WESTCROFT PARK
WHITCHURCH AVE
TURNWORTH CLO.
WHITCHURCH CLO.
BADBURY CLO.
TOLLERFORD ROAD
LODERS CL.
STEEPLE CL.
WINTERHAYES CL.
HOLYWELL CL.
WESHAM CL.
PORTESHAM CL.
WHITECROSS CL.
HARCOMBE CL.
PORTESHAM WAY
DEVHAM CL.
DRIVE
AVENUE
2
Plainfield Farm
BH18
ROAD
STEEPLETON
AIRETONS CL.
THORN RD.
EDGARTON RD.
COGDEANE RD.
WILLWOOD CL.
OVERCOMBE CL.
CORSCOMBE CL.
FURZEBROOK CL.
PILSDON
HAWKCHURCH GS.
MARSHWOOD
LOWER BARN ROAD
95
ONTMELL
GREENHAYES
Poole Grammar School Playing Fields
BERE RD.
STOURPAINE RD.
SANDHILLS CL.
BETTISCOMBE CL.
CHEDINGTON CL.
TARRANT CL.
CULLIFORD WAY
KNOWLTON
CRESCENT
CHALDON
3
BLANDFORD
B3074 ROAD
HASLER
HASLER RD.
HASLER RD.
HALSTOCK CR.
CRESCENT
REDHOAVE RD.
SIDNEY SMITH CT.
WALDITCH GS.
ROWBARROW CL.
PIMPERN
Neighbourhood Centre
CANFORD ROAD
YEATMINSTER RD.
YEATMINSTER CRES.
HERSTONE CL.
Montacute Sch.
CHETWODE WAY
METHUEN CL.
EDWINA DR.
CLYDE RD.
CRESCENT
37
MARSHAL
CANFORD
DARBY'S CORNER
TERENCE AV.
PLANTATION CT.
B3074 HEATH ROAD
REDHOAVE
THORNCOMBE CL.
ADASTRAL ROAD
Ad Astra First Sch.
SHERBORN
PUDDLETOWN RD.
WARNWELL
4
CRESCENT
FRENCH RD.
HILARY RD.
LAMBS CL.
BENISON RD.
APSLEY CRESCENT
Stanley Pearce Ho.
PLANTATION
CHILFROME CL.
HOLNEST RD.
STINSFORD RD.
WOODLAKE CL.
CHISWELL RD.
WRAXALL CL.
RYALL RD.
LENTHAY CL.
BREDY CL.
ROAD
CANFORD HEATH
Ashdown Sch. & Leisure Cen.
Haymoor Middle Sch.
ASHDOWN CL.
VERITY CRES.
LYNN RD.
CALDER RD.
ROAD
LANE
SOPERS
Play. Fld.
94
Sports Club
Ten. Cts.
Parkstone Grammar Sch. Playing Field
A349 PLANTATION
HOLLY HEDGE LA.
OYSTER
SANDYHURST CL.
WAYTOWN CL.
WITNEY ROAD
Hatch Pond
Endeavour Park
Sorting Office
ABINGDON RD.
DARBY'S LANE
NORTH
BH17
WARBURTON RD.
WARBURTON ROAD
BEAMISH ROAD
GRAY CL.
KELLAWAY
SAMPLES WY.
SCARF RD.
5
Indoor Bowls Club
HATCH POND ROAD
Works
STINSFORD ROAD
New Fields Business Pk.
COWLEY ROAD
ABINGDON RD.
NUFFIELD IND. EST.
Playing Fields
NICHOLSON CL.
BURBRIDGE CL.
WYKEHAM CL.
BADER ROAD
DUNDAS ROAD
MALAN CL.
Sub.
ADASTRAL SQ.
DOWNLANDS PL.
HANOVER GRN.
KELLY CL.
GOSLING CLO.
LORD CLO.
AARON CLO.
CABOT LANE
NUFFIELD INDUSTRIAL ESTATE
Works
KENNINGTON RD.
MORRIS RD.
AZTEC CEN.
HARWELL RD.
DIDCOT RD.
BANBURY RD.
BENSON RD.
Works
HODGES CL.
CRIBB CLO.
TAIT ROAD
MITCHELL ROAD
GIBSON ROAD
KINGSMILL ROAD
A3049
Superstore
Fleets Corner
NUFFIELD ROAD
Longspee Sch.
LEAROYD RD.
Tangmere PR.
Canford Heath First Sch.
KENYON CL.
KENYON ROAD
St. Edward's R.C. & C. of E. Sch.
Parr's Plantation
BH15
Superstore
Fleets Bridge
6
UPTON RD.
DORSET WAY
WIMBORNE
A35
BUSHELL RD.
BAILEY CRES.
COLLWOOD CL.
WORGRET RD.
TRIGON RD.
DARBY'S LA.
Canford Heath Mid. Sch.
Depot
A3049 WAY
DALE VALLEY ROAD
OAKDALE RD.
OLD FARM RD.
GREENFIELD RD.
MOOR VIEW RD.
Sub.
A3049
93
WAY
FLEETS LANE
FLEETWOOD CT.
CHORLEY WAY
STAPLE CLOSE LANE
HEATH ROAD
St. George's Playing Field
JOHNSTON ROAD
OAKDALE
ENFIELD ROAD
COBBS LANE
GREENFIELD FARM
MOOR VIEW
DALE VALLEY
CLOSE
FOXHOLES
Chapel
A
01
B
56
C
D

BH21
BH11
BH12
KNIGHTON HEATH GOLF COURSE
Bearwood Playing Field
Club House
Water Works
Filter Beds
BOURNEMOUTH
POOLE
Industrial Estate
Knighton Industrial Works
MANNINGS HEATH ROUNDABOUT
CANFORD WAY
RINGWOOD RD.
WALLISDOWN ROAD
Alderney
Sub.
Sub. ALDERNEY ROUNDABOUT
TA Centre
Alderney Community Hospital
Superstore
Depot
TOWER PARK
THE COURTYARD
Works
Leisure Complex
Factory
Works
ACORN BUSINESS PARK
TRADING EST.
Winchelsea Sch.
Playing Field
Alderney Middle Sch.
Trinidad House
The Martin Kemp-Welch School
Kemp Welch Leisure Centre
Playing Field
Pav.
Trinidad First Sch.
Library
Ralph Jessop Ct.
WAREHAM ROAD
Wessex Trade Centre
Factory
Factory
CHALWYN IND. EST.
Newtown Bus. Pk.
Works
Factory
Fox Holes
Cynthia House
Britannia Ct.
Newtown
Branksome Cemetery
Branksome Heath Mid.
Depot
THE BRANKSOME GDNS.
Rec. Grd.
Alder Recre Gro
Rossmo
HEATH ROAD
B3074
B3049
A3049
A348
A3049
B3068
B3068
03
04
E
F
G
H
39
96
1
2
3
4
5
6
95
94
93
40
23
57
05

40
Kinson
West Howe
Rossmore
Wallisdown
BH11
BH12
TURBARY COMMON
PARK AVENUE
KINGSWOOD
Knighton Heath Industrial Estate
Turbary Retail Pk.
Ringwood Rd. Retail Pk.
West Howe Ind. Est.
Dominion Cen.
Alderney Recreation Ground
Alderney Middle Sch.
Kemp Leisure Centre
St. Joseph's R.C. Combined Sch.
St. Brelades
Corbiere
Winchelsea Sch.
Playing Field
Evering Avenue
Oakmead Sch. (Technology College)
Sports Field
Sports Cen.
Ten. Cts.
Elmrise Prim. Sch.
Playground
Playing Field
Butcher's Coppice
Holloway Lane
Heathlands Jun. Sch. Play. Fld.
Sports Ground
Fernheath Valley
Kinson Cemetery
Kinson Swim. Pool
Kinson Common
Youth Cen.
Lib.
Wallisdown Heights
Wallisdown
BOURNEMOUTH POOLE
WALLISDOWN ROAD
Wallisdown Roundabout
Wallisdown Playing Field
Talbot Combined Sch.
Talbot Mdws.
Georgina Talbot Ho.
Langside Sch.
Royal Mail Sorting Off.
Alder Hills Industrial Park
Alder Hills Nature Reserve
Branksome Bus. Pk.
Superstore
Depot Factory
Comm. Cen.
ALDER ROAD
A3040
Rec. Grd.
Ralph Jessop Ct.
Herbert Ct.
Paddington Ct.
Fairway Est.
Industrial Estate
Depot
Works
Train Cen.
Works
Roundways
POOLE LANE ROUNDABOUT
A348
A3049
WALLISDOWN ROAD
Montrose Dr.
Kingswear
Heaton
Moorside
Rochester
Mount
Kinson
Road
Avenue
Wavell
Road
Tedder
Moorside
Bicton
Acton
Priestley
Laidlaw Cl.
Fern
Baverstock
Caton Cl.
Isaacs Cl.
Merrow Av.
Farnham
Winston Av.
Valley Vw.
Vine Fm.
Mickleham Cl.
Winton
Rossmore
Lincoln
Apollo
39
24
58
06
05
06
96
95
94
93
40

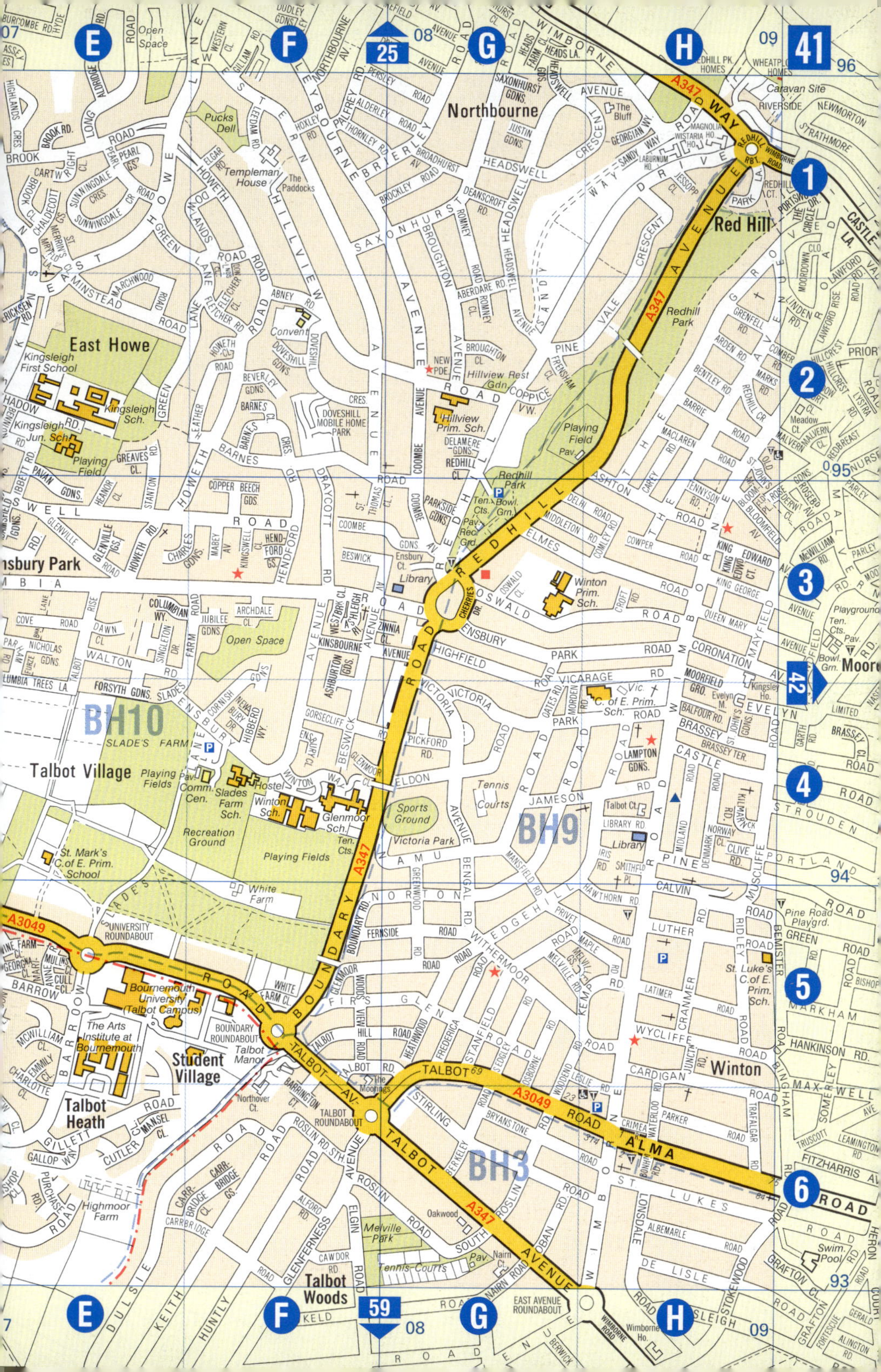
E
F
G
H
41
Open Space
Northbourne
Red Hill
1
East Howe
2
3
42
Moor
BH10
Talbot Village
4
BH9
BH3
5
Winton
6
Talbot Heath
Student Village
Talbot Woods
Bournemouth University (Talbot Campus)
The Arts Institute at Bournemouth
A3049 University Roundabout
A347
A347
A3049
WIMBORNE
WAY
REDHILL
ROAD
CASTLE LA.
BOUNDARY ROAD
TALBOT AVENUE
TALBOT
ROAD
ALMA ROAD
WIMBORNE ROAD
CHARMINSTER ROAD
St. Mark's C.of E. Prim. School
White Farm
Winton Sch.
Glenmoor Sch.
Sports Ground
Victoria Park
Tennis Courts
Recreation Ground
Playing Fields
Slades Farm Sch.
Comm. Cen.
Hostel
Kingsleigh First School
Kingsleigh Sch.
Kingsleigh Jun. Sch.
Playing Field
Pucks Dell
Templeman House
The Paddocks
Convent
Doveshill Mobile Home Park
Hillview Prim. Sch.
Hillview Rest Gdn
Coppice Vw.
Playing Field Pav.
Redhill Park
Redhill Park
Bowl. Grn.
Library
Ensbury Park
Winton Prim. Sch.
Moorfield
C. of E. Prim. Sch.
Library
Talbot Ct.
St. Luke's C. of E. Prim. Sch.
Pine Road Playgrd.
Talbot Manor
Talbot Roundabout
Boundary Roundabout
East Avenue Roundabout
Highmoor Farm
Melville Park
Swim. Pool
Caravan Site
Redhill Pk Homes
Wheatplot Homes
Riverside
Newmorton
Strathmore
Playground Ten. Cts. Pav.
Bowl. Grn.
The Bluff
Northbourne
Playing Field Pav.
07
08
09
96
95
94
93
25
59
42

42
A B C D
Muccleshell Farm
WHITELEGG WY
Caravan Site
RIVERSIDE
NEWMORTON
GRANBY
Muscliff
Rec. Gnd.
Nursery
Muscliff Park
Youth Cen.
Comm. Cen.
Ten. Cts.
ROI-MAR HOME PK
TAYLOR
LAVENDER
Cemetery
CAREYS
1
WIMBORNE RD
Red Hill
REDHILL
PARK
PORTSWOOD
CIRCLE RD
CASTLE LANE
A3060
REDBREAST RD
PRIORY VIEW
Moordown
BH9
WEST CASTLE ROAD
Broadway Park Sports Ground
Muscliff Prim. Sch.
BRADFORD
2
Red Hill
PRIORY VIEW
ROAD
FRANKLIN
NURSERY
FOREST
WINSTON
Musclff Park
3
KING GEORGE AVENUE
Moordown
Playground
Homeside Wood
CHARMINSTER
Pavilion
Playing Fields
Bournemouth School for Girls
Playing Field
Charminster
41
MOORFIELD GRO.
BRASSEY
Prim. Sch.
CAMDEN
UPLANDS
Bournemouth School
Sports Cen.
Tennis Courts
Bus Depot
4
STROUDEN
GRESHAM
ROAD
CHARMINSTER
COURT ROAD
SUTTON
B3063
Summerbee Firt & Jun. Schs.
North Cemetery Crematorium
Summerbee School
Playing Fields
PORTLAND
Loader Cl.
STROUDEN
Lib.
War Mem.
Strouden Park Playing Fields
BROAD
5
GREEN
ROAD
Pine Road Playgrd.
MARKHAM
FIRBANK
Queens Ct.
ASHLING
AVENUE BRACKENDALE
Winton
HANKINSON
ABBOTT
ACLAND
ROAD
QUEEN'S
AVENUE
MAURICE
PARK
MAX WELL
SOMERLEY
Winton Rec. Grd.
Pav.
ST. ALBANS
Cecil Ct.
ARCADIA
Queensmount
Park Vw. Ct.
ST. GEORGE'S
WEST
Playing Field
Miniature Rifle Range
6
ALMA
A3049
ST. LUKE'S
FITZHARRIS
Linwood Sch.
RICHMOND
WOOD
RICHMOND
PARK
AVENUE
Club House
BH12
Swim. Pool
Linwood Sch.
GRAFTON
KING
CHARMINSTER ROAD
RICHMOND
A3049
PARK
Warwick Ct.
Pinelands
Richmond
Sandon Lodge
Park Mansions
CROMER RD.
QUEENS
A B C D

11
E
F
G
H
13
43
96
Farm House
Throop
River Farm
Weir
Throop Mill
PIG SHOOT LANE
Playing
27
West Lodge
Ford
Leaden
Woodlands Cottage
Heron
Cts.
Grange
Hurn Court
The Bungalow
Weir
Fish Pond
BH23
1
North Road
Throop Farm
Blue Roof Farm
River
Weir
Weir
Stour
New Bridge
Stour
CHRISTCHURCH
BOURNEMOUTH
Village Green
2
95
HOLDENHURST
Vicarage
Holdenhurst
Manor Farm Barn
MANOR FARMYARD
Road
Play Area
HOLBURY CL.
GDNS
YEOMANS IND. PK.
Fair Acres
Valley Nurseries
Stockwell Nurseries
Westfield
Haunchwood
Road
Holdenhurst Farm
Church Hall
BH8
YEOMANS WAY
Townsend Open Space
Townsend
Manor House
Holdenhurst
Road
A338
Riverside
3
THE HAMPSHIRE SHOPPING CENTRE
P
P
P
P
P
P
WOODBURY AVENUE
HASTINGS
Eventide Homes
CULFORD CL.
STACEY GDS.
HEYLAR RD.
COWREY RD.
BARROW
BARROW DR.
MOUNTBATTEN
WY.
Rec. Grd.
IBBERTSON WAY
IBBERTSON CL.
ROAD
STONE GDNS.
WATTON
JEWELL
TYRRELL GS.
BIRCH DR.
HOPKINS CL.
Townsend Prim. Sch. & Comm. Cen.
Road
SWANSBURY DR.
NOYCE GDNS.
WILKINSON DR.
VICKERS CL.
Manor House
National Home (Elderly Nurses)
Avenue
44
L 471 A
N
E566
WILEVERLY RD.
IBBERTSON ROAD
JEWELL
Townsend
JEWELL DR.
Playg'rd
THROOP CL.
THROOP RD.
CHESHIRE
Crown & County Courts
Trouden fields
Comm. Cen
Lib.
VANGUARD
CRAIGMOOR RD.
E566
Craigmoor WY.
621
A3060
661
MIDWOOD AV.
INGLEWOOD AV.
MOUNT PLEASANT
CRAIGMOOR AV.
684
ROAD
BOURNEMOUTH MEML. HOMES
Castle Dene
DERWENT HOSP.
H
H
ROYAL BOURNEMOUTH HOSPITAL
LEIGH
DEANS
Everdene House
Superstore
4
94
Rec. Grd.
WORDSWORTH AVENUE
HIGHTREES AVENUE
BALMORAL AVENUE
LEYDENE CL.
MOUNT PLEASANT
LEYDENE
DEAN
LONGBOW DR.
CASTLE
A3060
LANE
Tringham House
SHEEP WASH
Raddon Hill
ersham
Open Space
SANDY MEAD
QUEENSWOOD
COPSEWOOD
LINKSIDE AV.
COOPER
AVENUE
DRIVE
WAY
LITTLEDOWN PARK
Football Pitches
Paddling Pool
Pav.
P
Littledown Leisure Centre
Riverside
kway
Playground
Cricket Pitch
P
P
P
5
Subway
A338
DRIVE
Offices
Offices
REGENT DRIVE
SOVEREIGN
COUNTESS GS.
SPRINGBANK RD.
SPRINGVALE
BEAUCHAMPS
HAZELTON GDS.
EVESHAM GDS.
CHANDRS GDS.
HATFIELD GDNS.
COWELL
TAN HOUSE CL.
PERRY CL.
ELISE CL.
SARAH
WALKWOOD AV.
WALKWOOD
BARTLET
Ten. Cts.
EAST
St. Peter's School
WESSEX
WALSINGHAM
WYN-TR
HAREWOOD
HAREWOOD ROAD
SUMMERFIELDS
Ten. Cts.
ELMGATE
MAXWELL
HENVY
The BEECHES
COWELL
HARES GRN.
WOODCOCKS CRES.
LECHLADE GS.
SEVENOAKS WAY
SHEPHERDS WAY
SPARKFORD CL.
HARTSBOURNE DR.
BOURTON
RENTHAM AV.
ELTHAM CL.
TRENTHAM AV.
Ten. Cts.
Littledown
BH7
Playing Field
AVENUE
AVENUE
WILLIAM
GAINSBOROUGH RD.
GLENCOE RD.
HAREWOOD AVENUE
HAREWOOD CRESCENT
LITTLEDOWN COMMON
SEVENOAKS
CYNE CL.
The Bicknell School
Porchester School
Avonbourne School
ROAD
WARNFORD
HAMBLEDON
St. Saviours CL.
COLEMORE
CHERITON AV.
HURSLE CL.
OVINGTON AV.
6
93
Littledown Road
Tennis Courts
Pav.
Bowl. Grn.
SWANMORE ROAD
'S PARK
COURSE
LEESON
BISHOP'S
THISTLEBARROW
HAYES AV.
BUCHANAN AV.
KING'S PARK
Tennis Cts.
61
PETERSFIELD
PETERSG PL.
SWAN WALTHAM
DURRINGTON
AVENUE
Wareham
RD.
CHRISTCHURCH RD.
ROPLEY CL.
E
Bournemouth AFC (Dean Court)
Football
F
Model Railway
G
H
13

44
96
13
44
Blackwater Hill
Town Common
Dudmoor Copse
Old
1
Blackwater Cotts
Blackwater Firs
BH8
A338
Blackwater
Footbridge
HESTAN CL
ORFORD CL
BLYTH CL
WHITBY CL
DRESWICK CL
ASTON
RYDA CL
DRIVE
St. Catherine's Hill
DUDMOOR
Briars Farm
FARM
ROAD
Plantation
FORELAND CL
VALENCIA CL
DURLSTON
DURLSTON CR
LEES CL
LYNTON CR
LYNTON CR
CHALFONT
GRASMERE
AMBLESIDE
MARLOW
MEAD
HIGHVIEW
WOODBURY CL
Reservoirs (covered)
St Catherine's Hill
Purification Works
2
HOLDENHURST
MANOR FARMYARD
Holdenhurst Fa
B3073
ST. CATHERINE'S WAY
VALLEY CL
Rifle Range
Paragon
95
CONIFER CL
SHRUB DR.
Weir
GLENDALE CT.
GLENDALE CL
OLD BARN
ROAD
HILLSIDE DRI.
SANDY LA.
HILL LA.
SURREY CL
MAR
IFORD BRIDGE GOLF COURSE
BH7
30
SANDY LA.
ST. CATHERINES
MARSH
NORFOLK AV
LINCOLN RD
HAMPSHIRE RD
3
Church Hall
RIVERSIDE
Grove Farm Meadow Caravan Park
DUKESFIELD
SQUIRRELS CL
STOUR WY.
SPRINGFIELD AV
KATTERNS CL
RIVERMEAD GDS
BOSLEY
BOSLEY CL
STOURCROFT DR.
PIPPIN CL
APPLE GROVE
GROVE
ST CATHS
ESSEX RD
NORMANTON CL
SUFFOLK RD
CAMBRIDGE GDS
RUTLAND RD
al Home y Nurses)
43
Recreation Ground
Grove Copse
ROAD OF FAIR MILE
274
225
WALCOTT
FLAMBA
AVENUE
STOUR
RIVER
CROSS
Jumpers Common
DARWIN CL
MELBOURNE AV
ALBION RD
ARCADIA CL
ENDFIELD RD
ADELAIDE
The Howard Social Cen.
KINGSWAY CL
4
Crown & County Courts
LINKS DRI.
BURFORD CL
WAY
WILTON CL
THE
CANBERRA AV
ELM AV
ENDFIELD
SYDNEY RD
BRISBANE
CROFTON CL
TCL
H
Leigh
94
Everdene House
AVENUE
RIVERSIDE
HURN
WAY
PERTH CL
CANBERRA
BRISBANE RD
BENDIGO RD
TIMBERLEY
ST CAIRNS
Fairmile Ho.
The Juniper Cen.
REGENT
Tringham House
Superstore
SHEEP WASH
RIVER
CEDAR AV
BECH AV
CHESTNUT AV
STOURVALE AV
SYRIE LA
THE GROVE
JUMPERS
LODGE RD.
HALEWOOD
Cemetery
GROVE RD
AVON RD
ACORN RD
TASMAN
5
CASTLE
LANE
A3060
IFORD BRIDGE GOLF COURSE
Ten. Cts.
AVENUE
Iford Sports Complex
Bowl. Grn.
Pav.
THE HURDLES
259
ELEANOR GDS
FITZMAURICE
GARDNER RD
DEVON RD
BARRACK ROAD
JUMPERS RD
182
ELIZABETH AV
YORK CLO
BURNETT RD
SHER
WALKWOOD
ELTHAM
Ten. Cts.
St. Peter's School
Driving Range
Club Ho.
New Iford Bridge
P
Recreation Ground
Iford Brdg
MAUNDEVILLE RD
MAUNDEVILLE
BURNETT RD
WINDSOR RD
CORBAR RD
SOMERSET RD
BERNARDS CL
BEAULIEU AV
BEAULIEU GDNS CARAVAN PARK
LANCER CL
HUSSAR CL
DRAGOON WAY
A35
Liberty Ct.
BAILEY DRIVE
Retail Park
Playing Field
BOURTON CL
ELTHAM AV
IFORD
BRIDLE
CASTLE LA
OLD BRIDGE RD
IFORD BRIDGE HOME PARK
CHRISTCHURCH
BOURNEMOUTH
The Stables
Bailey
6
Petersfield Rd
WARNFORD RD
DURRINGTON RD
HAMLEDON RD
MEON RD
Tennis Courts
Pav.
Bowl. Grn.
WARNFORD ROAD
CHERITON
HURSLEY CL
OVINGTON AV
OVINGTON GDS
BEDFORD RD
CROSSMEAD AV
ST. SAVIOURS CL
COLEMORE
ROPLEY RD
CHRISTCHURCH
A35
EAST ROAD
CORHAMPTON RD
IFORD RDBT
IFORD GDS
WATER LA
FORD RD
ASHFORD RD
DENMEAD RD
HARTING RD
IFORD LANE
BH6
Iford Meadows
Drains
Iford
93
SWANMORE
SWANMORE RD
HOLDENHURST ROAD
WILLOW CT.
WICK CL
RUSHMERE RD
SOUTH RD
BRIXTON RD
CARLYLE RD
CLINGAN RD
SHAKESPEARE RD
COLLINGBOURNE
BURNS RD
DICKENS RD
KING'S
STOUR
Works
Iford Playing Fields
HOME ESTATE
KING'S
MEADOW
13
A
B
C
62
14
D
Stourfield Jun. & Infs.
Community Cen.
KITTIWAKE CL
Rookery
KINGFISHER
Ramsey Ct.
Peel

45
96
1
2
3
46
4
5
6
15
E
F
G
Winkton
Holfleet Cottage
H
TIN LA.
Yard LA.
16
17
SALISBURY ROAD
BURLEY RD.
Weir
WINKTON GREEN
B3347
Homefield Sch.
Winkton House
JOPPS CORNER
Weir Sluices
238
0 95
94
93
OGBER
DUDMOOR FARM GOLF COURSE
Sandacres
Coward's Marsh
Winkton Common
Dairyhouse Farm
Drains
RIVER AVON
Drains
BH23
Aqueduct
Drains
RIVER
Ford
Drains
MILL STREAM
Old Stream
STONY LANE
161
184
114
MORLEY CL.
CHESTNUT
KIRKHM AV.
HARRISON CL.
CHEST NT.
CAMPBELL WAY
CAMPBELL PARK
CAMPBELL RD.
CAMPBELL RD.
Burton C. of E. Prim. Sch.
Play. Fld.
Burton Hall
FARWELL CL.
KATHERINE CL.
CHANCE CL.
PRIORY VIEW RD.
AVON VIEW RD.
WINKTON CL.
HEATH RD.
BURTON CROFT
BRINSONS CL.
BURTON HALL PL.
MOORCROFT CL.
Vicarage
VICARAGE WAY
PRESTON
THE LINDENS
BURTON
WOODSTOCK RD. Sch.
BURTON
SALISBURY ROAD
Burton Green Farm
COWLEY'S RD.
REDCLIFFE CLO.
SUMMFLD.
BURNHAM RD.
PITTMORE RD.
BAR-LNDS CL.
MEADOW LA.
PRIORY MEADOW RD.
FERN CL.
CRABTREE CL.
VINNEYS CL.
BODOWEN RD.
WHITEHAYES CLO.
WHITEHAYES RD.
FOOTNERS LA.
WHITEHAYES RD.
WHITEHAYES
TREEBYS CL.
BODOWEN RD.
HOLLY GDS.
SUMMER'S LA.
Waters Farm
Playing Field
MARTINS CL.
SHORTS CL.
HILL GORDON WY.
ALDER CL.
MEDLAR CL.
LA.
46
BURTON CL.
SANDY PLOT
LINESIDE
B3347
Burton Farm
STAPLECROSS LA.
Staple Cross Farm
A35 BY-PASS
IRVI WA
HILLA
MARSH LANE
AVENUE
AVENUE
AVE.
WILDFELL CLO.
VILLETTE CLO.
HAWORTH CLO.
CALKIN CL.
BRANWELL CLO.
ANNE CL.
BRONTE CL.
RIMBURY WAY
DEVEREL CL.
FAIRMILE
KNAPP MILL AV.
WATERMILL RD.
LATCH RD.
TIDEMILL RD.
KNAPP CL.
MILL ROAD
B3073
AVON EAST RD.
GROVE RD.
NEWCROFT CL.
PORTFIELD CLO.
PORTFIELD GDS.
ADDISCOMBE RD.
Christchurch Inf. Sch.
CLARENDON RD.
Christchurch
ARTHUR LA.
BELVEDERE RD.
TWYNHAM AV.
Winston Cl.
Kenilworth Cl.
Portfield Sch.
ST. STOUR RD.
BARGATES
ROAD
REID ST.
REID ST.
FAIRFIELD
FAIRFIELD
FAIRFIELD
Centenary Ho.
BEACONSFIELD RD.
Tabernacle
THE SAXON CEN.
FOUNTAIN
WORKS
Avon Trading Park
T.A. Centre Comm. Cen.
Works
Works
CHRISTCHURCH
CHRISTCHURCH
A35
Barlins
Works
AVON
Waterloo Bridge
MILHAMS CL.
HAM'S RD.
Saxon
DUCKING LANE
PURLEW
63
STONY LANE
PUREWELL
B3059
PUREWELL CROSS ROAD
ORCHID WY.
SCOTTS HILLS LA.
HAARLEM MS.
ROTTERDAM CT.
TILBURG RD.
UTRECHT CT.
AMSTERDAM RD.
MOFFAT RD.
SCOTTS HILLS
CAMERON RD.
Works
STREET
PELHAM
MARSH
DAIRY CL.
Purewell
Purewell Cross
COURT PARK
GROVELEY
BUS. PARK
93
Strete Mount
NORMANDY DRIVE
LE PATOUREL CL.
NORTON CL.
EDITH
MERE RD.
BINGHAM RD.
BURTON
REVERS
BONINGTON CL.
REDVERS RD.
DRAPER RD.
SLINN RD.
KNOWLES CL.
MARABOUT CL.
BATTEN CL.
MASTRS.
MILLER RD.
HAKING RD.
VICKERY WY.
TRYM CL.
SARAH SANDS CL.
TEASING WY.
ROEVERS LA.

46
17
96
A
Wayside
B
28
18
C
Waterditch
D
South Bockhampton
LYNDHURST
Hawthorn Farm
Hawthorn Farm
ROAD
Ford
1
Waterditch Farm
Keepers Cottage
HAWTHORN LANE
WATERDITCH
ROAD
HILL
2
PRESTON
LINDENS
95
Burton Rough
Burton Rough
HAMPSHIRE
DORSET
Donkey Bottom
Burton Green Farm
3
BH23
45
LA
HOLLY GDS
SALISBURY
SUMMERS
NEW FOREST
CHRISTCHURCH
4
Waters Farm
HAWTHORN ROAD
94
Farm
Stuarts Garden Land
WATERY LANE
River Mude
O.K. MOBILE HOME PARK
WESTFIELD GDNS
COLUMBINE CL
SNOWDROP GDS
BUTTERCUP
BURTON
MONKS WAY
Staplecross LA
Staple Cross
A35
BY-PASS
A35
SORRELL
SPEEDWELL DR
BELL
CL
YARROW CL
YARROW CL
SAFFRON
CLOVER CL
CLOVER
Superstore
Staple Cross Farm
HAMBURY
CHRISTCHURCH
Cheviot Ct Flats
DORSET ROAD
CHARLES RD
St Joseph's RC Prim. Sch.
Recn. Grd.
SORRELL COURT
SOMERFORD AV
BLUEBELL CL
BLUEBELL CL
SAFFRON
HONEYSUCKLE WAY
SAFFRON DR
CELANDI
5
IRVINE WAY
HILLARY RD
HUNT ROAD
EVEREST ROAD
EDWARD ROAD
SOUTHEY
Scott's Green
SOMERFORD
Somerford Bridge
ROAD
HIGHCLIFFE
ROAD
A337
Tennis Courts
Sports Ground
BONINGTON CL
KENSING WAY
The Grange Comp. Sch.
DRUITT ROAD
EDWARD ROAD
Comm. Cen.
194
Somerford
SEA VIXEN IND. EST.
Works
Weir
GRANGE RD. BUSINESS CENTRE
PRIORY INDUSTRIAL PARK
AIRSPEED RD
SARAH SANDS
VICKERY WY
TRUNK CL
REDVERS RD
DRAPER RD
Playing Field
AMETHYST ROAD
EDWARD
WILVERLEY
DELTA CL
GRANGE
HALIFAX WY
BRABAZON
VALIANT WY
MILLER RD.
BATTEN CL
HAKING RD.
CLIVE
MASTON CL.
MERE- DITH CL
Somerfield Jun. & Inf. Sch.
BINGHAM ROAD
PENNANT WY
B3059
CROFT RD.
NEWLANDS
CAXTON CL.
SOMERFORD BUSINESS PARK
HUGHS BUSINESS CENTRE
HUNTER CL.
DRIVE
SWORD
AUSTER
VULCAN
DONNINGTON DR.
6
KNOWLES RD.
MARABOUT CL.
Play Field
STONECHAT CT.
SILVER BUSINESS PARK
GREEN ACRE CARAVAN SITE
NEWLANDS RD.
WAY
PIPERS
COMET
VISCOUNT
BLENHEIM
STIRLING
RUNWAY
THE
WAY
PUREWELL CROSS RD.
NORTON CL
BINGHAM RD
Strete Mount
PARK GDS.
FRANCESCA CT.
Factory
Warehouse
DENNISTOUN AV
CAMPION GRO
LEYSIDE
AIRFIELD IND. EST.
Comm. Cen.
BEAVER IND.
CATALINA WY
DE HAVILLAND
STIRLING
BURE
93
THE BUTTERY
DAIRY CL.
Purewell Ct.
BERESFORD GDS
ROSEDALE PARK AV.
STROUD GDS
STROUD PARK AV.
BLACKBERRY
THE HAWTHORNS
AMBASSADOR IND. EST.
MALL
STIRLING WY
HOMAGE
17
PUREWELL
GROVELEY
A
BUS. CEN.
B
64
18
C
D
PELHAM
WAY

19
E
F
29
420
G
H
21
47
96
Derry Mount
1
Lodges
Shears Brook
Donkey Bottom
BURTON
Ford
COMMON
Lower Allensworth Wood
RINGWOOD
Rough Park
Dark Firs
Tilley's Plantation
The Avenue
Cricket Grd.
Hinton Admiral
A35
Hinton
2
Cranemoor Wood
095
Ford
Guss
Roeshot Belt
Roeshot Farm
STATION RD.
RINGWOOD
Cat Plantation
CRANEMOOR COMMON
ROAD
HINTON WOOD LA.
Hinton Admiral
RAILWAY
AMBERWOOD
3
AMBERWOOD GARDENS
ROESHOT HILL
A35
HINTON RD.
THE MEADWAY
HAVELOCK WAY
ROAD
SMUGGLERS
CLIVE
WOODHAYES
BUCKLAND GRO.
ROSSLEY CL.
CRANEMOOR CLO.
CRANEMOOR
CRANEMOOR GDNS.
THURSBY RD.
TALBOT
DUNBAR
CRES.
DRI.
PINEWOOD
48
ST.
VERNO
LANE
FOREST
TREESIDE
FOREST RISE
WESTBURY CLO.
WINGFIELD
WINSFORD CLO.
LODGE
BAYTREE WY.
Pav.
LANGLEY RD.
TERRINGTON LANE
HURSTBOURNE AVE.
ASHMORE GRO.
BROOKSIDE WY.
SILVERTON CL.
CHANTRY CL.
LATIMERS CL.
RD.
PINEWOOD
GLENAYR
WHIMBREL CLO.
HAZEL CLO.
MADA
AVE.
WOODFIELD
GARDENS
ROAD
Sports Ground
MARSTON GRO.
HOLMHURST AVE.
THURSBY RD.
SHEPHERD CLO.
ROTHERFIELD
NEWTON
4
Highcliffe Jun. Sch.
St. Marks C. of E. Inf. Sch.
CHEWTON COMMON
HOBURNE
MANNING AVE.
Tennis Courts
PARKSIDE
FOREST CLO.
FIELDWAY
NORTH
ROESHOT CRES.
LAKEWOOD RD.
THORNBURY
DRAEMAR
DRI.
94
Kingsbere Gdns.
HASLEMERE
HIGHCL
VERNO
CL.
MANNING
SMUGGLERS WOOD RD.
HOBURNE GDNS.
LAUREL CLO.
Highcliffe School Playing Field
GARDENS
CLOSE
WAY
NORTH
MOONRAKERS WY.
CARISBROOKE WY.
BIRCHWOOD CL.
HIGHHILL
WOOD
BRAEMAR
DENHAM WAY
COLEMERE
FELTON CRES.
GREEN
HASLEMERE
MERLEY
AV. DR.
CLEMATIS CL.
FOXGLOVE
PRIMROSE
TREFOIL WY.
WOODRUFF CL.
MALLOW CL.
Lilac Lodge
AVE.
SMUGGLERS WD.
BALFOUR CLO.
FARMDENE CL.
RIDGEFIELD
NEA CL.
HARRIS CL.
SMUGGLERS LANE
NEA MEADOW
Bowling Green
LANE STH.
COPSE WAY
CASTLE AVE.
EARLSDON
KILMINGTON
QUINTIN CL.
NORLEY WOOD
JULIA CL.
GERMAINE CL.
ANGELINE CL.
CRISPIN CL.
DRIVE
JESMOND
IMBER
5
BUCEHAYES
314
Community Centre
CORNFLOWER
SAFFRON DRIVE
HOBURNE
SMUGGLERS LANE
SAULFLAND PL.
SAULFLAND DR.
Hoburne Farm
ROWAN
ROWAN CL.
PRESTON WAY
CORNFORD WAY
BARNFIELD
BURN CL.
KNIGHTWOOD CLO.
BURE BROOK
CURZON WAY
NEA RD.
COPSE WAY
DRIVE
ROAD
AVENUE
WAY
LYME CRES.
ABBOTS
JESMOND AV.
HOBURNE LA.
HOBURNE CARAVAN PARK
Copse
High Pines
BELZAIRE
ST. GEORGES CL.
WOODLAND
PINES
Silverways
NEA
PINE CRES.
PINE CRES.
SILVER WAY
Claire Ct.
Diana Ct.
WORTLEY RD.
2
WHARNCLIFFE GDNS.
WATERFORD
6
ROAD
LYMINGTON
A337
ROAD
HUMPHREYS
Shelley Bri.
SHELLEY CLO.
46
Shelley Hamlets
HILL
106
Club House
167
ROTHESAY
RD.
OAKLEIGH CL.
BEACON DR.
REDAN CL.
MAPLE CL.
BEACON
WHARNCLIFFE DR.
Rec. Grd.
ELMWOOD WAY
ROAD
WESSEX
LANE
SEAWAY AVE.
WELLINGTON RD.
DUNEDIN GRO.
AUCKLAND GRO.
EAST CLIFF WAY
PRIORS CLO.
LYM. RD.
EAST CLIFF RD.
ST. GEORGES
HIGHCLIFFE CASTLE GOLF COURSE
RANELAGH RD.
ARUNDEL WAY
HIGH CLI
93
HYNESBURY
FRESHWATER AVENUE
FRESHWATER RD.
HM Coastguard Training Centre
SAVONCROFT
MEDINA
PENNY
Steamer Point Woodland
Highcliffe Castle
Steamer Lodge
65
420
CHRISTCHURCH
BAY
21
FRIARS CLIFF
E
F
G
H

48
96
21
A
B
22
C
D
Beckley Farm
30
BECK MOOR COPSE
Red House
ROAD
War Memorial
B3055
A35
1
Lodge
DARK LANE
Hinton House
Walkford Moor Copse
Walkford Brook
Hinton
2
Cranemoor Wood
95
Marlpit Copse
Meetinghouse Plantation
Castlefield Copse
Walkford Farm
CRANEMOOR COMMON
BH23
HAMPSHIRE
DORSET
240
3
PLANTATION DRIVE
WILLIAM CL.
GLENVILLE CL.
Walkford
WYNDHAM
BROAD LANDS CL.
AMBERWOOD DRI.
AMBERWOOD GARDENS
BECKLEY COPSE
GLENVILLE
MAY GS.
TRESILLIAN WY.
ROAD
SOLENT RD.
WYND HAM CL.
HOLLY LANE
HURST CL.
ROAD
ROAD
Chewton Glen Fm
ABBOT DUNBAR
47
CLOSE
ROAD PINEWOOD
DRIVE
HEATHER CLO.
TRESILLIAN CL.
CLINTON CL.
NICHOL AS CLO.
WALKFORD
ROAD
ROAD
CHRISTCHURCH
NEW FOREST
PINEWOOD
GLENAVON
ROAD
SOUTHWOOD CLO.
SOUTHWOOD
AVE. RD.
HEATH WAY
JACOBEAN CL.
SEA VIEW RD.
Walkford Brook
RD CLO.
Chewton Common
WALKFORD WAY
CHEWTON WAY
BRACKEN WY.
CHEWTON COMMON
Chewton Glen House Hotel
4
BRAEMAR
ROTHERFIELD RD.
CHEWTON COMMON
HIGHLAND AVE.
ARRAN WAY
BRACKEN WY.
ROAD
ACHEWTON
Lodge
Highcliffe Jun. Sch.
UP. GORDON RD.
UP. GORDON RD.
GORDON RD.
BRAMBLE LA.
94
FELTON CRES.
HASLEMERE
Kingsbere Gdns.
CHEWTON COMMON
Gordon Mt. Flats
ELPHINSTONE ROAD
Chewton Common
St. Marks C. of E. Inf. Sch.
HIGHCLIFFE
GORDON ROAD
SEATON CL.
SEATON RD.
HOLME RD.
ROAD
Chewton Farm Estate
The Weirs
CHRISTCHURCH
ANGELINE CL.
MERLEY
AV. DRI.
Camp Site
STANLEY RD.
Lib
POPLAR RD.
444
CHEWTON LODGE
MILL LANE
LORAINE AVE.
STUDLEY CLO.
DRI.
GLEN CL.
GLENDALES
WESTERN CL.
EAST CL.
5
CRISPIN CL.
GREEN WAY
IMBER DRI.
BUCEHAYES CL.
HIGHCLIFFE CORNER
A337
429
ROAD
ABINGDON
THE DELL
DRIVE
SELLWOOD WY.
BRAMSHAW WAY
STUDLEY CT.
BURLEY CL.
ROCK BOURNE
ELLINGHAM GDS.
SOPLEY CL.
MILLYFORD
LORRAINE
JESMOND
Community Centre
314
The Farthings
291
Stuart ROAD
JAYS CT.
BUTE DR.
MARRAT CT.
THE MEADOW
NAISH HOLIDAY VILLAGE
THE TRIANGLE
FIELD PLACE
THE CRES.
ROAD
SOUTHCLIFFE RD.
SOLENT CL.
BOLDRE CL.
NEACROFT RD.
VECTIS ROAD
WAY
WHARNCLIFFE
P
WORTLEY RD.
Claire Ct.
Diana Ct.
MONTAGU PARK
WATERFORD PL.
MONTAGU
Stella Ct.
Greystones
Penelope Ct.
GLENSIDE
Club Palma Apartments
PADDOCK
Ten. Cts. Playgrd.
BRICKENS WOOD
NORTH WOOD
SEA VIEW RD.
AMBER WOOD RD.
PURBECK ROAD
MARINE
AVENUE
BEACON DRI.
REDAN CL.
BEACON CL.
ELMWOOD WAY
WATERFORD GARDENS
Bermuda Ct.
Exeter Ct.
Kenneth Ct.
Alan Ct.
William Ct.
ROAD
KNIGHT WOOD RD.
BAY VIEW
SMUGGLERS VIEW
ISLAND VIEW
BRAMSHAW ISLAND VIEW
ISLAND VIEW RD.
BARTON
6
Rec. Grd.
HIGH CLIFF
Recreation Ground
P
Chewton ROAD
Lob's Hole
93
21
A
CHRISTCHURCH
B
BAY
22
C
D

49
E F 31 24 G H 49
96
1
NEW MILTON
Ballard School
Ballard Prep. Sch.
Great Ballard Lodge
Pond Copse
Lakeside Pines
The Fernmount Centre
Palmer
Winton Way
Marston
Ferndale
Oakwood
Barrs Wood Rd.
Brook Avenue North
Barrs Wood Dr.
Barrs Wd. Road
Larkhill Cl.
Lodge
Linford
Violet La.
2
New Milton
Station App.
Comm. Cen.
Oakwood Court
95
Chatsworth
Beechwood
Hatfield Ct.
Marryat
Kennard
Pond Cl.
Whitefield
Russell Cl.
Pegasus Ct.
Tanglewood
Orchard Ct.
Spencer
York
Lyon
Kenilworth
Warwick
Conway
Stirling
Duart Cl.
Jaundrells Cl.
Willowdene
Water-ford Rd.
Homewood
Oak
3
Queensway
Stem Lane Ind. Est.
Stem Lane Trad. Est.
Williams Ind. Pk.
Wick 1 Ind. Est.
Wick 2 Ind. Est.
Gore Rd. Ind. Est.
Gore Grange
Linnet Ct.
Liby!
New Milton Rec. Cen.
The Arnewood School
Crossmead
Wessex Av.
Derry
Homefield Ho.
Shelley Ho.
Byron Ho.
Eliot Ho.
Keats Ho.
Brian Gdns.
Waverley Ho.
Spencer
Charlotte Ct.
Rec. Ground
Elm
Forest Gdns.
Camellia
Hale
Grove
Ingle
Arnewood Ct.
Rothbury
Glenavon
Glengarry
4
BH25
Gore Farm
Comm. Cen.
Culver Rd.
Cemetery
Rectory
King George Mobile Home Park
Hall
Forest Arts Cen.
New Milton Jun. Sch.
New Milton Inf. Sch.
Old Milton
Old Milton Green
The Pde.
The Meadows
Caravan Site
Solent Lodge
Winston Ct.
Winston Pde.
Durland Cl.
Garden Court
Norris Gdns.
Dudley Pl.
Aspen
Cherry Tree Ct.
Everon Gdns.
Newlands Rd.
Yew Tree
Haysoms Cl.
Hazel Ct.
Green-wood
Tennis Club
Aysha
Ashington Pk.
A337
Milford
50
Silverstore
Football Pitch
Club Houses
Chiltern
Heathwood Ave.
Eldon Ave.
Eldon Clo.
Three Acre
Parkland Dri.
Southern
Wood Lawn Ave.
Moorland
Friars Wlk.
Highlands
Sunnyfield
Chestnut
Uplands
Westbury Clo.
Ashmore Ave.
Langton
Greenfield Gdns.
Penny Hedge
Royston Pl.
Newton
Seaway
Crooked
94
Byron Rd.
Knyghton Park
Seacroft Ave.
Pine Clo.
Coastguard Cotts.
Wavendon
Hengistbury
Seafield
Fairfield Rd.
Fairfield
Cliffe Rd.
Seaward
Westcliffe Bdgs.
Channel
Barton Wood Rd.
Beach
Keysworth Ave.
Barton Dri.
Island Vw.
Bracklesham Pl.
Blythswood
Lyrnic Clo.
White Knights
High Marryats
Barton Croft
Green Lane South
Durlston Court School
Lodge
Barton Common
Arlington Ct.
The Spinney
High Hills Rd.
The Willows
Silverdale
Martells
The Fairway
BARTON ON SEA
5
Harbour Ct.
West Marine Drive
Janred Ct.
White Horses Ho.
Sandmartin Clo.
West-minster Ct.
Marine Point
Marine Prospect
Aldbury Ct.
Barton Chase
Solent
Whale
Idol Phinp La.
Meadow Way
Willow Walk
Barton Common
Barton On Sea Golf Course
Club House
Greenside
6
First Marine Av.
Second Marine Av.
Marine Drive East
93
23 24 425
E F 31 24 G H
23 24 425
A337 Lymington Road
B3058 Station Road
Fernhill Lane

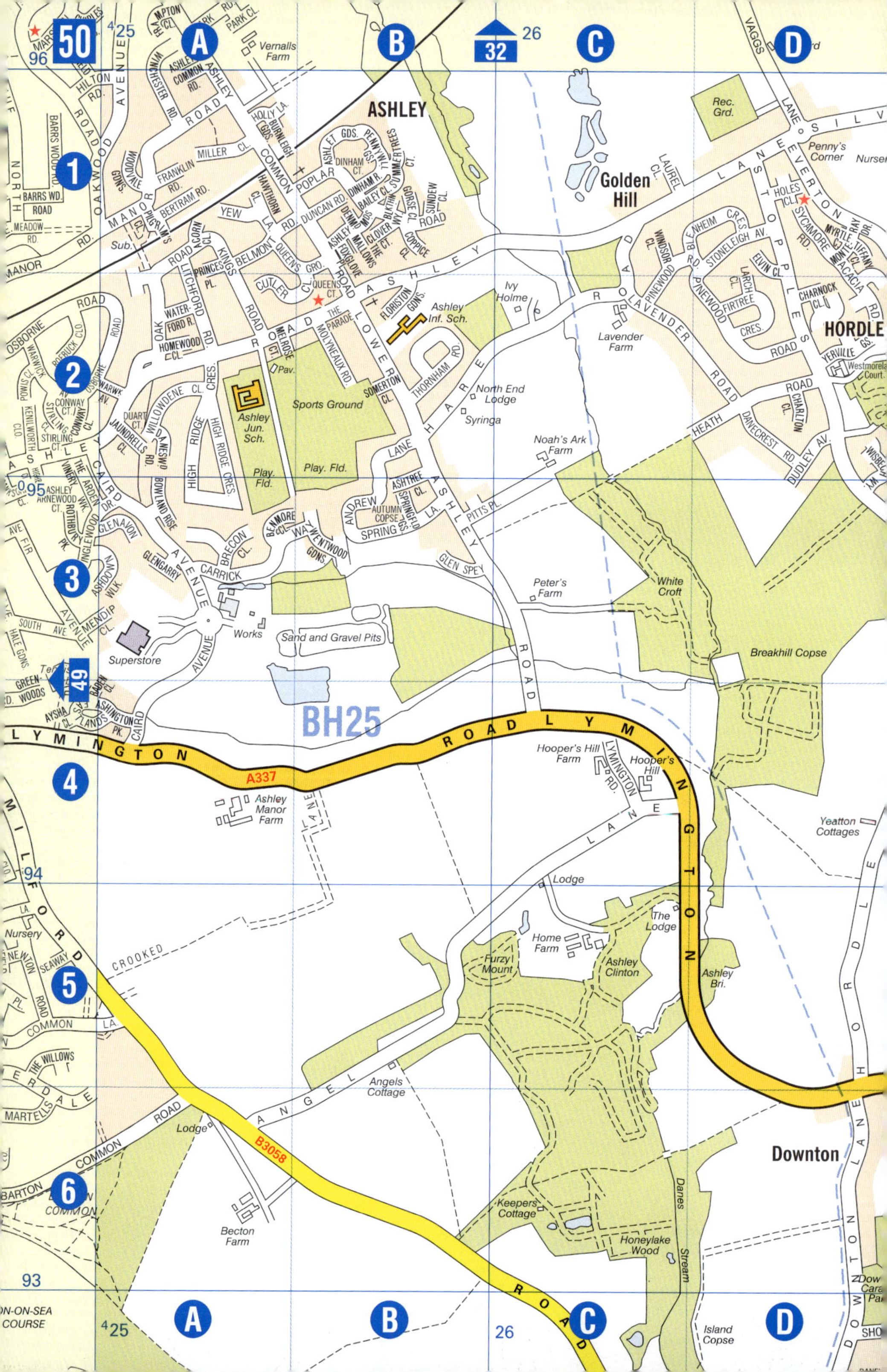

50
96
4 25
A
B
32 26
C
VAGGS
D
Vernalls Farm
ASHLEY
Rec. Grd.
Golden Hill
Penny's Corner
Nursery
SILV
HILTON RD.
BARRS WOOD
1
BARRS WD. ROAD
MEADOW RD.
MANOR
MILLER CL.
FRANKLIN RD.
BERTRAM RD.
YEW
Sub.
POPLAR
DINHAM CT.
DINHAM R.
ASHLEY COMMON RD.
CHICHESTER RD.
HAWTHORN CL.
DUNCAN RD.
GORSE CL.
SUNDEW CL.
COPPICE
LAUREL CL.
BLENHEIM CRES.
STONELEIGH AV.
ELVIN CL.
HOLES CL.
SYCAMORE RD.
MYRTLE
TIFFANY
MONTE RAY
ACACIA
HORDLE
Ashley Inf. Sch.
Ivy Holme
WINDSOR CL.
LAVENDER ROAD
PINEWOOD CL.
LARCH CL.
FIRTREE CL.
CHARNOCK CL.
YERVILLE GDNS.
Westmoreland Court.
2
WARWICK CT.
CONWAY CT.
STIRLING
STIRLING
JAUNDRELLS RD.
WILLOWDENE CL.
HIGH RIDGE CRES.
BELMONT
QUEENS GRO.
MELROSE CT.
MOLYNEAUX RD.
SOMERTON CL.
THORNHAM RD.
North End Lodge
Syringa
Lavender Farm
HEATH ROAD
DANECREST RD.
CHARLTON ROAD
DUDLEY AV.
95
Ashley Arnewood Ct.
ROTHBURY PK.
GLENAVON DR.
INGLEWOOD
Ashley Jun. Sch.
Play. Fld.
Sports Ground
Play. Fld.
ASHTREE CL.
SPRINGFLD. CL.
SPRINGFLD. GDS.
HARE LANE
PITTS PL.
Noah's Ark Farm
White Croft
3
FIR AVE.
SOUTH AVE.
HALE GDNS.
ASHDOWN WLK.
MENDIP CL.
GLENGARRY
CARRICK
BRECON CL.
BENMORE CL.
WENTWOOD GDNS.
WAY
ANDREW CLOSE
AUTUMN COPSE
SPRING
GLEN SPEY
Peter's Farm
Breakhill Copse
GREEN WOODS
49
AYSHA CL.
ISLANDS PK.
ASHINGTON LANDS
CADEN CL.
CAIRD
AVENUE
Superstore
Works
Sand and Gravel Pits
BH25
ROAD
Hooper's Hill Farm
Hooper's Hill
LYMINGTON
Yeatton Cottages
4
LYMINGTON
A337
Ashley Manor Farm
LANE
LYMINGTON RD.
MILFORD
94
Nursery
NEWTON
SEAWAY
CROOKED
Lodge
Home Farm
Furzy Mount
Ashley Clinton
The Lodge
Ashley Bri.
5
THE WILLOWS
MARTELLS
Lodge
ANGEL LANE
Angels Cottage
HORDLE
Downton
BARTON COMMON
COMMON ROAD
B3058
Keepers Cottage
Danes Stream
DOWNTON LANE
6
93
N-ON-SEA COURSE
4 25
A
B
26
ROAD
C
Becton Farm
Honeylake Wood
Island Copse
D

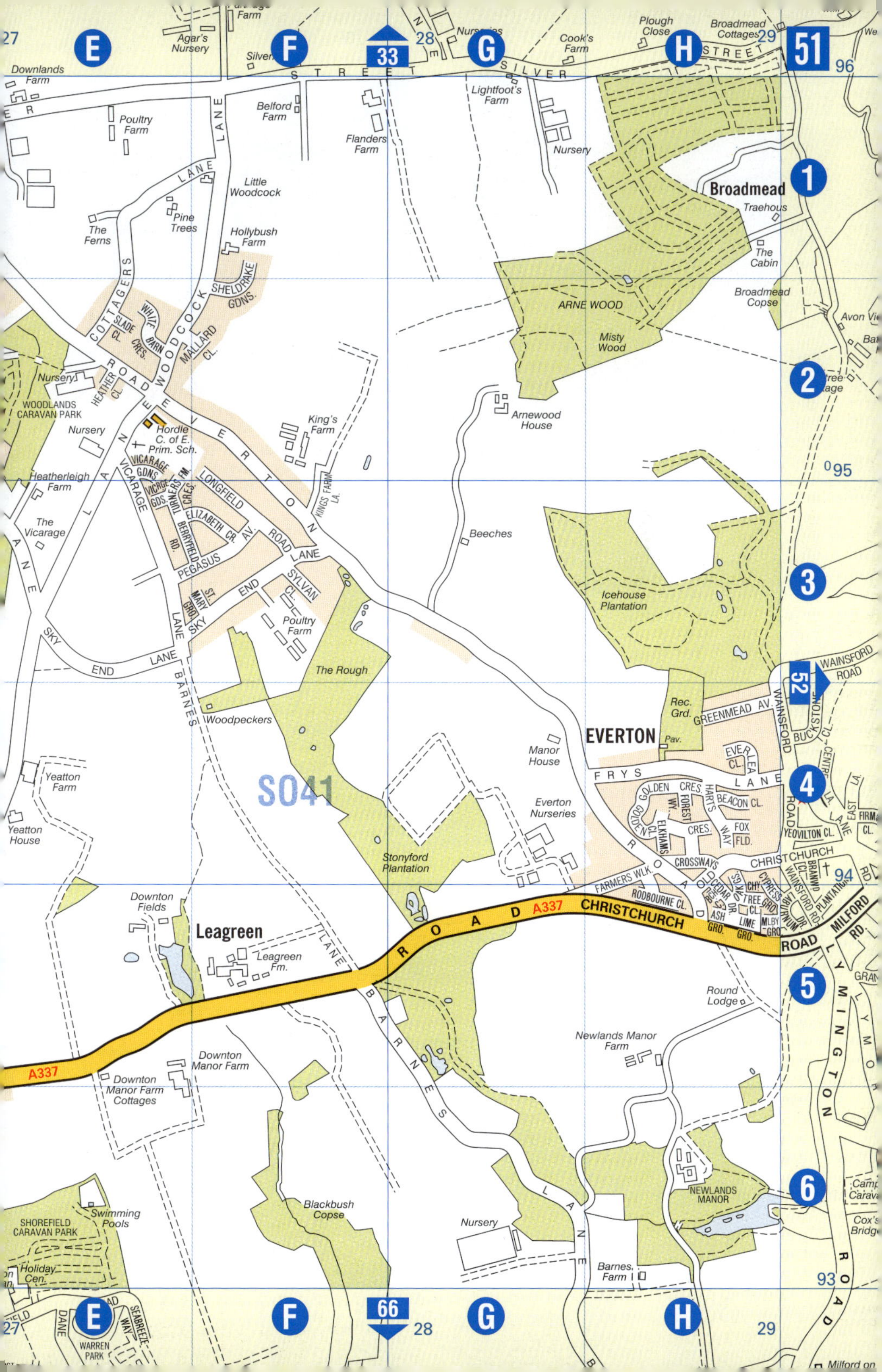
27
E
Agar's Nursery
F
Silver
33
28
Nurseries
G
Cook's Farm
SILVER
Plough Close
H
Broadmead Cottages
29
51
96
Downlands Farm
STREET
Lightfoot's Farm
Broadmead
1
Poultry Farm
Belford Farm
Flanders Farm
Nursery
Traehous
The Cabin
LANE
Little Woodcock
Broadmead Copse
Avon Vie
Ba
The Ferns
Pine Trees
Hollybush Farm
ARNE WOOD
Misty Wood
2
ree age
WOODCOCK
SHELDRAKE GDNS.
COTTAGERS
SLADE CL.
WHITE BARN CRES.
MALLARD CL.
ROAD
EVERTON
Nursery
Arnewood House
WOODLANDS CARAVAN PARK
HEATHER CL.
Hordle C. of E. Prim. Sch.
King's Farm
KINGS FARM LA.
95
Nursery
VICARAGE GDNS
VICARAGE GDS.
VICARAGE
TURNERS FM.
LONGFIELD
Heatherleigh Farm
BERRYFIELD RD.
ELIZABETH CR.
CRES.
AV.
LANE
Beeches
3
The Vicarage
PEGASUS
MARY GRO.
ST.
SYLVAN CL.
Icehouse Plantation
LANE
END
SKY
Poultry Farm
SKY END LANE
The Rough
WAINSFORD ROAD
52
Rec. Grd.
GREENMEAD AV.
WAINSFORD ROAD
BUCKSTONE
CENTR
Woodpeckers
SO41
EVERTON
Pav.
EVERLEA CL.
4
Yeatton Farm
Manor House
FRYS
LANE
EAST LA.
FIRM CL.
Yeatton House
Everton Nurseries
GOLDEN CRES.
HARTS
BEACON CL.
ROAD
YEOVILTON CL.
BARNES LANE
GOLDEN WY.
FOREST
FOX FLD.
ELKHAMS
CRES.
WAY
CHRISTCHURCH
Stonyford Plantation
CROSSWAYS
94
FARMERS WLK.
RODBOURNE CL.
OLD CEDAR DR.
ASH GRO.
CYPRESS GRO.
ICHY TREE GRO.
BRANW
WALNUT DR.
PLANTATN.
Leagreen
ROAD
A337
CHRISTCHURCH
LIME GRO.
MLBY GRO.
MILFORD RD.
Leagreen Fm.
ROAD
BARNES
ROAD
Round Lodge
5
LYMINGTON
GRAN
Downton Fields
Downton Manor Farm
Newlands Manor Farm
A337
Downton Manor Farm Cottages
BARNES LANE
6
SHOREFIELD CARAVAN PARK
Swimming Pools
Blackbush Copse
Nursery
NEWLANDS MANOR
Camp Carava
Cox's Bridge
Holiday Cen.
DANE
SEABREEZE WA
Barnes Farm
93
27
E
WARREN PARK
F
66
28
G
H
29
Milford on

52
29
96
95
0
51
94
93
29
Broadmead Copse
Traehous
The Cabin
Broadmead Copse
Avon View
Oaktree Cottage
Batchley Fm.
Batchley Copse
Mappleton
Wainsford Farm
Wainsford Bridge
Wainsford Copse
WAINSFORD
GREENMEAD AV.
BUCKSTONE CL.
CENTRE LA.
WEST LA.
EAST LANE
Knighton Caravan Park
Knightcrest Park
EVERTON
FIRMOUNT CL.
YEOVILTON CL.
ROAD
CHRISTCHURCH
ROBERTS CL.
BRANWD. CL.
WAINSFORD RD.
PLANTATION
THE GRANGE
GRANGE CL.
MILFORD
A337
ROAD MILFORD
CHRISTCHURCH ROAD
CYPRESS GRO.
LABURNUM DR.
CHY. TREE CL.
ASH GRO.
LIME GRO.
MLBY. GRO.
OLD ORCHARD DR.
FRYS CL.
HARTS CL.
BEACON CL.
FOX FLD.
CROSSWAYS
CRES.
WAY
EVER. CL.
RES.
Round Lodge
LYMINGTON ROAD
B3058
Braxton Farmhouse
Braxton Courtyard
NEWLANDS MANOR
Camping & Caravan Site
Cox's Bridge
Ford
Lymore
LYMORE VALLEY LANE
AGAR LANE
Milford on Sea
Ramley Ho.
34
30
Ramley Copse
Ramley Lodge
Upper Pennington
UPPER PENNINGTON COMMON
UPPER ROAD
DRAPPER ROAD
COMMON
MIDDLE ROAD
Upper Pennington
WAINSFORD ROAD
Lower Wainsford Copse
Wainsford Copse
Upper Rough
Orchard Cottage
Newlease Copse
Efford Horticultural Experimental Station
Efford House
Efford Farm House
Chain Lodge
Efford Horticultural Experimental Station
Newbridge Drive Cottages
Works
Weir
Efford Bridge
MILFORD
Great Newbridge Copse
Agarton Copse
Newbri. Cops
67
30
Avon Water
NORTHOVER RD.
BROWNINGS
HAZEL RD.
COMMON
Pinetops Nurseries
PINETOPS CL.
ST. MARKS RD.
YARRELL MEAD
YALDHURST LANE
Cowley Farm
Rec. Grd.
Hall
LODGE LAWN
EDWARDS CL.
THE SQUA
Pennington Common
ROAD
Furzey House
Widbury's Copse
SWANS FORD
SWAINS
CORBIN CRES.
CONIFER CL.
WEST CL.
PENNINGTON OVAL
BROOMHILL
EFFORD CL.
WILVERLEY CL.
BROADLY CL.
BLACKTHORN
JUNIPER CL.
HOWARDS MEAD
MEAD
MEAL
WAY
Corbin Ct.
EFFORD CT.
LITTLE DENE
DENESIDE
DENE COPS
HARF
POUN
ROAD
WAINSFORD
Wainsford Bridge
A B C D
1 2 3 4 5 6

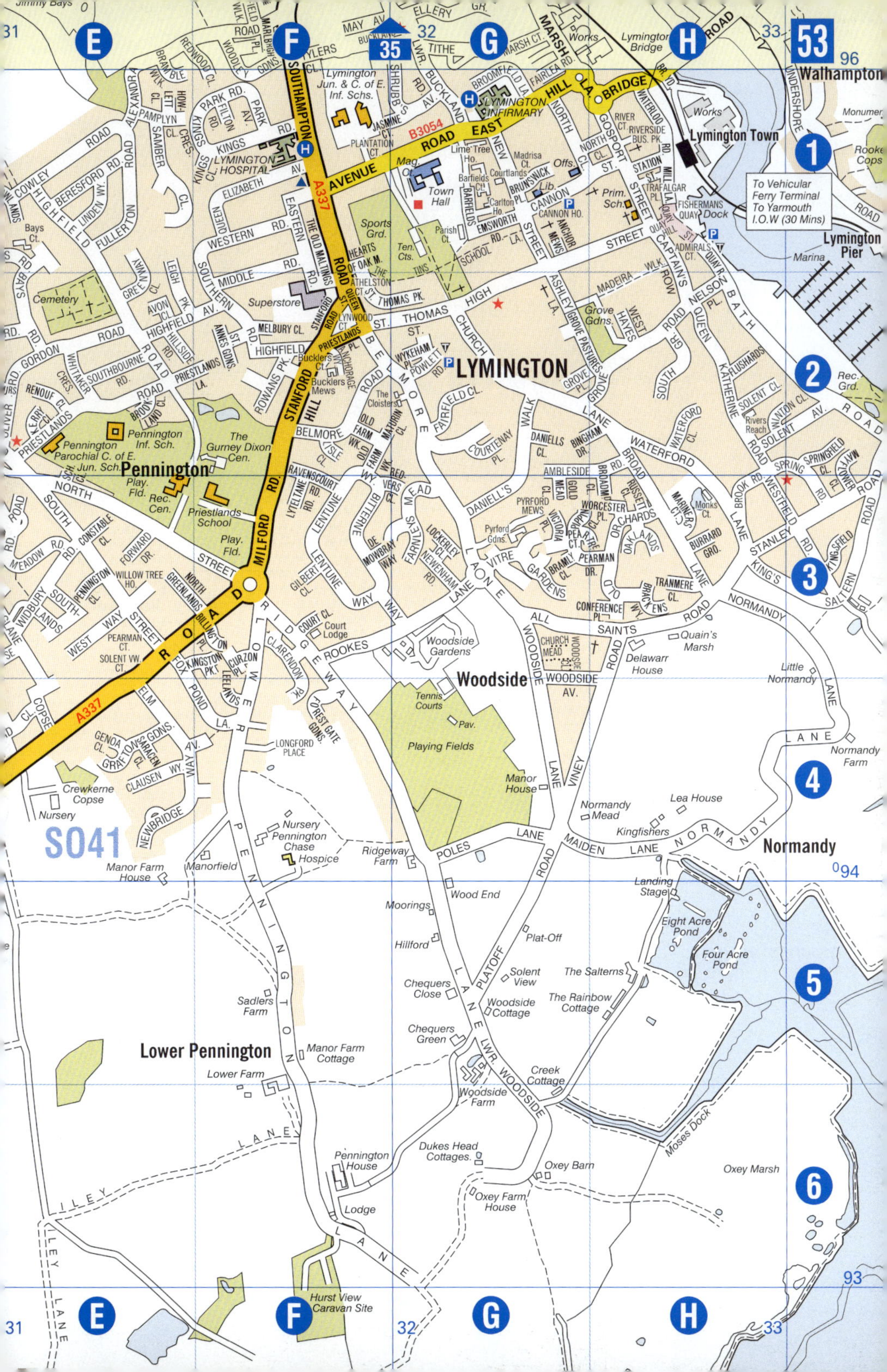

31
E
F
35
32
G
H
53
96
Walhampton
May Av.
Ellery Gr.
Tithe
Marsh Ct.
Works
Lymington Bridge
Road
33
Jimmy Bays
Tylers
Lymington Jun. & C. of E. Inf. Schs.
Jasmine Cl.
Shrubb's Road
Buckland Road
Broomfield La.
Fairlea Rd.
Hill
Marsh
La.
Bridge
Lymington Infirmary
Waterloo Rd.
River Ct.
Riverside Bus. Pk.
Works
Lymington Town
Undershore Road
Monumer
Rooke Cops
1
Redwood Cl.
Woodley
Marlborough Gdns.
Bramble
Park Rd.
Filton Cl.
Av.
Kings Rd.
Southampton Road
B3054
Road East
Plantation Ct.
Lime Tree Ho.
Madrisa Ct.
Offs.
North Cl.
Gosport Road
North St.
Station St.
Trafalgar Pl.
Mill Lane
Fishermans Quay
Admirals Ct.
To Vehicular Ferry Terminal To Yarmouth I.O.W (30 Mins)
Lymington Pier
Alexandra Road
Pamplyn Cl.
Howl. Lett Cl.
Samber Cl.
Kings Cres.
Lymington Hospital
Elizabeth Cl.
Avenue
A337
Mag. Ct.
Town Hall
Barfields
Courtlands
Brunswick Pl.
Carlton Pl.
Lib.
Prim. Sch.
Anchor Mews
Captain's Row
Quay St.
Marina
Cowley Road
Beresford Rd.
Linden Wy.
Fullerton Road
Western Road
Southern Rd.
Middle Rd.
The Old Maltings
Road
Hearts of Oak M.
The Athelston
Sports Grd.
Parish Ch.
Ten. Cts.
TINS
Emsworth Rd. La.
School La.
High Street
Ashley Grove Pastures
Madeira Wlk.
Grove Gdns.
West Hayes
Nelson Pl.
Queen
South
Solent Cl.
Rec. Grd.
2
Bays Ct.
Highfield
Greenway
Leigh Pk.
Highfield Av.
Avon Cl.
Hillside Rd.
Annes Gdns.
Melbury Cl.
Highfield
Stanford Rd.
Lynwood
Thomas Pk.
Thomas St.
Church Lane
Fairfield Cl.
Grove Pl.
Grove Lane
Waterford
Waterford Cl.
Broad Lane
Russett Cl.
Mariners Cl.
Monks Ct.
Rivers Reach
Solent Av.
Spring
Westfield Rd.
Springfield Cl.
Tower
Cemetery
Superstore
Queen St.
LYMINGTON
Wykeham Cl.
Powlett Rd.
Walk
Daniells Cl.
Bingham Dr.
Gold Mead
Broadway
Burrard Gro.
Stanley Road
King's Road
Salterns
3
Gordon Cres.
Whitaker Cl.
Southbourne Rd.
Priestlands Rd.
Priestlands La.
Rowans Pk.
Stanford Hill
Belmore Road
Ravenscourt Rd.
Lyttel Lane Rd.
De Mowbray Way
Bitterne Way
Farnleys Mead
Mead Lane
Daniell's Cl.
Pyrford Mews
Pyrford Gdns.
Victoria Rd.
Bramly Cl.
Pearman Dr.
Oaklands
Tranmere Cl.
Normandy Lane
Kingsfield
Saltern Av.
Renouf Cl.
Kerry Cl.
Priestlands
Brook Land Cl.
Pennington Parochial C. of E. Jun. Sch.
Pennington Inf. Sch.
The Gurney Dixon Cen.
Pennington
Play. Fld.
Rec. Cen.
Priestlands School
Play. Fld.
Belmore La.
Old Farm Wk.
Majorin Old Farm
The Cloisters
Courtenay Pl.
Worcester Pl.
Pea. R. Tree Ct.
Orchards
Blackens
Conference Pl.
All Saints
Road
Normandy Road
King's Road
Little Normandy
Lane
Normandy Farm
4
Oliver Rd.
Meadow Rd.
South Rd.
North Rd.
Constable Cl.
Forward Dr.
Willow Tree Ho.
Greenlands Road
North Street
Billington
Milford Road
Ridgeway
Clarendon
Curzon Cl.
Lelands
Court Cl.
Court Lodge
Rookes Lane
Woodside Gardens
Church Mead
Woodside Av.
Delawarr House
Viney Lane
Quain's Marsh
Lea House
Normandy Mead
Kingfishers
Normandy Lane
Normandy
0 94
Widbury Cl.
South Lane
West
Pennington Cl.
Pearman Ct.
Solent Vw. Ct.
A337
Elm Pk.
Fox Pond La.
Kingston Pk.
Forest Gate Gdns.
Longford Place
Woodside
Tennis Courts
Pav.
Playing Fields
Manor House
Maiden Lane
Landing Stage
Eight Acre Pond
Four Acre Pond
5
Genoa Cl.
Saracen Gdns.
Grafton Cl.
Clausen Wy.
Crewkerne Copse
Newbridge
Nursery
Manor Farm House
Manorfield
Pennington Lane
Nursery
Pennington Chase
Hospice
Ridgeway Farm
Poles Lane
Wood End
Moorings
Hillford
Platoff Lane
Solent View
The Salterns
The Rainbow Cottage
SO41
Lower Pennington
Manor Farm Cottage
Lower Farm
Chequers Close
Chequers Green
Woodside Cottage
Lwr. Woodside
Creek Cottage
Woodside Farm
Moses Dock
6
Iley Lane
Pennington House
Lodge
Dukes Head Cottages
Oxey Farm House
Oxey Barn
Oxey Marsh
Hurst View Caravan Site
Lane
31
E
F
32
G
H
33
93

54
97
98
93
A
B
C
D
36
1
2
3
4
5
6
92
93
91
90
BH16
SLOUGH
French's Farm
WATERY LANE
GREENWAY CR.
SEABANK CL.
BARN CL.
MARTINS CL.
SANDY LANE
BEACH ROAD
OTTER CL.
Upton Inf. Sch.
Upton Jun. Sch.
Sewage Pumping Station
Sewage Works
HEATHERDELL
MOORLAND RD.
HOLCOMBE RD.
BIRCHWOOD RD.
MOORLAND CR.
PEARCE RD.
CHELMSFORD RD.
CHERRY HILL CT.
RED CHERRY CT.
CHERRY HILL GRO.
WOOD COTE DR.
CHERRY HILL GDNS.
GREEN ACRE CL.
GWENLYN CL.
YARRELL'S CL.
PINE VIEW CL.
Yarrells Prep. Sch.
GUEST RD.
TEN. CTS.
OLD KILN RD.
Depot
VENTURA
THE VENTURA CENTRE
OLD KILN
ROPERS LA.
Pentre Cottages
BLANDFORD
ROAD
B3068
ALLEN'S LANE
OAK CL.
PETERS CL.
SANDY LANE
LYTCHETT BAY
Mud
Mud
Mud
Mud
Mud
Mud
Rock Lea River
SALTINGS RD.
FURZEY RD.
LYTCHETT BAY VIEW
SHORE GDNS.
SHORE AV.
SHORE CL.
BORDER DR.
BORDER
TREE HAMLETS
BOUND RD.
OLD RD.
BORDER RD.
STEPNELL REACH
Works
Works
WILLOW CL.
ALLENS RD.
ALLENS LANE
Works
PURBECK POOLE
Pavilion
Recreation Ground
Turlin Moor
Turlin Moor First Sch.
Turlin Moor Middle Sch.
Comm. Cen.
Hall
KELSWORTH RD.
Otter Island
Rock Lea Wood
Holton Clump
Holton Point
Rockley Viaduct
Rockley Point
EGMONT RD.
PETERELL CL.
EGMONT SOUTH CL.
EGMONT RD.
HAVEN RD.
FORELAND RD.
PATCHINS RD.
PATCHINS RD.
TURLIN RD.
RUSSELL CL.
SHIPSTAL CL.
REDHORN CL.
MIDDLEHERE CR.
FITZWORTH AVENUE
MARYLAND RD.
JUNCTION
Hamworthy
RICE GDNS.
GOATHORN RD.
CARTERS
GALLOWAY RD.
DAWKINS RD.
DAWKINS RD.
DAWKINS BUS. CEN.
FRESHWATER DR.
CARISBROOKE
FRESHWATER ROAD
HAMWORTHY
Works
Rifle Range
Ham Hill
Turlin Valley
Rockley Vale
ROCKLEY CARAVAN PARK
Club
Rockley Hill
Rockley Sands
Bay Hollow
NAPIER
Bay View
Purbeck View
Swimming Pool
WALCHEREN PL.
Ham Common
NAPIER ROAD
Amphibious Training Unit Royal Marines
Playing Field
Pav.
Ten. Cts.
Lake House
Depot
HOYAL
NATHEN
HERCULES
HESAMSON
GOLIATH RD.
DELILAH RD.
RUBENLO WY.
SOLOMON DR.
FORT MOORLAND PL.
NORMANDY PL.
SALERNO PL.
KANGAW PL.
Rockley Jetty
Mud
Wood Bar Looe
Depot
LAKE ROAD
LAKE DRIVE
LAKE AV.
Pier
Amphibious Training Unit Royal Marines
Pontoons
Slipway
Moriconium Quay
Marina
Lake
WAREHAM CHANNEL

UPTON COUNTRY PARK
Upton Park Farm
E
F LYTCHETT
MINSTER-&-UPTON-BY-PASS
A35
37
G
Creekmoor Bridge
THE ALPHA CEN.
FLEETSBRI. BUS. CEN.
H
55
93
01
Upton House
BH17
A3049
A349
WESSEX GATE RETAIL PARK
BROADSTONE WAY
HOLES-BAY-ROAD
A350
WILLIS WAY
SOVEREIGN BUSINESS PARK
FLEETS ESTATE
CHRISTOPHER WAY
CHRISTOPHER
1
Stanley Green
Boat House
Mud
Pergins Island
WILLIS WAY
WILLIS WAY
Manor Park
LANE
RECTORY RD.
PRESTON
CRES.
WHITE
STANLEY
2
DONNELL
PALMER
STANLEY RD.
STANLEY GREEN CRES.
STANLEY GREEN RD.
Tatnar Rec.
A350
STANLEY GREEN IND. EST.
92
Course of Roman Road
H o l e s   B a y
Creekmoor Lake
HOLES BAY
STERTE
STERTE M.
STERTE INDUSTRIAL EST.
STERTE AVENUE
STERTE AV. WEST
STERTE AV. EAST
Works
Works
3
Sterte CL.
RD. VIEW
Playing Fields
SYMES RD.
SYMES RD.
Vineyard Copse
SYMES RD.
Mud
PROMENADE
Sterte
Sterte
56
57
STERTE BAY
HEWITT RD.
FALCONER DRIVE
INGLESHAM
B3068
ROAD
HEWITT RD.
HARKWOOD DR.
HARKWOOD DR.
WOODLANDS
Cobbs Quay Marina
Upton Lake
4
ROAD
STERTE ROAD
POOLE
91
BECKHAMPTON
MANTON RD.
MANTON
RD.
MANTON AVE.
WOODLANDS CRES.
BH15
Mud
Channel
Mill
Warehc
Depot
Timber Yard
WINGATE GDS.
RIDGEMOUNT GDS.
DEAN CL.
HELIER
HALTER PATH
ST. MICHAELS
WOODLANDS AVENUE
Works
5
WEST QUAY
WEST ST.
WHITTLES WAY
MARSTON RD.
SLIP WAY
BUTTS
Works
CAVERSHAM
LAKE CRES.
HAMILTON CL.
HAMILTON RD.
BURGATE RD.
HINCHLIFFE RD.
HINCHLIFFE CL.
Carter Community School
ECCLES RD.
Quay West Marina
Works
Back Quay
WEST QUAY RD.
WILKINS WY.
GUILDHALL
NEW ORCHARD
HAY
DEAR ST.
ST.
6
ANNET CL.
ELIJAH RD.
Wareham Ct.
BENJAMIN RD.
JOSHUA CL.
Lulworth Ct.
COLES GDNS.
LEGION CL.
ALBANY GDS.
Playing Field
Hamworthy Rec. Grd.
Liby.
BLAND'S
TUCKERS
RIGLER RD.
ROAD
Works
Poole Bridge
A350
DEE WAY
WEST QUAY RD.
Barbers
St. Ga.
St. Clements
MARKET
CHURCH ST.
NEW ST.
HIGH ST.
CASTLE
STRAND ST.
Poole Quay
KUBS
COLES GDNS.
ROCKLEY
HOUNSLOW CL.
Hamworthy First Sch.
B3068
Timber Yard
Lifeboat Sta.
Little Channel
Ferry
Ballast Quay
The Bulwarks
Brownsea Foot Ferry
LULWORTH CL.
BRANKSEA CL.
PURBECK CL.
ASHMORE CR.
ASHMORE CR.
THE OLD ROPE WLK.
Hamworthy Middle Sch.
SHAPWICK RD.
BRIDGE APP.
NEW QUAY RD.
Lower Hamworthy
STATION RD.
THE QUAY
FERRY RD.
AVENUE
Paddling Pool Promenade
Hamworthy Park
Marina
NEW HARBOUR RD. WEST
NEW HARBOUR RD. WEST
NEW HARBOUR RD.
Freightliner Terminal
Ferry Passenger Terminal
PORT OF POOLE
E
F
G
H
99
00
90
Vehicular Ferry to:-
Cherbourg 4hrs. 15mins.
Guernsey 2hrs. 30mins.
(Fast Ferry, Summer Only)
Jersey 3hrs. 25mins.
(Fast Ferry, Summer Only)

56
93
01
02
38
OAKDALE
BH15
Poole High School
Longfleet
POOLE
Sterte
Poole
Stanley Green
Parr's Plantation
Cemetery
Chapel
Chapel
Parkstone Heights
POOLE PARK
Boating Lake
PARKSTONE BAY
Mud
Weston's Island
Weston's Point
Parkstone Marina
Parkstone Lake
PORT OF POOLE
Breakwater
The Bulwarks
Quay
New Quay
Wareham Ferry (Foot) May, Sept
Brownsea Island Ferry (Foot) May-Sept
Old Lifeboat House
Ballast Quay
Aquarium
Superstore
Dolphin Swimming Pool
Baiter Recreation Ground
Cycle Track
Promenade
Model Yacht Enclosure
Cricket Ground
Playing Field
Miniature Railway
Bournemouth & Poole College of F.E. Further Educat
Civic Cen.
Commercial Rd.
A35
A350
A35
A350
B3093
B3068
B3068
B3093
WIMBORNE ROAD
FERNSIDE ROAD
RINGWOOD ROAD
CONSTITUTION HILL
PARKSTONE ROAD
STERTE ROAD
BAY ROAD
HOLES BAY ROAD
TOWNGATE BRIDGE
NEWFOUNDLAND DRIVE
SELDOWN
MT. PLEASANT
WEST QUAY ROAD
WEST ST.
DORSET
Stanley Green First Sch.
Oakdale South Road Middle School
Tatnam Farm Rec. Grd.
St. Mary's Combined R.C. Sch.
Longfleet C. of E. Combined Sch.
Poole Hosp.
St. Mary's Maternity Hosp.
Football & Greyhound Stadium
Dolphin Centre
Bus Station
Bus Depot
Arts Cen.
Sports Cen.
Kingland Cres.
Fleets Estate
Sovereign Bus. Pk.
Willis Way
Manor Park
Sterte Industrial Est.
Stanley Green Ind. Est.
4
4
4
55

57
BH12
BH14
Upper Parkstone
Lower Parkstone
Parkstone
ASHLEY ROAD
BOURNEMOUTH ROAD
COMMERCIAL ROAD A35
POOLE ROAD A35
SANDBANKS ROAD
BLAKE ROAD B3369
SEA VIEW ROAD
B3061
B3068
B3369
Haskells Recreation Ground
Branksome Heath Mid. Sch.
Branksome Cemetery
Sylvan First Sch.
Sea View Cen. (Adult Training Cen.)
Day Centre
Purbeck Heights
Playing Field
Constitution Hill
Heatherlands First Sch.
Alexandra Park
Courthill First Sch.
Parkstone Cemetery
Baden Powell & St. Peter's C. of E. Middle Sch.
Whitecliff Recreation Ground
Dorset Lake Manor
Croquet Lawns
Tennis Cts.
Uplands School
Fairview Park
The Cheviots
Club House
Parkstone Golf Course
Overlinks Viewpoint
Ponds
Sailing Club Swimming Pool
Mud
Blue Lagoon
Boating Lake
Lilliput C. of E. First Sch.
Harbour Prospect
The Capstans
92
93
90
91
04
05
39
58
69
E F G H
1 2 3 4 5 6

58
93
405
58
A B 40 06 C D
Lincoln
Rossmore
Road
NEWLYN
SANCREED
R.C. Combined Sch.
WAY
CROMER DR.
ROAD
Factory
Alder Hills
Reserve
ARNHAM
FARNHAM RD.
WINSTON AV.
WINSTON AV.
MERROW AV.
The Mills
HERBERT RD.
NORTHMERE RD.
MORRISON AV.
HEATHER
PINE
BOYD RD.
WINSTON
AV.
COOKE
WINSTON PK.
CARROLL
FARNHAM ROAD
MAYFORD RD.
MAYFED RD.
SUNRIDGE RD.
1
BRANKSOME
Comm. Cen.
CONNAUGHT AVE
CENTRAL AVE
Comm. Cen.
A3040
DEREHAM WAY
YARMOUTH
COOKE
NORMAN PK.
NORMAN AV.
GDNS.
AVENUE
GUEST AV.
GUEST CL.
CORNELIA CRES.
WOLTERTON RD.
St. Aldhelm's C. of E. Combined Sch.
Bourne Valley
WREN CRES.
CHILTERN RD.
Chideock Ct.
Wharfdale
Recreation Ground
Pavs.
ROAD
DRIVE
SHERINGHAM
HOLT RD.
GUEST ROAD
CORNELIA CRES.
ING-WORTH RD.
DALLING RD.
Play. Fld.
Bourne Valley Nature Reserve
Gas Works
Fern B
BERESFORD
Playfields
ROAD
GLOUCESTER
BINNIE RD.
ROAD
ALDER ROAD
STALHAM RD.
RINTON
ALBY RD.
ROAD
COY
POND
Coy Pond
THWAITE
CRES.
Wolseley Road
Heatherlands First Sch.
DAVIS ROAD
GWYNNE
FRANCIS RD.
DOUGLAS RD.
GLAS GDNS.
BOUNTY'S
ROAD
WROXHAM RD.
HORNING RD.
GORLESTON RD.
ROAD
JAMES RD.
YARM. CL.
GORDON
HAVELOCK RD.
Coy Pond Gardens
ROAD
WREN
Sunny Hill
Sunny Hill Ct.
YBER RD.
BOB HANN CL.
LAYTON RD.
SHILLITO RD.
Davis Ct.
Emily Ct.
Hall
REDLANDS
POOLE COMMERCE CENTRE
CROMER CRESCENT
GORDON RD SOUTH
SURREY
ROAD
ERPINGHAM RD
NELSON
BRUNSTEAD PL.
IPSWICH RD.
ROAD
Crusader Ct.
Willow Cl.
ASHLEY
B3061 ROAD
CARNEGIE LIB.
LIBRARY
VALE CRESCENT
BEECH RD.
St. Aldhelms
WILLS RD.
Branksome
Bowling Alley
SILVER BIRCH CL.
COPPER BEECH CL.
PRINCESS
APPLE CL.
PEAR CL.
ROAD
BRUNSTEAD
ALEXANDRA
92
Alexandra Park
Pav
HIGH WOOD RD.
HARDY RD.
O VALE
VALE RD.
ROAD
ANGLEY RD.
DOYNE RD.
POOLE
Works
ROAD
ROAD
A35
339
Lindsay Hall
Burling Ter.
LINDUM
Lindum Pl.
EAGLE RD.
APPLE CL.
D Barons
Auburn Mans.
PRINCESS RD.
WESSEX
POOLE RD.
PRINCE
MILBURN
3
BOURNEMOUTH
PONSBY RD.
NORTH LODGE RD.
LODGE CT.
LODGE CLOSE
ARCHWAY RD.
Convent Monastery
The Victoria Sch.
The Gateway
Melton Ct.
VENTRY CL.
Darwin
AVON RD.
R322
Rutland Mnr.
Kilbride
The Oasis
Lindsay Mnr.
Broadway Gables
Broadway
250
Works
WILDERTON RD.
Pine Park Mansions
Cedar Grange
Lindsay Ct.
Pelham
Woodlands
HOLLY LODGE
Kelvedon
Pen Craig
Blenheim
Chartwell
Wood House
Westerham
SEAMOOR
WESTGATE PK.
WESTERHAM RD.
SEAMOOR
SEAMOOR PL.
ELDON PL.
Library
PARKSTONE
57
PENN HILL
SPUR RD.
CALEDON RD.
DELHI RD.
AV.
MAYFIELD AVENUE
AVENUE
ST. ALDHELM'S RD.
PINE
Branksome Bowling Grn.
Branksome Tennis Cts.
WITHINGHAM RD.
BALCOMBE ROAD
BURTON ROAD
Conifers
Belvoir Pk.
Kingsgate Park
Lingfield Grange
Western-gate
Greenacres
WESTERHAM
ROAD
R.L. STEVENSON AV.
Skerryvore RD.
PINEWOOD RD.
4
BH14
STEVENSON RD.
BIRCH CL.
AVENUE
BOULNOIS AV.
FRANKLAND CRES.
FRANKLAND CRES.
FRANKLAND AV.
ROAD
WESTERN
CLIFFS
ROAD
DOVER RD
DOVER CLO
PINE DRIVE
Chine
DRIVE
Ashton Ct.
Sunset Lodge
Dolphin Ct.
AVENUE
QUEENS
Ancrum Lodge
Rozel Manor
Fountain Court
GROVELEY RD.
Westbourne
PEMBROKE RD.
WARREN RD
DRURY RD
DENEWOOD RD
91
KINGS
CLIFTON ROAD
KINGS CRES.
AVENUE
ROAD
BH13
BURY ROAD
MORNISH ROAD
WESTERN
WEST GARDENS
BELGRAVE RD.
PINE DRIVE EAST
ORMONDE RD.
TOWER RD
HERBERT RD.
Comilla Ct.
BRANKSOME DENE RD.
ROSEMOUNT
ALUMDALE RD.
Alm. Gdns.
5
CANFORD CLIFFS
AVENUE
WIDDICOMBE AV.
OVER LINKS DRIVE
ROAD
Branksome Park
CHESTER RD.
EATON RD.
FOREST RD
MOTCOMBE RD.
The Pines
Dorset House
Evesham Ct.
B3065
TOWER
HAYDON RD.
WESTMINSTER RD.
TOWER RD EAST
CASSEL AV.
Zetland Ct.
BEAU
LINKS
LINKS VIEW AV.
HAIG AVENUE
BUCKLEY
CLEUCH
CERNE ABBAS
WESTMINSTER RD WEST
PINEWOOD RD
MOUNTBATTEN RD.
Skerryvore
6
Overlinks Viewpoint
Luscombe Valley
PARKSTONE GOLF COURSE
LAWRENCE DR.
CANFORD
MARTELLO ROAD
MARTELLO RD.
Branksome Park Wood
Berkeley Towers
DALKEITH RD.
DALKEITH ROAD
DALKEITH
Branksome Dene Chine
The Teak House
Zetland Ct.
90
405
406
A B 70 C D

59
93
Talbot Woods
BH3
BH2
BH1
BH4
Westbourne
West Cliff
BOURNEMOUTH
POOLE BAY
MEYRICK PARK GOLF COURSE
MEYRICK PARK
POOLE BOURNEMOUTH
Talbot Heath School
Pug's Hole
Playing Field
Tennis Courts
Recreation Ground
Bowling Greens
Club House
CEMETERY
Cricket Ground
Winter Gdns
The Pavilion
Bournemouth International Conference Centre
Oceanarium
Landing Stage
WIMBORNE ROAD
TALBOT AV.
WESSEX WAY
WEST CLIFF RD.
EXETER RD.
PRIORY RD.
CHAR-MINSTER RD.
LANSDOWNE
BATH RD.
PROMENADE
UNDERCLIFF DRIVE
OVERCLIFF DRIVE
A338
A347
A338
B3066
41
59
90
East Avenue Roundabout
St. Michael's Roundabout
East Avenue
West Cliff
Town Hall
Jetty
Groynes
Lifeguard Station
Admirals Walk
Mus. & Art Gallery
E F G H
1
2
3
4
5
6

BOURNEMOUTH
POOLE
Springbourne
East Cliff
BH8
BH1
BH3
Bournemouth

61
93
Avonbourne School
KINGS PARK
Bournemouth AFC (Dean Court)
Model Railway
Football Ground
Athletic Ground
Coach Park
Playground
Cricket Ground
Pav.
King's Park Prim. Sch.
Football Ground
Indoor Bowls Cen.
Depots
Warehouse
BH7
East Cemetery
Pokesdown
KINGS PARK COMMUNITY HOSP.
Pokesdown
Nursery
KINGS PARK
Wareham Ct.
Lascelles
Lascelles Ct.
Prim. Sch.
A35
Whittingham
BH6
SUNNYHILL
OXFORD
Pokesdown Prim. Sch.
SOUTHBOURNE
92
PARK
GRO.
NEW
DOUGLAS
CENTENARY WAY
Bus Sta.
SOVEREIGN CENTRE
ROYAL ARC CHRISTCHURCH
Lib.
St. James' Sq.
R.C. Prim. Sch.
College
Lib.
BEECH WOOD GS.
DARRACOTT
WEST
WOODSIDE RD.
PTER.
B3059 ROAD
SOUTHBOURNE
BEECH AV.
BRACKEN
62
SOUTHWOOD
BH5
WENTWORTH
WOODLAND WALK
GRASMERE
Wentworth College
Ten. Cts. Play. Fld.
WENTWORTH CL.
RAVINE
DINGLE
FISHERMAN'S WALK
SEAWARD
MONTAGUE
PORTMAN
ROTHERFLD. RD.
Shelley Park
Bowl. Grn.
OVERCLIFF
DRIVE
Play Area
Putting Grn.
FISHERMAN'S
SOUTHB
St. James
San Remo Towers
Marina Ct.
Mermaid Ct. Marina Twrs.
Ocean Heights
Carlinford
BOSCOMBE CLIFF RD.
BOSCOMBE
BOSCOMBE
Boscombe Cliff Gdns.
UNDERCLIFF RD.
THE MARINA
Honeycombe Chine
BOSCOMBE
Groynes
PROMENADE
Lift
Portman Ravine
91
Boscombe Pier
B A Y
90
E F G H
1 12 13

62
SOUTHBOURNE
WEST SOUTHBOURNE
TUCKTON
Iford Meadows
Iford Playing Fields
BMX Track
Rookery
Homelands
KING'S ESTATE
GLEADOWE
Tuckton
River Bridge
Pleasure Gardens
St. Peters School
Playing Field
Southbourne Sands
Putting Grn.
Play Area
Groynes
SOUTHBOURNE PROMENADE
Stourfield Jun. & Infs. Schs.
Comm. Cen.
Playground
A35
CHRISTCHURCH ROAD
SOUTHBOURNE GROVE
SOUTHBOURNE ROAD
B3059
BELLE VUE ROAD
B3059
TUCKTON ROAD
IFORD ROAD
STOUR
Needles

Christchurch
BARRACK
ROAD
RD.
AVENUE
STOUR
Portfield Sch.
Beaconsfield
BARGATES
CHRISTCHURCH BY-PASS
45
16
Barlins
63
93
E
F
G
H
17
FOUNTAIN WAY
HIGH
ROAD
A35
CHRISTCHURCH
Millhams
STREET
PUREWELL
1
Waterloo Bridge
Mill Stream
Pound La.
Portfield Sch.
Recreation Ground
Magdalen
Druitt Gdns
Castle (Rems.)
Constable's House
Town Bri.
Civic Offs.
Bowls Hall
Riversmeet Area
Twynham Comp. Sch.
Playing Fields
The Priory
Red Ho. Mus.
Holiday Camp
QUOMPS
The Quay
Priory Quay
Convent Meadows Caravan Park
Lock Marina
Clay Pool
BH23
RIVERSMEET GOLF COURSE
Playing Field
2
92
Stanpit Marsh Nature Reserve
Dorset Cricket Cen.
Hall
Riverlands
Broadwaters
Wick Farm
Pond
Drains
Mud
WICK
Golf Driving Range
HENGISTBURY HEAD
Drains
Drains
Drains
Grimbury Point
Crouch Hill
3
Grimbury Marsh
Mother Sillers Channel
Library
WICKMEADS
HENGIST PK. (CARAVAN PK.)
St. Katherine's C. of E. Prim. Sch.
Club House
64
Drains
BH6
SOLENT MEADS GOLF COURSE
SOLENT MEADS
CHRISTCHURCH
BOURNEMOUTH
Ferry (Fool)
Wick Hams
4
Groynes
White Pits
HENGISTBURY HEAD
91
5
Coastguard Lookout Station
Nurse
6
0
90
E
F
16
G
H
17
15

64
93
17
SOMER-FORD
BH23
STANPIT
CHRISTCHURCH
MUDEFORD
Mudeford Jun. Sch.
Dorset Cricket Cen.
Playing Field
Stanpit Marsh Nature Reserve
Drains
92
Mother Siller's Channel
63
CHRISTCHURCH HARBOUR
Blackberry Point
Mud
Mud
The Flats
CHRISTCHURCH BOURNEMOUTH
Ferry (Foot)
91
Mud
BH6
HENGISTBURY HEAD
Nursery
Hengistbury Head
Coastguard Lookout Station
Warren Hill
HENGISTBURY HEAD
Mudeford Quay
Lifeboat Station
Black Ho.
The Run
Ferry (Foot)
MUDEFORD SANDBANK
Breakwaters
SANDHILLS CARAVAN PARK
46
18
HUGH'S BUSINESS CENTRE
Comm. Cen.
BEAVER IND. EST.
AMBASSADOR IND. EST.
90
0
17
18
A
B
C
D
1
2
3
4
5
6

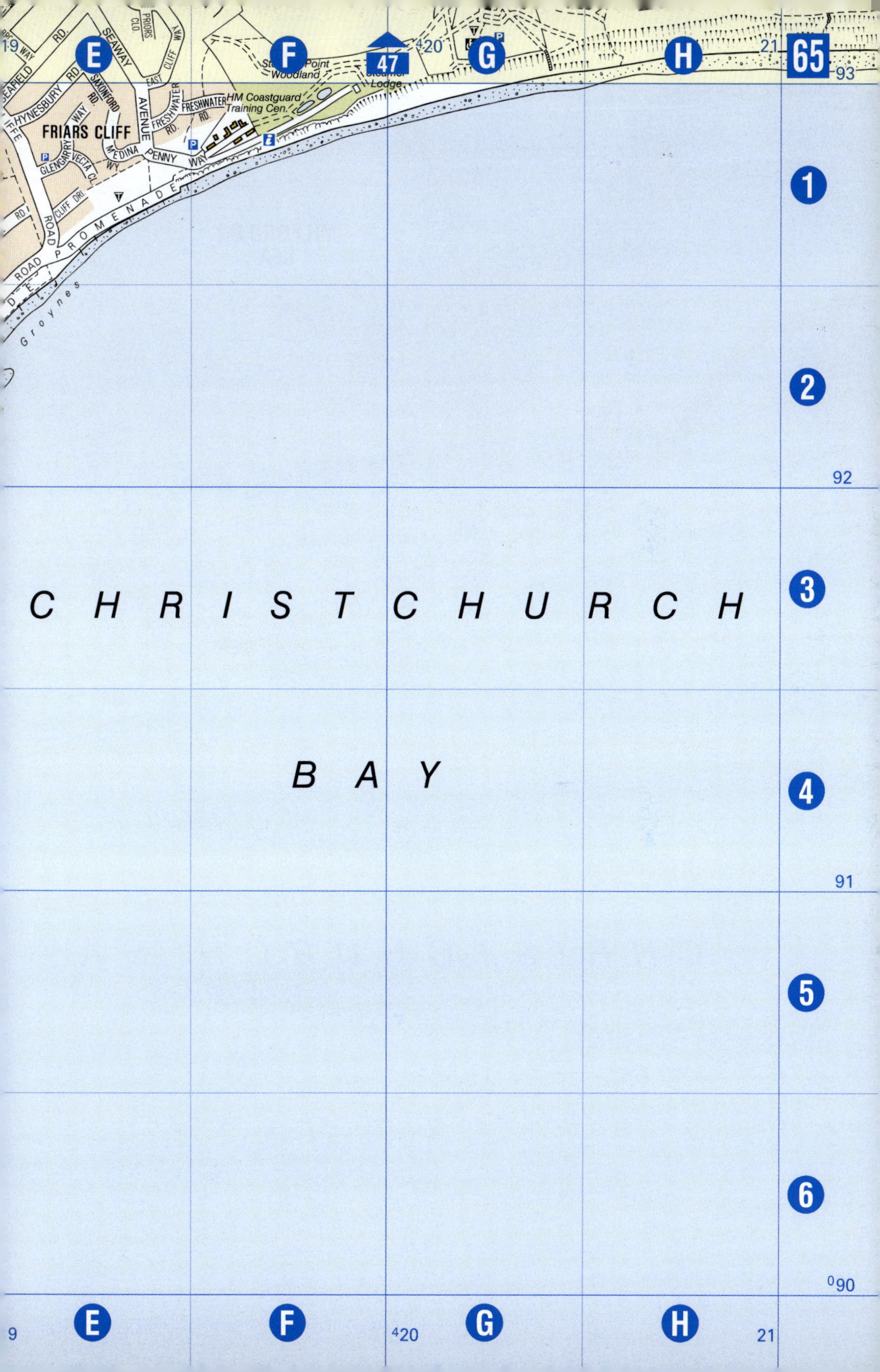
19 WAY RD.
PRIORS CLO.
SEAWAY
EAST CLIFF WAY
E
F
Start Point
Woodland
47
420
G
H
21
65
93
SEAFIELD RD.
HYNESBURY WAY
SAXONFORD RD.
FRESHWATER
FRESHWATER RD.
AVENUE
HM Coastguard
Training Cen.
Steamer
Lodge
FRIARS CLIFF
GLENGARRY WAY
VECTA CL.
MEDINA
PENNY WAY
1
RD.
CLIFF DRI.
ROAD
PROMENADE
Groynes
2
92
C H R I S T C H U R C H
3
B A Y
4
91
5
6
90
9
E
F
420
G
H
21
0

66
93
BH25
27
A
B
C
D
51
28
SHOREFIELD CARAVAN PARK
Swimming Pools
Copse
Nursery
Barnes Farm
Holiday Cen.
Downton Caravan Park
SHOREFIELD
SHOREFIELD ROAD
DANE RD
WARREN PARK
SEABREEZE WAY
Hordle Bridge
Danehurst
1
Hordle Manor Farm
Playing Fields
2
CLIFF
B3058
Hordle Cliff
WOODLAND VIEW
Ford
WEST ROAD
THE BUCKLERS
NTH. HEAD
PLESS ROAD
WESTMINSTER RD.
SEA WINDS
LYDGATE
Blackbush Copse
BLACKBUSH ROAD
Shorefield Copse
Pleasure Grounds
Studland Common
SHARVELLS DR.
STUDLAND
MILFORD ON SEA
GREENWAYS
ROAD
SHOREFIELD WAY
SHOREFIELD CRES.
GEORGE ROAD
SYCAMORE CL.
WAYSIDE CL.
VALLEY
MILL ROAD
VINEGAR HILL
NEW VALLEY BRIDGE
MEADOW
MANOR KITWALLS LANE
MANOR CL.
Rec. Grd.
BROADFIELDS
Addington Ct.
Blandford Ct.
DACRES
KEATS CL.
CHAUCER CL.
GLEBE FIELDS
DRYDEN PL.
WOLSEY WY.
SHELLEY AV.
WINDMILL CL.
CHAUCER DR.
ORCHARD MEADOW
KNOWLAND
KNOWLE DEAN
GREENBANK
Nursery
92
Camden Hurst
WHITBY RD
Solent Pines
GOS.
MARYLAND RD.
Maryland Ct.
Whitby Ct.
CORNWALLIS
VICTORIA RD.
Solent Ct.
Haven
Hurst Ct.
Osborne Ct.
Sea Pines
Totland Ct.
Pinehurst
ST. GEORGE'S HOSP.
VICTORIA
H
DE LA WARR RD.
HAMILTON CT.
ROOKCLIFF WY.
KENSINGTON PK.
HOLLY GDNS
OAKTREE CT.
KIVRNL. CT.
WOOD LANE
NEW WOOD LA.
KIVERNELL ROAD
Rookcliff
Park Ct.
WESTOVER
RAVENS
THE BOLTONS
SHINGLE BANK DR.
SHORE RD.
LUCERNE RD.
DANESTREAM RD.
Milford Bri.
OVERSTRAND
GILLIN
Milford Bri.
H
ROAD
Rook Cliff
P
Richmond Ct.
PARK LANE
NEEDLES POINT
SHORE CL.
White House
3
4
91
5
C H R I S T C H U R C H   B A Y
6
0
90
27
A
B
28
C
D

29
E
Cox's Bridge
Ford
Lymore
F
52
4 30
Agarton Copse
G
H
31
67
93
1
Milford on Sea C. of E. Primary School
LYMINGTON ROAD
B3058
SCHOOL
LYMORE VALLEY LANE
LYMORE LANE
AGARTON LANE
Lymore Farm
LYMEFIELDS
Knold
SO41
2
92
CT.
WLK.
CHURCH HILL
MILFORD
MILL LDS.
MILFIELDS
CHURCH HILL
Solent Flats
The Green
HIGH ST.
CARRINGTON
LYNDALE CL.
CARRINGTON CRES.
CARRINGTON PARK CL.
PARK RD.
Play Area
NORTHFIELD RD.
LAWN RD.
LAWN CL.
LAWN LANE
CHAMPION CL.
SOLENT WAY
EASTERN WAY
AUBREY CL.
Library
Vidle Van Farm
3
KEYHAVEN LANE
Aubrey Farm
Milford on Sea War Memorial Hospital
Milford Trading Estate
Laundry
SWALLOW CL.
GREBE
PLOVER DRIVE
NEW LANE
HARE WOOD GRN.
Aubrey House
Keyhaven Marshes
MANDERLEY
ISLAND VIEW CL.
CASTLE CL.
ROAD
P
P
Carrington Caravan Park
Sturt Pond
ROAD
NEW RD.
Keyhaven
SHIPWRIGHTS WK.
Keyhaven House
KEYHAVEN LANE
4
91
SALTGRASS LANE
Keyhaven Lake
5
Passenger Ferry to Hurst Castle (Summer only)
Hurst Beach
Mount Lake
6
0 90
E
F
4 30
G
H
31
29

68
01
A
B
02
C
D
1
FERRY ROAD
NEW
90
PORT OF POOLE
BH15
The Bulwarks
New Quay
Wareham Ferry (Foot)
Breakwater
House
56
Parkstone Lake
Marina
Vehicular Ferry to:-
Cherbourg 4hrs. 15mins.
Guernsey 2hrs. 30mins.
(Fast Ferry, Summer Only)
Jersey 3hrs. 25mins.
(Fast Ferry, Summer Only)
Brownsea Island Ferry (Foot) May to September
M a i n
2
POOLE
PURBECK
89
P O O L E   H A R B O U R
W y c h   C h a n n e l
3
Mud
Mud
Mud
4
Mud
Wellington Hill
Seymer's Hill
Seymer's House
Cambridge Wood
Pipers Folly
Oxford Wood
St. Andrews Terrace
Columbine Hill
Cabbage Hill
Harlequin Hill
St. Peters Hill
Venetia Park
St. Georges Hill
St. Andrew's Hill
Maryland
The Sanctuary
The Villa
Elizabeth Hill
West Lake
Lonsdale Wood
Middle
East Lake
Nature Reserve
Pantaloon Hill
Nature Trail
Pottery Pier
Rough Brake
Street
Wilderness
Middle
88
Clown Hill
BROWNSEA   ISLAND
Street
St. Michael's Mount
The Pens
Swindale
Bentinck Hill
St. Mary's Church
Green Dale
Saddle Back
Rocket Corner
Pheasant Hill
5
BH15
Vinery Hill
Gravel Hill
Church Hill
Red Hill
Lincoln Cliff
Devil's Den
Harley Wood
Branksea (on site of)
Farm Cottages
William Pit
St. Mark's Lodge
Rose Cottage
South Shore Lodge
St. Anne's Hill
Oak Corner
Portland Hill
Barnes Bottom
Caroline Cliff
Mud
Harry Point
W H I T E   G R O U N D   L A K E
6
Mud
Landing Stage
Mud
FURZEY   ISLAND
87
01
A
B
Mud
02
C
D
Wind

E
F
G
H
04
05
69
090
57
Swimming Pool
Mud
SANDBANKS
BLAKE
BROWN SEA AV.
PARKSTONE
ROAD
Blue Lagoon
THE CAPSTANS
LAGOON
SEA W.
BROWN-
GREENWOOD AV.
FAIRWAY RD.
COMPTON
AV.
Lilliput C. of E. First Sch.
LILLIPUT
GOLF COURSE
P
Boating Lake
WAY
Lagoon Cl.
SALTERNS CT.
280
LAKE AVE.
ANTHONY'S
HURST HILL
HURST CRES.
DEAN
SWIFT
HARBOUR PROSPECT
AVENUE
BINGHAM
1
Canford Cliffs
Compton
Salterns Point
SALT-o-ERNS
DORSET CRES.
GARDENS
FIRS LANE
LILLIPUT
GULLIVER
CL.
Lilliput
ROAD
LAGOON CLO.
13
Marina
Yacht Club
P
B3369
AVALON
ROAD
BH14
2
Pin Bottom
DORNIE RD.
NAIRN
INVERNESS RD.
NAIRN ROAD
89
ROA
Groynes
Hospice
CRICHEL
MOUNT
MINTERNE
ROAD
MOUNT GRACE
DRIVE
THE DRIVE
RD
CHADD
71
Landing Stage
Landing Stage
Minterne Grange
Witley
LITTLE COURT
ALINGTON CL.
Reserve
BRUDENELL
BRUDENELL RD.
PIN
Evening Hill
Harbour Watch
ALINGTON
ROAD
Nature
SHORE
FLAG FARM
Waters Edge
B3065
HAVEN
82
ST. ANN HOSPIT
H
Channel
East Dorset Sailing Club
ROAD
HARBR.
210
CHADDESLEY
HIVE GDNS.
3
CHADDESLEY GLEN
GLEN
Little Fosters
SHORE
ROAD
70
P
4
19
P
B3369
Groynes
88
Brownsea Island Ferry (Foot) May–Sept.
BROWNSEA ROAD
89
SANDBANKS
ROAD
Sandbanks Pav.
Putt. Grn.
PROMENADE
5
Cottages
Sch
Piers
Piers
Jetty
Boat House
THE
Towans
P
B3369
Pier
OLD COASTGUARD RD.
28
17
ROAD
SANDBANKS
Dune Crest
SANDBANKS
Brownsea Island Ferry (Foot)
PANORAMA
GRASMERE
ROAD
SEACOMBE
SALTER ROAD
SUMMERHILL
ROAD
38
121
Fairwinds
BH13
6
North Haven Point
PANORAMA
RD
57
120
Woodrising
HAVEN CT. 80
BANKS
FERRY WY.
SANDBANKS BUS. CEN.
Golden Gates
P
Carina Ct.
MIDWAY PATH
Groynes
Ferry (Vehicular)
Groynes
E
F
G
H
04
05
87
LAWRE
DR.

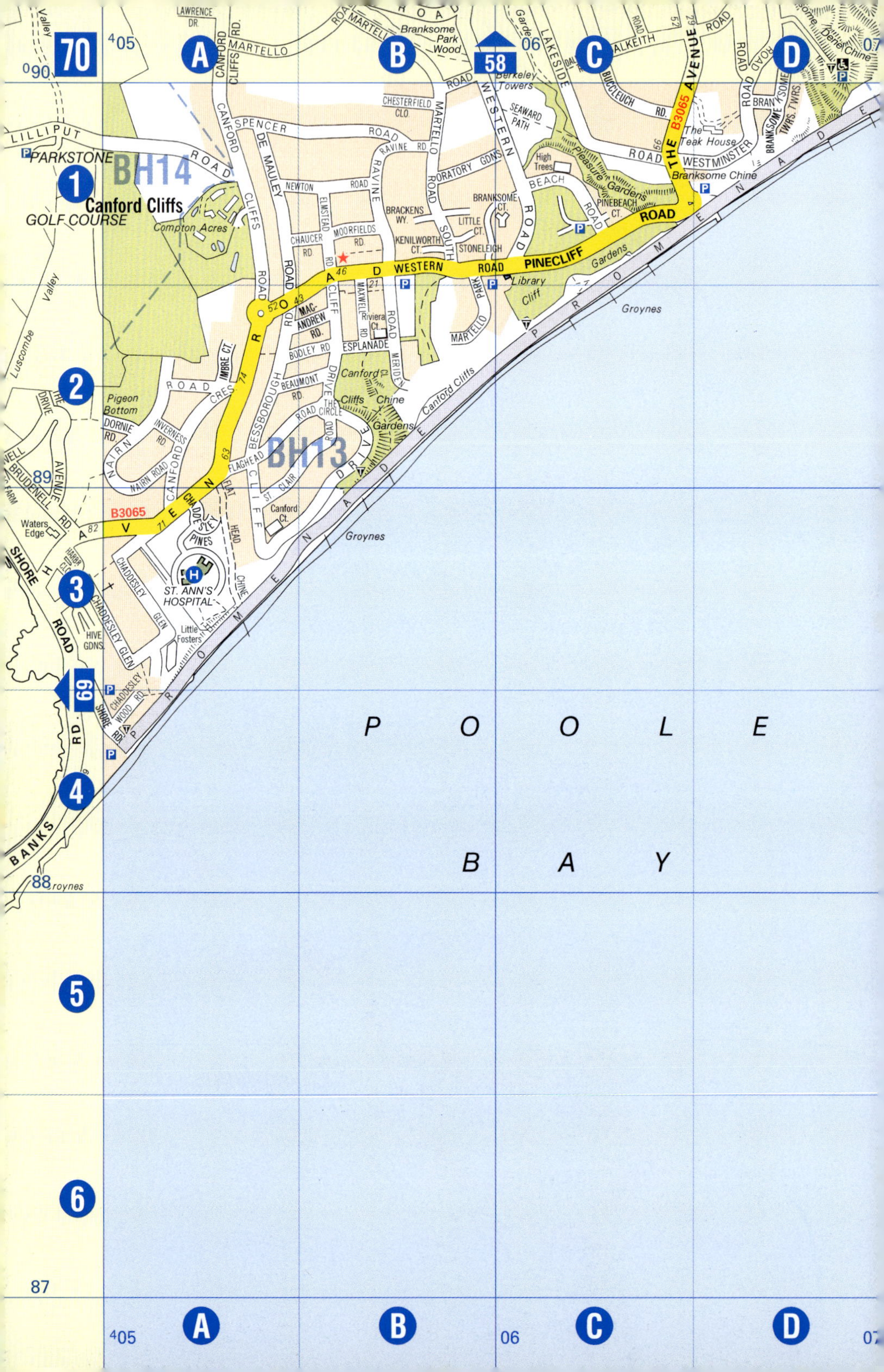

70
405
090
LAWRENCE DR.
A
B
BRANKSOME PARK WOOD
58
06
C
CALKEITH
D
DENE Chine
MARTELLO
CANFORD CLIFFS RD.
ROAD
MARTELLO
LAKESIDE
THE AVENUE
ROAD
ROAD
BRANKSOME
LILLIPUT
PARKSTONE
BH14
1
Canford Cliffs
GOLF COURSE
CHESTERFIELD CLO.
ROAD
SPENCER
DE MAULEY
CANFORD
CLIFFS
ROAD
NEWTON ROAD
RAVINE RD.
RAVINE
MARTELLO ROAD
WESTERN
ORATORY GDNS.
ROAD
SEAWARD PATH
Berkeley Towers
BUCCLEUCH RD.
56
B3065
The Teak House
WESTMINSTER
Branksome Chine
ROAD
BRANKSOME TWRS. TWRS.
High Trees
Pleasure Gardens
ROAD
Compton Acres
BRACKENS WY.
BRANKSOME
CT.
BEACH
PINEBEACH CT.
ROAD
Valley
Luscombe
Valley
CHAUCER RD.
ELMSTEAD RD.
MOORFIELDS RD.
A 46
D
WESTERN
ROAD
PINECLIFF
Gardens
ROAD
KENILWORTH CT.
SOUTH
LITTLE CT.
STONELEIGH
Library
Cliff
Groynes
CLIFF RD.
52
43
MAC-ANDREW RD.
P
MAXWELL RD.
Riviera Ct.
21
ROAD
MERIDEN
MARTELLO
PARK
P
2
Pigeon Bottom
THE
DRIVE
DORNIE RD.
INVERNESS RD.
NAIRN ROAD
ROAD
IMBRE CT.
74
CRES.
BESSBOROUGH
BEAUMONT RD.
ROAD
CIRCLE
Canford Cliffs Chine
Gardens
BH13
BRUDENELL
89
AVENUE
RD.
A 82
NAIRN RD.
CANFORD
63
FLAGHEAD
CLIFF
ST. CLAIR
DRIVE
THE
Canford Ct.
Groynes
Waters Edge
B3065
V
71
CHADDESLEY
PINES
FLAT HEAD CHINE
CLIFF
N
A
D
E
SHORE
ROAD
HARBR.
3
CHADDESLEY GLEN
St. ANN'S HOSPITAL
Little Fosters
HIVE GDNS.
CHADDESLEY GLEN
CHADDESLEY WOOD RD.
69
ROAD
SHORE RD.
P
BANKS
4
88
Groynes
POOLE
BAY
5
6
87
405
A
B
06
C
D
07

71
E F G H
RUSHPOLE WOOD 31
29 430 30
Burnt Hill
Blackwater Farm
Bunker's Hill
Norlands
Blackwater House
FENWICK HOSPITAL
Oak Cottage
Coppice Close
Oak Bank
Pikeshill
Pikes Hill Avenue
Westwood Rd.
Broughton Rd.
Foldsgate
Robertshaw House
Police HQ
FAIR CROSS
River Beaulieu
NEW FOREST
GOLF COURSE
DUNCES ARCH INCLOSURE
09
New Forest Golf Club
Dunces Arch
Thatched Cottage Pk.
Northerwood House
Northerwood Inclosure
NORTHERWOOD PARK
Pike's Hill
Cranleigh Paddock
Garden Cl.
Northerwood Av.
The Cottage
Craig-Ny-Baa
Knightwood Lodge
Knightwood Cl.
Elcombes Cl.
Racecourse Vw.
Queens Rd.
Clarence Rd.
Empress Rd.
Forest Gds.
Kings Cl.
The Custards Rd.
Pemberton Rd.
Custards
Football Pav.
Football Grd.
SO43
Queens Rd.
Princes Cres.
Cemetery
ROMSEY ROAD A337
A337
HIGH STREET
Lyndhurst C. of E. Inf. Sch.
WELLANDS
High Street
The Queen's House
LYNDHURST
CHURCH LA.
Lib.
Mus.
Rufus Ct.
Holmfield
War Mem.
Bolton's Bench
Cricket Ground Pav.
SOUTHAMPTON RD.
A35
2
3
108
BOURNEMOUTH RD.
A35
BOURNEMOUTH RD.
Cuffnels Lodge
Deerleap
Hawks Lease
Haskells Cl.
South Lawns
Sandy La.
CHAPEL LANE
Shrubbs Hill Gdns.
Shrubbs Hill
Great Mead
Dearing Cl.
The Coppice
The Meadows
Shaggs Mdw.
Gosport La.
Appletree Ct. (New Forest District Council)
The Bench
Yew Tree Manor
BEAULIEU
B3056
Beverley
Ravens Nest
4
RD.
Little Paddocks
Tanglewood
Angel's Farm
Oak Cl.
Cedarmount Hill
Goose Grn.
Vernall's Farm
Brooklands
Goose Green
IRONS HILL WALK
NEW FOREST
Foxlease Park
A337
GOOSE GREEN LANE
Wilverley Lodge
Wilverley Coach House
Beechen Lane
Hilary
BEECHEN LANE
PONDHEAD INCLOSURE
5
07
PINKNEY
WILVERLEY PARK
Pinkney Farm
Wilverley Park Cottage
Philip's Hill
Foxlease House
Hall
Clayhill
6
High Coxlease Inclosure
High Coxlease
Coxlease Sch.
A337
BRICK KILN INCLOSURE
PARK GROUND INCLOSURE
E F G H
29 30 430 31

72
OBER HEATH
A
28
B
C
29
D
BLACK KNOWL
Aldridgehill Cottage
Ober Corner
Willis's Plantation
Caravan Site
1
ALDRIDGEHILL INCLOSURE
Aldridge Hill
03
Catherston Stud (Riding School)
Black Knoll House
Ober Water
Beachern Wood
New Cottage
Oberleigh
RHINEFIELD WALK
Beachern Wood Cottage
2
Whitefield Moor
P
RHINEFIELD
P
RHINEFIELD
RHINEFIELD
OBERFIELD RD.
WHITEMOOR RD.
NEW FOREST
BROADLANDS ROAD
FOREST PARK ROAD
OBER
RHINEFIELD
Black Knoll House
ROAD
NORTH
Ober Lodge
THE COPPICE
MOORLANDS CL.
NEW FOREST DRIVE
MDW. CREST WOOD
KNOWLE RD.
Forest Park
3
FOREST GLADE CL.
Thatchby
FOREST DR.
WOODBURY
FOREST VW.
ARMSTRONG
BROADLANDS RD.
ARMSTRONG LANE
ARMSTRONG CL.
The Weirs House
WEIRS
NORTH
Thornacre
WEIRS
102
North Weirs
White Moor
The Weir
Furzey Cottage
BURLEY
Edgemoor House
Linden House
Ford Cottage
Ford
Pound Farm
4
SOUTH
Forest View
SO42
Five Thorns Hill
WEIRS
South Weirs
ROAD
Furzy Hill
Peartree Cottage
BURLEY
WEIRS
Laurel Cottage
The Weirs Cottage
SOUTH
5
The Lodge
Weirfield Holt
Worthys Farm
Barnfield
Farm Cottage
The Bungalow
BURLEY
Trenley Lawn
01
Blackhamsley Hammock
Hincheslea Wood
Hincheslea Bog
Blackhamsley House
Club House
6
BROCKENHURST MANOR GOLF COURSE
Lymington Junction
Hincheslea Bog
A
28
Blackhamsley Hill
B
Gatehouse Cottage
Cater's Cottage
C
29
D
Latch Co.

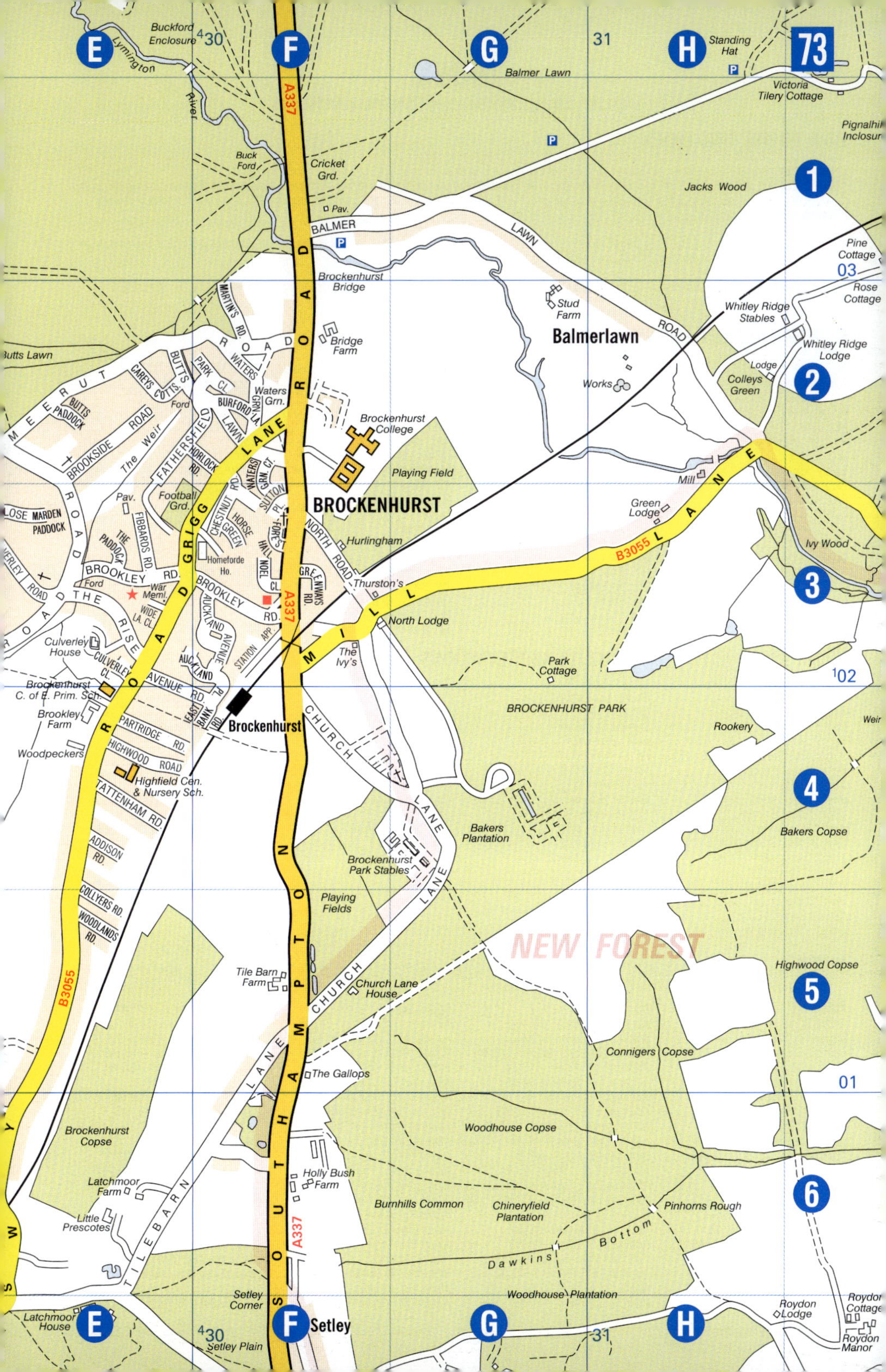
E
F
G
H
73
Buckford Enclosure
Lymington River
430
Standing Hat
Victoria Tilery Cottage
Pignalhill Inclosure
1
Jacks Wood
Pine Cottage
03
Buck Ford
Cricket Grd.
Pav.
BALMER
Brockenhurst Bridge
Rose Cottage
Whitley Ridge Stables
Whitley Ridge Lodge
Stud Farm
Balmerlawn
LAWN ROAD
Lodge
Colleys Green
2
Butts Lawn
Bridge Farm
Waters
PARK CL.
BURFORD
Waters Grn. La.
Waters Grn.
Brockenhurst College
Works
Mill
E
Ivy Wood
MEERUT
BUTTS PADDOCK
CAREYS COTTS.
BUTTS
BROOKSIDE ROAD
The Weir
Ford
FATHERSFIELD
MORLOCK RD.
GRIGG LANE
Playing Field
Green Lodge
LANE
3
LOSE MARDEN PADDOCK
Pav.
Football Grd.
THE PADDOCK
FIBBARDS RD.
CHESTNUT RD.
HORSE GREEN
SUTTON RD.
WATERS
NOEL CL.
BROCKENHURST
Hurlingham
B3055 LANE
WAVERLEY ROAD
BROOKLEY
Ford
War Meml.
WIDE LA. CL.
Homeforde Ho.
HALL
NORTH ROAD
GREENWAYS RD.
Thurston's
B3055
THE RISE
ROAD
BROOKLEY RD.
AUCKLAND AVENUE
STATION APP.
A337
North Lodge
Park Cottage
02
Culverley House
CULVERLEY CL.
AUCKLAND PL.
The Ivy's
Brockenhurst C. of E. Prim. Sch.
AVENUE RD.
EAST BANK RD.
Brockenhurst
BROCKENHURST PARK
Rookery
Brookley Farm
PARTRIDGE RD.
CHURCH LANE
Weir
Woodpeckers
HIGHWOOD ROAD
4
Highfield Cen. & Nursery Sch.
TATTENHAM RD.
Bakers Plantation
Bakers Copse
ADDISON RD.
SOUTHAMPTON
Brockenhurst Park Stables
NEW FOREST
COLLYERS RD.
Playing Fields
WOODLANDS RD.
CHURCH LANE
Highwood Copse
B3055
CHURCH LANE
5
Tile Barn Farm
Church Lane House
Connigers Copse
01
SWAY
Brockenhurst Copse
A337
The Gallops
Woodhouse Copse
Latchmoor Farm
Holly Bush Farm
6
Little Prescotes
TILEBARN
Burnhills Common
Chineryfield Plantation
Pinhorns Rough
Dawkins Bottom
Latchmoor House
Setley Corner
Woodhouse Plantation
Roydon Lodge
Roydon Cottage
E
430
F
Setley
G
31
H
Setley Plain
Roydon Manor

INDEX

Including Streets and Selected Subsidiary Addresses

HOW TO USE THIS INDEX

1. Each street name is followed by its Posttown or Postal Locality and then by its map reference; e.g. Abbey Rd. *W Mr* —1E **19** is in the West Moors Postal Locality and is to be found in square 1E on page **19**. The page number being shown in bold type. A strict alphabetical order is followed in which Av., Rd., St., etc. (though abbreviated) are read in full and as part of the street name; e.g. Abbotsbury Rd. appears after Abbey Rd. but before Abbots Clo.

2. Streets and a selection of Subsidiary names not shown on the Maps, appear in the index in *Italics* with the thoroughfare to which it is connected shown in brackets; e.g. *Ashbourne Ct. Bourn* —4A **60** *(off Lorne Pk. Rd.)*

3. Map references shown in brackets; e.g. Adelaide La. *Bourn* —4H **59** (3H **5**) refer to entries that also appear on the large scale pages 4 & 5.

GENERAL ABBREVIATIONS

All : Alley	Ct : Court	Lit : Little	Rd : Road
App : Approach	Cres : Crescent	Lwr : Lower	Shop : Shopping
Arc : Arcade	Cft : Croft	Mc : Mac	S : South
Av : Avenue	Dri : Drive	Mnr : Manor	Sq : Square
Bk : Back	E : East	Mans : Mansions	Sta : Station
Boulevd : Boulevard	Embkmt : Embankment	Mkt : Market	St : Street
Bri : Bridge	Est : Estate	Mdw : Meadow	Ter : Terrace
B'way : Broadway	Fld : Field	M : Mews	Trad : Trading
Bldgs : Buildings	Gdns : Gardens	Mt : Mount	Up : Upper
Bus : Business	Gth : Garth	Mus : Museum	Va : Vale
Cvn : Caravan	Ga : Gate	N : North	Vw : View
Cen : Centre	Gt : Great	Pal : Palace	Vs : Villas
Chu : Church	Grn : Green	Pde : Parade	Vis : Visitors
Chyd : Churchyard	Gro : Grove	Pk : Park	Wlk : Walk
Circ : Circle	Ho : House	Pas : Passage	W : West
Cir : Circus	Ind : Industrial	Pl : Place	Yd : Yard
Clo : Close	Info : Information	Quad : Quadrant	
Comn : Common	Junct : Junction	Res : Residential	
Cotts : Cottages	La : Lane	Ri : Rise	

POSTTOWN AND POSTAL LOCALITY ABBREVIATIONS

Ashtn : Ashington	*Cor M* : Corfe Mullen	*Lyn* : Lyndhurst	*St L* : St Leonards
Ashy : Ashley	*Cowg* : Cowgrove	*Lyt Mi* : Lytchett Minster	*South* : Southbourne
Ashy H : Ashley Heath	*Crow* : Crow	*Mil S* : Milford on Sea	*Sway* : Sway
Bart S : Barton on Sea	*Down* : Downton	*Nea* : Neacroft	*T Leg* : Three Legged Cross
Bcn H : Beacon Hill	*Evtn* : Everton	*New M* : New Milton	*Tip* : Tiptoe
Blash : Blashford	*Fern* : Ferndown	*N'brne* : Northbourne	*Uptn* : Upton
Bock : Bockhampton	*Fern I* : Ferndown Ind. Est.	*Oak* : Oakdale	*Ver* : Verwood
Bold : Boldre	*Furz* : Furzehill	*Oss* : Ossemsley	*Wal* : Walhampton
Bosc : Boscombe	*H'wthy* : Hamworthy	*Park* : Parkstone	*Walk* : Walkford
Bourn : Bournemouth	*Hang* : Hangersley	*Parl* : Parley	*Wat* : Waterloo
Brnk : Branksome	*Highc* : Highcliffe	*Penn* : Pennington	*W Mr* : West Moors (Ferndown)
Brnk P : Branksome Park	*Hight* : Hightown	*Pilf* : Pilford	*W Moor* : West Moors (Wimborne)
Brans : Bransgore	*High H* : Hightown Hill	*Pill* : Pilley	*W Parl* : West Parley
Broad : Broadstone	*Hint* : Hinton	*Poole* : Poole	*Wim* : Wimborne
Broc : Brockenhurst	*Hord* : Hordle	*P'mre* : Portmore	*Wink* : Winkton
Burt : Burton	*Hurn* : Hurn	*Poul* : Poulner	
Can C : Canford Cliffs	*Key* : Keyhaven	*Ring* : Ringwood	
Christ : Christchurch	*L'ton* : Lymington	*St I* : St Ives	

INDEX

Aaron Clo. *Poole* —6D **38**
Abbey Gdns. *Wim* —4D **16**
Abbey Rd. *W Mr* —1E **19**
Abbotsbury Rd. *Broad* —6E **21**
Abbots Clo. *Highc* —6H **47**
Abbott Clo. *Bourn* —5A **42**
Abbott Rd. *Bourn* —5A **42**
Abbotts Way. *W Mr* —1E **19**
Aberdare Rd. *Bourn* —2G **41**
Abingdon Dri. *Highc* —5C **48**
Abingdon Rd. *Poole* —5B **38**
Abinger Rd. *Bourn* —1G **61**
Abney Rd. *Bourn* —2F **41**
Acacia Av. *Ver* —5G **7**
Acacia Rd. *Hord* —1D **50**
Acland Rd. *Bourn* —5B **42**
Acorn Bus. Pk. *Poole* —5F **39**
Acorn Clo. *Christ* —5D **44**
Acorn Clo. *New M* —1A **50**
Acorn Clo. *St L* —4A **12**
Acorns, The. *Wim* —5A **16**

Acorn Way. *Ver* —3E **7**
Acres Rd. *Bourn* —3D **40**
Acton Rd. *Bourn* —4D **40**
Adamsfield Gdns. *Bourn* —3E **41**
Adastral Rd. *Poole* —4C **38**
Adastral Sq. *Poole* —5D **38**
Addington Ct. *Mil S* —2D **66**
Addington Pl. *Christ* —1H **63**
Addiscombe Rd. *Christ* —6E **45**
Addison Rd. *Broc* —4E **73**
Addison Sq. *Ring* —4D **8**
Adelaide Clo. *Christ* —5D **44**
Adelaide La. *Bourn* —4H **59** (3H **5**)
Adelaide Rd. *Poole* —4B **56** (1D **4**)
Adeline Rd. *Bourn* —3E **61**
Adlam's La. *Sway* —1D **32**
Admirals Ct. *L'ton* —1H **53**
Admirals Wlk. *Bourn* —5F **59**
Admiralty Rd. *Bourn* —4D **62**
Agars La. *Hord* —5E **33**
Agarton La. *Mil S* —1F **67**

Aggis Farm Rd. *Ver* —3C **6**
Aireton's Clo. *Broad* —2A **38**
Airfield Ind. Est. *Christ* —6C **46**
Airfield Rd. *Christ* —6B **46**
Airfield Way. *Christ* —6B **46**
Airspeed Rd. *Christ* —6D **46**
Akeshill Clo. *New M* —6H **31**
Alan Ct. *Christ* —6B **48**
Albany. *Bourn* —4C **60**
Albany Clo. *Bart S* —4F **49**
Albany Dri. *T Leg* —1A **10**
Albany Gdns. *Poole* —5F **55**
Albany Pk. *Poole* —5H **37**
Albemarle Rd. *Bourn* —6H **41**
Albert Rd. *Bourn* —4H **59** (3G **5**)
Albert Rd. *Cor M* —6D **20**
Albert Rd. *Fern* —4A **18**
  (in two parts)
Albert Rd. *New M* —2F **49**
Albert Rd. *Poole* —2H **57**
Albion Clo. *Poole* —6F **39**

Albion Rd. *Christ* —4D **44**
Albion Way. *Ver* —3B **6**
Alby Rd. *Poole* —2B **58**
Alcester Rd. *Poole* —1H **57**
Aldbury Ct. *New M* —6G **49**
Alder Clo. *Burt* —4H **45**
Alder Cres. *Poole* —6B **40**
Alder Hills. *Poole* —6C **40**
Alder Hills Ind. Pk. *Poole* —6B **40**
Alderley Rd. *Bourn* —1F **41**
Alderney Av. *Poole* —4G **39**
Alderney Roundabout. *Poole*
  —3H **39**
Alder Rd. *Poole* —2A **58**
Aldis Gdns. *Poole* —5E **55**
Aldridge Rd. *Bourn* —1E **41**
Aldridge Rd. *Fern* —6C **18**
Aldridge Way. *Fern* —6D **18**
Alexander Clo. *Christ* —1A **64**
Alexandra Lodge. *Bourn* —4A **60**
Alexandra Rd. *Bourn* —2A **62**

Alexandra Rd. *L'ton* —1E **53**
Alexandra Rd. *Poole* —3G **57**
Alexandria Ct. *Fern* —6B **18**
Alford Rd. *Bourn* —6F **41**
Alington Clo. *Poole* —2G **69**
Alington Rd. *Bourn* —1A **60**
Alington Rd. *Poole* —2G **69**
Alipore Clo. *Poole* —4H **57**
Allenby Clo. *Poole* —3H **37**
Allenby Rd. *Poole* —4H **37**
Allen Ct. *Wim* —4E **15**
Allen Rd. *Wim* —5E **15**
Allens La. *Poole* —2D **54**
Allens Rd. *Poole* —1C **54**
Allenview Rd. *Wim* —3E **15**
All Saints Rd. *L'ton* —3G **53**
Alma Rd. *Bourn* —6H **41**
Almer Rd. *Poole* —4E **55**
Almond Gro. *Poole* —6H **39**
Alpha Cen., The. *Poole* —6H **37**
Alpine Rd. *Ring* —6E **13**
Alton Rd. *Bourn* —4D **40**
Alton Rd. *Poole* —4F **57**
Alton Rd. E. *Poole* —5H **57**
Alum Chine Rd. *Bourn* —4D **58**
Alumdale Rd. *Bourn* —5D **58**
Alumhurst Rd. *Bourn* —4D **58**
Alvandi Gdns. *New M* —2H **49**
Alverton Av. *Poole* —4C **56**
Alyth Rd. *Bourn* —1E **59**
Ambassador Clo. *Christ* —1C **64**
Ambassador Ind. Est. *Christ*
—1C **64**
Amberley Clo. *Highc* —5G **47**
Amberley Ct. *Bourn* —4A **60**
Amber Rd. *Cor M* —1C **36**
Amberwood. *Fern* —3C **18**
Amberwood. *New M* —6C **48**
Amberwood Dri. *Walk* —3H **47**
Amberwood Gdns. *Walk* —3A **48**
Ambleside. *Christ* —2B **44**
Ambleside Rd. *L'ton* —2G **53**
Ambury La. *Christ* —5A **46**
Amesbury Rd. *Bourn* —1A **62**
Amethyst Rd. *Christ* —6B **46**
Ameysford Rd. *Fern* —6A **10**
(in two parts)
Ameys La. *Fern* —2D **18**
Amira Ct. *Bourn* —3E **5**
Ampfield Rd. *Bourn* —2D **42**
Ampress La. *L'ton* —5F **35**
Amsterdam Sq. *Christ* —1G **63**
Anchorage Way. *L'ton* —2F **53**
Anchor Clo. *Bourn* —6B **24**
Anchor Clo. *Christ* —2C **64**
Anchor M. *L'ton* —1G **53**
Anchor Rd. *Bourn* —6B **24**
Ancrum Lodge. *Poole* —4D **58**
Andbourne Ct. *Bourn* —4D **62**
Anderwood Dri. *Sway* —1F **33**
Andover Clo. *Christ* —6D **46**
Andrew La. *New M* —3B **50**
Andrews Clo. *Bourn* —2C **40**
Androse Gdns. *Ring* —5B **8**
Angeline Clo. *Highc* —5H **47**
Angel La. *Fern* —6H **17**
Angel La. *New M* —6A **50**
Anglia Ct. *Bourn* —4E **5**
Anjou Clo. *Bourn* —6H **23**
Anne Clo. *Christ* —4E **45**
Annerley Rd. *Bourn* —3C **60**
Annet Clo. *Poole* —5E **55**
Anson Clo. *Christ* —1B **64**
Anson Clo. *Ring* —3E **9**
Anstey Clo. *Bourn* —5C **24**
Anstey Rd. *Bourn* —6C **24**
Anthony's Av. *Poole* —1F **69**
Antler Dri. *New M* —1E **49**
Anvil Cres. *Broad* —6E **21**
Apollo Clo. *Poole* —6H **39**
Apple Clo. *Poole* —3C **58**
Apple Gro. *Christ* —3C **44**
Appleslade Way. *New M* —6H **31**
Appletree Clo. *Bourn* —2A **62**
Appletree Clo. *New M* —4G **49**

Appletree Ct. *Lyn* —4G **71**
Apple Tree Gro. *Fern* —3C **18**
Approach Rd. *Poole* —4F **57**
April Clo. *Bourn* —1C **40**
April Ct. *Bourn* —1C **40**
Apsley Cres. *Poole* —4H **37**
Aragon Way. *Bourn* —6B **26**
Arcade, The. *Bourn*
—4H **59** (4H **5**)
Arcadia Av. *Bourn* —6B **42**
Arcadia Rd. *Christ* —4D **44**
Archdale Clo. *Bourn* —3F **41**
Archway Rd. *Poole* —3A **58**
Arden Rd. *Bourn* —2H **41**
Arden Wlk. *New M* —3H **49**
Ardmore Rd. *Poole* —3F **57**
Argyle Rd. *Christ* —2A **64**
Argyll Rd. *Bourn* —3E **61**
Argyll Rd. *Poole* —1H **57**
Ariel Clo. *Bourn* —3F **63**
Ariel Dri. *Bourn* —3F **63**
Ark Dri. *Fern* —6D **18**
Arley Rd. *Poole* —5E **57**
Arlington Ct. *New M* —5H **49**
Armstrong Clo. *Broc* —3D **72**
Armstrong La. *Broc* —3D **72**
Armstrong Rd. *Broc* —3D **72**
Arne Av. *Poole* —6A **40**
Arne Cres. *Poole* —6A **40**
Arne Vw. Clo. *Uptn* —6B **36**
Arnewood Bri. Rd. *Sway* —4C **32**
Arnewood Ct. *Bourn*
—5G **59** (5E **5**)
Arnewood Rd. *Bourn* —3A **62**
Arnold Clo. *W Mr* —4C **10**
Arnold Rd. *W Mr* —4C **10**
Arnolds Clo. *Bart S* —5F **49**
Arran Way. *Walk* —4B **48**
Arrowsmith La. *Wim* —4C **22**
Arrowsmith Rd. *Wim* —6B **22**
Arthur Clo. *Bourn* —2H **59**
Arthur La. *Christ* —6E **45**
Arthur Rd. *Christ* —6E **45**
Arundel Clo. *New M* —2E **49**
Arundel Way. *Highc* —6H **47**
Ascham Rd. *Bourn* —2B **60**
Ascot Rd. *Broad* —1G **37**
Ashbourne Ct. Bourn —4A **60**
(off Lorne Pk. Rd.)
Ashbourne Rd. *Bourn* —2H **61**
Ashburn Gth. *Hight* —5F **9**
Ashburton Gdns. *Bourn* —4F **41**
Ash Clo. *Poole* —5B **36**
Ashdene Clo. *Wim* —4F **15**
Ashdown. *Bourn* —5F **59**
Ashdown Clo. *Poole* —4C **38**
Ashdown Wlk. *New M* —3A **50**
Ashford Rd. *Bourn* —6B **44**
Ash Gro. *Evtn* —5H **51**
Ash Gro. *Ring* —4E **9**
Ashington La. *Ashtn* —1G **21**
Ashington Pk. *New M* —4A **50**
Ashleigh Ri. *Bourn* —3F **41**
Ashlet Gdns. *New M* —1B **50**
Ashley Arnwood Ct. *New M*
—3H **49**
Ashley Clo. *Bourn* —1E **61**
Ashley Clo. *Ring* —5F **9**
Ashley Comn. Rd. *New M* —6A **32**
Ashley Ct. *Fern* —1E **19**
Ashley Dri. N. *Ashy H* —1B **12**
(in two parts)
Ashley Dri. S. *Ashy H* —2B **12**
Ashley Dri. W. *Ashy H* —2B **12**
Ashley Heath Ind. Est. *T Leg*
—1F **11**
Ashley La. *L'ton* —2G **53**
Ashley La. *New M & Hord* —2B **50**
Ashley Meadows. *New M* —1B **50**
Ashley Pk. *Ashy H* —1C **12**
Ashley Rd. *Bourn* —1E **61**
Ashley Rd. *New M* —3H **49**
Ashley Rd. *Poole* —2F **57**
Ashling Clo. *Bourn* —5C **42**
Ashling Cres. *Bourn* —5B **42**

Ashmeads Clo. *Wim* —3A **16**
Ashmeads Way. *Wim* —3A **16**
Ashmede. *Bourn* —5E **59**
Ashmore. *Wim* —5F **15**
Ashmore Av. *Bart S* —5H **49**
Ashmore Av. *Poole* —6F **55**
Ashmore Cres. *Poole* —6F **55**
Ashmore Gro. *Christ* —4G **47**
Ashridge Av. *Bourn* —6F **25**
Ashridge Gdns. *Bourn* —6F **25**
Ashridge Pde. *Bourn* —6F **25**
Ashton Ct. *Poole* —5C **58**
Ashton Rd. *Bourn* —3H **41**
Ashtree Clo. *New M* —3B **50**
Ashurst Rd. *Bourn* —2D **42**
Ashurst Rd. *W Mr* —4C **10**
Ashwood Dri. *Broad* —1A **38**
Aspen Dri. *Ver* —3F **7**
Aspen Gdns. *Poole* —5B **40**
Aspen Pl. *New M* —4H **49**
Aspen Rd. *Poole* —6B **40**
Aspen Way. *Poole* —6B **40**
Asquith Clo. *Christ* —2H **63**
Astbury Av. *Poole* —5B **40**
Aston Mead. *Christ* —1C **44**
Athelstan Rd. *Bourn* —2C **62**
Athelston Ct. *L'ton* —2F **53**
Aubrey Clo. *Mil S* —3F **67**
Auburn Mans. *Poole* —3D **58**
Auckland Av. *Broc* —3F **73**
Auckland Pl. *Broc* —3E **73**
Auckland Rd. *Christ* —6E **47**
Audemer Ct. *Ring* —3E **9**
Austen Av. *Bourn* —5F **25**
Auster Clo. *Christ* —6D **46**
Austin Av. *Poole* —6F **57**
Austin Clo. *Bourn* —2D **60**
Autumn Clo. *Fern* —2H **17**
Autumn Copse. *New M* —3B **50**
Autumn Rd. *Bourn* —2H **39**
Avalon. *Poole* —1G **69**
Avebury Av. *Bourn* —5G **25**
Avenue Ct. *Poole* —4C **58**
Avenue La. *Bourn* —4G **59** (4F **5**)
Avenue Rd. *Bourn* —4G **59** (4E **5**)
Avenue Rd. *Broc* —3E **73**
Avenue Rd. *Christ* —6D **44**
Avenue Rd. *L'ton* —1F **53**
Avenue Rd. *New M* —2G **49**
Avenue Rd. *Walk* —4C **48**
Avenue Rd. *Wim* —5F **15**
Avenue Shop. Cen., The. *Bourn*
—4G **59** (4F **5**)
Avenue, The. *Bourn* —3H **41**
Avenue, The. *Poole* —1C **70**
Avenue, The. *W Mr* —4B **10**
Aviation Pk. *Hurn* —2F **27**
Aviation Pk. W. *Hurn* —2D **26**
Avon Av. *Ring* —4F **13**
Avon Bldgs. *Christ* —6F **45**
Avon Castle Dri. *Ring* —3F **13**
Avon Causeway. *Hurn* —4H **27**
Avoncliffe Rd. *Bourn* —4C **62**
Avon Clo. *Bourn* —1D **60**
Avon Clo. *L'ton* —2E **53**
Avon Ct. *Poole* —3C **58**
Avon Gdns. *Brans* —2D **28**
Avon Ho. *Bourn* —5G **59** (6E **5**)
Avon M. *Bourn* —1C **60**
Avon Pk. *Ring* —1F **13**
Avon Rd. *Bourn* —1C **60**
Avon Rd. *W Mr* —6C **10**
Avon Rd. E. *Christ* —5E **45**
Avon Rd. W. *Christ* —5D **44**
Avon Run Clo. *Christ* —2D **64**
Avon Run Rd. *Christ* —2D **64**
Avon Trad. Pk. *Christ* —6E **45**
Avon Vw. Pde. *Burt* —2G **45**
Avon Vw. Rd. *Burt* —2G **45**
Avon Wharf. *Christ* —1G **63**
Award Rd. *Wim* —4F **17**
Axford Clo. *Bourn* —2E **43**
Aylesbury Rd. *Bourn* —3D **60**
Aysha Clo. *New M* —4H **49**
Azalea Clo. *St I* —2C **12**

Aztec Cen. *Poole* —5B **38**
Azura Clo. *T Leg* —1F **11**

Back La. *Sway* —1G **33**
Badbury Clo. *Broad* —2A **38**
Badbury Vw. *Wim* —4F **15**
Badbury Vw. Rd. *Cor M* —3D **20**
Baden Clo. *New M* —4H **49**
Bader Rd. *Poole* —5C **38**
Badgers Clo. *Ashy H* —2B **12**
Badgers Clo. *Sway* —1G **33**
Badgers Copse. *New M* —5A **32**
Badgers Wlk. *Fern* —2C **18**
Badger Way. *Ver* —4D **6**
Bailey Clo. *New M* —1B **50**
Bailey Cres. *Poole* —6A **38**
Bailey Dri. *Christ* —6D **44**
Baiter Gdns. *Poole* —6A **56** (5C **4**)
Baker Rd. *Bourn* —6B **24**
Bakers Farm Rd. *Ver* —2C **6**
Balcombe Rd. *Poole* —4C **58**
Baldwin Clo. *Christ* —1H **63**
Balena Clo. *Poole* —5G **37**
Balfour Clo. *Christ* —5F **47**
Balfour Rd. *Bourn* —4H **41**
Ballam Clo. *Poole* —6C **36**
Ballard Clo. *New M* —1H **49**
Ballard Clo. *Poole* —6B **56** (5C **4**)
Ballard Rd. *Poole* —6A **56** (5C **4**)
Ballards Pas. *Poole* —5A **56** (4B **4**)
Ball La. *Poole* —6A **56** (5B **4**)
Balmer Lawn Rd. *Broc* —1F **73**
Balmoral Av. *Bourn* —4E **43**
Balmoral Ho. *Bourn* —4F **59**
Balmoral Rd. *Poole* —4G **57**
Balmoral Wlk. *New M* —2F **49**
Balston Rd. *Poole* —1E **57**
Balston Ter. *Poole* —5H **55** (4A **4**)
Banbury Rd. *Poole* —6A **38**
Bank Chambers. Poole —3A **58**
(off Penn Hill Av.)
Bank Clo. *Christ* —1F **63**
Bankhill Dri. *L'ton* —6F **35**
Bankside. *L'ton* —5F **35**
Bankside Rd. *Bourn* —2A **42**
Banks Rd. *Poole* —6F **69**
Bankview. *L'ton* —5F **35**
Banstead Rd. *Broad* —6G **21**
Barberry Way. *Ver* —4G **7**
Barbers Ga. *Poole* —6H **55** (5A **4**)
Barbers Piles. *Poole*
—6H **55** (5A **4**)
Barbers Wharf. *Poole* —5A **4**
Barfields. *L'ton* —1G **53**
Barfields Ct. *L'ton* —1G **53**
Bargates. *Christ* —6E **45**
Baring Rd. *Bourn* —3E **63**
Barlands Clo. *Burt* —3G **45**
Barn Clo. *Poole* —6A **36**
Barnes Clo. *Bourn* —2F **41**
Barnes Cres. *Bourn* —2F **41**
Barnes Cres. *Wim* —5G **15**
Barnes La. *Hord* —4E **51**
(in two parts)
Barnes Rd. *Bourn* —2F **41**
Barnfield. *Christ* —5F **47**
Barn Rd. *Broad* —2H **37**
Barnsfield Rd. *St L* —5C **12**
Barns Rd. *Fern* —3E **19**
Barons Ct. *Poole* —3D **58**
Barons Rd. *Bourn* —5H **23**
Barrack La. *Crow* —6G **9**
Barrack Rd. *Christ* —5B **44**
Barrack Rd. *W Parl* —2A **26**
Barrie Rd. *Bourn* —2H **41**
Barrington Ct. *Bourn* —6F **41**
Barrow Dri. *Bourn* —3F **43**
Barrowgate Rd. *Bourn* —2C **42**
Barrowgate Way. *Bourn* —2D **42**
Barrow Rd. *Bourn* —3F **43**
Barrows La. *Sway* —4F **33**
Barrow Vw. *Fern* —3H **17**
Barrow Way. *Bourn* —3F **43**
Barrs Av. *New M* —1G **49**

Barrs Wood Dri. *New M* —1H **49**
Barrs Wood Rd. *New M* —1H **49**
Barry Gdns. *Broad* —6F **21**
Barters La. *Broad* —2F **37**
Bartlett Dri. *Bourn* —5H **43**
Bartley Ct. *Wim* —4D **14**
Barton Chase. *Bart S* —6F **49**
Barton Comn. La. *New M* —5H **49**
Barton Comn. Rd. *New M* —6H **49**
Barton Ct. Av. *Bart S* —6F **49**
Barton Ct. Rd. *New M* —4G **49**
Barton Cft. *Bart S* —6G **49**
Barton Dri. *Bart S* —5F **49**
Barton Grn. *Bart S* —6H **49**
Barton Ho. *Bart S* —6E **49**
Barton La. *Bart S* —5D **48**
Barton Lodge. *Poole* —2F **57**
Bartonside Rd. *New M* —5C **48**
Barton Way. *Bart S* —5F **49**
Barton Wood Rd. *Bart S* —6E **49**
Bascott Clo. *Bourn* —4C **40**
Bascott Rd. *Bourn* —4B **40**
Bashley Comn. Rd. *New M*
—4G **31**
Bashley Cross Rd. *New M* —6D **30**
Bashley Dri. *New M* —5H **31**
Bashley Rd. *New M* —4G **31**
Bassett Rd. *Poole* —1F **57**
Batchelor Cres. *Bourn* —2B **40**
Batchelor Rd. *Bourn* —2B **40**
Batcombe Clo. *Bourn* —2A **40**
Bath Hill Ct. *Bourn* —4A **60** (4H **5**)
Bath Hill Roundabout. *Bourn*
—5A **60** (5H **5**)
Bath Rd. *Bourn* —5H **59** (5H **5**)
Bath Rd. *L'ton* —2H **53**
Batten Clo. *Christ* —6H **45**
Baverstock Rd. *Poole* —5D **40**
Bay Clo. *Poole* —1B **54**
Bay Clo. *T Leg* —2A **10**
Bay Hog La. *Poole* —5H **55** (4A **4**)
Bays Ct. *L'ton* —1E **53**
Bays Rd. *Penn* —1D **52**
Baytree Way. *Christ* —4F **47**
Bay Vw. *New M* —6C **48**
Beach Av. *Bart S* —6F **49**
Beach Rd. *Poole* —1C **70**
Beach Rd. *Uptn* —1A **54**
Beacon Clo. *Evtn* —4H **51**
Beacon Dri. *Highc* —6H **47**
Beacon Gdns. *Broad* —2E **37**
Beacon Hill La. *Cor M* —2B **36**
Beacon Pk. Cres. *Poole* —5A **36**
Beacon Pk. Rd. *Poole* —6A **36**
Beacon Rd. *Bourn* —5G **59** (5F **5**)
Beacon Rd. *Broad* —2E **37**
Beacon Rd. *Poole* —6B **36**
Beaconsfield Rd. *Christ* —6F **45**
Beaconsfield Rd. *Poole* —2H **57**
Beacon Way. *Broad* —2E **37**
Beamish Rd. *Poole* —5D **38**
Bear Cross Av. *Bourn* —5A **24**
Bear Cross Roundabout. *Bourn*
—5B **24**
Beatty Clo. *Ring* —3E **9**
Beatty Rd. *Bourn* —4B **42**
Beauchamps Gdns. *Bourn*
—5G **43**
Beau Ct. *New M* —2G **49**
Beaucroft La. *Wim* —3G **15**
Beaucroft Rd. *Wim* —3G **15**
Beaufort Clo. *Christ* —6D **46**
Beaufort Dri. *Wim* —4E **15**
Beaufort M. *Wim* —5D **14**
Beaufort Rd. *Bourn* —2A **62**
Beaufoys Av. *Fern* —2A **18**
(in two parts)
Beaufoys Clo. *Fern* —2A **18**
Beaufoys Ct. *Fern* —3A **18**
Beaulieu Av. *Christ* —6C **44**
Beaulieu Clo. *New M* —2E **49**
Beaulieu Gdns. Cvn. Pk. *Christ*
—6C **44**
Beaulieu Rd. *Bourn* —6D **58**
Beaulieu Rd. *Christ* —6C **44**

Beaulieu Rd. *Lyn* —3G **71**
Beaumont Rd. *Poole* —2A **70**
Beaver Ind. Est. *Christ* —1C **64**
Beccles Clo. *Poole* —5F **55**
Becher Rd. *Poole* —3A **58**
Beckhampton Rd. *Poole* —4E **55**
Beckley Copse. *Walk* —3A **48**
Becton La. *Bart S* —4H **49**
Becton Mead. *Bart S* —4H **49**
Bedale Way. *Poole* —2D **56**
Bedford Cres. *Bourn* —6A **44**
Bedford Rd. N. *Poole* —3G **39**
Bedford Rd. S. *Poole* —3G **39**
Beech Av. *Bourn* —3A **62**
Beech Av. *Christ* —5B **44**
Beechbank Av. *Poole* —4E **37**
Beech Clo. *Broad* —1E **37**
Beech Clo. *Evtn* —5H **51**
Beech Clo. *Ver* —4C **6**
Beech Ct. *Wim* —5G **15**
Beechcroft La. *Ring* —3D **8**
Beechcroft M. Ring —3D **8**
(off Beechcroft La.)
Beechen La. *Lyn* —5G **71**
Beeches, The. *Bourn* —5G **43**
Beechey Rd. *Bourn* —2A **60**
Beech La. *St L* —5A **12**
Beechwood Av. *Bourn* —3F **61**
Beechwood Av. *New M* —1E **49**
Beechwood Clo. *Broad* —2G **37**
Beechwood Ct. *Bourn*
—4G **59** (5F **5**)
Beechwood Gdns. *Bourn* —3G **61**
Beechwood Rd. *W Mr* —6D **10**
Belben Clo. *Poole* —3H **39**
Belben Rd. *Poole* —3G **39**
Belfield Rd. *Bourn* —3E **63**
Belgrave Rd. *Poole* —5C **58**
Belle Vw. Mans. *Bourn* —4C **62**
Belle Vue Clo. *Bourn* —3B **62**
Belle Vue Cres. *Bourn* —3D **62**
Belle Vue Gdns. *Bourn* —3D **62**
Belle Vue Gro. *W Mr* —5D **10**
Belle Vue Rd. *Bourn* —3B **62**
Belle Vue Rd. *Poole* —4G **57**
Belle Vue Wlk. *W Parl* —1G **25**
Bellflower Clo. *Christ* —5D **46**
Bell Heather Clo. *Poole* —5B **36**
Bell La. Poole —6A **56** (5B **4**)
(off High St.)
Belmont Av. *Bourn* —3C **42**
Belmont Clo. *Ver* —4E **7**
Belmont Rd. *New M* —1A **50**
Belmont Rd. *Poole* —2F **57**
Belmore La. *L'ton* —2F **53**
Belmore Rd. *L'ton* —2F **53**
Belvedere Rd. *Bourn* —1A **60**
Belvedere Rd. *Christ* —6E **45**
Belvoir Pk. *Poole* —4D **58**
Bemister Rd. *Bourn* —5A **42**
Benbow Cres. *Poole* —3A **40**
Benbridge Av. *Bourn* —6B **24**
Bendigo Rd. *Christ* —5C **44**
Benellen Av. *Bourn* —3E **59**
Benellen Gdns. *Bourn* —3E **59**
Benellen Rd. *Bourn* —2E **59**
Benellen Towers. *Bourn* —3E **59**
Bengal Rd. *Bourn* —4G **41**
Benjamin Rd. *Poole* —5E **55**
Benmoor Rd. *Poole* —5G **37**
Benmore Clo. *New M* —3A **50**
Benmore Rd. *Bourn* —4A **42**
Bennets All. *Poole* —5A **4**
Bennett Ho. Bourn —3E **59**
(off Westbourne Clo.)
Bennett Rd. *Bourn* —1B **60**
Bennion Rd. *Bourn* —2E **41**
Benridge Clo. *Broad* —2G **37**
Benson Clo. *Brans* —2D **28**
Benson Rd. *Poole* —6B **38**
Bentley Rd. *Bourn* —2H **41**
Bere Clo. *Poole* —3B **38**
Beresford Clo. *Poole* —1H **57**
Beresford Gdns. *Christ* —1A **64**
Beresford Rd. *Bourn* —3H **61**

Beresford Rd. *L'ton* —1E **53**
Beresford Rd. *Poole* —1H **57**
Berkeley Av. *Poole* —5G **39**
Berkeley Clo. *Ver* —2C **6**
Berkeley Ct. *W Mr* —5C **10**
Berkeley Rd. *Bourn* —6G **41**
Berkley Av. *W Parl* —6B **18**
Bermuda Ct. *Highc* —6A **48**
Bernards Clo. *Christ* —5C **44**
Berne Ct. *Bourn* —4A **60**
Berrans Av. *Bourn* —5C **24**
Berryfield Rd. *Hord* —3E **51**
Bertram Rd. *New M* —1A **50**
Berwick Rd. *Bourn* —1G **59**
Berwyn Ct. *Broad* —1G **37**
Bessborough Rd. *Poole* —2A **70**
Bessemer Clo. *Ver* —5G **7**
Beswick Av. *Bourn* —4F **41**
Bethany Ct. *Poole* —6C **40**
Bethany Ho. *Bourn* —2D **60**
Bethia Clo. *Bourn* —1D **60**
Bethia Rd. *Bourn* —6D **42**
Betsy Clo. *Brans* —2D **28**
Betsy La. *Brans* —2D **28**
Bettiscombe Clo. *Poole* —3C **38**
Beverley Gdns. *Bourn* —2F **41**
Bexington Clo. *Bourn* —2A **40**
Bickerley Gdns. *Ring* —5B **8**
Bickerley Grn. *Ring* —5B **8**
Bickerley Rd. *Ring* —4B **8**
Bickerley Ter. *Ring* —4B **8**
Bicknell Ho. Bourn —4E **59**
(off Westbourne Clo.)
Bicton Rd. *Bourn* —2D **40**
Billington Pl. *Penn* —3F **53**
Bindon Clo. *Poole* —6A **40**
Bingham Av. *Poole* —2G **69**
Bingham Clo. *Christ* —6A **46**
Bingham Clo. *Ver* —5F **7**
Bingham Dri. *L'ton* —2G **53**
Bingham Dri. *Ver* —5E **7**
Bingham Rd. *Bourn* —5A **42**
Bingham Rd. *Christ* —6A **46**
Bingham Rd. *Ver* —5E **7**
Binnie Rd. *Poole* —2A **58**
Birch Av. *Burt* —2G **45**
Birch Av. *New M* —5E **31**
Birch Av. *W Parl* —2H **25**
Birch Clo. *Cor M* —5D **20**
Birch Clo. *Poole* —4A **58**
Birch Clo. *St L* —4H **11**
Birchdale Rd. *Wim* —4F **15**
Birch Dri. *Bourn* —3G **43**
Birch Gro. *New M* —4G **49**
Birch Gro. *W Mr* —5B **10**
Birch Rd. *St I* —3D **12**
Birch Wlk. *Fern* —6D **18**
Birchwood Clo. *Christ* —5G **47**
Birchwood M. *Poole* —4H **57**
Birchwood Rd. *Park* —4H **57**
Birchwood Rd. *Uptn* —1B **54**
Birchy Hill. *Sway* —2G **33**
Birds Hill Gdns. *Poole* —4C **56**
Birds Hill Rd. *Poole* —3C **56**
Birkdale Ct. *Broad* —6G **21**
Birkdale Rd. *Broad* —6G **21**
Bishop Clo. *Poole* —6E **41**
Bishop Ct. *Ring* —4C **8**
Bishop Rd. *Bourn* —5A **42**
Bishops Clo. *Bourn* —6F **43**
Bitterne Way. *L'ton* —3F **53**
Bitterne Way. *Ver* —4E **7**
Blackberry La. *Christ* —1B **64**
Blackbird Clo. *Poole* —5E **37**
Blackbird Way. *Brans* —3E **29**
Blackburn Rd. *Poole* —1F **57**
Blackbush Rd. *Mil S* —1B **66**
Blackfield La. *W Mr* —4C **10**
Blackfield Rd. *Bourn* —2D **42**
Black Hill. *Ver* —3E **7**
Black Moor Rd. *Ver* —4G **7**
Blacksmith Clo. *Cor M* —6D **20**
Blackthorn Clo. *Penn* —3D **52**
Blackthorn Way. *New M* —1B **50**
Blackthorn Way. *Ver* —4F **7**

Blackwater. *Lyn* —1E **71**
Blackwater Dri. *Wim* —4B **22**
Blair Av. *Poole* —3G **57**
Blair Clo. *New M* —2E **49**
Blake Dene Rd. *Poole* —6F **57**
Blake Hill Av. *Poole* —6H **57**
Blake Hill Cres. *Poole* —6G **57**
Blandford Clo. *Poole* —5F **55**
Blandford Ct. *Mil S* —2D **66**
Blandford Rd. *Cor M* —2B **20**
Blandford Rd. *Poole* —6C **36**
Blandford Rd. *Wim* —2A **14**
Blandford Rd. N. *Bcn H & Poole*
—3A **36**
Blaney Way. *Cor M* —5C **20**
Blenheim. *Poole* —4C **58**
Blenheim Ct. *Christ* —5D **44**
Blenheim Cres. *Hord* —1C **50**
Blenheim Dri. *Christ* —6D **46**
Blind La. *Wim* —3D **14**
Bloomfield Av. *Bourn* —3H **41**
Bloomfield Pl. *Bourn* —3H **41**
Bloxworth Rd. *Poole* —5B **40**
Bluebell Clo. *Christ* —5D **46**
Bluebell La. *Poole* —4F **37**
Bluff, The. *Bourn* —1H **41**
Blyth Clo. *Christ* —1B **44**
Blythe Rd. *Cor M* —5D **20**
Blythswood Ct. *New M* —6F **49**
Bob Hann Clo. *Poole* —2H **57**
Bockhampton Rd. *Bock* —6A **28**
Bodley Rd. *Poole* —2A **70**
Bodorgan Rd. *Bourn*
—3H **59** (2G **5**)
Bodowen Clo. *Burt* —3H **45**
Bodowen Rd. *Burt* —3H **45**
Bognor Rd. *Broad* —1F **37**
Boldre Clo. *New M* —5D **48**
Boldre Clo. *Poole* —6H **39**
Boldre La. *Bold* —4F **35**
Boleyn Cres. *Bourn* —1C **42**
Bolton Clo. *Bourn* —4C **62**
Bolton Cres. *Fern* —3E **19**
Bolton Rd. *Bourn* —4C **62**
Boltons, The. *Mil S* —3D **66**
Bond Av. *W Mr* —3B **10**
Bond Clo. *Sway* —1F **33**
Bond Rd. *Poole* —2D **56**
Bonham Rd. *Bourn* —6H **41**
Bonington Clo. *Christ* —5A **46**
Border Dri. *Poole* —2C **54**
Border Rd. *Poole* —2C **54**
Boreham Rd. *Bourn* —2B **62**
Borley Rd. *Poole* —5G **37**
Borthwick Rd. *Bourn* —2E **61**
Boscombe Cliff Rd. *Bourn* —4E **61**
Boscombe Cres. *Bourn* —3E **61**
Boscombe Gro. Rd. *Bourn*
—2D **60**
Boscombe Overcliff Dri. *Bourn*
—4F **61**
Boscombe Promenade. *Bosc*
—4E **61**
Boscombe Spa Rd. *Bourn* —3D **60**
Bosley Clo. *Christ* —3C **44**
Bosley Way. *Christ* —3C **44**
Bosworth M. *Bourn* —1B **42**
Boulnois Av. *Poole* —4A **58**
Boundary Dri. *Wim* —3F **15**
Boundary La. *St L* —6G **11**
Boundary Rd. *Bourn* —5F **41**
(in two parts)
Boundary Roundabout. *Poole*
—5F **41**
Boundway. *Sway* —2C **32**
Bounty's La. *Poole* —2A **58**
Bourne Av. *Bourn* —4G **59** (2E **5**)
Bourne Clo. *Bourn* —4F **59**
Bourne Ct. *Bourn* —4H **59** (3G **5**)
Bourne Ct. *Wim* —4F **15**
Bournemouth Central Bus. Pk.
Bourn —2C **60**
Bournemouth Ho. *Bourn* —4B **60**
Bournemouth International Airport.
Hurn —3E **27**

Bournemouth International Cen.
Roundabout. *Bourn.* —5G **5**
Bournemouth Memorial Homes.
Bourn —4F **43**
Bournemouth Rd. *Lyn* —3E **71**
Bournemouth Rd. *Poole* —3F **57**
Bournemouth Sta. Roundabout.
Bourn —3B **60**
Bournemouth W. Roundabout.
Bourn —3F **59**
Bourne Pines. *Bourn* —1H **5**
Bourne River Ct. *Bourn* —3F **59**
Bourne Valley Rd. *Poole* —3C **58**
Bournewood Dri. *Bourn* —3E **59**
Bourton Gdns. *Bourn* —5H **43**
Bouverie Clo. *Bart S* —4F **49**
Boveridge Gdns. *Bourn* —1B **42**
Bovington Clo. *Poole* —4D **38**
Bowden Rd. *Poole* —3G **39**
Bower Rd. *Bourn* —5D **42**
Bowland Ri. *New M* —3A **50**
Bowling Grn. All. *Poole* —4B **4**
Box Clo. *Poole* —6H **37**
Boyd Rd. *Poole* —1B **58**
Brabazon Dri. *Christ* —6D **46**
Brabazon Rd. *Wim* —2D **22**
Brabourne Av. *Fern* —5A **18**
Bracken Clo. *Ashy H* —3H **11**
Brackendale Rd. *Bourn* —5C **42**
Bracken Glen. *Poole* —2C **56**
Brackenhill. *Poole* —6C **58**
Brackenhill Rd. *Wim* —2A **16**
Bracken Rd. *Bourn* —3A **62**
Bracken Rd. *Fern* —2H **17**
Brackens Way. *L'ton* —3H **53**
Brackens Way. *Poole* —1B **70**
Bracken Way. *Walk* —4B **48**
Bracklesham Pl. *Bart S* —6F **49**
Brackley Clo. *Hurn* —3G **27**
Bradburne Rd. *Bourn*
—4G **59** (3E **5**)
Bradford Rd. *Bourn* —1C **42**
Bradpole Rd. *Bourn* —3E **43**
Bradstock Clo. *Poole* —5B **40**
Braemar Av. *Bourn* —3E **63**
Braemar Clo. *Bourn* —3E **63**
Braemar Dri. *Highc* —4G **47**
Braeside Rd. *St L* —3A **12**
Braeside Rd. *W Mr* —4C **10**
Braidley Rd. *Bourn* —3G **59** (1F **5**)
Brailswood Rd. *Poole* —3B **56**
Braishfield Gdns. *Bourn* —3D **42**
Bramble La. *Highc* —4B **48**
Bramble Wlk. *L'ton* —6E **35**
Bramble Way. *Brans* —2D **28**
Bramley Clo. *L'ton* —3G **53**
Bramley Ct. *Fern* —3A **18**
Bramley Rd. *Bourn* —6E **25**
Bramley Rd. *Fern* —3A **18**
Brampton Ct. *Bourn*
—4G **59** (3F **5**)
Brampton Rd. *Poole* —1B **56**
Bramshaw. *New M* —6C **48**
Bramshaw Gdns. *Bourn* —2D **42**
Bramshaw Way. *New M* —5D **48**
Branders Clo. *Bourn* —3E **63**
Branders La. *Bourn* —2E **63**
Brandon Ct. Poole —3D *58*
(off Poole Rd.)
Branksea Av. *Poole* —6D **54**
Branksea Clo. *Poole* —6E **55**
Branksome Bldgs. *Bourn* —4E **5**
Branksome Bus. Pk. *Poole*
—6B **40**
Branksome Clo. *New M* —3H **49**
Branksome Ct. *Poole* —1B **70**
Branksome Dene Rd. *Bourn*
—5D **58**
Branksome Hill Rd. *Bourn* —1D **58**
Branksome Towers. *Poole* —1D **70**
Branksome Wood Gdns. *Bourn*
—3F **59**
Branksome Wood Rd.
Poole & Bourn —2D **58**
Bransgore Gdns. *Brans* —2D **28**

Branwell Clo. *Christ* —4E **45**
Branwood Clo. *Evtn* —4A **52**
Brassey Clo. *Bourn* —4A **42**
Brassey Rd. *Bourn* —4H **41**
Brassey Ter. *Bourn* —4H **41**
Braxton Courtyard. *Mil S* —6A **52**
Breach La. *Ring* —3G **9**
Breamore Clo. *New M* —2E **49**
Brecon Clo. *Bourn* —5G **25**
Brecon Clo. *New M* —3A **50**
Bredy Clo. *Poole* —4B **38**
Bremble Clo. *Poole* —3G **39**
Brendon Clo. *Bourn* —3E **43**
Briar Clo. *Christ* —1B **64**
Briar Clo. *Poole* —2C **56**
Briarswood Rd. *Poole* —6C **36**
Briar Way. *Wim* —4B **16**
Brickenswood. *New M* —6C **48**
Brickfield La. *Wal* —6H **35**
Brickyard La. *Cor M* —3A **20**
Brickyard La. *Fern* —3G **17**
Brickyard La. *Ver* —2B **6**
Bridge App. *Poole* —6H **55**
Bridge Pl. *Bourn* —4F **25**
Bridge Rd. *L'ton* —1H **53**
Bridges Clo. *W Mr* —4D **10**
Bridges, The. *Ring* —4A **8**
Bridge St. *Christ* —1G **63**
Bridgewater Rd. *Poole* —1H **57**
Bridge Yd. *L'ton* —1H **53**
Bridle Clo. *Uptn* —6D **36**
Bridle Cres. *Bourn* —5A **44**
Bridle Way. *Wim* —3B **16**
Bridleways. *Ver* —3C **6**
Bridport Rd. *Poole* —5B **40**
Bridport Rd. *Ver* —3D **6**
Brierley Av. *W Parl* —2G **25**
Brierley Clo. *Bourn* —6G **25**
Brierley Rd. *Bourn* —1F **41**
Brightlands Av. *Bourn* —3D **62**
Brighton Rd. *Sway* —1E **33**
Bright Rd. *Poole* —1C **56**
Brinsons Clo. *Burt* —2G **45**
Brisbane Rd. *Christ* —4C **44**
Britannia Ct. *Poole* —6F **39**
Britannia Rd. *Poole* —4E **57**
Britannia Way. *Christ* —6D **46**
Brixey Clo. *Poole* —6G **39**
Brixey Rd. *Poole* —6G **39**
Broad Av. *Bourn* —4D **42**
Broadfields Clo. *Mil S* —2D **66**
Broadhurst Av. *Bourn* —1G **41**
Broadlands Av. *Bourn* —3D **62**
Broadlands Clo. *Bourn* —2D **42**
Broadlands Clo. *Walk* —3B **48**
Broadlands Rd. *Broc* —2D **72**
Broad La. *L'ton* —2H **53**
Broadly Clo. *Penn* —3D **52**
Broadmayne Rd. *Poole* —6B **40**
Broadmead Clo. *L'ton* —3H **53**
Broad Mead Rd. *T Leg* —1B **10**
Broadmoor Rd. *Cor M* —5B **20**
Broadshard Ct. *Ring* —2C **8**
Broadshard La. *Ring* —2C **8**
Broads, The. *Wim* —3B **14**
Broadstone Way. *Poole & Broad*
—3F **37**
Broadwater Av. *Poole* —5F **57**
Broadway. *South* —3D **62**
Broadway Gables. *Poole* —3H **57**
Broadway Gdns. *Wim* —5E **15**
Broadway La. *Bourn* —2C **42**
Broadway, The. *Broad* —1G **37**
Broadway, The. *N'brne* —5F **25**
Brockenhurst Rd. *Bourn* —3B **42**
Brockenhurst Rd. *New M* —2G **31**
Brockhills La. *New M* —6A **32**
Brockley Rd. *Bourn* —1G **41**
Brocks Pine. *St L* —4B **12**
Brog St. *Cor M* —2C **20**
Brombys, The. *Poole* —4C **4**
Bronte Av. *Christ* —4E **45**
Brook Av. *New M* —1G **49**
Brook Av. N. *New M* —6H **31**
Brook Clo. *Bourn* —1E **41**

Brookdale Clo. *Broad* —1G **37**
Brookdale Farm. *Broad* —1G **37**
Brook Dri. *Ver* —5F **7**
Brookland Clo. *Penn* —2E **53**
Brook La. *Cor M* —5C **20**
Brook La. *Nea* —4D **28**
Brookley Rd. *Broc* —3E **73**
Brooklyn Ct. *New M* —2F **49**
Brook Pk. Ind. Est. *Wim* —6G **15**
Brook Rd. *Bourn* —1E **41**
Brook Rd. *L'ton* —3H **53**
Brook Rd. *Poole* —2G **57**
Brook Rd. *Wim* —5G **15**
Brooks Clo. *Ring* —5D **8**
Brookside Clo. *Brans* —2C **28**
Brookside Rd. *Brans* —2C **28**
Brookside Rd. *Broc* —2E **73**
Brookside Rd. *Wim* —5H **15**
Brookside Way. *Highc* —4G **47**
Brook Vw. *W Mr* —4B **10**
Brook Way. *Christ* —6E **47**
Broomfield Ct. *Fern* —4C **18**
Broomfield La. *L'ton* —1G **53**
Broomhill Clo. *Penn* —3D **52**
Broom Rd. *Poole* —4F **39**
Broughton Av. *Bourn* —1G **41**
Broughton Clo. *Bourn* —2G **41**
Broughton Rd. *Lyn* —2F **71**
Brownen Rd. *Bourn* —5B **42**
Browning Av. *Bourn* —3F **61**
Browning Rd. *Poole* —1H **57**
Brownings Clo. *Penn* —1C **52**
Brownsea Av. *Cor M* —5D **20**
Brownsea Clo. *New M* —2E **49**
Brownsea Ct. *Poole* —1F **69**
Brownsea Rd. *Poole* —6F **69**
Brownsea Vw. Av. *Poole* —6F **57**
Brownsea Vw. Clo. *Poole* —6G **57**
Brudenell Av. *Poole* —2H **69**
Brudenell Rd. *Poole* —2H **69**
Brunel Clo. *Ver* —5G **7**
Brune Way. *W Parl* —6B **18**
Brunstead Pl. *Poole* —3D **58**
Brunstead Rd. *Poole* —3C **58**
Brunswick Pl. *L'ton* —1G **53**
Bryanstone Rd. *Bourn* —6G **41**
Bryant Rd. *Poole* —5C **40**
Bryony Clo. *Broad* —3E **37**
Bub La. *Christ* —1A **64**
Buccaneers Clo. *Christ* —1H **63**
Buccleuch Rd. *Poole* —6C **58**
Bucehayes Clo. *Highc* —5A **48**
Buchanan Av. *Bourn* —1E **61**
Buckingham Ct. *Poole* —4B **56**
Buckingham Mans. *Bourn* —4A **60**
Buckingham Rd. *Poole* —6H **39**
Buckingham Wlk. *New M* —2E **49**
Buckland Dene. *L'ton* —6F **35**
Buckland Gro. *Christ* —3G **47**
Buckland Rd. *Poole* —2G **57**
Buckland Ter. *Poole* —2G **57**
Buckland Vw. *L'ton* —6F **35**
Bucklers Ct. *L'ton* —2F **53**
Bucklers M. *L'ton* —2F **53**
Bucklers, The. *Mil S* —2A **66**
Bucklers Way. *Bourn* —2D **42**
Buckstone Clo. *Evtn* —4A **52**
Buckthorn Clo. *Poole* —4F **37**
Buffalo M. *Poole* —5H **55** (4A **4**)
Bugdens La. *Ver* —3D **6**
(in two parts)
Buldowne Wlk. *Sway* —1F **33**
Bullfinch Clo. *Poole* —4F **37**
Bull La. *Poole* —6A **56** (5B **4**)
Bunting Rd. *Fern* —1H **17**
Burbridge Clo. *Poole* —5C **38**
Burcombe La. *Hang* —2G **9**
Burcombe Rd. *Bourn* —6E **25**
Burdock Clo. *Christ* —4D **46**
Bure Clo. *Christ* —1D **64**
Bure Ct. *Christ* —1D **64**
Bure Haven Dri. *Christ* —1C **64**
Bure Homage Gdns. *Christ*
—1D **64**
Bure Homage La. *Christ* —1C **64**

Bure La. *Christ* —2D **64**
Bure Pk. *Christ* —1D **64**
Bure Rd. *Christ* —1D **64**
Burford Clo. *Christ* —4B **44**
Burford Ct. *Bourn* —4B **60**
Burford La. *Broc* —2F **73**
Burgess Clo. *Bourn* —1B **40**
Burleigh Rd. *Bourn* —1B **62**
Burley Clo. *New M* —5D **48**
Burley Clo. *Ver* —4C **6**
Burley Rd. *Brans* —4C **28**
Burley Rd. *Broc* —5A **72**
Burley Rd. *Poole* —1G **57**
Burley Rd. *Wink & Bock*
—1G **45** (5A **28**)
Burling Ter. *Poole* —3C **58**
Burlington Arc. *Bourn*
—4H **59** (3H **5**)
Burnaby Ct. *Bourn* —6D **58**
Burnaby Rd. *Bourn* —6E **59**
Burnbake Rd. *Ver* —4D **6**
Burnbrae Rd. *W Parl* —2F **25**
Burn Clo. *Ver* —5F **7**
Burnett Av. *Christ* —5C **44**
Burnett Rd. *Christ* —6D **44**
Burngate Rd. *Poole* —5E **55**
Burnham Dri. *Bourn* —6C **42**
Burnham Rd. *Burt* —3G **45**
Burnleigh Gdns. *New M* —1A **50**
Burnside. *Christ* —5F **47**
Burns Rd. *Bourn* —6B **44**
Burnt Ho. La. *Brans* —2C **28**
Burnt Ho. La. *Pill* —2H **35**
Burrard Gro. *L'ton* —3H **53**
Burrows La. *Ver* —1D **6**
Burtley Rd. *Bourn* —4C **62**
Burton Clo. *Ashy H* —2H **11**
Burton Clo. *Burt* —4G **45**
Burtoncroft. *Burt* —2G **45**
Burton Hall Pl. *Burt* —2G **45**
Burton Rd. *Christ* —6A **46**
Burton Rd. *Poole* —4C **58**
Burt's Hill. *Wim* —3E **15**
Bury Rd. *Poole* —6A **58**
Bushell Rd. *Poole* —6A **38**
Bushey Rd. *Bourn* —4C **42**
Bushmead Dri. *Ashy H* —2A **12**
Bute Dri. *Highc* —6B **48**
Butlers La. *Ring* —2E **9**
Buttercup Dri. *Christ* —4D **46**
Buttery, The. *Christ* —6H **45**
Button's La. *Poole* —6A **56** (5B **4**)
Butts Lawn. *Broc* —2E **73**
Butts Paddock. *Broc* —2E **73**
Byron Ct. *Fern* —4B **18**
Byron Ho. *New M* —3G **49**
Byron Rd. *Bart S* —5E **49**
Byron Rd. *Bourn* —3F **61**
Byron Rd. *Wim* —3E **15**

Cabot La. *Poole* —5G **37**
Cabot Way. *New M* —2F **49**
Cadhay Clo. *New M* —2F **49**
Cadnam Way. *Bourn* —2D **42**
Cadogan Rd. *Ring* —4D **8**
Caernarvon Ho. Bourn
(off Norwich Av.) —4G *29* (3E *5*)
Caesar's Way. *Broad* —1E **37**
Caird Av. *New M* —3A **50**
Cairns Clo. *Christ* —5D **44**
Caister Clo. *Fern* —3A **18**
Calder Rd. *Poole* —5D **38**
Caledonian Clo. *Christ* —6D **46**
Caledon Rd. *Poole* —4H **57**
Calkin Clo. *Christ* —4E **45**
Calluna Rd. *Poole* —5F **39**
Calmore Clo. *Bourn* —2D **42**
Calpe Av. *Lyn* —2F **71**
Calvin Rd. *Bourn* —5H **41**
Cambridge Gdns. *Christ* —3D **44**
Cambridge Rd. *Bourn* —4F **59**
Camden Clo. *Bourn* —4B **42**
Camden Hurst. *Mil S* —3B **66**
Camellia Clo. *T Leg* —1A **10**

Camellia Gdns. *New M* —3H **49**
Cameron Rd. *Christ* —6H **45**
Cammel Rd. *W Parl* —1F **25**
Campbell Rd. *Bourn* —2E **61**
Campbell Rd. *Burt* —2G **45**
Campion Gro. *Christ* —1B **64**
Campion Way. *L'ton* —6G **35**
Canberra Rd. *Christ* —5C **44**
Candys Clo. *Cor M* —1E **21**
Candy's La. *Cor M* —1D **20**
Canford Av. *Bourn* —4B **40**
Canford Bottom. *Wim* —3B **16**
Canford Cliffs Av. *Poole* —5H **57**
Canford Cliffs Rd. *Poole* —6A **58**
Canford Ct. *Poole* —3A **70**
Canford Cres. *Poole* —2A **70**
Canford Gdns. *Bourn* —4C **40**
Canford Heath Rd. *Poole* —3A **38**
Canford Magna. *Wim* —1E **23**
Canford Rd. *Bourn* —4C **40**
Canford Rd. *Poole* —3B **56** (1D **4**)
Canford Vw. Dri. *Wim* —3B **16**
Canford Way. *Poole* —3F **39**
Cannon Clo. *Broad* —4F **37**
Cannon Hill Gdns. *Wim* —2B **16**
Cannon Hill Rd. *Wim* —2A **16**
(in two parts)
Cannon Ho. *L'ton* —1G **53**
Cannon St. *L'ton* —1G **53**
Canons Wlk. *Mil S* —2D **66**
Canterbury Clo. *W Mr* —6D **10**
Canute Dri. *Brans* —2D **28**
Canute Ho. *Poole* —5B **4**
Capella Ct. *Bourn* —5H **59** (5H **5**)
Capesthorne. *Christ* —2D **64**
Capstone Pl. *Bourn* —1D **60**
Capstone Rd. *Bourn* —1B **60**
Captain's Row. *L'ton* —1H **53**
Caradon Pl. *Ver* —2B **6**
Carbery Av. *Bourn* —3B **62**
Carbery Gdns. *Bourn* —2C **62**
Carbery La. *Bourn* —3A **62**
Carbery Row. Bourn —3A **62**
(off Carbery La.)
Cardigan Rd. *Bourn* —5H **41**
Cardigan Rd. *Poole* —2B **58**
Carey Rd. *Bourn* —3H **41**
Careys Cotts. *Broc* —2E **73**
Careys Rd. *Bourn* —1D **42**
Carina Ct. *Poole* —6F **69**
Carisbrooke Ct. *New M* —2F **49**
Carisbrooke Cres. *Poole* —4D **54**
Carisbrooke Way. *Christ* —4G **47**
Carlinford. *Bourn* —4F **61**
Carlton Av. *Bart S* —5D **48**
Carlton Gro. *Poole* —2H **57**
Carlton Ho. *L'ton* —1G **53**
Carlton Mt. *Bourn* —4G **59** (5F **5**)
Carlton Rd. *Bourn* —3C **60**
Carlyle Rd. *Bourn* —1B **62**
Carnarvon Rd. *Bourn* —3E **61**
Carnegie Clo. *Poole* —2H **57**
Caroline Av. *Christ* —1A **64**
Caroline Rd. *Bourn* —2D **40**
Carpenter Clo. *L'ton* —6F **35**
Carrbridge Clo. *Bourn* —6F **41**
Carrbridge Gdns. *Bourn* —6F **41**
Carrbridge Rd. *Bourn* —6E **41**
Carrick Way. *New M* —3A **50**
Carrington Cvn. Pk. *Mil S* —4F **67**
Carrington Clo. *Mil S* —2E **67**
Carrington La. *Mil S* —2E **67**
Carroll Av. *Fern* —4C **18**
Carroll Clo. *Poole* —1C **58**
Carsworth Way. *Poole* —3E **39**
Carters Av. *Poole* —3D **54**
Carters La. *Poole* —5A **56** (4B **4**)
Cartref Clo. *Ver* —3D **6**
Cartwright Clo. *Bourn* —1E **41**
Carvers Ind. Est. *Ring* —4B **8**
Carvers La. *Ring* —4C **8**
Carysfort Rd. *Bourn* —3D **60**
Cashmoor Pl. *Poole* —6B **40**
Caslake Clo. *New M* —4F **49**
Cassel Av. *Poole & Bourn* —6D **58**

Castle Av. *Highc* —5G **47**
Castle Clo. *Mil S* —4E **67**
Castledene Cres. *Poole* —5E **57**
Castle Ga. Clo. *Bourn* —3C **42**
Castle Hill. *Poole* —3F **57**
Castle La. E. *Bourn* —4G **43**
Castle La. W. *Bourn* —1A **42**
Castlemain Av. *Bourn* —2A **62**
Castleman Ct. *W Mr* —4B **10**
Castleman Way. *Ring* —5C **8**
Castle M. *Ring* —2E **13**
Castle Pde. *Bourn* —6B **44**
Castle Rd. *Bourn* —4H **41**
Castle St. *Christ* —1F **63**
Castle St. *Poole* —6A **56** (5B **4**)
Castleton Av. *Bourn* —5F **25**
Castlewood. *Ring* —2F **13**
Catalina Clo. *Christ* —1C **64**
Catalina Dri. *Poole* —6B **56**
Caton Clo. *Poole* —5D **40**
Cattistock Rd. *Bourn* —3E **43**
Cavan Cres. *Poole* —4H **37**
Cavendish Corner Mobile Home Pk.
Ring —3D **8**
Cavendish Pl. *Bourn* —2A **60**
Cavendish Rd. *Bourn*
—2H **59** (1H **5**)
Caversham Clo. *Poole* —4E **55**
Cawdor Rd. *Bourn* —6F **41**
Caxton Clo. *Christ* —6B **46**
Cecil Av. *Bourn* —6B **42**
Cecil Clo. *Cor M* —5E **21**
Cecil Ct. *Bourn* —5B **42**
Cecil Hill. *Bourn* —5B **42**
Cecil Rd. *Bourn* —3E **61**
Cecil Rd. *Poole* —1H **57**
Cedar Av. *Bourn* —5F **25**
Cedar Av. *Christ* —5B **44**
Cedar Av. *St L* —4A **12**
Cedar Clo. *Poole* —5B **36**
Cedar Dri. *Evtn* —5H **51**
Cedar Dri. *Wim* —4B **16**
Cedar Gdns. *New M* —4E **49**
Cedar Grange. *Poole* —3C **58**
Cedar Mnr. *Bourn* —4E **59**
Cedarmount. *Lyn* —4F **71**
Cedar Pk. *Wim* —2F **17**
Cedar Pl. *Brans* —2D **28**
Cedars, The. *Bourn* —3E **59**
Cedar Trade Pk. *Wim* —3F **17**
Cedar Way. *Fern* —1A **18**
Celandine Clo. *Christ* —5D **46**
Cellars Farm Rd. *Bourn* —4E **63**
Cemetery Av. *Poole* —1D **56**
Cemetery Rd. *Wim* —4D **14**
Centenary Clo. *Sway* —1G **33**
Centenary Ho. *Christ* —6F **45**
Centenary Way. *Bourn* —2E **61**
Central Av. *Cor M* —4D **20**
Central Av. *Poole* —1A **58**
Central Dri. *Bourn* —3G **59** (1F **5**)
(BH2)
Central Dri. *Bourn* —1F **61**
(BH7)
Centre La. *Evtn* —4A **52**
Centre Pl. *Ring* —4B **8**
Cerne Abbas. *Poole* —6C **58**
Cerne Clo. *Bourn* —1B **42**
Chaddesley Glen. *Poole* —3H **69**
Chaddesley Pines. *Poole* —3A **70**
Chaddesley Wood Rd. *Poole*
—4A **70**
Chaffey Clo. *Ring* —3E **9**
Chaffinch Clo. *New M* —3F **49**
Chaffinch Clo. *Poole* —4F **37**
Chalbury Clo. *Poole* —3E **39**
Chaldecott Gdns. *Bourn* —1E **41**
Chaldon Rd. *Poole* —3D **38**
Chalfont Av. *Christ* —2B **44**
Chalice Clo. *Poole* —3E **57**
Chalwyn Ind. Est. *Poole* —6E **39**
Champion Clo. *Mil S* —3F **67**
Chander Clo. *Fern* —5B **18**
Chandlers Clo. *Bourn* —5H **43**
Chandos Av. *Poole* —5C **40**

Channel Ct. *New M* —6E **49**
Chant Clo. *Christ* —6H **45**
Chantry Clo. *Highc* —4H **47**
Chantry, The. *Bourn* —3A **60**
Chapel Clo. *Cor M* —5C **20**
Chapel Ga. *Parl* —3C **26**
Chapel La. *Brans* —3C **28**
Chapel La. *Cor M* —6C **20**
Chapel La. *Hurn* —2C **26**
Chapel La. *Lyn* —3E **71**
Chapel La. *Poole* —5A **56** (3B **4**)
Chapel La. *Sway* —2H **33**
Chapel La. *Wim* —4D **14**
Chapel Ri. *Ring* —5F **13**
Chapel Rd. *Poole* —3E **57**
Charborough Rd. *Broad* —2H **37**
Charing Clo. *Ring* —5C **8**
Charles Cres. *New M* —6H **31**
Charles Gdns. *Bourn* —3E **41**
Charles Keightley Ct. *Wim* —6F **15**
Charles Rd. *Christ* —5B **46**
Charles Rd. *Poole* —3B **56**
Charlotte Clo. *Christ* —1C **64**
Charlotte Clo. *Poole* —5E **41**
Charlotte Ct. *New M* —3G **49**
Charlton Clo. *Bourn* —1C **42**
Charlton Clo. *Hord* —2D **50**
Charltons, The. *Bourn* —2H **59**
Charminster Av. *Bourn* —4B **42**
Charminster Clo. *Bourn* —3B **42**
Charminster Pl. *Bourn* —3B **42**
Charminster Rd. *Bourn* —1A **60**
Charmouth Gro. *Poole* —3E **57**
Charnock Clo. *Hord* —2D **50**
Charnwood Av. *Bourn* —2B **42**
Charnwood Clo. *W Mr* —5C **10**
Charnwood Ho. *Bourn* —4D **62**
Charter Rd. *Bourn* —5H **23**
Chartwell. *Poole* —4D **58**
Chaseside. *Bourn* —5G **43**
Chase, The. *Ring* —2F **13**
Chase, The. *Ver* —3F **7**
Chatsworth Rd. *Bourn* —1B **60**
Chatsworth Rd. *Poole* —2F **57**
Chatsworth Way. *New M* —2E **49**
Chaucer Clo. *Wim* —3E **15**
Chaucer Dri. *Mil S* —2D **66**
Chaucer Rd. *Poole* —1B **70**
Cheam Rd. *Broad* —1F **37**
Cheddington Rd. *Bourn* —1A **42**
Chedington Clo. *Poole* —3C **38**
Chelmsford Rd. *Poole* —6B **36**
Cheltenham Rd. *Poole* —2G **57**
Chene Rd. *Wim* —5F **15**
Chequers Clo. *Penn* —2D **52**
Cherford Rd. *Bourn* —3D **40**
Cherita Ct. *Poole* —1D **56**
Cheriton Av. *Bourn* —5A **44**
Cheriton Way. *Wim* —3E **15**
Cherrett Clo. *Bourn* —1B **40**
Cherries Dri. *Bourn* —3G **41**
Cherry Clo. *Poole* —2F **57**
Cherry Gro. *Fern* —3A **18**
Cherry Hill Gdns. *Poole* —1B **54**
Cherry Hill Gro. *Poole* —1B **54**
Cherry Tree Clo. *Evtn* —5H **51**
Cherry Tree Clo. *St L* —4H **11**
Cherry Tree Ct. *New M* —4H **49**
Cherry Tree Dri. *New M* —6E **31**
Cherry Tree Wlk. *Bourn* —5F **59**
Cheshire Dri. *Bourn* —4G **43**
Chesildene Av. *Bourn* —2D **42**
(in two parts)
Chesildene Dri. *Bourn* —2C **42**
Chessel Av. *Bourn* —2F **61**
Chesnut Clo. *Broc* —3F **73**
Chesterfield Clo. *Poole* —1B **70**
Chesterfield Ct. *Bourn* —4C **60**
Chester Rd. *Poole* —5C **58**
Chestnut Av. *Bart S* —5G **49**
Chestnut Av. *Bourn* —3A **62**
Chestnut Av. *Christ* —5B **44**
Chestnut Gro. *Wim* —3E **17**
Chestnut Way. *Burt* —2G **45**
Chetnole Clo. *Poole* —4E **39**

Chetwode Way. *Poole* —3H **37**
Cheviot Ct. Flats. *Christ* —5A **46**
Cheviots, The. *Poole* —4G **57**
Cheviot Way. *Ver* —4D **6**
Chewton Comn. Rd. *Highc*
—4A **48**
Chewton Farm Est. *Christ* —5C **48**
Chewton Farm Rd. *Walk* —4C **48**
Chewton Lodge. *Highc* —5B **48**
Chewton Way. *Walk* —4B **48**
Cheyne Gdns. *Bourn* —5E **59**
Chichester Rd. *Ring* —2E **9**
Chichester Wlk. *Wim* —2C **22**
Chichester Way. *Christ* —2C **64**
Chickerell Clo. *Bourn* —1B **42**
Chideock Clo. *Poole* —1A **58**
Chideock Ct. *Poole* —1A **58**
Chigwell Rd. *Bourn* —4B **42**
Chilcombe Rd. *Bourn* —2H **61**
Chilfrome Clo. *Poole* —4A **38**
Chiltern Clo. *Bart S* —4F **49**
Chiltern Clo. *Bourn* —2D **58**
Chiltern Dri. *Bart S* —5E **49**
Chiltern Dri. *Ver* —3D **6**
Chine Cres. *Bourn* —5F **59**
Chine Cres. Rd. *Bourn* —5F **59**
Chine Wlk. *W Parl* —1G **25**
Chisels La. *Brans* —5D **28**
Chislehurst Flats. *Bourn* —4E **59**
Chiswell Rd. *Poole* —4B **38**
Chorley Clo. *Poole* —1A **56**
Chris Cres. *Poole* —6C **36**
Christchurch Bay Rd. *Bart S*
—6F **49**
Christchurch By-Pass. *Christ*
—6F **45**
Christchurch Rd. *Bourn* —4B **60**
Christchurch Rd. *Down* —5H **51**
Christchurch Rd. *Fern & W Parl*
—1D **24**
Christchurch Rd. *Hurn* —5H **27**
Christchurch Rd. *New M* —5D **48**
Christchurch Rd. *Ring* —4B **8**
Christopher Cres. *Poole* —1A **56**
Christophers. *Wim* —2B **22**
Churchfield. *Ver* —3C **6**
Churchfield Ct. *Poole* —4C **56**
Churchfield Cres. *Poole* —3C **56**
Churchfield Rd. *Poole* —4C **56**
Church Hill. *Mil S* —2E **67**
Church Hill. *Ver* —3C **6**
Churchill Ct. *Bourn* —3E **61**
Churchill Ct. *New M* —3F **49**
Churchill Cres. *Poole* —1G **57**
Churchill Gdns. *Poole* —2G **57**
Churchill Rd. *Bourn* —2D **60**
Churchill Rd. *Poole* —2G **57**
Churchill Rd. *Wim* —6F **15**
Church La. *Bold & Pill* —1H **35**
Church La. *Broc* —4F **73**
Church La. *Christ* —1F **63**
Church La. *L'ton* —2G **53**
Church La. *Lyn* —3F **71**
Church La. *New M* —4F **49**
Church La. *Sway* —2F **33**
Church La. *W Parl* —5H **25**
Church La. Corner. *Pill* —2H **35**
Church Mead. *L'ton* —3G **53**
Church M. *Poole* —3F **57**
Churchmoor Rd. *Wim* —4A **16**
Church Rd. *Bourn* —4D **62**
Church Rd. *Fern* —3A **18**
Church Rd. *Poole* —3E **57**
Church Rd. *T Leg* —1A **10**
Church St. *Christ* —1F **63**
Church St. *Poole* —6H **55** (5A **4**)
Church St. *Wim* —4D **14**
Cinnamon La. *Poole*
—6H **55** (5A **4**)
Circle, The. *Bourn* —1A **42**
Circle, The. *Poole* —2B **70**
Claire Ct. *Highc* —6A **48**
Clare Lodge Clo. *Brans* —2C **28**
Claremont Av. *Bourn* —3B **42**
Claremont Rd. *Bourn* —3B **42**

Clarence Pk. Rd. *Bourn* —1G **61**
Clarence Pl. *Christ* —5E **45**
Clarence Rd. *Lyn* —3F **71**
Clarence Rd. *Poole* —4E **57**
Clarendon Clo. *Broad* —1G **37**
Clarendon Pk. *L'ton* —3F **53**
Clarendon Rd. *Bourn* —5E **59**
Clarendon Rd. *Broad* —2E **37**
Clarendon Rd. *Christ* —6E **45**
Clarks Clo. *Ring* —4C **8**
Clausen Way. *Penn* —4E **53**
Clayford Av. *Fern* —2H **17**
Clayford Clo. *Poole* —3B **38**
Claylake Dri. *Ver* —4E **7**
Cleeves Clo. *Poole* —3H **39**
Clematis Clo. *Christ* —5E **47**
Clement M. *Bourn* —4D **58**
Cleveland Clo. *Bart S* —6D **48**
Cleveland Ct. *Bourn* —5F **59**
Cleveland Gdns. *Bourn* —2C **60**
Cleveland Rd. *Bourn* —2D **60**
Cliff Cres. *New M* —6F **49**
Cliff Dri. *Christ* —1E **65**
Cliff Dri. *Poole* —2B **70**
Cliffe Rd. *Bart S* —6E **49**
Clifford Rd. *Bourn* —4A **42**
Cliff Rd. *Mil S* —1A **66**
Cliff Ter. *New M* —6F **49**
Clifton Gdns. *Fern* —5A **18**
Clifton Rd. *Bourn* —4B **62**
Clifton Rd. *Poole* —5H **57**
Clingan Rd. *Bourn* —1B **62**
Clinton Clo. *Walk* —3B **48**
Clinton Rd. *L'ton* —6G **35**
Cliveden Clo. *Fern* —2A **18**
Clive Rd. *Bourn* —4H **41**
Clive Rd. *Christ* —3F **47**
Cloisters, The. *L'ton* —2F **53**
Cloisters, The. *Ring* —5E **9**
Close, The. *Ashy* —3F **13**
Close, The. *Broad* —2E **37**
Close, The. *New M* —5H **49**
Close, The. *Ring* —4B **8**
Close, The. *St I* —3C **12**
Close, The. *Sway* —1E **33**
Clough's Rd. *Ring* —4D **8**
Clover Clo. *Christ* —5D **46**
Clover Ct. *New M* —1B **50**
Clover Dri. *Poole* —4F **37**
Clovers, The. *Poole* —5C **40**
Clowes Av. *Bourn* —4F **63**
Clyde Rd. *Poole* —3H **37**
Coach Ho. Pl. *Bourn* —2A **60**
Coastguard Cotts. *Bart S* —5E **49**
Coastguard Way. *Christ* —2B **64**
Cobbs La. *Poole* —1C **56**
Cobb's Rd. *Wim* —3G **15**
Cobham Rd. *Bourn* —2A **42**
Cobham Rd. *Fern I* —3F **17**
Cobham Way. *Wim* —2C **22**
Cockerell Clo. *Wim* —2D **22**
Cogdean Clo. *Cor M* —3E **21**
Cogdeane Rd. *Poole* —3B **38**
Cogdean Wlk. *Cor M* —3E **21**
Cogdean Way. *Cor M* —3E **21**
Colborne Av. *Wim* —4H **15**
Colborne Clo. *L'ton* —6G **35**
Colborne Clo. *Poole* —6B **56**
Colbourne Clo. *Brans* —3C **28**
Colehill Cres. *Bourn* —2B **42**
Colehill La. *Wim* —2G **15**
Coleman Rd. *Bourn* —2C **40**
Colemere Gdns. *Highc* —4H **47**
Colemore Rd. *Bourn* —6A **44**
Coleridge Grn. *Christ* —5B **46**
Coles Av. *Poole* —5E **55**
Coles Gdns. *Poole* —5E **55**
Colin Clo. *Cor M* —6D **20**
College Rd. *Bourn* —3G **61**
College Rd. *Ring* —4C **8**
Collingbourne Av. *Bourn* —1B **62**
Collingwood Rd. *W Moor* —1C **10**
Collins La. *Ring* —4C **8**
Collwood Clo. *Poole* —6A **38**
Collyers Rd. *Broc* —5E **73**

Colman Ct. *Bourn* —4C **60**
Colonnade Rd. *Bourn* —2G **61**
Colonnade Rd. W. *Bourn* —2G **61**
Colt Clo. *Wim* —3B **16**
Columbian Way. *Bourn* —3E **41**
Columbia Rd. *Bourn* —3D **40**
Columbia Trees La. *Bourn* —4E **41**
Columbine Clo. *Christ* —4D **46**
Colville Clo. *Bourn* —2G **61**
Colville Rd. *Bourn* —2G **61**
Comber Rd. *Bourn* —2H **41**
Comet Way. *Christ* —6C **46**
Comley Rd. *Bourn* —3H **41**
Commercial Rd. *Bourn*
—4G **59** (4E **5**)
Commercial Rd. *Poole* —3D **56**
Compton Av. *Poole* —5H **57**
Compton Beeches. *St I* —2C **12**
Compton Clo. *Ver* —3D **6**
Compton Cres. *W Mr* —6E **11**
Compton Dri. *Poole* —5G **57**
Compton Gdns. *Poole* —5G **57**
Compton Rd. *New M* —3G **49**
Condor Clo. *T Leg* —1F **11**
Coneygar La. *Fern* —6G **17**
Conference Pl. *L'ton* —3H **53**
Conifer Av. *Poole* —5F **57**
Conifer Clo. *Christ* —2B **44**
Conifer Clo. *St L* —3H **11**
Conifer Clo. *W Parl* —2H **25**
Conifer Cres. *Penn* —2D **52**
Conifers. *Bourn* —4D **58**
Coniston Av. *Bourn* —5A **24**
Coniston Clo. *Ver* —4C **6**
Coniston Rd. *Ring* —5D **8**
Connaught Clo. *New M* —4E **49**
Connaught Cres. *Poole* —1A **58**
Connaught Rd. *Bourn* —2H **61**
Connell Rd. *Poole* —2A **56**
Consort Clo. *Poole* —2G **57**
Consort Ho. *Fern* —3B **18**
Constitution Hill Gdns. *Poole*
—2E **57**
Constitution Hill Rd. *Poole*
—3D **56**
Convent Meadows Cvn. Pk. *Christ*
—2G **63**
Convent Wlk. *Christ* —1G **63**
Conway Clo. *New M* —2H **49**
Conway Ct. *New M* —2H **49**
Conways Dri. *Poole* —3E **57**
Cook Clo. *Ring* —3E **9**
Cooke Gdns. *Poole* —1B **58**
Cooke Rd. *Poole* —1B **58**
Cook Row. *Wim* —5D **14**
Coombe Av. *Bourn* —3G **41**
Coombe Gdns. *Bourn* —3F **41**
Coombe La. *Sway* —2H **33**
Cooper Dean Dri. *Bourn* —4F **43**
Coopers La. *Ver* —1D **6**
Copeland Dri. *Poole* —5F **57**
Copper Beech Clo. *Poole* —3C **58**
Copper Beeches. *Bourn*
—2H **59** (1H **5**)
Copper Beech Gdns. *Bourn*
—3F **41**
Coppercourt Leaze. Wim —5E **15**
(off Poole Rd.)
Coppice Av. *Fern* —2H **17**
Coppice Clo. *New M* —1B **50**
Coppice Clo. *St I* —3B **12**
Coppice, The. *Broc* —2C **72**
Coppice, The. *Christ* —1D **64**
Coppice Vw. *Bourn* —2G **41**
Copse Av. *New M* —3H **49**
Copse Clo. *Poole* —4D **56**
Copse Rd. *New M* —3H **49**
Copse Rd. *Ver* —3D **6**
Copse Way. *Christ* —5G **47**
Copsewood Av. *Bourn* —4E **43**
Copythorne Clo. *Bourn* —3D **42**
Corbar Rd. *Christ* —5C **44**
Corbiere Av. *Poole* —4H **39**
Corbin Av. *Fern* —3E **19**
Corbin Ct. *Penn* —3D **52**

Corbin Rd. *Penn* —2D **52**
Corfe Halt Clo. *Cor M* —1E **21**
Corfe Lodge Rd. *Cor M & Broad*
—1C **36**
Corfe Vw. Rd. *Cor M* —6C **20**
Corfe Vw. Rd. *Poole* —4F **57**
Corfe Way. *Broad* —2E **37**
Corhampton Rd. *Bourn* —1H **61**
Cornelia Cres. *Poole* —1C **58**
Cornflower Dri. *Christ* —4E **47**
Cornford Way. *Christ* —5F **47**
Cornilla Ct. *Poole* —5D **58**
Cornish Gdns. *Bourn* —4F **41**
Cornmarket Ct. Wim —4D **14**
(off West St.)
Cornwallis Rd. *Mil S* —3B **66**
Coronation Av. *Bourn* —3H **41**
Coronation Av. *Poole* —6B **36**
Coronation Clo. *Ver* —2D **6**
Coronation Rd. *Ver* —2D **6**
Corporation Rd. *Bourn* —2B **60**
Corscombe Clo. *Poole* —3C **38**
Cortry Clo. *Poole* —6C **40**
Cotes Av. *Poole* —2E **57**
Cotlands Rd. *Bourn* —3B **60**
Cotswold Clo. *Ver* —4D **6**
Cottage Gdns. *Poole* —2G **57**
Cottagers La. *Hord* —2E **51**
Cotton Clo. *Broad* —6F **21**
Countess Clo. *Wim* —3C **22**
Countess Gdns. *Bourn* —5F **43**
Court Clo. *Christ* —6A **46**
Court Clo. *L'ton* —3F **53**
Courtenay Dri. *Wim* —3E **15**
Courtenay Pl. *L'ton* —2G **53**
Courtenay Rd. *Poole* —3F **57**
Courthill Rd. *Poole* —3G **57**
Courtlands. *L'ton* —1G **53**
Courtleigh Mnr. *Bourn* —3D **60**
Court Lodge. *L'ton* —3F **53**
Courtney Pl. *Cor M* —6C **20**
Court Rd. *Bourn* —4B **42**
Courtyard, The. Bourn —4F **59**
(off Wharfdale Rd.)
Courtyard, The. *Poole* —4G **39**
Covena Rd. *Bourn* —1B **62**
Coventry Clo. *Cor M* —1C **36**
Coventry Cres. *Poole* —3G **37**
Cove Rd. *Bourn* —3E **41**
Cowdrey Gdns. *Bourn* —3F **43**
Cowdry's Fld. *Wim* —3D **14**
Cowell Dri. *Bourn* —5G **43**
Cowgrove Rd. *Wim* —4A **14**
Cowley Rd. *L'ton* —1E **53**
Cowley Rd. *Poole* —5B **38**
Cowleys Rd. *Burt* —3G **45**
Cowper Av. *New M* —4G **49**
Cowper Rd. *Bourn* —3H **41**
Cowpitts La. *Ring* —1E **9**
Cowslip Rd. *Broad* —4E **37**
Cox Av. *Bourn* —1B **42**
Cox Clo. *Bourn* —1B **42**
Coxstone La. *Ring* —5C **8**
Coy Pond Rd. *Poole* —2C **58**
Crabbswood La. *Sway* —3C **32**
Crab Orchard Way. *T Leg* —6C **6**
Crabton Clo. Rd. *Bourn* —3F **61**
Crabtree Clo. *Burt* —3G **45**
Cracklewood. *Fern* —1E **19**
Craigmoor Av. *Bourn* —3E **43**
Craigmoor Clo. *Bourn* —4F **43**
Craigmoor Way. *Bourn* —3E **43**
Craigside Rd. *St L* —4H **11**
Craigwood Dri. *Fern* —4C **18**
Cranborne Cres. *Poole* —5A **40**
Cranborne Pl. *New M* —2E **49**
Cranborne Rd. *Bourn*
—5G **59** (5F **5**)
Cranborne Rd. *Wim* —3E **15**
Cranbourne Ct. Poole —3E **39**
(off Sherborn Cres.)
Cranbrook M. *Poole* —1F **57**
Cranbrook Rd. *Poole* —2F **57**
Crane Dri. *Ver* —2C **6**
Cranemoor Av. *Christ* —3G **47**

Cranemoor Clo. *Christ* —3G **47**
Cranemoor Gdns. *Highc* —3H **47**
Cranes M. *Poole* —4B **56** (1D **4**)
Crane Way. *T Leg* —1F **11**
Cranfield Av. *Wim* —4F **15**
Cranleigh Clo. *Bourn* —2C **62**
Cranleigh Ct. *Bourn* —2C **62**
Cranleigh Gdns. *Bourn* —2C **62**
Cranleigh Paddock. *Lyn* —2F **71**
Cranleigh Rd. *Bourn* —1B **62**
Cranmer Rd. *Bourn* —5H **41**
Crantock Gro. *Bourn* —3F **43**
Cranwell Clo. *Bourn* —1A **40**
Cranwell Clo. *Brans* —2D **28**
Crawshaw Rd. *Poole* —5F **57**
Creasey Rd. *Bourn* —6C **24**
Creech Rd. *Poole* —2G **57**
Creedy Path. *Christ* —1F **63**
Creekmoor La. *Poole* —4F **37**
Crescent Ct. Bart S —6F **49**
(off Crescent Dri.)
Crescent Ct. *Bourn* —5F **59**
Crescent Dri. *Bart S* —6F **49**
Crescent Rd. *Bourn*
—4G **59** (3E **5**)
Crescent Rd. *Poole* —3A **58**
Crescent Rd. *Ver* —3E **7**
Crescent Rd. *Wim* —5E **15**
Crescent, The. *New M* —5D **48**
Crescent Wlk. *W Parl* —2G **25**
Cresta Gdns. *W Parl* —1G **25**
Crest Rd. *Poole* —1G **57**
Cribb Clo. *Poole* —6C **38**
Crichel Mt. Rd. *Poole* —2G **69**
Crichel Rd. *Bourn* —5A **42**
Cricket Chambers. *Bourn* —3A **60**
Cricket Clo. *Christ* —2B **64**
Crimea Rd. *Bourn* —6H **41**
Cringle Av. *Bourn* —3E **63**
Crispin Clo. *Highc* —5H **47**
Criterion Arc. *Bourn*
—4H **59** (4G **5**)
Crittall Clo. *Sway* —1G **33**
Crockford Clo. *New M* —6H **31**
Croft Clo. *Cor M* —4D **20**
Crofton Clo. *Christ* —4C **44**
Croft Rd. *Bourn* —3H **41**
Croft Rd. *Christ* —6B **46**
Croft Rd. *Nea* —5D **28**
Croft Rd. *Poole* —1F **57**
Croft Rd. *Ring* —2E **9**
Cromer Gdns. *Poole* —2B **58**
Cromer Rd. *Bourn* —6D **42**
Cromer Rd. *Poole* —3B **58**
Cromwell Pl. *Bourn* —2H **61**
Cromwell Rd. *Bourn* —2H **61**
Cromwell Rd. *Poole* —2H **57**
Cromwell Rd. *Wim* —5F **15**
Crooked La. *New M* —5A **50**
Crosby Rd. *Bourn* —6E **59**
Crossmead Av. *New M* —3G **49**
Cross Way. *Christ* —4B **44**
Crossways. *Evtn* —4H **51**
Crossways, The. *Poole* —6C **36**
Crow Arch La. *Ring* —5D **8**
Crow Arch La. Ind. Est. *Ring*
—6D **8**
Crow La. *Crow* —5E **9**
Crown Clo. *Poole* —2G **57**
Crown Hill Ct. *Poole* —3C **56**
Crown Mead. *Wim* —5E **15**
(in two parts)
Crown Wlk. *Bourn* —3E **61**
Crusader Ct. *Bourn* —3D **58**
Crusader Rd. *Bourn* —1H **39**
Cruse Clo. *Sway* —1F **33**
Cruxton Farm Courtyard. *Wim*
—1B **22**
Cucklington Gdns. *Bourn* —1B **42**
Cuckoo Hill Way. *Brans* —2E **29**
Cuckoo Rd. *Poole* —5E **39**
Cudnell Av. *Bourn* —5B **24**
Cul-de-Sac. *New M* —5C **48**
Culford Clo. *Bourn* —3F **43**
Cull Clo. *Poole* —5E **41**

Culliford Cres. *Poole* —3C **38**
Cull La. *New M* —5H **31**
(in two parts)
Cullwood La. *New M* —6A **32**
Culverhayes Clo. *Wim* —3D **14**
Culverhayes Pl. *Wim* —3D **14**
Culverhayes Rd. *Wim* —3D **14**
Culverley Clo. *Broc* —3E **73**
Culver Rd. *New M* —3F **49**
Cumnor Rd. *Bourn* —4A **60**
Cunningham Clo. *Bourn* —2C **40**
Cunningham Clo. *Christ* —1C **64**
Cunningham Clo. *Ring* —3E **9**
Cunningham Cres. *Bourn* —2C **40**
Cunningham Pl. *Bourn* —2C **40**
Curlew Clo. *Fern* —2H **17**
Curlew Rd. *Bourn* —3D **42**
Curlew Rd. *Christ* —1C **64**
Curlews, The. *Ver* —4E **7**
Curlieu Rd. *Poole* —1B **56**
Curtis Rd. *Poole* —2G **57**
Curzon Pl. *Penn* —3F **53**
Curzon Rd. *Bourn* —1D **60**
Curzon Rd. *Poole* —4E **57**
Curzon Way. *Christ* —5F **47**
Custards, The. *Lyn* —2G **71**
Cuthburga Rd. *Wim* —4E **15**
Cuthbury Clo. *Wim* —5C **14**
Cuthbury Gdns. *Wim* —4C **14**
Cutler Clo. *New M* —2A **50**
Cutler Clo. *Poole* —6E **41**
Cutlers Pl. *Wim* —4A **16**
Cynthia Clo. *Poole* —6F **39**
Cynthia Ho. *Poole* —6F **39**
Cynthia Rd. *Poole* —6F **39**
Cypress Gro. *Evtn* —4H **51**
Cyril Rd. *Bourn* —1C **60**

Dacombe Clo. *Uptn* —6C **36**
Dacombe Dri. *Poole* —6C **36**
Dacres Wlk. *Mil S* —2D **66**
Dairy Clo. *Christ* —6H **45**
Dairy Clo. *Cor M* —1B **36**
Dakota Clo. *Christ* —6D **46**
Dale Clo. *Poole* —1D **56**
Dale Rd. *Poole* —1D **56**
Dales Clo. *Wim* —3C **16**
Dales Dri. *Wim* —4B **16**
Dales La. *Hurn* —4E **27**
Dale Valley Rd. *Poole* —6C **38**
Dalewood Av. *Bourn* —6A **24**
Dalkeith Arc. *Bourn*
—4H **59** (3H **5**)
Dalkeith La. *Bourn* —4H **59** (3H **5**)
Dalkeith Rd. *Cor M* —1D **36**
Dalkeith Rd. *Poole* —6C **58**
(in two parts)
Dalkeith Steps. *Bourn* —3H **5**
Dalling Rd. *Poole* —2C **58**
Dalmeny Rd. *Bourn* —4E **63**
Damerham Rd. *Bourn* —2D **42**
Danecourt Clo. *Poole* —3D **56**
Danecourt Rd. *Poole* —3D **56**
Danecrest Rd. *Hord* —2D **50**
Dane Dri. *W Parl* —6C **18**
Danehurst. *Mil S* —1A **66**
Danehurst New Rd. *Tip* —3A **32**
Dane Rd. *Mil S* —1A **66**
Danesbury Av. *Bourn* —3D **62**
Danes Clo. *Bart S* —6G **49**
Danestream Clo. *Mil S* —3D **66**
Danestream Ct. *Mil S* —3E **67**
Daneswood Rd. *New M* —2A **50**
Daniel Gdns. *Poole* —5C **4**
Daniells Clo. *L'ton* —2G **53**
Daniell's Wlk. *L'ton* —3G **53**
Daniels Ct. *Ring* —4A **8**
Dansie Clo. *Poole* —3F **57**
Darby's Clo. *Poole* —1B **56**
Darbys Corner. *Poole* —3A **38**
Darby's La. *Poole* —6B **38**
Darby's La. N. *Poole* —6B **38**
Dark La. *Hint* —1A **48**
Dark La. *New M* —1F **49**

Darley Rd. *Fern* —6A **18**
Darracott Rd. *Bourn* —3G **61**
Darrian Ct. *Poole* —6B **36**
Darwin Av. *Christ* —4C **44**
Darwin Ct. *Poole* —3C **58**
Davenport Clo. *Poole* —6C **36**
David's La. *Ring* —2E **13**
David Way. *Poole* —5D **54**
Davies Ct. *Poole* —2A **58**
Davis Fld. *New M* —3F **49**
Davis Rd. *Poole* —2A **58**
Dawkins Bus. Cen. *Poole* —4D **54**
Dawkins Rd. *Poole* —3D **54**
Dawkins Way. *New M* —3G **49**
Dawn Chorus. *Poole* —4F **57**
Dawn Clo. *Bourn* —3E **41**
Daws Av. *Bourn* —4C **40**
Daylesford Clo. *Poole* —5E **57**
Day's Ct. *Wim* —5F **15**
(in two parts)
Deacon Gdns. *Bourn* —6C **24**
Deacon Rd. *Bourn* —6C **24**
Dean Clo. *Poole* —4E **55**
Dean Pk. Cres. *Bourn*
—3H **59** (2H **5**)
Dean Pk. Rd. *Bourn*
—3H **59** (2H **5**)
Deans Ct. *Mil S* —2D **66**
Dean's Ct. La. *Wim* —5E **15**
Deanscroft Rd. *Bourn* —1G **41**
Deans Gro. *Wim* —2F **15**
Deansleigh Rd. *Bourn* —4H **43**
Deans Rd. *Bourn* —2H **61**
Deans, The. *Bourn* —3H **59** (1H **5**)
Dean Swift Cres. *Poole* —1G **69**
Dear Hay La. *Poole* —5A **56** (4B **4**)
Dearing Clo. *Lyn* —3F **71**
Decies Rd. *Poole* —2F **57**
De Courtenai Clo. *Bourn* —6H **23**
Deepdene La. *Bourn* —6A **24**
Deer La. *L'ton* —4F **35**
Deerleap Way. *New M* —5H **31**
Deer Pk. Clo. *New M* —1F **49**
Dee Way. *Poole* —6H **55** (5A **4**)
De Haviland Clo. *Wim* —1D **22**
De Havilland Way. *Christ* —2B **64**
Delamere Gdns. *Bourn* —2G **41**
De La Warr Rd. *Mil S* —3C **66**
Delft M. *Christ* —1H **63**
Delhi Clo. *Poole* —4H **57**
Delhi Rd. *Bourn* —3G **41**
Delilah Rd. *Poole* —5D **54**
De Lisle Rd. *Bourn* —6H **41**
Delkeith Ct. *Fern* —5B **18**
Dell Clo. *Broad* —2E **37**
Dell, The. *New M* —5C **48**
Delph Rd. *Wim* —3B **22**
Delta Clo. *Christ* —6C **46**
De Mauley Rd. *Poole* —1A **70**
De Montfort Rd. *Wim* —2B **22**
De Mowbray Way. *L'ton* —3F **53**
Denby Rd. *Poole* —3B **56**
Dene Clo. *Ring* —2E **9**
Deneside Copse. *Penn* —3D **52**
Deneve Av. *Poole* —4A **38**
Dene Wlk. *W Parl* —2G **25**
Denewood Copse. *W Mr* —4B **10**
Denewood Rd. *Bourn* —4D **58**
Denewood Rd. *W Mr* —3B **10**
Denham Clo. *Poole* —2C **38**
Denham Dri. *Highc* —4H **47**
Denholm Clo. *Ring* —2F **9**
Denison Rd. *Poole* —4A **38**
Denmark La. *Poole* —4B **56** (2D **4**)
Denmark Rd. *Bourn* —4H **41**
Denmark Rd. *Poole*
(in two parts) —4B **56** (2D **4**)
Denmead. *New M* —1B **50**
Denmead Rd. *Bourn* —6B **44**
*Dennets La. Poole —6H **55** (5A **4**)*
(off High St.)
Dennis Rd. *Cor M* —6D **20**
(in two parts)
Dennistoun Av. *Christ* —6B **46**
Derby Rd. *Bourn* —3C **60**

De Redvers Rd. *Poole* —5G **57**
Dereham Way. *Poole* —1B **58**
Derritt La. *Brans* —3A **28**
Derry Brian Gdns. *New M* —3G **49**
Derwent Clo. *Bourn* —3A **42**
Derwent Clo. *Fern* —3E **19**
Derwent Rd. *New M* —6H **31**
Derwentwater Rd. *Wim* —1B **22**
Deverel Clo. *Christ* —5E **45**
Devon Rd. *Christ* —5C **44**
Devon Rd. *Poole* —2C **56**
Deweys La. *Ring* —4B **8**
Dewlands Pk. *Ver* —3B **6**
Dewlands Rd. *Ver* —4B **6**
Dewlands Way. *Ver* —3C **6**
Dewlish Clo. *Poole* —3E **39**
Dial Clo. *Brans* —1F **29**
Diana Clo. *Fern* —3B **18**
Diana Ct. *Highc* —6A **48**
Diana Way. *Cor M* —4E **21**
Dibden Clo. *Bourn* —2D **42**
Dickens Rd. *Bourn* —6C **44**
Didcot Rd. *Poole* —6B **38**
Dilly La. *Bart S* —5G **49**
Dingle Rd. *Bourn* —3H **61**
Dingley Rd. *Poole* —1B **56**
Dinham Ct. *New M* —1B **50**
Dinham Rd. *New M* —1B **50**
Diprose Rd. *Cor M* —4E **21**
Disraeli Rd. *Christ* —1H **63**
Ditchbury. *L'ton* —5F **35**
Doe Copse Way. *New M* —1E **49**
Doe's La. *Ver* —3B **6**
Dogdean. *Wim* —2E **15**
Dogwood Rd. *Broad* —3E **37**
Dolbery Rd. N. *Poole* —3H **39**
Dolbery Rd. S. *Poole* —4G **39**
Dolphin Av. *Bourn* —6G **25**
Dolphin Cen. *Poole* —5A **56** (3C **4**)
Dolphin Ct. *Poole* —5D **58**
Dolphin Pl. *Bart S* —6G **49**
Dominion Cen. *Bourn* —2A **40**
Dominion Rd. *Bourn* —2A **40**
Donnelly Rd. *Bourn* —2D **62**
Donnington Dri. *Christ* —6D **46**
Donoughmore Rd. *Bourn* —3D **60**
Dorchester Gdns. *Poole* —2C **56**
Dorchester Rd. *Oak* —1B **56**
Dorchester Rd. *Poole* —6A **36**
Dornie Rd. *Poole* —2A **70**
Dorset Av. *Fern* —5A **18**
Dorset Ho. *Poole* —5C **58**
Dorset Lake Av. *Poole* —1F **69**
Dorset Lake Mnr. *Poole* —5E **57**
Dorset Rd. *Bourn* —2E **59**
Dorset Rd. *Christ* —5B **46**
Dorset Way. *Poole* —6A **38**
Douglas Av. *Christ* —1D **62**
Douglas Clo. *Poole* —5C **36**
Douglas Ct. *Christ* —1D **62**
Douglas Gdns. *Poole* —2A **58**
Douglas M. *Bourn* —2A **62**
Douglas M. *Poole* —5B **36**
Douglas Rd. *Bourn* —3C **62**
Douglas Rd. *Poole* —2A **58**
Doulton Gdns. *Poole* —5F **57**
Doussie Clo. *Poole* —5A **36**
Dover Clo. *Poole* —4C **58**
Dover Rd. *Poole* —4C **58**
Doveshill Cres. *Bourn* —2F **41**
Doveshill Gdns. *Bourn* —2F **41**
Doveshill Mobile Home Pk. *Bourn*
—2F **41**
Dowlands Clo. *Bourn* —1F **41**
Dowlands Rd. *Bourn* —1F **41**
Downey Clo. *Bourn* —3B **40**
Downlands Pl. *Poole* —5C **38**
Downton Clo. *Bourn* —2C **42**
Downton La. *Down* —6D **50**
Doyne Rd. *Poole* —3A **58**
Dragoon Way. *Christ* —6D **44**
Drake Clo. *Christ* —1B **64**
Drake Clo. *New M* —2F **49**
Drake Clo. *Ring* —2F **9**
Drake Ct. *Poole* —6A **56** (5B **4**)

Drake Rd. *Poole* —6A **56** (5B **4**)
Drakes Rd. *Fern* —6D **18**
Draper Rd. *Bourn* —1C **40**
Draper Rd. *Christ* —6A **46**
Draycott Rd. *Bourn* —3F **41**
Dreswick Clo. *Christ* —1B **44**
Drew Clo. *Poole* —6E **41**
Drive, The. *Poole* —2H **57**
(BH12)
Drive, The. *Poole* —2H **69**
(BH13)
Droxford Rd. *Bourn* —1H **61**
Druids Clo. *W Parl* —1F **25**
Druitt Rd. *Christ* —5B **46**
Drummond Rd. *Bourn* —3D **60**
Drury Rd. *Bourn* —5D **58**
Dryden Clo. *Ashy H* —2A **12**
Dryden Pl. *Mil S* —2D **66**
Duart Ct. *New M* —2A **50**
Ducking Stool La. *Christ* —1F **63**
Duck Island La. *Ring* —5B **8**
Duck La. *Bourn* —6B **24**
(Dalewood Av.)
Duck La. *Bourn* —1B **40**
(Poole La.)
Dudley Av. *Hord* —2D **50**
Dudley Gdns. *Bourn* —6F **25**
Dudley Pl. *New M* —4G **49**
Dudley Rd. *Bourn* —6F **25**
Dudmoor Farm Rd. *Christ* —1D **44**
Dudmoor La. *Christ* —1D **44**
Dudsbury Av. *Fern* —5B **18**
Dudsbury Cres. *Fern* —5B **18**
Dudsbury Gdns. *W Parl* —3G **25**
Dudsbury Rd. *W Parl* —2F **25**
Dudsway Ct. *Fern* —5B **18**
Dugdell Clo. *Fern* —3D **18**
Dukes Dri. *Bourn* —6A **24**
Dukesfield. *Christ* —3B **44**
Dulsie Rd. *Bourn* —1E **59**
Dunbar Cres. *Walk* —3H **47**
Dunbar Rd. *Bourn* —1G **59**
Duncan Rd. *New M* —1B **50**
Duncliff Rd. *Bourn* —3E **63**
Dundas Rd. *Poole* —5C **38**
Dune Crest. *Poole* —6G **69**
Dunedin Clo. *Fern* —6H **17**
Dunedin Dri. *Fern* —6H **17**
Dunedin Gdns. *Fern* —6H **17**
Dunedin Gro. *Christ* —6E **47**
Dunford Clo. *New M* —4E **49**
Dunford Rd. *Poole* —2H **57**
Dunkeld Rd. *Bourn* —1F **59**
Dunlin Clo. *Christ* —2D **64**
Dunnock Clo. *Fern* —1H **17**
Dunstans La. *Poole* —1D **56**
Dunyeats Rd. *Broad* —1H **37**
Dunyeats Roundabout. *Poole*
—6B **22**
Durdells Av. *Bourn* —5C **24**
Durdells Gdns. *Bourn* —6C **24**
Durland Clo. *New M* —4G **49**
Durley Chine. *Bourn* —5F **59**
Durley Chine Ct. *Bourn* —5F **59**
Durley Chine Rd. *Bourn* —4F **59**
Durley Chine Rd. S. *Bourn* —5F **59**
Durley Gdns. *Bourn* —5F **59**
Durley Rd. *Bourn* —5G **59** (5E **5**)
Durley Rd. S. *Bourn*
—5F **59** (5E **5**)
Durlston Cres. *Christ* —1B **44**
Durlston Rd. *Poole* —5G **57**
Durnstown. *Sway* —1G **33**
Durrant Rd. *Bourn* —3G **59** (2F **5**)
Durrant Rd. *Poole* —4G **57**
Durrant Way. *Sway* —1F **33**
Durrington Pl. *Bourn* —1H **61**
Durrington Rd. *Bourn* —1H **61**
Durweston Clo. *Bourn* —2B **42**

Eaglehurst. *Poole* —3C **58**
(off Poole Rd.)
Eagle Rd. *Poole* —3C **58**
Earle Rd. *Bourn* —6E **59**

Earles Rd. *T Leg* —2A **10**
Earlham Dri. *Poole* —3G **57**
Earlsdon Way. *Highc* —5G **47**
East Av. *Bourn* —1E **59**
East Av. *New M* —6C **48**
E. Av. Roundabout. *Bourn* —1G **59**
E. Bank Rd. *Broc* —4F **73**
E. Borough. *Wim* —3D **14**
  (in two parts)
Eastbrook Row. *Wim* —5E **15**
E. Cliff Promenade. *Bourn*
        —5A **60** (5H **5**)
E. Cliff Way. *Christ* —6E **47**
East Clo. *Bart S* —5D **48**
Eastcott Clo. *Bourn* —5G **43**
Eastern Rd. *L'ton* —1F **53**
Eastern Way. *Mil S* —3F **67**
Easter Rd. *Bourn* —3A **42**
Eastfield Ct. *Ring* —4E **9**
Eastfield La. *Ring* —4E **9**
East Hill. *L'ton* —1G **53**
E. Howe La. *Bourn* —2E **41**
Eastlake Av. *Poole* —1F **57**
Eastlands. *New M* —4H **49**
East La. *Evtn* —4A **52**
E. Overcliff Dri. *Bourn* —5A **60**
East Quay. *Poole* —6A **56** (5C **4**)
E. Quay Rd. *Poole* —6A **56** (5B **4**)
East St. *Poole* —5A **56** (4C **4**)
East St. *Wim* —5E **15**
E. View Rd. *Ring* —4D **8**
East Way. *Bourn* —4B **42**
East Way. *Cor M* —6D **20**
Eastwood Av. *Fern* —3C **18**
Eastworth Rd. *Ver* —2C **6**
Eaton Rd. *Poole* —5C **58**
Ebblake Ind. Est. *Ver* —5H **7**
Ebenezer La. *Ring* —4B **8**
Ebor Clo. *W Parl* —1G **25**
Ebor Rd. *Poole* —1H **57**
Eccles Rd. *Poole* —5G **55**
Eden Gro. *Wim* —6F **15**
Edgarton Rd. *Poole* —2B **38**
Edgehill Rd. *Bourn* —5G **41**
Edgemoor Rd. *W Mr* —6E **11**
Edifred Rd. *Bourn* —1A **42**
Edmondsham Ho. *Bourn*
        —4G **59** (4F **5**)
Edmondsham Rd. *Ver* —1C **6**
Edmunds Clo. *Bart S* —4F **49**
Edward May Ct. *Bourn* —1C **40**
Edward Rd. *Bourn* —2D **40**
  (in two parts)
Edward Rd. *Christ* —5B **46**
Edward Rd. *Poole* —2G **57**
Edwards Clo. *L'ton* —2D **52**
Edwina Clo. *Ring* —2E **9**
Edwina Dri. *Poole* —3H **37**
Efford Ct. *Penn* —3D **52**
Efford Way. *Penn* —3D **52**
Egdon Ct. *Poole* —6B **36**
Egdon Dri. *Wim* —3C **22**
Egerton Gdns. *Bourn* —1D **60**
Egerton Rd. *Bourn* —1D **60**
Egmont Clo. *Ring* —5E **13**
Egmont Dri. *Ring* —5F **13**
Egmont Gdns. *Ring* —5F **13**
Egmont Rd. *Poole* —3B **54**
Elcombes Clo. *Lyn* —3F **71**
Elderberry La. *Christ* —1B **64**
Eldon Av. *Bart S* —5E **49**
Eldon Clo. *Bart S* —5E **49**
Eldon Pl. *Bourn* —4D **58**
Eldon Rd. *Bourn* —4G **41**
Eleanor Dri. *Bourn* —6H **23**
Eleanor Gdns. *Christ* —5C **44**
Elfin Dri. *Fern* —2A **18**
Elgar Rd. *Bourn* —1F **41**
Elgin Rd. *Bourn* —6F **41**
Elgin Rd. *Poole* —6F **57**
  (in two parts)
Elijah Clo. *Poole* —5E **55**
Eliot Ho. *New M* —3G **49**
Elise Clo. *Bourn* —5H **43**
Elizabeth Av. *Christ* —5D **44**

Elizabeth Ct. *Bourn* —4A **60**
Elizabeth Cres. *Hord* —3F **51**
Elizabeth Gdns. *Christ* —6F **47**
Elizabeth Rd. *Poole* —4B **56** (1D **4**)
  (BH15)
Elizabeth Rd. Poole —6C *36*
  (off Douglas Clo., BH16)
Elizabeth Rd. *Wim* —3E **15**
Elkhams Clo. *Evtn* —4H **51**
Ellerslie Chambers. *Bourn*
        —4H **59** (4H **5**)
Ellery Gro. *L'ton* —6G **35**
Ellesfield Dri. *W Parl* —6B **18**
Ellingham Rd. *New M* —5D **48**
Elliott Rd. *Bourn* —2A **40**
Elm Av. *Christ* —4C **44**
Elm Av. *New M* —3G **49**
Elm Av. *Penn* —4E **53**
Elm Ct. *New M* —3G **49**
Elmers Way. *Brans* —2D **28**
Elmes Rd. *Bourn* —3G **41**
Elm Gdns. *Bourn* —2E **59**
Elmgate Dri. *Bourn* —6F **43**
Elmhurst Rd. *Bourn* —6C **24**
Elmhurst Rd. *W Mr* —6D **10**
Elmhurst Way. *W Mr* —6D **10**
Elmore Dri. *Ashy H* —1A **12**
Elms Av. *Poole* —6E **57**
Elms Clo. *Poole* —6E **57**
Elmsdown Ct. *Ring* —4B **8**
Elmstead Rd. *Poole* —1B **70**
Elmsway. *Bourn* —3C **62**
Elm Tree Wlk. *W Parl* —3G **25**
Elmwood Way. *Highc* —6H **47**
Elphinstone Rd. *Highc* —5B **48**
Eltham Clo. *Bourn* —5H **43**
Elvin Clo. *Hord* —1D **50**
Elwyn Rd. *Bourn* —2C **60**
Elysium Ct. *Fern* —6C **18**
Embankment Way. *Ring* —5D **8**
Emberley Clo. *Fern* —2E **19**
Emerald Clo. *Ashy H* —1A **12**
Emerson Clo. *Poole*
        —5A **56** (4C **4**)
Emerson Rd. *Poole*
        —5A **56** (4C **4**)
Emily Clo. *Christ* —4D **44**
Emily Ct. *Poole* —2A **58**
Empress Rd. *Lyn* —3F **71**
Emsworth Rd. *L'ton* —1G **53**
Encombe Clo. *Poole* —5B **40**
Endeavour Pk. *Poole* —4B **38**
Endeavour Pk. *Ring* —5D **8**
Endfield Clo. *Christ* —4D **44**
Endfield Rd. *Bourn* —3A **42**
Endfield Rd. *Christ* —4C **44**
Enefco Ho. *Poole* —6A *56* (5A *4*)
  (off Quay, The)
Enfield Av. *Poole* —1C **56**
Enfield Cres. *Poole* —1C **56**
Enfield Rd. *Poole* —1C **56**
Englands Way. *Bourn* —1H **39**
Ensbury Av. *Bourn* —4F **41**
Ensbury Clo. *Bourn* —4F **41**
Ensbury Ct. *Bourn* —3G **41**
Ensbury Pk. Rd. *Bourn* —3G **41**
Enterprise Way. *Hurn* —2C **26**
Enyon M. *Ring* —5B **8**
Erica Dri. *Wim* —5D **20**
Ericksen Rd. *Bourn* —2E **41**
Erinbank Mans. *Bourn* —4C **60**
Erpingham Rd. *Poole* —3C **58**
Esmonde Way. *Poole* —5D **38**
Esplanade. *Can C* —2B **70**
Essex Av. *Christ* —4D **44**
Ethelbert Rd. *Wim* —5F **15**
Eton Gdns. *Bourn* —3E **59**
Ettrick Rd. *Poole* —6C **58**
Eucalyptus Av. *St L* —5C **12**
Euston Gro. *Ring* —5C **8**
Evans Clo. *Ashy H* —1A **12**
Evans Clo. *Bourn* —4B **40**
Evelyn M. *Bourn* —4H **41**
Evelyn Rd. *Bourn* —4H **41**
Evening Glade. *Fern* —5C **18**

Eventide Homes. *Bourn* —3E **43**
Everdene Ho. *Bourn* —4H **43**
Everest Rd. *Christ* —5A **46**
Everglades Clo. *Fern* —2B **18**
Evergreen Clo. *T Leg* —2A **10**
Evergreens. *Ashy H* —2A **12**
Evering Av. *Poole* —4G **39**
Evering Gdns. *Poole* —4G **39**
Everlea Clo. *Evtn* —4H **51**
Everon Gdns. *New M* —3H **49**
Evershot Rd. *Bourn* —3E **43**
Everton Rd. *Hord & Evtn* —1D **50**
Evesham Clo. *Bourn* —5H **43**
Evesham Ct. *Poole* —5C **58**
Exbury Dri. *Bourn* —6B **24**
Excelsior Rd. *Poole* —4G **57**
Exeter Ct. *Highc* —6B **48**
Exeter Cres. *Bourn* —5H **59** (4G **5**)
Exeter Grange. *Bourn* —5G **5**
Exeter La. *Bourn* —4H **59** (4G **5**)
Exeter Pk. Mans. *Bourn* —5G **5**
Exeter Pk. Rd. *Bourn*
        —5H **59** (5G **5**)
Exeter Rd. *Bourn* —4H **59** (4G **5**)
Exton Rd. *Bourn* —6A **44**

Factory Rd. *Poole* —6C **36**
Fairfield. *Christ* —6F **45**
Fairfield Clo. *Christ* —6F **45**
Fairfield Clo. *L'ton* —2G **53**
Fairfield Clo. *Wim* —4H **15**
Fairfield Rd. *Bart S* —6E **49**
Fairfield Rd. *Wim* —5F **15**
Fairhaven Ct. *Bourn* —3E **61**
Fairies Dri. *Fern* —6D **18**
Fair Lea. *Bourn* —5G **59** (6E **5**)
Fairlea Rd. *L'ton* —1G **53**
Fairlie. *Ring* —2E **9**
Fairlie Pk. *Ring* —2D **8**
Fairmile Ho. *Christ* —5D **44**
Fairmile Rd. *Christ* —3C **44**
Fairthorn Ct. *Bourn*
        —3H **59** (1G **5**)
Fairview Cres. *Broad* —6G **21**
Fairview Dri. *Broad* —6G **21**
Fairview Pk. *Poole* —4G **57**
Fairview Rd. *Broad* —6G **21**
Fairway Dri. *Christ* —1D **62**
Fairway Est. *Bourn* —1H **39**
Fairway Rd. *Poole* —1G **69**
Fairways. *Fern* —3D **18**
Fairway, The. *New M* —6H **49**
Fairwinds. *Poole* —6F **69**
Fairwood Rd. *Ver* —4G **7**
Falcon Dri. *Christ* —2C **64**
Falconer Dri. *Poole* —3E **55**
Falkland Sq. *Poole* —5A **56** (3C **4**)
Fallows, The. *New M* —6H **31**
Fancy Rd. *Poole* —5F **39**
Farcroft Rd. *Poole* —2F **57**
Farm Clo. *Ring* —3C **8**
Farmdene Clo. *Christ* —5F **47**
Farmers Wlk. *Evtn* —5H **51**
Farmers Wlk. *Wim* —3D **14**
Farm La. *Christ* —2C **64**
Farm La. N. *Bart S* —5G **49**
Farm La. S. *Bart S* —6G **49**
Farm Rd. *W Mr* —5B **10**
Farnham Rd. *Poole* —6C **40**
Farnleys Mead. *L'ton* —3G **53**
Farriers Clo. *Wim* —3B **16**
Farrington. *Bourn* —5E **59**
Farthings, The. *Highc* —5A **48**
Farwell Clo. *Burt* —2G **45**
Farwell Rd. *Poole* —3G **39**
Fathersfield. *Broc* —2E **73**
Fawcett Rd. *New M* —3F **49**
Fawley Grn. *Bourn* —2D **42**
Fawn Gdns. *New M* —1F **49**
Fayrewood Ct. *Ver* —2D **6**
Felton Ct. *Poole* —2D **56**
Felton Cres. *Highc* —5H **47**
Felton Rd. *Poole* —2D **56**
Fenleigh Clo. *Bart S* —4H **49**

Fenn Bank. *Bourn* —4H **59** (3G **5**)
Fennel Gdns. *L'ton* —6F **35**
Fenton Rd. *Bourn* —1A **62**
Fenwick Ct. *Bourn* —2B **60**
Fern Barrow. *Poole* —5D **40**
Fern Clo. *Burt* —3G **45**
Ferncroft Gdns. *Bourn* —6F **25**
Ferncroft Rd. *Bourn* —6F **25**
Ferndale Rd. *New M* —6H **31**
Ferndown Cen. *Fern* —4B **18**
Ferndown Ind. Est. *Wim* —2G **17**
Fernglade. *New M* —2G **49**
Fernheath Clo. *Bourn* —3C **40**
Fernheath Rd. *Bourn* —2C **40**
Fernhill Clo. *Poole* —3E **39**
Fernhill Fields. *New M* —6G **31**
Fernhill Flats. *Bourn*
        —4H **59** (3G **5**)
Fernhill La. *New M* —6G **31**
Fernhill Rd. *New M* —2G **49**
Fernlea Av. *Fern* —5B **18**
Fernlea Clo. *Ashy H* —3A **12**
Fernlea Clo. *Fern* —5B **18**
Fernlea Gdns. *Fern* —5B **18**
Fernmount Cen., The. *New M*
        —6G **31**
Fernside Av. *Poole* —3D **56**
Fernside Pk. Ind. Est. *Wim*
        —2G **17**
Fernside Rd. *Bourn* —5F **41**
Fernside Rd. *Poole* —2B **56**
Fernside Rd. *W Mr* —6C **10**
Fernway Clo. *Wim* —5B **16**
Fernwood Clo. *St I* —2D **12**
Ferris Av. *Bourn* —3C **42**
Ferris Clo. *Bourn* —3D **42**
Ferris Pl. *Bourn* —3D **42**
Ferry Rd. *Bourn* —4D **62**
Ferry Rd. *Poole* —6H **55** (6A **4**)
Ferry Way. *Poole* —6F **69**
Feversham Av. *Bourn* —4E **43**
Fibbards Rd. *Broc* —3E **73**
Field Pl. *New M* —5D **48**
Field Pl. *Ver* —2C **6**
Field Wlk. *L'ton* —6F **35**
Fieldway. *Christ* —4F **47**
Field Way. *Cor M* —3E **21**
Fieldway. *Ring* —3D **8**
Filton Rd. *L'ton* —1F **53**
Finchfield Av. *Bourn* —5B **24**
Fir Av. *New M* —3H **49**
Firbank Rd. *Bourn* —5B **42**
Fir Clo. *Lyn* —4F **71**
Fir Clo. *W Mr* —4C **10**
Firmain Rd. *Poole* —4H **39**
Firmount Clo. *Evtn* —4A **52**
Firs Glen Rd. *Bourn* —5F **41**
Firs Glen Rd. *Ver* —4D **6**
Firs Glen Rd. *W Mr* —5C **10**
Firshill. *Christ* —4G **47**
Firside Rd. *Cor M* —1C **36**
Firs La. *Poole* —1F **69**
Firs, The. *Bourn* —3A **60**
First Marine Av. *Bart S* —6F **49**
Firs Way. *Poole* —6C **36**
Fir Tree Clo. *St L* —5H **11**
Firtree Cres. *Hord* —2D **50**
Fir Tree La. *Christ* —4F **47**
Fir Va. Rd. *Bourn* —4H **59** (3H **5**)
Fishermans Av. *Bourn* —3H **61**
Fishermans Bank. *Christ* —2A **64**
Fishermans Quay. *L'ton* —1H **53**
Fishermans Rd. *Poole*
        —6A **56** (5B **4**)
Fishermans Wlk. *Bourn* —4A **62**
Fitzharris Av. *Bourn* —6A **42**
Fitzmaurice Rd. *Christ* —5C **44**
Fitzpain Clo. *W Parl* —1F **25**
Fitzpain Rd. *W Parl* —1F **25**
Fitzwilliam Clo. *Bourn* —6A **24**
Fitzworth Av. *Poole* —3C **54**
Flag Farm. *Poole* —2H **69**
Flag Head Chine. *Poole* —3A **70**
Flaghead Rd. *Poole* —2A **70**
Flambard Av. *Christ* —4D **44**

Flambard Rd. *Poole* —5G **57**
Flazen Clo. *Bourn* —2H **39**
Fleetsbridge Bus. Cen. *Poole* —6H **37**
Fleetsbridge Retail Pk. *Poole* —1H **55**
Fleets Corner. *Poole* —6E **15**
Fleets Est. *Poole* —1H **55**
Fleets La. *Poole* —6H **37**
Fletcher Clo. *Bourn* —2F **41**
Fletcher Rd. *Bourn* —2F **41**
Fleur De Lys Pk. *Pill* —2H **35**
Flexford La. *Sway* —5G **33**
Floral Farm. *Wim* —1D **22**
Florence Rd. *Bourn* —3E **61**
Florence Rd. *Poole* —3G **57**
Florin Mall. *Bourn* —3E **61**
  (off Royal Arc.)
Floriston Gdns. *New M* —2B **50**
Flower Ct. *Wim* —6F **15**
Flushards. *L'ton* —2H **53**
Foldsgate Clo. *Lyn* —2F **71**
Folly Farm La. *Ashy* —1E **13**
Fontmell Rd. *Broad* —3A **38**
Footners La. *Burt* —3G **45**
Ford Clo. *Fern* —2D **18**
Ford La. *Fern* —2E **19**
Foreland Clo. *Christ* —1B **44**
Foreland Rd. *Poole* —3B **54**
Forelle Cen., The. *Ver* —5G **7**
Forest Clo. *Christ* —4F **47**
Forest Clo. *Ver* —5H **7**
Forest Ct. *New M* —3H **49**
Forest Edge Clo. *Ashy H* —2H **11**
Forest Edge Dri. *Ashy H* —2H **11**
Forest Edge Rd. *Crow* —6G **9**
Forest Gdns. *Lyn* —3F **71**
Forest Ga. Gdns. *L'ton* —4F **53**
Forest Glade Clo. *Broc* —3C **72**
Forest Hall. *Broc* —3F **73**
Foresthills Ct. *Ring* —5F **9**
Forest Ho. *Bourn* —5A **60**
Forestlake Av. *Ring* —5F **9**
Forest La. *High H* —5G **9**
Forest La. *Ver* —2C **6**
Forest Links Rd. *Fern* —6A **10**
Forest Oak Dri. *New M* —6G **31**
Forest Pk. Rd. *Broc* —2D **72**
Forest Pines. *New M* —1G **49**
Forest Ri. *Christ* —3F **47**
Forest Rd. *Poole* —6C **58**
Forest Rd. *W Mr* —4D **10**
Forestside Gdns. *Ring* —2E **9**
Forestside, The. *Ver* —4H **7**
Forest Vw. *Broc* —3C **72**
Forest Vw. *New M* —5D **30**
Forest Vw. Clo. *Bourn* —3A **42**
Forest Vw. Dri. *Wim* —3G **17**
Forest Vw. Rd. *Bourn* —2A **42**
Forest Way. *Christ* —3F **47**
Forest Way. *Evtn* —4H **51**
Forest Way. *Wim* —4G **17**
Forge La. *Ver* —4B **6**
Forsyth Gdns. *Bourn* —4E **41**
Fort Cumberland Pl. *Poole* —5D **54**
Fortescue Rd. *Bourn* —1A **60**
Fortescue Rd. *Poole* —6H **39**
Forward Dri. *Penn* —3E **53**
Fountain Ct. *Poole* —5D **58**
Fountain Way. *Christ* —1F **63**
Four Wells Rd. *Wim* —2A **16**
Foxbury Rd. *St L* —6B **12**
  (in two parts)
Foxcote Gdns. *New M* —2F **49**
Foxcroft Dri. *Wim* —4B **16**
Foxes Clo. *Ver* —4D **6**
Fox Fld. *Evtn* —4H **51**
Foxglove Clo. *Christ* —5E **47**
Foxglove Pl. *New M* —1B **50**
Foxhills. *Ver* —3F **7**
Foxholes Rd. *Bourn* —3D **62**
Foxholes Rd. *Poole* —1D **56**
Fox La. *Wim* —4C **16**
  (in two parts)
Fox Pond La. *Penn* —3E **53**

Foxwold Ho. *Bourn* —3D **62**
Foxwood Av. *Christ* —2B **64**
Frampton Clo. *New M* —6A **32**
Frampton Pl. *Ring* —4B **8**
Frampton Rd. *Bourn* —5A **42**
Francesca Ct. *Christ* —6A **46**
Frances Rd. *Bourn* —3B **60**
Francis Av. *Bourn* —2H **39**
Francis Rd. *Poole* —2A **58**
Frankland Cres. *Poole* —4A **58**
Franklin Rd. *Bourn* —2A **42**
Franklin Rd. *New M* —1A **50**
Franklyn Clo. *Poole* —6B **36**
Frankston Rd. *Bourn* —3A **62**
Franks Way. *Poole* —6F **39**
Fraser Rd. *Poole* —4B **40**
Freda Rd. *Christ* —1D **62**
Frederica Rd. *Bourn* —5G **41**
Freemans Clo. *Wim* —4B **16**
Freemans La. *Wim* —4B **16**
Fremington Ct. *New M* —2H **49**
French Rd. *Poole* —4H **37**
French's Farm Rd. *Poole* —6A **36**
Frensham Clo. *Bourn* —2G **41**
Freshwater Dri. *Poole* —4D **54**
Freshwater Rd. *Christ* —1E **65**
Friars Rd. *Christ* —1D **64**
Friars Wlk. *Bart S* —5G **49**
  (in two parts)
Fritham Gdns. *Bourn* —2D **42**
Frobisher Av. *Poole* —4B **40**
Frobisher Clo. *Christ* —1B **64**
Frobisher Clo. *Ring* —3E **9**
Fromond Clo. *L'ton* —6G **35**
Frost Rd. *Bourn* —1B **40**
Froud Way. *Cor M* —1C **36**
Fryer Clo. *Bourn* —6D **24**
Fryers Copse. *Wim* —3C **16**
Fryers Rd. *T Leg* —2A **10**
Frys La. *Evtn* —4H **51**
Fullerton Rd. *L'ton* —1E **53**
Fulmar Rd. *Christ* —2C **64**
Fulwood Av. *Bourn* —6A **24**
Furlong M. *Ring* —4B **8**
Furlong Shop. Cen., The. *Ring* —4B **8**
Furlong, The. *Ring* —4B **8**
Furnell Rd. *Poole* —6B **56** (5D **4**)
Furze Bank La. *Bourn* —3E **41**
Furzebrook Clo. *Poole* —2C **38**
Furze Cft. *New M* —4G **49**
Furzehill. *Wim* —1E **15**
Furze Hill Dri. *Poole* —6G **57**
Furzelands Rd. *T Leg* —2A **10**
Furzey Rd. *Poole* —1B **54**
Furzy Whistlers Clo. *Brans* —2D **28**

G

Gainsborough Av. *New M* —6H **31**
Gainsborough Ct. *Bourn* —2H **61**
Gainsborough Rd. *Ashy H* —2A **12**
Gainsborough Rd. *Bourn* —6F **43**
Gallop Way. *Poole* —6E **41**
Galloway Rd. *Poole* —3D **54**
Gallows Dri. *W Parl* —2F **25**
Galton Av. *Christ* —1D **62**
Garden Clo. *Lyn* —3E **71**
Garden Clo. *New M* —4G **49**
Garden Ct. *Bourn* —1D **60**
Garden Ct. Cotts. *W Mr* —4B **10**
Garden Ho. *Bourn* —4A **60**
Garden La. *St L* —4A **12**
Gardens Ct. *Poole* —4C **56**
Gardens Cres. *Poole* —1F **69**
Gardens Rd. *Poole* —1F **69**
Garden Wlk. *Fern* —2C **18**
Gardner Rd. *Christ* —5C **44**
Gardner Rd. *Ring* —5D **8**
Garfield Av. *Bourn* —2D **60**
Garland Rd. *Poole* —3B **56**
Garrow Dri. *L'ton* —6G **35**
Garsdale Clo. *Bourn* —5C **24**
Garth Clo. *St L* —3H **11**

Garth Rd. *Bourn* —4A **42**
Gateway, The. *Poole* —3B **58**
Gaydon Ri. *Bourn* —1A **40**
Geneva Av. *Bourn* —2B **62**
Genoa Clo. *Penn* —4E **53**
George Rd. *Cor M* —4D **20**
George Rd. *Mil S* —2C **66**
George Roundabout, The. *Poole* —4B **56** (2D **4**)
Georges M. *Cor M* —4D **20**
Georgian Clo. *Ring* —3C **8**
Georgian Way. *Bourn* —1H **41**
Georgina Clo. *Poole* —5E **41**
Georgina Talbot Ho. *Poole* —5D **40**
Gerald Rd. *Bourn* —1A **60**
Germaine Clo. *Highc* —5H **47**
Gervis Cres. *Poole* —3E **57**
Gervis Pl. *Bourn* —4H **59** (4G **5**)
Gervis Rd. *Bourn* —4A **60**
Gibson Rd. *Poole* —6C **38**
Giddylake. *Wim* —3E **15**
Gilbert Clo. *L'ton* —3F **53**
Gilbert Rd. *Bourn* —1D **60**
Gillam Rd. *Bourn* —6F **25**
Gillett Rd. *Poole* —6E **41**
Gillingham Clo. *Bourn* —2C **42**
Gillingham Rd. *Mil S* —3D **66**
Gilpin Clo. *Pill* —2H **35**
Gilpin Hill. *Sway* —1F **33**
Gilpin Pl. *Sway* —1E **33**
Gipsy La. *Ring* —3D **8**
Gladdis Rd. *Bourn* —1B **40**
Gladelands Clo. *Broad* —1E **37**
Gladelands Mobile Home Pk. *Fern* —2D **18**
Gladelands Way. *Broad* —1E **37**
Glade, The. *Ashy H* —2A **12**
Gladstone Clo. *Christ* —1H **63**
Gladstone Rd. *Bourn* —2F **61**
Gladstone Rd. *Poole* —2G **57**
Gladstone Rd. E. *Bourn* —2F **61**
Gladstone Rd. W. *Bourn* —2E **61**
Glamis Av. *Bourn* —6G **25**
Gleadowe Av. *Christ* —1D **62**
Glebefields. *Mil S* —2D **66**
Glenair Av. *Poole* —4E **57**
Glenair Cres. *Poole* —4E **57**
Glenair Rd. *Poole* —4E **57**
Glenavon. *New M* —3A **50**
Glenavon Rd. *Highc* —4H **47**
Glen Clo. *Bart S* —5D **48**
Glencoe Rd. *Bourn* —6F **43**
Glencoe Rd. *Poole* —2H **57**
Glendale Av. *Fern* —3B **18**
Glendale Clo. *Christ* —2B **44**
Glendale Clo. *Wim* —4E **15**
Glendale Ct. *Christ* —2B **44**
Glendale Rd. *Bourn* —3E **63**
Glendales. *Bart S* —5D **48**
Glendene Pk. *New M* —5E **31**
Glendon Av. *Bourn* —5E **25**
Glen Dri. *New M* —5C **48**
Gleneagles. *Christ* —1D **62**
Gleneagles Av. *Poole* —5H **57**
Gleneagles Clo. *Fern* —3D **18**
Glenferness Av. *Bourn* —3E **59**
Glen Fern Rd. *Bourn* —4A **60** (3H **5**)
Glengariff Rd. *Poole* —5G **57**
Glengarry. *New M* —3A **50**
Glengarry Way. *Christ* —1E **65**
Glenives Clo. *St I* —3B **12**
Glenmeadows Dri. *Bourn* —6D **24**
Glenmoor Clo. *Bourn* —4F **41**
Glenmoor Rd. *Bourn* —5F **41**
Glenmoor Rd. *W Parl* —6A **18**
Glen Mt. Dri. *Park* —2F **57**
Glen Rd. *Bourn* —3E **61**
Glen Rd. *Poole* —2F **57**
Glenroyd Gdns. *Bourn* —3C **62**
Glenside. *New M* —6B **48**
Glen Spey. *New M* —3B **50**
Glen, The. *Poole* —1H **57**
Glenville Clo. *Walk* —3B **48**
Glenville Gdns. *Bourn* —3E **41**

Glenville Rd. *Bourn* —3E **41**
Glenville Rd. *Walk* —3A **48**
Glenwood Clo. *W Mr* —5C **10**
Glenwood La. *W Mr* —5C **10**
Glenwood Rd. *Ver* —4D **6**
Glenwood Rd. *W Mr* —5C **10**
Glenwood Way. *W Mr* —5C **10**
Glissons. *Fern* —1C **24**
Globe La. *Poole* —5A **56** (4C **4**)
  (in two parts)
Gloucester Rd. *Bourn* —1F **61**
Gloucester Rd. *Poole* —2A **58**
Glynville Clo. *Wim* —2A **16**
Glynville Ct. *Wim* —2A **16**
Glynville Rd. *Wim* —2A **16**
Goathorn Clo. *Poole* —3D **54**
Godmanston Clo. *Poole* —4E **39**
Godshill Clo. *Bourn* —2D **42**
Golden Cres. *Evtn* —4H **51**
Golden Gates. *Poole* —6F **69**
Goldenleas Dri. *Bourn* —2H **39**
Goldfinch Clo. *New M* —3F **49**
Goldfinch Rd. *Poole* —5E **37**
Gold Mead Clo. *L'ton* —3G **53**
Golf Links Rd. *Broad* —6H **21**
Golf Links Rd. *Fern* —1G **25**
Goliath Rd. *Poole* —5D **54**
Good Rd. *Poole* —6G **39**
Gooseberry La. *Ring* —4B **8**
Goose Grn. *Lyn* —4F **71**
Gordleton Ind. Est. *Penn* —6B **34**
Gordon Mt. *Christ* —4B **48**
Gordon Mt. Flats. *Christ* —5A **48**
Gordon Rd. *Bourn* —3D **60**
Gordon Rd. *Highc* —5A **48**
Gordon Rd. *Penn* —2E **53**
Gordon Rd. *Poole* —2C **58**
Gordon Rd. *Wim* —5G **15**
Gordon Rd. S. *Poole* —2C **58**
Gordon Way. *Burt* —4G **45**
Gore Grange. *New M* —3F **49**
Gore Rd. *New M* —3D **48**
Gore Rd. Ind. Est. *New M* —3E **49**
Gorey Rd. *Poole* —4H **39**
Gorleston Rd. *Poole* —2B **58**
Gorley Rd. *Ring* —3E **9**
Gorsecliff Ct. *Bourn* —3D **60**
Gorsecliff Rd. *Bourn* —4F **41**
Gorse Clo. *New M* —1B **50**
Gorse Clo. *St L* —3H **11**
Gorsefield Rd. *New M* —6H **31**
Gorse Hill Clo. *Poole* —2C **56**
Gorse Hill Cres. *Poole* —2C **56**
Gorse Hill Rd. *Poole* —2C **56**
Gorseland Ct. *Fern* —6B **18**
Gorse La. *Poole* —6C **36**
Gorse Rd. *Cor M* —6C **20**
Gort Rd. *Bourn* —2D **40**
Gort Rd. *Poole* —4G **37**
Gosling Clo. *Poole* —5D **38**
Gosport La. *Lyn* —3G **71**
Gosport St. *L'ton* —1H **53**
Gough Cres. *Poole* —4H **37**
Grace Darling Ho. *Poole* —5D **4**
Grafton Clo. *Bourn* —6A **42**
Grafton Clo. *Christ* —1H **63**
Grafton Gdns. *Penn* —4E **53**
Grafton Rd. *Bourn* —1A **60**
Grammar School La. *Wim* —5D **14**
Granby Rd. *Bourn* —1A **42**
Grand Av. *Bourn* —3A **62**
Grand Pde. *Bourn* —5E **25**
Grand Pde. *Poole* —5A **4**
Grange Clo. *Evtn* —5A **52**
Grange Ct. *Bourn* —4B **60**
Grange Gdns. *Poole* —6A **40**
Grange Rd. *Bourn* —4B **62**
Grange Rd. *Broad* —1G **37**
Grange Rd. *Christ* —6D **46**
Grange Rd. *St L* —5H **11**
Grange Rd. Bus Cen. *Christ* —6C **46**
Grange, The. *Evtn* —5A **52**
Grantham Rd. *Bourn* —2E **61**
Grantley Rd. *Bourn* —3F **61**

Grants Av. *Bourn* —1D **60**
Grants Clo. *Bourn* —1D **60**
Granville Pl. *Bourn* —3H **5**
Granville Rd. *Bourn* —2G **61**
Granville Rd. *Poole* —2F **57**
Grasmere Clo. *Christ* —2B **44**
Grasmere Gdns. *New M* —6H **31**
Grasmere Rd. *Bourn* —3G **61**
Grasmere Rd. *Poole* —6F **69**
Gravel Hill. *Poole & Wim* —3A **38**
Gravel La. *Ring* —4B **8**
(in two parts)
Gray Clo. *Poole* —5D **38**
Graycot Clo. *Bourn* —6E **25**
Grayson Ct. *Fern* —5C **18**
Gray's Yd. *Poole* —5B **4**
Greatmead. *Lyn* —4F **71**
Greaves Clo. *Bourn* —2E **41**
Grebe Clo. *Christ* —1C **64**
Grebe Clo. *Mil S* —3E **67**
Grebe Clo. *Poole* —5E **37**
Green Acre. *Bart S* —5G **49**
Grn. Acre Cvn. Site. *Christ*
—6B **46**
Greenacre Clo. *Poole* —1C **54**
Greenacres. *Poole* —4C **58**
Greenacres Clo. *Bourn* —5G **25**
Grn. Acres Clo. *Ring* —2F **13**
Greenbanks Clo. *Mil S* —2D **66**
Green Bottom. *Wim* —2A **16**
Green Clo. *Poole* —6B **56** (5D **4**)
Greenclose La. *Wim* —4F **15**
Greenfield Gdns. *Bart S* —5H **49**
Greenfield Rd. *Poole* —1C **56**
Greenfields. *Poole* —5B **40**
Greenfinch Clo. *Poole* —4F **37**
Greenfinch Wlk. *Hight* —5E **9**
Green Gdns. *Poole* —6B **56** (5D **4**)
(in two parts)
Greenhayes. *Broad* —3A **38**
Greenhayes Ri. *Wim* —4E **15**
Greenhill Clo. *Wim* —3F **15**
Greenhill La. *Wim* —3F **15**
Greenhill Rd. *Wim* —3F **15**
Green La. *Bart S* —5H **49**
Green La. *Bourn* —1E **41**
Green La. *Christ* —6A **30**
Green La. *Crow* —6E **9**
Green La. *Fern* —2C **24**
Green La. *Oss* —2D **30**
Green La. *Ring* —4C **8**
Green Loaning. *Christ* —2B **64**
Greenmead Av. *Evtn* —4H **51**
Green Pk. *Bourn* —4D **60**
Green Rd. *Bourn* —5A **42**
Green Rd. *Poole* —5A **56** (4C **4**)
Greenside Ct. *Bart S* —6G **49**
Greensleeves Av. *Broad* —5H **21**
Greensome Dri. *Fern* —3D **18**
Green, The. *Bourn* —2E **59**
Greenway Clo. *L'ton* —2E **53**
Greenway Cres. *Poole* —6A **36**
Greenways. *Highc* —5H **47**
Greenways. *Mil S* —2C **66**
Greenways Av. *Bourn* —2C **42**
Greenways Ct. *Fern* —6C **18**
Greenways Rd. *Broc* —3F **73**
Greenwood Av. *Fern* —3B **18**
Greenwood Av. *Poole* —6G **57**
Greenwood Copse. *St I* —3B **12**
Greenwood Rd. *Bourn* —4G **41**
Greenwoods. *New M* —4H **49**
Greenwood Way. *St I* —3C **12**
Grenfell Rd. *Bourn* —2H **41**
Grenville Clo. *Ring* —2F **9**
Grenville Ct. *Bourn* —3F **59**
Grenville Ct. *Poole* —5A **56** (4C **4**)
Grenville Rd. *Wim* —5F **15**
Gresham Rd. *Bourn* —4A **42**
Greycot Clo. *T Leg* —2A **10**
Greystoke Av. *Bourn* —6B **24**
Griffin Ct. *Wim* —6F **15**
Griffiths Gdns. *Bourn* —6D **24**
Grigg La. *Broc* —3E **73**
Grosvenor Clo. *Ashy H* —2H **11**

Grosvenor Ct. *Bourn* —3D **60**
Grosvenor Gdns. *Bourn* —3E **61**
Grosvenor M. *L'ton* —6F **35**
Grosvenor Rd. *Bourn* —4E **59**
Grove Farm Mdw. Cvn. Pk. *Christ*
—3B **44**
Groveley Bus. Cen. *Christ* —1A **64**
Groveley Rd. *Bourn* —5D **58**
Groveley Rd. *Christ* —1A **64**
Grovely Av. *Bourn* —3F **61**
Grove Pastures. *L'ton* —2G **53**
Grove Pl. *L'ton* —2G **53**
Grove Rd. *Bart S* —6F **49**
Grove Rd. *Bourn* —4A **60**
Grove Rd. *L'ton* —2H **53**
Grove Rd. *Poole* —1F **57**
Grove Rd. *Wim* —5F **15**
Grove Rd. E. *Christ* —5E **45**
Grove Rd. W. *Christ* —5D **44**
Grove, The. *Bourn* —2H **41**
Grove, The. *Christ* —4C **44**
Grove, The. *Fern* —5A **18**
Grove, The. *Ver* —4E **7**
Grower Gdns. *Bourn* —1C **40**
Guernsey Rd. *Poole* —4H **39**
Guest Av. *Poole* —1B **58**
Guest Clo. *Poole* —1C **58**
Guest Rd. *Poole* —6B **36**
Guildhall Ct. *Poole* —5H **55** (4A **4**)
Guildhill Rd. *Bourn* —3C **62**
Gulliver Clo. *Poole* —1G **69**
Gulliver Ct. *Wim* —4E **15**
Gundrymoor Trad. Est. *W Moor*
—1C **10**
Gunville Cres. *Bourn* —2B **42**
Gurjun Clo. *Poole* —5A **36**
Gurney Rd. *Cor M* —5E **21**
Gussage Rd. *Poole* —5A **40**
Guy's Clo. *Ring* —4D **8**
Gwenlyn Rd. *Poole* —1C **54**
Gwynne Rd. *Poole* —2A **58**

Haarlem M. *Christ* —6H **45**
Hadden Rd. *Bourn* —5D **42**
Hadley Way. *Broad* —2E **37**
Hadow Rd. *Bourn* —2E **41**
Hadrian Clo. *Fern* —1F **25**
Hadrian Way. *Cor M* —3E **21**
Haglane Copse. *Penn* —3E **53**
Hahnemann Rd. *Bourn*
—5G **59** (5E **5**)
Haig Av. *Poole* —6A **58**
Hainault Dri. *Ver* —3E **7**
Haking Rd. *Christ* —6H **45**
Hale Av. *New M* —3H **49**
Halebrose Ct. *Bourn* —4C **62**
Hale Gdns. *New M* —3H **49**
Halewood Way. *Christ* —5D **44**
Halifax Way. *Christ* —6D **46**
Hall Rd. *Bourn* —2B **40**
Halstock Cres. *Poole* —3B **38**
Halter Path. *Poole* —4E **55**
(in two parts)
Halter Ri. *Wim* —3C **16**
Halton Clo. *Brans* —3D **28**
Hambledon Gdns. *Bourn* —1A **62**
Hambledon Rd. *Bourn* —6H **43**
Hamble Rd. *Poole* —6D **38**
Hamilton Clo. *Bourn* —2D **60**
Hamilton Clo. *Christ* —3B **64**
Hamilton Clo. *Poole* —5E **55**
Hamilton Ct. *Bourn* —2B **60**
Hamilton Ct. *Mil S* —3C **66**
Hamilton Cres. *Poole* —5E **55**
Hamilton Rd. *Bourn* —2D **60**
Hamilton Rd. *Cor M* —6E **21**
Hamilton Rd. *Poole* —5E **55**
Hamilton Way. *New M* —3E **49**
Ham La. *Wim* —5B **16**
Hampden La. *Bourn* —2H **61**
Hampreston Rd. *Fern* —1C **24**
Hampshire Clo. *Christ* —3D **44**
Hampshire Ct. *Bourn*
—4G **59** (3G **5**)

Hampshire Hatches La. *Ring*
—3H **13**
Hampshire Ho. *Bourn* —3G **5**
Hampshire Shop. Cen., The. *Bourn*
—3E **43**
Hampton Ct. *Bourn* —3F **59**
Hampton Dri. *Ring* —2D **8**
Handley Ct. *Ring* —4B **8**
Hanham Rd. *Cor M* —6D **20**
Hanham Rd. *Wim* —4E **15**
Hankinson Rd. *Bourn* —5A **42**
Hanlon Ct. *Bourn* —1C **40**
Hannah Way. *Penn* —5B **34**
Hannington Pl. *Bourn* —2G **61**
Hannington Rd. *Bourn* —2G **61**
Hanover Grn. *Poole* —5D **38**
Hanover Ho. *Poole* —4B **56**
Harbeck Rd. *Bourn* —2C **42**
Harbour Clo. *Poole* —3H **69**
Harbour Ct. *Bart S* —6E **49**
Harbour Cres. *Christ* —2A **64**
Harbour Hill Cres. *Poole* —2C **56**
Harbour Hill Rd. *Poole* —3C **56**
Harbour Prospect. *Poole* —1G **69**
Harbour Rd. *Bourn* —4E **63**
Harbour Vw. Clo. *Poole* —2E **57**
Harbour Vw. Ct. *Christ* —2F **63**
Harbour Vw. Rd. *Poole* —2E **57**
Harbour Watch. *Poole* —2G **69**
Harcombe Clo. *Poole* —2C **38**
Harcourt Rd. *Bourn* —2G **61**
Hardy Clo. *New M* —2F **49**
Hardy Clo. *W Mr* —6D **10**
Hardy Cres. *Wim* —6F **15**
Hardy Rd. *Poole* —3H **57**
Hardy Rd. *W Mr* —6D **10**
Hare Rd. *New M & Hord* —2B **50**
Hares Grn. *Bourn* —5G **43**
Harewood Av. *Bourn* —6F **43**
Harewood Cres. *Bourn* —6F **43**
Harewood Gdns. *Bourn* —6F **43**
Hare Wood Grn. *Key* —3G **67**
Harewood Pl. *Bourn* —1H **61**
Harford Clo. *Penn* —4D **52**
Harford Rd. *Poole* —5G **39**
Harkwood Dri. *Poole* —3E **55**
Harland Rd. *Bourn* —3E **63**
Harleston Vs. *Wim* —5F **15**
Harness Clo. *Wim* —3B **16**
Harraby Grn. *Broad* —2G **37**
Harrier Dri. *Wim* —1B **22**
Harriers Clo. *Christ* —5F **47**
Harrison Av. *Bourn* —1D **60**
Harrison Clo. *Burt* —2G **45**
Harrison Way. *W Mr* —4C **10**
Harris Way. *New M* —5A **32**
Harrow Clo. *Nea* —4D **28**
Harrow Rd. *Brans & Nea* —4C **28**
Harry Barrows Clo. *Ring* —5C **8**
Hart Clo. *New M* —1F **49**
Harting Rd. *Bourn* —6B **44**
Hartnell Ct. *Cor M* —6D **20**
Hartsbourne Dri. *Bourn* —5H **43**
Harts Way. *Evtn* —4H **51**
Hartwell Rd. *Poole* —6B **38**
Harvester Way. *L'ton* —5F **35**
Harvey Rd. *Bourn* —2G **61**
Harvey Rd. *Wim* —3C **22**
(in two parts)
Harwell Rd. *Poole* —6B **38**
Haskells Clo. *Lyn* —4E **71**
Haskells Rd. *Poole* —6F **39**
Haslemere Av. *Highc* —5H **47**
Haslemere Pl. *Christ* —4A **48**
Hasler Rd. *Poole* —3A **38**
Haslop Rd. *Wim* —2A **16**
Hastings Rd. *Bourn* —3F **43**
Hastings Rd. *Poole* —3H **37**
Hatch Pond Rd. *Poole* —5A **38**
Hatfield Ct. *New M* —2E **49**
Hatfield Gdns. *Bourn* —5H **43**
Hathaway Rd. *Bourn* —3B **62**
Hatherden Av. *Poole* —2D **56**
Havelock Rd. *Poole* —2C **58**
Havelock Way. *Christ* —3F **47**

Haven Ct. *Mil S* —3C **66**
Haven Ct. *Poole* —6F **69**
Haven Gdns. *New M* —3H **49**
Haven Rd. *Cor M* —5C **20**
Haven Rd. *Poole* —3H **69**
Haverstock Rd. *Bourn* —3B **42**
Haviland Ct. *Bourn* —2F **61**
Haviland Rd. *Bourn* —3F **61**
Haviland Rd. *Fern I* —2G **17**
Haviland Rd. E. *Bourn* —2F **61**
Hawden Rd. *Bourn* —4C **40**
Hawkchurch Gdns. *Poole* —3C **38**
Hawk Clo. *Wim* —2A **16**
Hawker Clo. *Wim* —2D **22**
Hawkins Clo. *Ring* —2E **9**
Hawkins Rd. *Poole* —4B **40**
Hawkwood Rd. *Bourn* —3E **61**
Haworth Clo. *Christ* —4E **45**
Hawthorn Clo. *New M* —1A **50**
Hawthorn Dri. *Poole* —4F **37**
Hawthorn Dri. *Sway* —1F **33**
Hawthorn Rd. *Bock & Burt*
—1B **46**
Hawthorn Rd. *Bourn* —5H **41**
Hawthorns, The. *Christ* —1B **64**
Haydon Rd. *Poole* —6D **58**
Hayes Av. *Bourn* —1E **61**
Hayes Clo. *Wim* —5A **16**
Hayes La. *Wim* —5B **16**
Hayeswood Rd. *Wim* —3A **16**
Haymoor Rd. *Poole* —6D **38**
Haynes Av. *Poole* —3B **56**
Haysoms Clo. *New M* —4H **49**
Hayward Cres. *Ver* —4C **6**
Haywards Farm Clo. *Ver* —4C **6**
Haywards La. *Cor M* —3C **20**
Hayward Way. *Ver* —4B **6**
Hazel Clo. *Christ* —4E **47**
Hazel Ct. *New M* —4H **49**
Hazeldene. *Broad* —1G **37**
Hazel Dri. *Fern* —1A **18**
Hazell Av. *Bourn* —3D **40**
Hazel Rd. *Penn* —1C **52**
Hazelton Clo. *Bourn* —5G **43**
Hazelwood Av. *New M* —1E **49**
Hazelwood Dri. *Ver* —5F **7**
Hazlebury Rd. *Poole* —6G **37**
Hazlemere Dri. *St L* —4A **12**
Headlands Bus. Pk. *Blash* —1C **8**
Heads Farm Clo. *Bourn* —6G **25**
Heads La. *Bourn* —6G **25**
Headswell Av. *Bourn* —1G **41**
Headswell Cres. *Bourn* —1G **41**
Headswell Gdns. *Bourn* —6G **25**
Heanor Clo. *Bourn* —3E **41**
Hearts of Oak M. *L'ton* —1F **53**
Heath Av. *Poole* —1B **56**
Heath Clo. *Wim* —2B **16**
Heathcote Rd. *Bourn* —3F **61**
Heatherbank Rd. *Bourn* —4E **59**
Heatherbrae La. *Poole* —1B **54**
Heather Clo. *Bourn* —1D **42**
Heather Clo. *Cor M* —5E **21**
Heather Clo. *Hord* —2E **51**
Heather Clo. *St L* —4A **12**
Heather Clo. *Walk* —4A **48**
Heatherdell. *Poole* —1B **54**
Heatherdown Rd. *W Mr* —6E **11**
Heatherdown Way. *W Mr* —6E **11**
Heather Dri. *Fern* —2B **18**
Heatherlands Ri. *Poole* —2H **57**
Heatherlea Rd. *Bourn* —3B **62**
Heather Lodge. *New M* —2G **49**
Heather Rd. *Bourn* —2F **41**
Heather Vw. Rd. *Poole* —6B **40**
Heather Way. *Fern* —2B **18**
Heath Farm Clo. *Fern* —6A **18**
Heath Farm Rd. *Fern* —6A **18**
Heath Farm Way. *Fern* —6A **18**
Heathfield Av. *Poole* —5C **40**
Heathfield Rd. *W Mr* —6D **10**
Heathfield Way. *W Mr* —6D **10**
Heathlands Av. *W Parl* —1F **25**
Heathlands Clo. *Burt* —2G **45**
Heathlands Clo. *Ver* —3E **7**

Heath Rd. *Hord* —2D **50**
Heath Rd. *St L* —3H **11**
Heath Rd. *Walk* —4B **48**
Heathwood Av. *Bart S* —5E **49**
Heathwood Rd. *Bourn* —5G **41**
Heathy Clo. *Bart S* —5F **49**
Heaton Rd. *Bourn* —3D **40**
Heavytree Rd. *Poole* —3F **57**
Heckford La. *Poole* —4B **56** (1D **4**)
Heckford Rd. *Cor M* —6C **20**
Heckford Rd. *Poole*
—3B **56** (1D **4**)
Hedgerley. *New M* —5H **49**
Heights App. *Poole* —6C **36**
Heights Rd. *Poole* —5C **36**
Helic Ho. *Wim* —4E **15**
Helyar Rd. *Bourn* —3F **43**
Henbest Clo. *Wim* —4C **16**
Henbury Clo. *Cor M* —5D **20**
Henbury Clo. *Poole* —3E **39**
Henbury Ri. *Cor M* —5D **20**
Henbury Vw. Rd. *Cor M* —5C **20**
Hendford Gdns. *Bourn* —3F **41**
Hendford Rd. *Bourn* —3F **41**
Hengistbury Rd. *Bart S* —5E **49**
Hengistbury Rd. *Bourn* —4D **62**
Hengist Pk. *Bourn* —3F **63**
Hengist Rd. *Bourn* —3D **60**
Henley Gdns. *Bourn* —6G **43**
Hennings Pk. Rd. *Poole* —2B **56**
Henville Rd. *Bourn* —2C **60**
Herbert Av. *Poole* —5G **39**
Herbert Ct. *Poole* —5H **39**
Herberton Rd. *Bourn* —2A **62**
Herbert Rd. *Bourn* —5D **58**
Herbert Rd. *New M* —2H **49**
Hercules Rd. *Poole* —4D **54**
Hermitage Rd. *Poole* —1E **57**
Herm Rd. *Poole* —4H **39**
Heron Clo. *Sway* —2F **33**
Heron Ct. Rd. *Bourn* —6A **42**
Heron Dri. *Wim* —2A **16**
Herons Mead. *Bourn* —6D **26**
Herstone Clo. *Poole* —4D **38**
Hesketh Clo. *St I* —2C **12**
Hestan Clo. *Christ* —1B **44**
Heston Way. *W Mr* —4B **10**
Hewitt Rd. *Poole* —3E **55**
Heysham Rd. *Broad* —2G **37**
Heytesbury Rd. *Bourn* —1B **62**
Hibberd Way. *Bourn* —4F **41**
Hibbs Clo. *Poole* —6C **36**
Hickes Clo. *Bourn* —1B **40**
Hickory Clo. *Poole* —5A **36**
Highbridge Rd. *Poole* —4G **57**
Highbury Clo. *New M* —2H **49**
Highcliffe Corner. *Christ* —5B **48**
Highcliffe Rd. *Christ* —5C **46**
Higher Blandford Rd.
Cor M & Broad —4E **21**
Higher Merley La. *Cor M* —3E **21**
Highfield. *L'ton* —2F **53**
Highfield Av. *L'ton* —2E **53**
Highfield Av. *Ring* —3C **8**
Highfield Clo. *Cor M* —6E **21**
Highfield Clo. *Sway* —1F **33**
Highfield Dri. *Ring* —2C **8**
Highfield Gdns. *Sway* —1F **33**
Highfield Rd. *Bourn* —3G **41**
Highfield Rd. *Cor M* —1E **37**
Highfield Rd. *L'ton* —1E **53**
Highfield Rd. *Ring* —3C **8**
Highfield Rd. *W Mr* —3B **10**
High Howe Clo. *Bourn* —1A **40**
High Howe Gdns. *Bourn* —1A **40**
High Howe La. *Bourn* —1A **40**
Highland Av. *Christ* —4B **48**
Highland Rd. *Poole* —2F **57**
Highland Rd. *Wim* —3F **15**
Highlands Cres. *Bourn* —1E **41**
Highlands Rd. *Bart S* —5G **49**
Highland Vw. Clo. *Wim* —4F **15**
High Marryats. *Bart S* —6G **49**
High Mead. *Fern* —1C **24**
High Mead La. *Fern* —2C **24**

Highmoor Clo. *Cor M* —6D **20**
Highmoor Clo. *Poole* —4F **57**
Highmoor Rd. *Bourn* —4C **40**
Highmoor Rd. *Cor M* —6D **20**
Highmoor Rd. *Poole* —4G **57**
High Oaks Gdns. *Bourn* —1A **40**
High Pk. Rd. *Broad* —1E **37**
High Pines. *Christ* —6F **47**
High Ridge Cres. *New M* —2A **50**
High St. *Ashy H* —1A **12**
High St. *Christ* —1F **63**
High St. *L'ton* —2G **53**
High St. *Lyn* —3F **71**
High St. *Mil S* —3E **67**
High St. *Poole* —6H **55** (5A **4**)
(in two parts)
High St. *Ring* —4B **8**
High St. *Wim* —4D **14**
High St. N. *Poole* —4B **56** (2D **4**)
Hightown Gdns. *Ring* —5D **8**
Hightown Hill. *Ring* —5F **9**
Hightown Rd. *Ring* —5C **8**
Hightown Trad. Est. *Ring* —5D **8**
High Trees. *Poole* —1C **70**
Hightrees Av. *Bourn* —4E **43**
High Trees Wlk. *Fern* —2B **18**
Highview Clo. *Christ* —2C **44**
Highview Gdns. *Poole* —6G **39**
High Way. *Broad* —2F **37**
Highwood La. *Ring* —1G **9**
Highwood Rd. *Broc* —4E **73**
Highwood Rd. *Poole* —3A **58**
Hilary Rd. *Poole* —4A **38**
Hilda Rd. *Poole* —1A **58**
Hiley Rd. *Poole* —1A **56**
Hillary Clo. *Lyn* —5G **71**
Hillary Rd. *Christ* —5A **46**
Hillbourne Rd. *Poole* —3G **37**
Hillbrow Rd. *Bourn* —1H **61**
Hill Clo. *Brans* —3C **28**
Hillcrest Av. *Fern* —1A **18**
Hillcrest Clo. *Bourn* —2A **42**
Hillcrest Rd. *Bourn* —2A **42**
Hillcrest Rd. *Cor M* —6C **20**
Hillcrest Rd. *Poole* —2E **57**
Hillditch. *L'ton* —5F **35**
Hill La. *Brans* —3A **46**
(Hawthorn Rd.)
Hill La. *Brans* —3C **28**
(Wiltshire Rd.)
Hillman Rd. *Poole* —2H **57**
Hill Mdw. *Ver* —5E **7**
Hillside Dri. *Christ* —1B **44**
Hillside Gdns. *Cor M* —1C **36**
Hillside M. *Cor M* —1C **36**
Hillside Rd. *Cor M* —1C **36**
Hillside Rd. *L'ton* —2E **53**
Hillside Rd. *Poole* —4B **40**
Hillside Rd. *Ver* —2D **6**
Hill St. *Poole* —5A **56** (4B **4**)
Hill Ter. *Wim* —1E **23**
Hilltop Clo. *Fern* —2H **17**
Hilltop Rd. *Cor M* —6E **21**
Hilltop Rd. *Fern* —2H **17**
Hillview Rd. *Bourn* —1F **41**
Hill Vw. Rd. *Fern* —2A **18**
Hill Way. *Ashy H* —2B **12**
Hiltom Rd. *Ring* —4D **8**
Hilton Clo. *Poole* —1E **57**
Hilton Rd. *New M* —1H **49**
Hinchliffe Clo. *Poole* —5F **55**
Hinchliffe Rd. *Poole* —5F **55**
Hinton Rd. *Bourn*
—4H **59** (3H **5**)
Hinton Wood. *Bourn* —5A **60**
Hinton Wood Av. *Christ* —3G **47**
Hinton Wood La. *Hint* —3G **47**
Hive Gdns. *Poole* —3H **69**
Hives Way. *L'ton* —5F **35**
Hobart Rd. *New M* —3F **49**
Hobbs Pk. *St L* —3B **12**
Hobbs Rd. *Poole* —5G **39**
Hoburne Cvn. Pk. *Christ* —5E **47**
Hoburne Gdns. *Christ* —4E **47**
Hoburne La. *Christ* —4E **47**

Hodges Clo. *Poole* —6C **38**
Hogue Av. *Bourn* —6F **25**
Holbury Clo. *Bourn* —2E **43**
Holcombe Rd. *Poole* —1B **54**
Holdenhurst Av. *Bourn* —1A **62**
Holdenhurst Rd. *Bourn* —4B **60**
(Landsowne Cres.)
Holdenhurst Rd. *Bourn* —2F **43**
(Throop Rd.)
Holes Bay Rd. *Poole*
—1H **55** (1A **4**)
Holes Clo. *Hord* —1D **50**
Hollands Wood Dri. *New M*
—6G **31**
Holland Way. *Broad* —6F **21**
Hollenden. *Poole* —3C **58**
Hollies Clo. *Sway* —2F **33**
Holloway Av. *Bourn* —6B **24**
Holly Clo. *Poole* —6A **36**
Holly Clo. *St L* —3H **11**
Holly Ct. *Bourn* —4F **59**
Holly Ct. *Poole* —3B **56**
Holly Gdns. *Burt* —4H **45**
Holly Gdns. *Mil S* —2C **66**
Holly Grn. Ri. *Bourn* —1A **40**
Holly Gro. *Ver* —4C **6**
Holly Hedge La. *Poole* —5A **38**
Holly La. *New M* —1A **50**
Holly La. *Walk* —3C **48**
Holly La. *Wim* —4A **14**
Holly Lodge. *Poole* —3C **58**
Hollywood La. *L'ton* —6F **35**
Holm Clo. *Ring* —2E **9**
Holme Rd. *Highc* —5B **48**
Holmfield Av. *Bourn* —6A **44**
Holm Hill La. *Christ* —4B **30**
Holmhurst Av. *Highc* —4G **47**
Holmsley Clo. *Penn* —3D **52**
Holmsley Rd. *New M* —1D **30**
Holmwood Gth. *Hight* —5F **9**
Holnest Rd. *Poole* —4B **38**
Holt Rd. *Poole* —1B **58**
Holt Rd. *T Leg* —2A **10**
Holworth Clo. *Bourn* —2A **40**
Holywell Clo. *Poole* —2B **38**
Homedale Ho. *Bourn* —2H **59**
Homedene Ho. *Poole* —4B **56**
Home Farm Rd. *Ver* —3C **6**
Home Farm Way. *Ver* —3C **6**
Homefield Ho. *New M* —3G **49**
Homeforde Ho. *Broc* —3F **73**
Homelake Ho. *Poole* —4F **57**
Homelands Est. *Christ* —1D **62**
Homelands Ho. *Fern* —4B **18**
Homeleigh Ho. *Bourn* —2A **60**
Home Oak Clo. *Ver* —2C **6**
Homeoaks Ho. *Bourn* —2H **59**
Home Rd. *Bourn* —5D **24**
Homeside Rd. *Bourn* —3A **42**
Homeview Ho. *Poole* —4B **56**
Homewood Clo. *New M* —2A **50**
Honeybourne Cres. *Bourn*
—3E **63**
Honeysuckle La. *Poole* —4F **37**
Honeysuckle Way. *Christ* —5D **46**
Hood Clo. *Bourn* —4D **40**
Hood Cres. *Bourn* —4D **40**
Hooke Clo. *Poole* —3E **39**
Hop Clo. *Poole* —6A **36**
Hopkins Clo. *Bourn* —3G **43**
Horace Rd. *Bourn* —3E **61**
Hordle La. *Hord* —5D **50**
Horlock Rd. *Broc* —2F **73**
Hornbeam Way. *Wim* —4G **15**
Horning Rd. *Poole* —2B **58**
Horsa Clo. *Bourn* —3C **62**
Horsa Ct. *Bourn* —3C **62**
Horsa Rd. *Bourn* —3C **62**
Horseshoe Clo. *Wim* —3B **16**
Horseshoe Common Roundabout.
Bourn —3H **5**
Horseshoe Ct. *Bourn*
—3H **59** (2H **5**)
Horseshoe, The. *Poole* —5G **69**
Horsham Av. *Bourn* —5E **25**

Horton Clo. *Bourn* —2C **42**
Horton Rd. *Ashy H* —1G **11**
Horton Rd. *T Leg* —2A **10**
Horton Way. *Ver* —4B **6**
Hosier's La. *Poole* —6H **55** (5A **4**)
Hosker Rd. *Bourn* —2H **61**
Houlton Rd. *Poole* —3C **56**
Hounds Way. *Wim* —4B **16**
Hounslow Clo. *Poole* —5F **55**
Howard Clo. *Christ* —1B **64**
Howard Rd. *Bourn* —6C **42**
Howard Rd. *Ver* —3D **6**
(in two parts)
Howards Mead. *Penn* —3D **52**
Howe Clo. *Christ* —2B **64**
Howe Clo. *New M* —2F **49**
Howe La. *Ver* —4C **6**
Howell Ho. *Wim* —2H **15**
Howeth Clo. *Bourn* —2F **41**
Howeth Rd. *Bourn* —3E **41**
Howlett Clo. *L'ton* —1E **53**
Howton Clo. *Bourn* —6E **25**
Howton Rd. *Bourn* —6E **25**
Hoxley Rd. *Bourn* —1F **41**
Hoyal Rd. *Poole* —4D **54**
Hudson Clo. *Poole* —3G **39**
Hudson Clo. *Ring* —3E **9**
Hudson Davies Clo. *Pill* —2H **35**
Hughs Bus. Cen. *Christ* —6C **46**
Hull Cres. *Bourn* —1H **39**
Hull Rd. *Bourn* —1H **39**
Hull Way. *Bourn* —1H **39**
Humber Rd. *Fern* —3E **19**
Humphrey's Bri. *Christ* —6E **47**
Hundred La. *P'mre* —4H **35**
Hungerfield Clo. *Brans* —2C **28**
Hungerford Rd. *Bourn* —2D **42**
Hunger Hill. *Poole* —3B **4**
Hunter Clo. *Christ* —6C **46**
Hunter Clo. *Wim* —3C **16**
Hunters Clo. *Ver* —4G **7**
Huntfield Rd. *Bourn* —3B **42**
Huntingdon Dri. *Wim* —2C **22**
Huntingdon Gdns. *Christ* —3D **44**
Huntly Rd. *Bourn* —1F **59**
Hunt Rd. *Christ* —5A **46**
Hunt Rd. *Poole* —3C **56**
Huntvale Rd. *Bourn* —2B **42**
Hurdles Mead. *Mil S* —1H *53*
(off Gosport St.)
Hurdles Mead. *Mil S* —4D **66**
(Hurst Rd.)
Hurdles, The. *Christ* —5C **44**
Hurn Clo. *Ring* —1F **13**
Hurn Ct. La. *Hurn* —5F **27**
Hurn La. *Ring* —1F **13**
Hurn Rd. *Christ* —1B **44**
Hurn Rd. *Ring* —1F **13**
Hurn Way. *Christ* —4B **44**
Hursley Clo. *Bourn* —5A **44**
Hurstbourne Av. *Christ* —4G **47**
Hurst Clo. *Walk* —3C **48**
Hurst Ct. *Mil S* —3C **66**
Hurstdene Rd. *Bourn* —3C **42**
Hurst Hill. *Poole* —1G **69**
Hurst Rd. *Mil S* —4D **66**
Hurst Rd. *Ring* —2C **8**
Hussar Clo. *Christ* —6D **44**
Hyacinth Clo. *Poole* —4F **37**
Hyde Clo. *Sway* —1F **33**
Hyde Rd. *Bourn* —6E **25**
Hyde, The. *New M* —1E **49**
Hynesbury Rd. *Christ* —1E **65**
Hythe Rd. *Poole* —6E **39**

Ibbertson Clo. *Bourn* —3F **43**
Ibbertson Rd. *Bourn* —4F **43**
Ibbertson Way. *Bourn* —3F **43**
Ibbett Rd. *Bourn* —3E **41**
Ibsley Clo. *Bourn* —1C **60**
Iddesleigh Rd. *Bourn* —1H **59**
Iford Clo. *Bourn* —1C **62**
Iford Gdns. *Bourn* —6A **44**
Iford La. *Bourn* —6B **44**

Iford Roundabout. *Bourn* —6A **44**
Iley La. *Mil S* —2H **67**
Ilford Bri. Home Pk. *Bourn*
—6B **44**
Imber Dri. *Highc* —5H **47**
Imbre Ct. *Poole* —2A **70**
Inglegreen Clo. *New M* —4F **49**
Inglesham Way. *Poole* —3E **55**
Inglewood Av. *Bourn* —4F **43**
Inglewood Dri. *New M* —3H **49**
Ingram Wlk. *Wim* —5F **15**
Ingworth Rd. *Poole* —2C **58**
Insley Cres. *Broad* —6E **21**
Inveravon. *Christ* —2B **64**
Inverclyde Rd. *Poole* —3F **57**
Inverleigh Rd. *Bourn* —1A **62**
Inverness Rd. *Poole* —2A **70**
Ipswich Rd. *Poole & Bourn*
—3D **58**
Iris Rd. *Bourn* —4H **41**
Irvine Way. *Christ* —5A **46**
Irving Rd. *Bourn* —3A **62**
Isaacs Clo. *Poole* —6D **40**
Island Vw. *New M* —6C **48**
Island Vw. Av. *Christ* —1D **64**
Island Vw. Clo. *Mil S* —4E **67**
Island Vw. Ct. *New M* —6F **49**
Island Vw. Rd. *New M* —6D **48**
Ivamy Pl. *Bourn* —3B **40**
Ivor Rd. *Cor M* —1D **36**
Ivor Rd. *Poole* —6G **55**
Ivy Clo. *St L* —3H **11**
Ivy Ho. *Bourn* —4F **59**
Ivy Rd. *Wim* —3B **22**
Iwerne Clo. *Bourn* —1B **42**

Jacklin Ct. *Broad* —6H **21**
Jackson Gdns. *Poole* —1G **57**
Jackson Rd. *Poole* —1G **57**
Jacobean Clo. *Walk* —4B **48**
Jacobs Rd. *Poole* —5E **55**
Jacqueline Rd. *Poole* —6F **39**
Jameson Rd. *Bourn* —4G **41**
James Rd. *Poole* —2C **58**
Janred Ct. *Bart S* —6E **49**
Jasmine Ct. *L'ton* —1F **53**
Jaundrells Clo. *New M* —2A **50**
Jays Ct. *Christ* —5B **48**
Jealous La. *L'ton* —1C **34**
Jefferson Av. *Bourn* —1D **60**
Jellicoe Clo. *Poole* —2D **56**
Jellicoe Dri. *Christ* —1B **64**
Jennings Rd. *Poole* —5G **57**
Jephcote Rd. *Bourn* —1B **40**
Jersey Clo. *Poole* —4H **39**
Jersey Rd. *Poole* —4H **39**
Jesmond Av. *Highc* —5H **47**
Jessica Av. *Ver* —2B **6**
Jessopp Clo. *Bourn* —1H **41**
Jessopp Rd. *Wim* —3B **16**
Jewell Rd. *Bourn* —3F **43**
Jimmy Brown Av. *W Mr* —2C **10**
Johnson Rd. *Fern I* —2G **17**
Johnstone Rd. *Christ* —1A **64**
Johnston Rd. *Poole* —6B **38**
Jolliffe Av. *Poole* —3B **56**
Jolliffe Rd. *Poole* —3B **56**
Jonathan Clo. *L'ton* —6G **35**
Jopps Corner. *Burt* —1G **45**
Jordans La. *Sway* —1G **33**
Joshua Clo. *Poole* —5E **55**
Jowitt Dri. *New M* —3F **49**
Joyce Dickson Clo. *Ring* —5D **8**
Joys Rd. *T Leg* —2A **10**
Jubilee Clo. *Cor M* —4E **21**
Jubilee Clo. *Ring* —3E **9**
Jubilee Ct. *Sway* —2F **33**
Jubilee Cres. *Poole* —2H **57**
Jubilee Gdns. *Bourn* —3F **41**
Jubilee Rd. *Cor M* —4E **21**
Jubilee Rd. *Poole* —2H **57**
Julia Clo. *Highc* —5H **47**
Julian's Rd. *Wim* —5C **14**
Julyan Av. *Poole* —5C **40**

Jumpers Av. *Christ* —5C **44**
Jumpers Rd. *Christ* —5D **44**
Junction Rd. *Bourn* —5H **41**
Junction Rd. *Poole* —3C **54**
Juniper Cen., The. *Christ* —5D **44**
Juniper Clo. *Fern* —1A **18**
Juniper Clo. *Penn* —3D **52**
Juniper Clo. *T Leg* —2A **10**
Jupiter Way. *Cor M* —3E **21**
(in two parts)
Justin Gdns. *Bourn* —1G **41**

Kamptee Copse. *New M* —5H **31**
Kangaw Pl. *Poole* —5D **54**
Katherine Chance Clo. *Burt*
—2G **45**
Katterns Clo. *Christ* —3C **44**
Keats Av. *Mil S* —2D **66**
Keats Ho. *New M* —3G **49**
Keeble Clo. *Bourn* —5F **25**
Keeble Cres. *Bourn* —5F **25**
Keeble Rd. *Bourn* —5F **25**
Keel Ho. *Poole* —2D **4**
Keepers La. *Wim* —4E **17**
Keighley Av. *Broad* —3F **37**
Keith Rd. *Bourn* —1E **59**
Kellaway Rd. *Poole* —5D **38**
Kelly Clo. *Poole* —5D **38**
Kelsall Gdns. *New M* —2G **49**
Kemp Rd. *Bourn* —5H **41**
Kenilworth Clo. *New M* —2H **49**
Kenilworth Ct. *Christ* —6E **45**
Kenilworth Ct. *Poole* —1B **70**
Kennard Ct. *New M* —2F **49**
Kennard Rd. *New M* —1F **49**
Kennart Rd. *Poole* —6H **37**
Kenneth Ct. *Christ* —6B **48**
Kennington Rd. *Poole* —5B **38**
Ken Rd. *Bourn* —3C **62**
Kensington Dri. *Bourn* —3F **59**
Kensington Pk. *Mil S* —3C **66**
Kent Rd. *Poole* —1A **58**
Kenyon Clo. *Poole* —6C **38**
Kenyon Rd. *Poole* —6C **38**
Keppel Clo. *Ring* —4D **8**
Kerley Rd. *Bourn* —5G **59** (5F **5**)
Kerry Clo. *Penn* —2E **53**
Kestrel Clo. *Fern* —2H **17**
Kestrel Clo. *Poole* —5B **36**
Kestrel Ct. *Ring* —3C **8**
Kestrel Dri. *Christ* —1C **64**
Keswick Ct. *New M* —6H **31**
Keswick Rd. *Bourn* —3F **61**
Keswick Rd. *New M* —6H **31**
Keswick Way. *Ver* —4C **6**
Keverstone Ct. *Bourn* —4D **60**
Keyes Clo. *Christ* —1B **64**
Keyes Clo. *Poole* —4B **40**
Keyhaven Rd. *Mil S* —3E **67**
Key La. *Poole* —5A **4**
Keysworth Av. *Bart S* —5F **49**
Keysworth Rd. *Poole* —3C **54**
Khyber Rd. *Poole* —2H **57**
Kilbride. *Poole* —3C **58**
Kilmarnock Rd. *Bourn* —4H **41**
Kilmington Way. *Highc* —5G **47**
Kiln Clo. *Cor M* —1C **36**
Kimberley Clo. *Christ* —5D **44**
Kimberley Rd. *Bourn* —1A **62**
Kimberley Rd. *Poole* —4F **57**
Kimber Rd. *Bourn* —2B **40**
Kimmeridge Av. *Poole* —5F **39**
King Clo. *St I* —3B **12**
Kingcup Clo. *Broad* —3E **37**
King Edward Av. *Bourn* —3H **41**
Kingfisher Clo. *Bourn* —1C **62**
Kingfisher Clo. *W Mr* —5D **10**
Kingfisher Pk. *W Moor* —1C **10**
Kingfishers, The. *Ver* —4E **7**
Kingfisher Way. *Christ* —2C **64**
Kingfisher Way. *Ring* —1D **8**
King George Av. *Bourn* —3H **41**
King George Mobile Home Pk.
New M —4F **49**

King John Av. *Bourn* —5H **23**
King John Clo. *Bourn* —6H **23**
Kingland Cres. *Poole*
—5A **56** (3C **4**)
Kingland Rd. *Poole* —5B **56** (3D **4**)
King Richard Dri. *Bourn* —6G **23**
King's Arms La. *Ring* —4B **8**
Kings Arms Row. *Ring* —4B **8**
King's Av. *Christ* —1D **62**
Kings Av. *Poole* —5H **57**
Kingsbere Av. *Bourn* —3D **40**
Kingsbere Rd. *Poole* —2C **56**
Kingsbridge Rd. *Poole* —4G **57**
Kingsbury's La. *Ring* —4B **8**
Kings Clo. *L'ton* —1F **53**
Kings Clo. *Lyn* —3F **71**
Kings Clo. *W Mr* —6C **10**
Kings Cres. *L'ton* —1F **53**
Kings Cres. *Poole* —5A **58**
Kings Farm La. *Hord* —3F **51**
Kingsfield. *L'ton* —3H **53**
Kingsfield. *Ring* —5C **8**
Kingsgate. *Poole* —4D **58**
Kings La. *Sway* —4H **33**
Kingsley Av. *Bourn* —3E **63**
Kingsley Clo. *Bourn* —3E **63**
Kingsley Ho. *Bourn* —4H **41**
Kingsmead Ct. *Wim* —4D **14**
Kingsmill Rd. *Poole* —6C **38**
Kings Pk. *Bourn* —1E **61**
Kings Pk. Dri. *Bourn* —1G **61**
(Central Dri.)
Kings Pk. Dri. *Bourn* —1E **61**
(Holdenhurst Rd.)
Kings Pk. Rd. *Bourn* —1E **61**
King's Rd. *Bourn* —6A **42**
Kings Rd. *L'ton* —1F **53**
Kings Rd. *New M* —1A **50**
King's Saltern Rd. *L'ton* —3H **53**
Kingston Pk. *Penn* —3F **53**
Kingston Rd. *Poole* —3B **56**
King St. *Wim* —5D **14**
Kingsway. *Fern* —1H **17**
Kingsway Clo. *Christ* —4D **44**
Kingswell Clo. *Bourn* —3F **41**
Kingswell Gdns. *Bourn* —3D **40**
Kingswell Gro. *Bourn* —3D **40**
Kingswell Rd. *Bourn* —3D **40**
Kinross Rd. *Bourn* —1G **59**
Kinsbourne Av. *Bourn* —3F **41**
Kinson Av. *Poole* —6E **39**
Kinson Gro. *Bourn* —5E **25**
Kinson Pk. Rd. *Bourn* —5F **25**
Kinson Rd. *Bourn* —4C **40**
Kinston Pottery Ind. Est. *Poole*
—1E **57**
Kiosks, The. *Poole* —5B **4**
Kipling Rd. *Poole* —2F **57**
Kirby Clo. *Poole* —1D **56**
Kirby Way. *Bourn* —3B **62**
Kirkham Av. *Burt* —2G **45**
Kirkway. *Broad* —1H **37**
Kitchener Cres. *Poole* —4H **37**
Kitchers Clo. *Sway* —1F **33**
Kitscroft Rd. *Bourn* —6E **25**
Kittiwake Clo. *Bourn* —1B **62**
Kitwalls La. *Mil S* —1D **66**
Kivernell Pl. *Mil S* —2C **66**
Kivernell Rd. *Mil S* —3C **66**
Kiwi Clo. *Poole* —4C **56**
Knapp Clo. *Christ* —5E **45**
Knapp Mill Av. *Christ* —5E **45**
Knightcrest Pk. *Evtn* —4A **52**
Knighton Heath Clo. *Bourn*
—1A **40**
Knighton Heath Ind. Est. *Bourn*
—3A **40**
Knighton Heath Rd. *Bourn* —1A **40**
Knighton La. *Wim* —4H **23**
Knighton Pk. *New M* —5E **49**
Knightsbridge Ct. *Bourn* —5F **5**
Knights Rd. *Bourn* —6H **23**
Knightstone Gro. *W Mr* —5B **10**
Knightwood. *New M* —6C **48**
Knightwood Av. *Lyn* —3F **71**

Knightwood Clo. *Christ* —5F **47**
Knightwood Clo. *Lyn* —3F **71**
Knobcrook Rd. *Wim* —3D **14**
Knole Gdns. *Bourn* —3D **60**
Knole Rd. *Bourn* —2D **60**
Knoll Gdns. *St I* —3B **12**
Knoll La. *Cor M* —3B **20**
Knowland Dri. *Mil S* —2D **66**
Knowle Rd. *Broc* —2D **72**
Knowles Clo. *Christ* —6A **46**
Knowlton Gdns. *Bourn* —1B **42**
Knowlton Rd. *Poole* —3D **38**
Knyveton Rd. *Bourn* —3B **60**
Kyrchil La. *Wim* —3H **15**
Kyrchil Way. *Wim* —2H **15**

Labrador Dri. *Poole*
—6B **56** (5D **4**)
Laburnum Clo. *Fern* —3H **17**
Laburnum Clo. *Ver* —4G **7**
Laburnum Dri. *Evtn* —5A **52**
Laburnum Ho. *Bourn* —1H **41**
Lacey Cres. *Poole* —1E **57**
Lacy Clo. *Wim* —3E **15**
Lacy Dri. *Wim* —3E **15**
Ladysmith Clo. *Christ* —6A **46**
Lagado Clo. *Poole* —1G **69**
Lagland Ct. *Poole* —6A **56** (5B **4**)
Lagland St. *Poole* —5A **56** (3C **4**)
Lagoon Clo. *Poole* —1F **69**
Lagoon Rd. *Poole* —1F **69**
Laidlaw Clo. *Poole* —5D **40**
Lake Av. *Poole* —6D **54**
Lake Cres. *Poole* —4E **55**
Lake Dri. *Poole* —5C **54**
(in two parts)
Lake Gro. Rd. *New M* —1F **49**
Lake Rd. *Bourn* —5D **24** .
Lake Rd. *Poole* —6D **54**
Lake Rd. *Ver* —5E **7**
Lakeside. *Hight* —5E **9**
Lakeside Pines. *New M* —1H **49**
Lakeside Rd. *Poole* —6C **58**
Lakeview Dri. *Hight* —5F **9**
Lakewood Rd. *Highc* —4G **47**
Lambs Clo. *Poole* —4A **38**
Lambs Grn. La. *Cor M* —1F **21**
Lampton Gdns. *Bourn* —4H **41**
Lancaster Clo. *Broad* —6F **21**
Lancaster Clo. *Christ* —6E **47**
Lancaster Dri. *Broad* —6E **21**
Lancaster Dri. *Ver* —3C **6**
Lancaster Rd. *Wim* —1G **17**
Lancer Clo. *Christ* —6D **44**
Lander Clo. *Poole* —6B **56** (5D **4**)
Landford Gdns. *Bourn* —3D **42**
Landford Way. *Bourn* —3D **42**
Landseer Rd. *Bourn* —4E **59**
Lanes, The. *New M* —6G **31**
Lane, The. *Bourn* —2C **60**
Langdon Ct. *Poole* —3H **57**
Langdon Rd. *Poole* —3G **57**
Langley Chase. *Ring* —2C **12**
Langley Rd. *Christ* —4G **47**
Langley Rd. *Poole* —3A **58**
Langside Av. *Poole* —5C **40**
Langton Clo. *Bart S* —5H **49**
Langton Rd. *Bourn* —2F **61**
Lansdowne Ct. *Bourn* —4C **60**
Lansdowne Cres. *Bourn* —4A **60**
Lansdowne Gdns. *Bourn* —3A **60**
Lansdowne Rd. *Bourn* —2A **60**
Lansdown Roundabout, The.
Bourn —4A **60**
Lapwing Rd. *Wim* —2A **16**
Lara Clo. *Bourn* —2D **42**
Larch Clo. *Hord* —2D **50**
Larch Clo. *Poole* —4E **37**
Larch Clo. *St I* —3C **12**
Larch Way. *Fern* —1A **18**
Lark Rd. *Christ* —1C **64**
Larks Clo. *Fern* —2H **17**
Larksfield Av. *Bourn* —2C **42**
Larkshill Clo. *New M* —1H **49**

Larks Ri. *Fern* —2H **17**
Lascelles Ct. *Bourn* —1H **61**
Lascelles Rd. *Bourn* —1H **61**
Latch Farm Av. *Christ* —5E **45**
Latimer Rd. *Bourn* —5H **41**
Latimers Clo. *Highc* —4H **47**
Laundry La. *Mil S* —3E **67**
Laurel Clo. *Christ* —4F **47**
Laurel Clo. *Cor M* —5D **20**
Laurel Clo. *Hord* —1C **50**
Laurel Clo. *St L* —3A **12**
Laurel Dri. *Broad* —1H **37**
Laurel Gdns. *Broad* —1A **38**
Laurel La. *St L* —4A **12**
Laurels, The. *Fern* —2A **18**
Lavender Clo. *Ver* —4G **7**
Lavender Dri. *Bourn* —1D **42**
Lavender Rd. *Hord* —2C **50**
Lavender Wlk. *Bourn* —1D **42**
Lavender Way. *Broad* —2D **36**
Lavinia Rd. *Poole* —6G **39**
Lawford Ri. *Bourn* —2A **42**
Lawford Rd. *Bourn* —1A **42**
Lawn Clo. *Mil S* —3E **67**
Lawn Ct. *Bourn* —3F **59**
Lawn Rd. *Mil S* —3E **67**
Lawn Rd. *Penn* —2D **52**
Lawns Clo. *Wim* —3C **16**
Lawns Rd. *Wim* —3B **16**
Lawns, The. *Christ* —5B **48**
Lawn Vw. *New M* —6D **30**
Lawrence Ct. *Bourn* —1C **60**
Lawrence Dri. *Poole* —6A **58**
Lawrence Rd. *Ring* —1E **9**
Lawson Rd. *Poole* —1F **57**
Layard Dri. *Wim* —2B **22**
Laymoor La. *Wim* —4D **16**
Layton Ct. *Poole* —2H **57**
Layton Rd. *Poole* —2H **57**
Leamington Rd. *Bourn* —6A **42**
Leap Hill Rd. *Bourn* —1G **61**
Learoyd Rd. *Poole* —6B **38**
Lea, The. *Ver* —4E **7**
Lea Way. *Bourn* —5A **24**
Lechlade Gdns. *Bourn* —5G **43**
Ledbury Rd. *Christ* —2B **64**
Ledgard Clo. *Poole* —3F **57**
Lee Ct. *Fern* —4B **18**
Leedam Rd. *Bourn* —1F **41**
Leelands. *Penn* —4F **53**
Lees Clo. *Christ* —1B **44**
Leeson Dri. *Fern* —2H **17**
Leeson Rd. *Bourn* —6E **43**
Legg La. *Wim* —5F **15**
Legion Clo. *Poole* —5E **55**
Legion Rd. *Poole* —5E **55**
Leicester Rd. *Poole* —3A **58**
Leigham Va. Rd. *Bourn* —3B **62**
Leigh Comn. *Wim* —4G **15**
Leigh Gdns. *Wim* —5F **15**
Leigh La. *Wim* —4G **15**
Leigh Pk. *L'ton* —1E **53**
Leigh Rd. *New M* —2G **49**
Leigh Rd. *Wim* —5E **15**
Leighton Lodge. *Bourn* —3F **59**
Lentham Clo. *Poole* —4B **38**
Lentune Way. *L'ton* —3F **53**
Le Patourel Clo. *Christ* —6H **45**
Leslie Rd. *Bourn* —5H **41**
Leslie Rd. *Poole* —4E **57**
Leven Av. *Bourn* —2F **59**
Leven Clo. *Bourn* —3F **59**
Levet's La. *Poole* —5H **55** (4A **4**)
Lewens Clo. *Wim* —5E **15**
Lewens La. *Wim* —5E **15**
Lewesdon Dri. *Broad* —1F **37**
Leybourne Av. *Bourn* —6E **25**
(in two parts)
Leybourne Clo. *Bourn* —6E **25**
Leydene Av. *Bourn* —4F **43**
Leydene Clo. *Bourn* —4F **43**
Leyland Rd. *Poole* —3A **40**
Leyside. *Christ* —6B **46**
Liberty Clo. *T Leg* —1F **11**
Liberty Ct. *Christ* —6D **44**

Library Rd. *Bourn* —4H **41**
Library Rd. *Fern* —4B **18**
Library Rd. *Poole* —2A **58**
Lilac Clo. *Ring* —3D **8**
Lilliput Ct. *Poole* —4F **57**
Lilliput Rd. *Poole* —1G **69**
Lime Clo. *Poole* —1D **56**
Lime Gro. *Evtn* —5H **51**
Lime Tree Ho. *L'ton* —1G **53**
Limited Rd. *Bourn* —4A **42**
Linbrook Almshouses. *Ring*
—1E **9**
Linbrook Ct. *Ring* —2C **8**
Lin Brook Dri. *Ring* —1E **9**
Linbrook Vw. *Ring* —1H **9**
Lincoln Av. *Bourn* —1D **60**
Lincoln Av. *Christ* —3D **44**
Lincoln Rd. *Poole* —6H **39**
Lindbergh Rd. *Wim* —1G **17**
Linden Clo. *W Parl* —2F **25**
Linden Ct. *Ring* —3B **8**
Linden Gdns. *Ring* —3B **8**
Linden Rd. *Bourn* —2A **42**
Linden Rd. *Poole* —1G **57**
Linden Rd. *W Parl* —2F **25**
Lindens, The. *Burt* —2H **45**
Linden Way. *L'ton* —1E **53**
Lindsay Gdns. *Poole* —3C **58**
Lindsay Mnr. *Poole* —3C **58**
Lindsay Pk. *Poole* —3C **58**
Lindsay Rd. *Poole* —3B **58**
Lindsey Ct. *Fern* —6A **18**
Lindurn Ct. *Poole* —3C **58**
Lineside. *Burt* —5G **45**
Linford Clo. *New M* —1G **49**
Linford Rd. *Ring* —2E **9**
Lingdale Rd. *Bourn* —1B **62**
Lingfield Grange. *Poole* —4D **58**
Ling Rd. *Poole* —5E **39**
Lingwood Av. *Christ* —1A **64**
Linhorns La. *New M* —6G **31**
Link Mall. *Poole* —5B **56** (3D **4**)
(off Dolphin Cen.)
Link Ri. *Cor M* —5E **21**
Links Dri. *Christ* —4B **44**
Linkside Av. *Bourn* —5E **43**
Links Rd. *Poole* —5H **57**
Links Vw. Av. *Poole* —6H **57**
Linmead Dri. *Bourn* —5C **24**
Linnet Clo. *Hight* —5E **9**
Linnet Ct. *New M* —3F **49**
Linnet Rd. *Poole* —5F **37**
Linnies La. *Sway* —4E **33**
Linthorpe Rd. *Poole* —3C **56**
Linwood Rd. *Bourn* —6B **42**
Lionheart Clo. *Bourn* —6H **23**
Lions Hill Way. *Ashy H* —3G **11**
Lions La. *Ashy H* —2H **11**
Lions Wood. *St L* —3A **12**
Lisle Clo. *L'ton* —2F **53**
Litchford Rd. *New M* —1A **50**
Lit. Barrs Dri. *New M* —1H **49**
Lit. Burn. *Sway* —1F **33**
Little Ct. *Poole* —1B **70**
(BH13)
Little Ct. *Poole* —2G **69**
(BH14)
Littlecroft Av. *Bourn* —2B **42**
Lit. Croft Rd. *Poole* —1F **57**
Lit. Dene Copse. *Penn* —3D **52**
Lit. Dewlands. *Ver* —3B **6**
Littledown Av. *Bourn* —6E **43**
Littledown Dri. *Bourn* —6E **43**
Lit. Forest Mans. *Bourn* —4A **60**
Lit. Forest Rd. *Bourn* —2F **59**
Lit. Fosters. *Poole* —3A **70**
Lit. Lonnen. *Wim* —1H **15**
Littlemead Clo. *Poole* —6G **37**
Littlemoor Av. *Bourn* —1H **39**
Livingstone Rd. *Bourn* —3H **61**
Livingstone Rd. *Christ* —6H **45**
Livingstone Rd. *Poole* —1F **57**
Livingstone Rd. *Wim* —5G **15**
Llewellin Clo. *Poole* —5C **36**
Llewellin Ct. *Poole* —6C **36**

Loch Rd. *Poole* —2A **58**
Lockerley Clo. *L'ton* —3G **53**
Locksley Dri. *Fern* —6A **18**
Lockyers Dri. *Fern* —3D **18**
Lockyers Rd. *Cor M* —3E **21**
Loders Clo. *Poole* —2B **38**
Lodge Clo. *Poole* —3A **58**
Lodge Ct. *Poole* —3A **58**
Lodge Rd. *Christ* —5C **44**
Lodge Rd. *Penn* —2D **52**
Loewy Cres. *Poole* —3H **39**
Lombard Av. *Bourn* —2B **62**
Lombardy Clo. *Ver* —4F **7**
London Tavern Cvn. Pk., The. *Ring*
—3E **9**
Lone Pine Dri. *W Parl* —6C **18**
Lone Pine Mobile Homes Pk. *Fern*
—6D **18**
Lone Pine Way. *W Parl* —1H **25**
Longacre Dri. *Fern* —5A **18**
Longbarrow Clo. *Bourn* —4F **43**
Longespee Rd. *Wim* —3B **22**
Longfield Dri. *Bourn* —5C **24**
Longfield Dri. *W Parl* —3G **25**
Longfield Rd. *Hord* —3F **51**
Longfleet Dri. *Poole* —4B **38**
(in two parts)
Longfleet Dri. *Wim* —5D **22**
Longfleet Rd. *Poole* —4B **56**
Longford Pl. *Penn* —4F **53**
Long La. *Ring* —6D **8**
Long La. *Wim* —2F **15**
Longleat Gdns. *New M* —2E **49**
Longmeadow La. *Poole* —6E **37**
Long Rd. *Bourn* —1E **41**
Lonnen Rd. *Wim* —2H **15**
Lonnen Wood Clo. *Wim* —1A **16**
Lonsdale Rd. *Bourn* —6H **41**
Loraine Av. *Highc* —5C **48**
Lord Clo. *Poole* —6D **38**
Lorne Pk. Rd. *Bourn* —4A **60**
Love La. *Mil S* —3D **66**
Lwr. Ashley Rd. *New M* —2B **50**
Lwr. Blandford Rd. *Broad* —2H **37**
Lwr. Buckland Rd. *L'ton* —6F **35**
Lwr. Golf Links Rd. *Broad* —6H **21**
Lwr. Meadend Rd. *Sway* —2D **32**
Lwr. Pennington La. *Penn*
—3F **53**
Lwr. Woodside. *L'ton* —5G **53**
Lowther Gdns. *Bourn* —2C **60**
Lowther Rd. *Bourn* —1A **60**
Lucas Rd. *Poole* —1G **57**
(BH12)
Lucas Rd. *Poole* —6H **55**
(BH15)
Lucerne Av. *Bourn* —2B **62**
Lucerne Rd. *Mil S* —3D **66**
Luckham Clo. *Bourn* —3B **42**
Luckham Gdns. *Bourn* —3C **42**
Luckham Pl. *Bourn* —3B **42**
Luckham Rd. *Bourn* —3B **42**
Luckham Rd. E. *Bourn* —3B **42**
Lucky La. *Pill* —2H **35**
Lulworth Av. *Poole* —6E **55**
Lulworth Clo. *Poole* —6E **55**
Lulworth Ct. *Poole* —5E **55**
Lulworth Cres. *Poole* —6E **55**
Lumby Dri. *Ring* —3D **8**
Lumby Dri. Cvn. Pk. *Ring* —3D **8**
Luscombe Rd. *Poole* —5G **57**
Luther Rd. *Bourn* —5H **41**
Lych Ga. Ct. *Ring* —5E **9**
Lydford Gdns. *Bourn* —3C **40**
Lydford Rd. *Bourn* —3C **40**
Lydgate. *Mil S* —2A **66**
Lydlinch Clo. *W Parl* —2F **25**
Lydwell Clo. *Bourn* —6B **24**
Lyell Rd. *Poole* —1G **57**
Lyme Cres. *Highc* —5H **47**
Lymefields. *Mil S* —1E **67**
Lymington Rd. *Christ & Highc*
—6E **47**
Lymington Rd. *Evtn & Mil S*
—5A **52**

Lymington Rd. *New M & Evtn*
(in two parts) —4G **49**
Lymore La. *Evtn & Mil S* —5A **52**
Lymore Valley. *Mil S* —6A **52**
Lyndale Clo. *Mil S* —2E **67**
Lyndhurst Rd. *Bock* —1B **46**
Lyndhurst Rd. *Christ & Hint*
—5C **46**
Lyne's La. *Ring* —4B **8**
Lynn Rd. *Poole* —5D **38**
Lynric Clo. *Bart S* —6G **49**
Lynton Cres. *Christ* —2B **44**
Lynwood Clo. *Fern* —2B **18**
Lynwood Ct. *L'ton* —2F **53**
Lynwood Dri. *Wim* —3C **22**
Lyon Av. *New M* —2H **49**
Lyon Rd. *Poole* —3A **40**
Lysander Clo. *Christ* —6D **46**
Lystra Rd. *Bourn* —2A **42**
Lytchett Dri. *Broad* —3F **37**
Lytchett Minster & Upton By-Pass.
Lyt Mi & Poole —5A **36**
Lytchett Way. *Poole* —1B **54**
Lyteltane Rd. *L'ton* —3F **53**
Lytham Rd. *Broad* —2G **37**
Lytton Rd. *Bourn* —2C **60**

Mabey Av. *Bourn* —3F **41**
MacAndrew Rd. *Poole* —2B **70**
Macaulay Rd. *Broad* —1G **37**
McIntyre Rd. *Hurn* —3F **27**
McKinley Rd. *Bourn* —5E **59**
Maclaren Rd. *Bourn* —2H **41**
Maclean Rd. *Bourn* —2B **40**
McWilliam Clo. *Poole* —5E **41**
McWilliam Rd. *Bourn* —3A **42**
Madeira Rd. *Bourn* —4A **60**
Madeira Rd. *Poole* —2H **57**
Madeira Wlk. *L'ton* —2H **53**
Madeline Clo. *Poole* —6F **39**
Madeline Cres. *Poole* —6F **39**
Madison Av. *Bourn* —1D **60**
Madrisa Ct. *L'ton* —1G **53**
Magdalen La. *Christ* —1E **63**
Magna Clo. *Bourn* —5B **24**
Magna Gdns. *Bourn* —5B **24**
Magna Rd. *Wim & Bourn* —3E **23**
Magnolia Clo. *Bourn* —2E **63**
Magnolia Clo. *Ver* —5G **7**
Magnolia Ct. *Bourn* —4F **59**
Magnolia Ho. *Bourn* —1H **41**
Magpie Clo. *Bourn* —2C **42**
Magpie Gro. *New M* —3F **49**
Mag's Barrow. *W Parl* —1G **25**
Maiden La. *L'ton* —4G **53**
Maidment Clo. *Bourn* —1A **40**
Main Rd. *Wal* —5H **35**
Maitlands, The. *Bourn* —5F **59**
Majorca Mans. *Bourn*
—4G **59** (3E **5**)
Malan Clo. *Poole* —5C **38**
Malcomb Clo. *Bourn* —4E **63**
Mallard Clo. *Bourn* —4C **42**
Mallard Clo. *Christ* —1C **64**
Mallard Clo. *Hord* —2E **51**
Mallard Rd. *Bourn* —4D **42**
Mallard Rd. *Wim* —2A **16**
Mallory Clo. *Christ* —5B **46**
Mallow Clo. *Broad* —2E **37**
Mallow Clo. *Christ* —5E **47**
Mallows, The. *New M* —1B **50**
Malmesbury Ct. *Bourn* —1C **60**
Malmesbury Pk. Pl. *Bourn* —2C **60**
Malmesbury Pk. Rd. *Bourn*
—1A **60**
Malmesbury Rd. *St L* —4A **12**
Maloren Way. *W Mr* —6E **11**
Malthouse. *Poole* —5A **56** (4B **4**)
Maltings, The. *Poole* —4C **56**
Malvern Clo. *Bourn* —2A **42**
Malvern Rd. *Bourn* —2A **42**
Manchester Rd. *Sway* —1F **33**
Mandale Clo. *Bourn* —1C **40**
Mandale Rd. *Bourn* —2B **40**

Manderley. *Mil S* —4E **67**
Manning Av. *Christ* —4E **47**
Mannings Heath Rd. *Poole* —3F **39**
Mannings Heath Roundabout.
 Poole —3F **39**
Mannington Pl. *Bourn* —4E **5**
Mannington Way. *W Mr* —5B **10**
Manor Av. *Poole* —5G **39**
Manor Clo. *Fern* —4C **18**
Manor Clo. *Mil S* —1D **66**
Manor Ct. *Ring* —3B **8**
Mnr. Farm Clo. *New M* —4F **49**
Mnr. Farm Rd. *Bourn* —5D **24**
Manor Farmyard. *Bourn* —2H **43**
Manor Gdns. *Ring* —3B **8**
Manor Gdns. *Ver* —3D **6**
Manor La. *Ver* —4D **6**
Manor Pk. *Poole* —2H **55**
Manor Rd. *Bourn* —4B **60**
Manor Rd. *Christ* —1E **63**
Manor Rd. *Mil S* —1D **66**
Manor Rd. *New M* —2G **49**
Manor Rd. *Ring* —4C **8**
Manor Rd. *Ver* —3D **6**
Manor Way. *Ver* —2D **6**
Mansel Clo. *Poole* —6E **41**
Mansfield Av. *Poole* —3G **57**
Mansfield Clo. *Poole* —3G **57**
Mansfield Clo. *W Parl* —1F **25**
Mansfield Rd. *Bourn* —4G **41**
Mansfield Rd. *Poole* —3G **57**
Mansfield Rd. *Ring* —4B **8**
Manton Clo. *H'wthy* —4E **55**
Manton Rd. *Poole* —4E **55**
 (in two parts)
Maple Clo. *Bart S* —6H **49**
Maple Clo. *Highc* —6H **47**
Maple Dri. *Fern* —1A **18**
Maple Rd. *Bourn* —5H **41**
Maple Rd. *Poole* —4B **56** (1D **4**)
Mapperton Clo. *Poole* —3D **38**
Marabout Clo. *Christ* —6A **46**
Marchwood Rd. *Bourn* —2E **41**
Marden Paddock. *Broc* —3E **73**
Margards La. *Ver* —4B **6**
 (in two parts)
Marian Clo. *Cor M* —1C **36**
Marianne Rd. *Poole* —5E **41**
Marianne Rd. *Wim* —2A **16**
Marian Rd. *Cor M* —1C **36**
Marie Clo. *Poole* —6H **39**
Marina Ct. *Bourn* —4E **61**
Marina Dri. *Poole* —6F **57**
Marina, The. *Bourn* —4E **61**
Marina Towers. *Bosc* —4E **61**
Marina Vw. *Christ* —2D **62**
Marine Dri. *Bart S* —6E **49**
Marine Dri. E. *Bart S* —6F **49**
Marine Dri. W. *Bart S* —6D **48**
Marine Point. *Bart S* —6F **49**
Marine Prospect. *Bart S* —6F **49**
Marine Rd. *Bourn* —4B **62**
Mariners Ct. *L'ton* —3H **53**
Market Clo. *Poole* —5A **56** (4B **4**)
Market Pl. *Ring* —4B **8**
Market St. *Poole* —6H **55** (5A **4**)
Market Way. *Wim* —5F **15**
Markham Av. *Bourn* —5F **25**
Markham Clo. *Bourn* —4F **25**
Markham Rd. *Bourn* —5A **42**
Mark's La. *New M* —5G **31**
Marks Rd. *Bourn* —2H **41**
Marlborough Ct. Poole —3D **58**
 (off Poole Rd.)
Marlborough Ct. *Wim* —4E **15**
Marlborough Mans. *Bourn*
 —1H **61**
Marlborough Pl. *L'ton* —6F **35**
Marlborough Pl. *Wim* —4F **15**
Marlborough Rd. *Bourn* —4E **59**
Marlborough Rd. *Poole* —3G **57**
Marley Av. *New M* —1E **49**
Marley Clo. *New M* —2F **49**
Marley Mt. *Sway* —2C **32**
Marline Rd. *Poole* —1H **57**

Marlott Rd. *Poole* —2A **56**
Marlow Dri. *Christ* —2B **44**
Marlpit Dri. *Walk* —3A **48**
Marlpit La. *New M* —3G **31**
Marmion Grn. *Christ* —6B **46**
Marnhull Rd. *Poole* —3B **56**
Marpet Clo. *Bourn* —5B **24**
Marquis Way. *Bourn* —6G **23**
Marram Clo. *L'ton* —5G **35**
Marryat Ct. *Christ* —6B **48**
Marryat Ct. *New M* —2F **49**
Marryat Rd. *New M* —2F **49**
Marshal Rd. *Poole* —4H **37**
Marshfield. *Wim* —2H **15**
Marsh La. *Christ* —3D **44**
 (Fairmile Rd., in two parts)
Marsh La. *Christ* —1H **63**
 (Purewell, in two parts)
Marsh La. *L'ton* —5F **35**
Marsh La. *Poole* —6A **36**
Marshwood Av. *Poole* —3D **38**
Marston Clo. *New M* —6H **31**
Marston Gro. *Christ* —4G **47**
Marston Rd. *New M* —6H **31**
Marston Rd. *Poole* —5H **55** (4A **4**)
Martello Pk. *Poole* —2B **70**
Martello Rd. *Poole* —6A **58**
Martello Rd. S. *Poole* —6B **58**
Martells, The. *New M* —6H **49**
Martin Clo. *Poole* —6F **37**
Martindale Av. *Wim* —4B **16**
 (in two parts)
Martingale Clo. *Uptn* —6D **36**
Martins Clo. *Fern* —2C **18**
Martins Dri. *Fern* —1C **18**
Martin's Hill Clo. *Burt* —4G **45**
Martins Hill La. *Burt* —4G **45**
Martins Rd. *Broc* —2F **73**
Martins Way. *Fern* —2C **18**
Marwell Clo. *Bourn* —6G **43**
Maryland Ct. *Mil S* —3B **66**
Maryland Gdns. *Mil S* —3B **66**
Maryland Rd. *Poole* —3C **54**
Mary La. *W Mr* —5C **10**
Mary Mitchell Clo. Ring —4B **8**
 (off Bickerley Rd.)
Masters Ct. *Bourn* —4F **59**
Masterson Clo. *Christ* —6H **45**
Matcham La. *Hurn* —4H **27**
Matlock Rd. *Fern* —6A **18**
Maturin Clo. *L'ton* —2F **53**
Maundeville Cres. *Christ* —5B **44**
Maundeville Rd. *Christ* —5C **44**
Maureen Clo. *Poole* —6F **39**
Maurice Rd. *Bourn* —5D **42**
Mavis Rd. *Bourn* —4B **42**
Maxwell Rd. *Bourn* —6A **42**
Maxwell Rd. *Broad* —2D **36**
Maxwell Rd. *Poole* —2B **70**
May Av. *L'ton* —6F **35**
Mayfair Ct. *Bourn* —5E **59**
Mayfair Gdns. *Bourn* —1C **40**
Mayfield Av. *Poole* —4A **58**
Mayfield Clo. *Fern* —3A **18**
Mayfield Dri. *Fern* —3A **18**
Mayfield Rd. *Bourn* —3H **41**
Mayfield Way. *Fern* —3A **18**
Mayflower Clo. *L'ton* —2H **53**
Mayford Rd. *Poole* —1D **58**
May Gdns. *Bourn* —2A **40**
May Gdns. *Walk* —3B **48**
May La. *Pill* —2H **35**
Maylyn Rd. *Bcn H* —3A **36**
Mead Clo. *Broad* —4G **37**
Mead End Rd. *Sway* —2D **32**
Meadowbank. *Poole* —5C **36**
Meadow Clo. *Brans* —3C **28**
Meadow Clo. *Ring* —2D **8**
Meadow Clo. *W Parl* —2F **25**
Meadow Ct. *Bourn* —2A **42**
Meadow Ct. Clo. *Bourn* —2A **42**
Mdw. Crest Wood. *Broc* —2C **72**
Mdw. Farm La. *Cor M* —3D **20**
Meadow Gro. *Ver* —4F **7**
Meadow Land. *Christ* —1B **64**

Meadowlands. *L'ton* —1D **52**
Meadowlands. *Ring* —6C **8**
Meadow La. *Burt* —3G **45**
 (in two parts)
Meadow Ri. *Broad* —6F **21**
Meadow Rd. *New M* —1H **49**
Meadow Rd. *Penn* —3E **53**
Meadow Rd. *Ring* —3D **8**
Meadows Cvn. Site, The. *New M*
 —4F **49**
Meadows Clo. *Poole* —5C **36**
Meadows Dri. *Poole* —6C **36**
Meadowsweet Rd. *Poole* —5E **37**
Meadow, The. *Lyn* —4F **71**
Meadow, The. *New M* —5C **48**
Mdw. View Rd. *Bourn* —1A **40**
Meadow Way. *Bart S* —6G **49**
Meadow Way. *Ring* —3D **8**
Meadow Way. *Ver* —4E **7**
Mead Rd. *Penn* —3D **52**
Meadway, The. *Christ* —3F **47**
Medina Way. *Christ* —1E **65**
Medlar Clo. *Burt* —4H **45**
Medway Rd. *Fern* —3E **19**
Meerut Rd. *Broc* —2E **73**
Meeting Ho. La. *Ring* —4B **8**
Melbourne Rd. *Bourn* —1C **60**
Melbourne Rd. *Christ* —4C **44**
Melbury Av. *Poole* —6H **39**
Melbury Clo. *Fern* —5B **18**
Melbury Clo. *L'ton* —2F **53**
Mellstock Rd. *Poole* —2A **56**
Melrose Ct. *New M* —2A **50**
Melton Ct. *Poole* —3C **58**
Melverley Gdns. *Wim* —4F **15**
Melville Gdns. *Bourn* —5G **41**
Melville Rd. *Bourn* —5G **41**
Mendip Clo. *New M* —3H **49**
Mendip Clo. *Ver* —4D **6**
Mendip Rd. *Ver* —3D **6**
Mentone Rd. *Poole* —4E **57**
Meon Rd. *Bourn* —1H **61**
Meredith Clo. *Christ* —6A **46**
Meriden Clo. *Poole* —2B **70**
Meridians, The. *Christ* —1D **62**
Merino Way. *W Mr* —6D **10**
Merlewood Clo. *Bourn*
 —3H **59** (1G **5**)
Merley Ct. Touring Pk. *Wim*
 —2H **21**
Merley Dri. *Highc* —5A **48**
Merley Gdns. *Wim* —2B **22**
Merley Ho. La. *Wim* —2H **21**
Merley La. *Wim* —2B **22**
Merley Pk. Rd. *Ashtn* —3F **21**
Merley Ways. *Wim* —1A **22**
Merlin Clo. *Hight* —5E **9**
Merlin Way. *Christ* —2C **64**
Mermaid Ct. *Bosc* —4E **61**
Merriefield Av. *Broad* —6H **21**
Merriefield Clo. *Broad* —5H **21**
Merriefield Dri. *Broad* —5H **21**
Merrifield. *Wim* —1G **15**
Merritown La. *Hurn* —4D **26**
Merrivale Av. *Bourn* —2C **62**
Merrow Av. *Poole* —6D **40**
Merryfield Clo. *Brans* —3C **28**
Merryfield Clo. *Ver* —3D **6**
Merryfield La. *Bourn* —1E **41**
Merryweather Est. *Ring* —3E **9**
Merton Gro. *Ring* —3B **8**
Methuen Clo. *Bourn* —2C **60**
Methuen Rd. *Bourn* —2B **60**
Methuen Rd. *Poole* —3H **37**
Mews, The. *Bourn* —4F **59**
Meyrick Clo. *Brans* —4C **28**
Meyrick Pk. Cres. *Bourn* —1H **59**
Meyrick Pk. Mans. *Bourn*
 —3H **59** (2G **5**)
Meyrick Rd. *Bourn* —4B **60**
Michelgrove Rd. *Bourn* —4E **61**
Michelmersh Grn. *Bourn* —3D **42**
Mickleham Clo. *Poole* —5D **40**
Middlebere Cres. *Poole* —3C **54**
Middle Comn. Rd. *Penn* —2C **52**

Middlehill Dri. *Wim* —3B **16**
Middlehill Rd. *Wim* —2H **15**
Middle La. *Ring* —4C **8**
Middle Rd. *Bourn* —6E **25**
Middle Rd. *L'ton* —2F **53**
Middle Rd. *Poole* —1C **56**
Middle Rd. *Sway* —1F **33**
Middle Rd. *Tip* —3B **32**
Middleton Rd. *Bourn* —3G **41**
Middleton Rd. *Ring* —3C **8**
Midland Rd. *Bourn* —4H **41**
Midway Path. *Poole* —6G **69**
Midwood Av. *Bourn* —4F **43**
Milborne Cres. *Poole* —6A **40**
Milbourne Rd. *Fern* —3A **18**
Milburn Clo. *Bourn* —3E **59**
Milburn Rd. *Bourn* —3D **58**
Mildenhall. *Bourn* —5F **59**
Milestone Rd. *Poole* —1B **56**
Milford Clo. *W Mr* —5D **10**
Milford Ct. *Mil S* —3E **67**
Milford Cres. *Mil S* —2E **67**
Milford Dri. *Bourn* —6B **24**
Milford Pl. *Mil S* —4E **67** ·
Milford Rd. *Evtn & Penn* —5A **52**
Milford Rd. *L'ton* —3F **53**
Milford Rd. *New M* —4H **49**
Milford Trad. Est. *Mil S* —3E **67**
Millbank Ho. *Wim* —4E **15**
Miller Clo. *New M* —1A **50**
Miller Rd. *Christ* —6H **45**
Millfield. *Poole* —6G **37**
Millhams Clo. *Bourn* —5D **24**
Millhams Dri. *Bourn* —5D **24**
Millhams Rd. *Bourn* —4C **24**
Millhams St. *Christ* —1F **63**
Millhams St. N. *Christ* —1F **63**
Mill Hill Clo. *Poole* —4F **57**
Mill La. *Broc* —3F **73**
Mill La. *Highc* —5B **48**
 (Lymington Rd.)
Mill La. *Highc* —5H **27**
 (Parley La.)
Mill La. *L'ton* —1H **53**
Mill La. *Penn* —4H **33**
Mill La. *Poole* —5F **57**
 (in two parts)
Mill La. *Wim* —4D **14**
Mill Mdw. *Mil S* —2C **66**
Mill Rd. *Christ* —5E **45**
Mill Rd. N. *Bourn* —2D **42**
Mill Rd. S. *Bourn* —3D **42**
Mills, The. *Poole* —1A **58**
Millstream Clo. *Poole* —6G **37**
Millstream Clo. *Wim* —5E **15**
Millstream Trad. Est. *Ring* —6C **8**
Mill St. *Cor M* —1A **20**
Millyford Clo. *New M* —5D **48**
Milne Rd. *Poole* —4H **37**
Milner Rd. *Bourn* —5E **59**
Milton Clo. *Poole* —4H **57**
Milton Ct. *Fern* —4B **18**
Milton Gro. *New M* —3H **49**
Milton Mead. *New M* —3F **49**
Milton Rd. *Bourn* —2A **60**
Milton Rd. *Poole* —4H **57**
Milton Rd. *Wim* —3E **15**
Milverton Clo. *Christ* —4G **47**
Mimosa Av. *Wim* —3B **22**
Minstead Rd. *Bourn* —2E **41**
Minster Pk. *W Moor* —2C **10**
Minster Vw. *Wim* —4E **15**
Minster Way. *Poole* —5B **36**
Minterne Grange. *Poole* —2G **69**
Minterne Rd. *Bourn* —3A **42**
Minterne Rd. *Christ* —1A **64**
Minterne Rd. *Poole* —2G **69**
Mission La. *Broad* —3G **37**
Mission Rd. *Broad* —3G **37**
Mitchell Clo. *Bart S* —6G **49**
Mitchell Rd. *Fern I* —2G **17**
Mitchell Rd. *Poole* —5D **38**
Moat Ct. *Bourn* —2D **58**
Moat La. *Bart S* —4F **49**
 (in two parts)

Oban Rd. *Bourn* —6G **41**
Oberfield Rd. *Broc* —2C **72**
Ober Rd. *Broc* —2D **72**
Ocean Heights. *Bourn* —4F **61**
Okeford Rd. *Broad* —3A **38**
O.K. Mobile Home Pk. *Christ* —5D **46**
Old Barn Clo. *Christ* —3B **44**
Old Barn Clo. *Ring* —4E **9**
Old Barn Farm Rd. *T Leg* —2E **11**
Old Barn Rd. *Christ* —3B **44**
Old Bound Rd. *Poole* —1C **54**
Old Bridge Rd. *Bourn* —5B **44**
Old Christchurch La. *Bourn* —4H **59** (3H **5**)
Old Christchurch Rd. *Bourn* (in two parts) —4H **59** (4G **5**)
Old Christchurch Rd. *Evtn* —4H **51**
Old Coastguard Rd. *Poole* —5F **69**
Old Farm Clo. *Poul* —1E **9**
Old Farmhouse M. L'ton —6G **35** (off Lwr. Buckland Rd.)
Old Farm Rd. *Poole* —1C **56**
Old Farm Wlk. *L'ton* —2F **53**
Old Forge Rd. *Wim* —3F **17**
Old Ham La. *Wim* —4C **16**
Old Highways M. *Wim* —5G **15**
Old Kiln Rd. *Poole* —6D **36**
Old Maltings, The. *L'ton* —1F **53**
Old Mnr. Clo. *Wim* —5G **15**
Old Mkt. Rd. *Cor M* —3A **20**
Old Mill Flats. *Ring* —5B **8**
Old Milton Grn. *New M* —4F **49**
Old Milton Rd. *New M* —4F **49**
Old Orchard. *Poole* —6A **56** (5B **4**) (in three parts)
Old Orchards. *L'ton* —3H **53**
Old Orchard Shop. Cen. Poole (off Princess Rd.) —3C **58**
Old Orchard Shop. Cen. *Poole* (Old Orchard) —6A **56** (5B **4**)
Old Pines Clo. *Fern* —5C **18**
Old Priory Rd. *Bourn* —3D **62**
Old Rectory Clo. *Cor M* —2D **20**
Old Rd. *Wim* —5D **14**
Old Rope Wlk., The. *Poole* —6F **55**
Old St Johns M. *Bourn* —2H **41**
Old Sawmill Clo. *Ver* —2B **6**
Old School Clo. *Fern* —4A **18**
Old School Clo. *Poole* —3E **57**
Old Stacks Gdns. *Ring* —5E **9**
Old Town M. *Poole* —4B **4**
Old Vicarage Clo. *Bourn* —5G **25**
Old Vicarage La. *Sway* —2G **33**
Old Wareham Rd. *Bcn H & Cor M* —3A **36**
Old Wareham Rd. *Poole* —6E **39**
Oliver Rd. *Penn* —2E **53**
Olivers Rd. *Wim* —3A **16**
Olivers Way. *Wim* —3A **16**
Onslow Gdns. *Wim* —3F **15**
Ophir Gdns. *Bourn* —2B **60**
Ophir Rd. *Bourn* —2B **60**
Oratory Gdns. *Poole* —1B **70**
Orchard Av. *Poole* —5D **56**
Orchard Clo. *Christ* —1E **63**
Orchard Clo. *Cor M* —4D **20**
Orchard Clo. *Fern* —4C **18**
Orchard Clo. *Ring* —3C **8**
Orchard Ct. *New M* —2H **49**
Orchard Ct. *Ver* —4E **7**
Orchard Gro. *New M* —4G **49**
Orchard La. *Cor M* —4D **20**
Orchard Leigh. *New M* —3H **49**
Orchard St. *Bourn* —4G **59** (4F **5**)
Orchard, The. *Bourn* —5H **23**
Orchard, The. *Brans* —3E **29**
Orchard, The. *Mil S* —3D **66**
Orchard Wlk. *Bourn* —4G **59** (4F **5**)
Orcheston Rd. *Bourn* —1B **60**
Orchid Way. *Christ* —6G **45**
Orford Clo. *Christ* —1B **44**
Ormonde Rd. *Poole* —5C **58**
Osborne Ct. *Mil S* —3C **66**

Osborne Rd. *Bourn* —5G **41**
Osborne Rd. *New M* —2G **49**
Osborne Rd. *Poole* —4F **57**
Osborne Rd. *Wim* —5F **15**
Osprey Clo. *Christ* —2C **64**
Ossemsley S. Dri. *New M* —3E **31**
Oswald Clo. *Bourn* —3G **41**
Oswald Rd. *Bourn* —3G **41**
Otterbourne. *Bourn* —3F **59**
Otter Clo. *Poole* —1B **54**
Otter Clo. *Ver* —4E **7**
Otter Rd. *Poole* —1D **56**
Otters Wlk. *New M* —5H **31**
Overbury Rd. *Poole* —4G **57**
Overcliffe Mans. *Bourn* —4C **60**
Overcombe Clo. *Poole* —2C **38**
Over Links Dri. *Poole* —5H **57**
Overstrand Cres. *Mil S* —4D **66**
Ovington Av. *Bourn* —6A **44**
Ovington Gdns. *Bourn* —6A **44**
Owls Rd. *Bourn* —4D **60**
Owls Rd. *Ver* —3E **7**
Oxey Clo. *New M* —4G **49**
Oxford Av. *Bourn* —2H **61**
Oxford La. *Bourn* —5D **24**
Oxford Rd. *Bourn* —3B **60**
Oxford Ter. *Sway* —1F **33**

Paddington Clo. *Bourn* —1H **39**
Paddington Gro. *Bourn* —2H **39**
Paddock. *New M* —6C **48**
Paddock Clo. *Park* —1F **57**
Paddock Clo. *St I* —3B **12**
Paddock Clo. *Wim* —3G **17**
Paddock Gdns. *L'ton* —6F **35**
Paddock Gro. *Ver* —4E **7**
Paddocks, The. *Bourn* —1F **41**
Paddock, The. *Broc* —3E **73**
Padfield Clo. *Bourn* —1C **62**
Padget Rd. *Ring* —2E **9**
Paget Clo. *Wim* —2A **16**
Paget Rd. *Bourn* —1C **40**
Paisley Rd. *Bourn* —1A **62**
Palfrey Rd. *Bourn* —1F **41**
Palma Apartments. *New M* —6C **48**
Palmer Pl. *New M* —1G **49**
Palmer Rd. *Poole* —2A **56**
Palmerston Av. *Christ* —1H **63**
Palmerston Clo. *Poole* —6D **36**
Palmerston M. *Bourn* —2E **61**
Palmerston Rd. *Bourn* —2E **61**
Palmerston Rd. *Poole* —3H **57**
Palmerston Rd. *Uptn* —6C **36**
Pamplyn Clo. *L'ton* —1E **53**
Panorama Rd. *Poole* —6F **69**
Pans Corner. *Fern* —6D **18**
Parade, The. *Bourn* —4C **62**
Parade, The. *Cor M* —6D **20**
Parade, The. *New M* —2B **50** (Ashley Rd.)
Parade, The. *New M* —4F **49** (Southern La.)
Parade, The. *Wat* —4H **37**
Paradise St. *Poole* —6H **55** (5A **4**)
Pardy's Hill. *Cor M* —3C **20**
Parham Clo. *New M* —2E **49**
Parham Rd. *Bourn* —3E **41**
Parish Ct. *L'ton* —1G **53**
Parish Rd. *Poole* —4C **56**
Park Av. *Bourn* —5E **25**
Park Av. *L'ton* —1F **53**
Park Clo. *Broc* —2F **73**
Park Clo. *Burt* —2G **45**
Park Clo. *Mil S* —3E **67**
Park Clo. *New M* —6A **32**
Park Ct. *Mil S* —3C **66**
Park Ct. *Poole* —4D **58**
Park Dri. *Ver* —2C **6**
Parker Rd. *Bourn* —6H **41**
Park Gdns. *Christ* —6A **46**
Park Ga. M. *Bourn* —4E **5**
Pk. Homer Dri. *Wim* —2H **15**

Pk. Homer Rd. *Wim* —2H **15**
Pk. Lake Rd. *Poole* —5C **56**
Parkland Clo. *Ver* —5H **7**
Parkland Dri. *Bart S* —5F **49**
Park La. *Bourn* —1H **41**
Park La. *Mil S* —3C **66**
Park La. *Wim* —5E **15**
Park Mans. *Bourn* —6C **42**
Park Pl. *Poole* —3D **56**
Park Rd. *Bourn* —3A **60**
Park Rd. *L'ton* —1F **53**
Park Rd. *Mil S* —3E **67**
Park Rd. *New M* —6A **32** (Ashley Comn. Rd.)
Park Rd. *New M* —4F **49** (Christchurch Rd.)
Park Rd. *Poole* —4D **56**
Parkside. *Christ* —4F **47**
Parkside. *Ring* —5C **8**
Parkside Gdns. *Bourn* —3G **41**
Parkside Rd. *Poole* —3G **57**
Parkstone Av. *Poole* —3G **57**
Parkstone Heights. *Poole* —2D **56** (in two parts)
Parkstone Rd. *Poole* —4B **56** (2D **4**)
Park, The. *New M* —6C **48**
Parkview. *Bourn* —3G **59** (2F **5**)
Park Vw. *New M* —3G **49**
Park Vw. *Poole* —4C **56**
Pk. View Ct. *Bourn* —6C **42**
Park Way. *W Mr* —5B **10**
Parkway Dri. *Bourn* —5D **42**
Parkway Retail Pk. *Bourn* —3C **60**
Parkwood La. Bourn —2H **61** (off Hosker Rd.)
Parkwood Rd. *Bourn* —2G **61**
Parkwood Rd. *Wim* —5E **15**
Parley Clo. *W Parl* —2H **25**
Parley La. *Parl* —3B **26**
Parley Rd. *Bourn* —3A **42**
Parmiter Dri. *Wim* —5G **15**
Parmiter Rd. *Wim* —5G **15**
Parmiter Way. *Wim* —5G **15**
Parr Ho. *Poole* —3E **57**
Parr St. *Poole* —3E **57**
Parsonage Barn La. *Ring* —3C **8**
Parsonage Rd. *Bourn* —4A **60** (4H **5**)
Partridge Clo. *Christ* —2C **64**
Partridge Dri. *Poole* —6F **57**
Partridge Grn. *New M* —5H **31**
Partridge Rd. *Broc* —4E **73**
Partridge Wlk. *Poole* —6G **57**
Pascoe Clo. *Poole* —3E **57**
Passford Hill. *L'ton* —4F **35**
Patchins Rd. *Poole* —3B **54** (in two parts)
Pauls La. *Sway* —3H **33**
Pauncefote Rd. *Bourn* —2G **61**
Pauntley Rd. *Christ* —1A **64**
Pavan Gdns. *Bourn* —3E **41**
Payne Clo. *W Mr* —2C **10**
Peace Clo. *Brans* —3C **28**
Pearce Av. *Poole* —6E **57**
Pearce Gdns. *Poole* —6E **57**
Pearce Rd. *Poole* —1B **54**
Pearcesmith Ct. *Bart S* —6E **49**
Pear Clo. *Poole* —3D **58**
Pearl Gdns. *Bourn* —1E **41**
Pearl Rd. *Bourn* —1E **41**
Pearman Ct. *Penn* —3E **53**
Pearman Dri. *L'ton* —3H **53**
Pearson Av. *Poole* —2F **57**
Pearson Gdns. *Bourn* —5F **25**
Pear Tree Clo. *Brans* —3D **28**
Peartree Ct. *L'ton* —3G **53**
Peckham Av. *New M* —3G **49**
Peddlars Wlk. *Ring* —4B **8**
Peel Clo. *Poole* —2G **57**
Peel Ct. *Christ* —1D **62**
Pegasus Av. *Hord* —3E **51**
Pegasus Ct. *Bourn* —2A **60**
Pegasus Ct. *New M* —2G **49**
Pelham. *Poole* —3C **58**

Pelham Clo. *Christ* —1H **63**
Pelican Mead. *Hight* —5E **9**
Pembroke Rd. *Bourn* —5D **58**
Pembroke Rd. *Poole* —6H **39**
Pen Craig. *Poole* —4D **58**
Penelope Ct. *Christ* —6B **48**
Pengelly Av. *Bourn* —6G **25**
Pennant Way. *Christ* —6B **46**
Penn Clo. *Bart S* —4E **49**
Penn Ct. *W Mr* —5B **10**
Penn Hill Av. *Poole* —4H **57**
Pennine Way. *Ver* —4D **6**
Pennington Clo. *Penn* —3E **53**
Pennington Clo. *W Mr* —6B **10**
Pennington Cres. *W Mr* —5B **10**
Pennington Oval. *Penn* —3D **52**
Pennington Rd. *W Mr* —6B **10**
Penny Hedge. *New M* —5H **49**
Penny La. *Bourn* —3E **61**
Penny's Ct. *Fern* —4B **18**
Penny's Wlk. *Fern* —4B **18**
Penny Way. *Christ* —1E **65**
Pennywell Gdns. *New M* —1B **50**
Penrith Clo. *Ver* —4C **6**
Penrith Rd. *Bourn* —3G **61**
Penrose Rd. *Fern* —3B **18**
Percy Rd. *Bourn* —3E **61**
Peregrine Rd. *Christ* —1C **64**
Pergin Cres. *Poole* —6H **37**
Pergin Way. *Poole* —6H **37**
Perryfield Gdns. *Bourn* —5H **43**
Perry Gdns. *Poole* —6A **56** (5C **4**) (in two parts)
Persley Rd. *Bourn* —1F **41**
Perth Clo. *Christ* —4C **44**
Peter Grant Way. *Fern* —4A **18**
Peters Clo. *Poole* —1C **54**
Petersfield Pl. *Bourn* —6H **43**
Petersfield Rd. *Bourn* —1G **61** (in two parts)
Petersham Rd. *Poole* —5F **37**
Peters Rd. *Fern* —6D **18**
Petit Rd. *Bourn* —2A **42**
Petwyn Clo. *Fern* —3E **19**
Peverell Rd. *Poole* —3B **54**
Peveril Clo. *Ashy H* —1B **12**
Phelipps Rd. *Cor M* —4D **20**
Phyldon Clo. *Poole* —2F **57**
Phyldon Rd. *Poole* —1F **57**
Pickard Rd. *Fern* —2D **18**
Pickering Clo. *Broad* —3G **37**
Pickford Rd. *Bourn* —4G **41**
Pier App. *Bourn* —5H **59** (5H **5**)
Pig Shoot La. *Hurn* —1F **43**
Pikes Hill Av. *Lyn* —2E **71**
Pilford Heath Rd. *Wim* —1A **16**
Pilford La. *Pilf* —1A **16**
Pilgrim Pk. Homes. *Ring* —3E **9**
Pilgrim's Clo. *New M* —1A **50**
Pilgrims Way. *Poole* —6G **37**
Pilley Hill. *Pill* —2G **35**
Pilley St. *Pill* —2H **35**
Pilot Hight Rd. *Bourn* —1C **40**
Pilsdon Dri. *Poole* —3C **38**
Pimpern Clo. *Poole* —3C **38**
Pine Av. *Bourn* —3A **62**
Pine Av. *Poole* —6B **40**
Pinebeach Ct. *Poole* —1C **70**
Pinecliffe Av. *Bourn* —3A **62**
Pinecliffe Rd. *New M* —6C **48**
Pinecliff Rd. *Poole* —1C **70**
Pine Clo. *Bart S* —5E **49**
Pine Clo. *Fern* —2A **18**
Pine Cres. *Highc* —6G **47**
Pine Dri. *Poole* —4B **58** (in two parts)
Pine Dri. *St I* —3B **12**
Pine Dri. E. *Poole* —5C **58**
Pine End. *Fern* —6D **18**
Pine Glen Av. *Fern* —1A **18**
Pine Grange. *Bourn* —4A **60**
Pineholt Clo. *St I* —2C **12**
Pinehurst. *Mil S* —3C **66**
Pinehurst Av. *Christ* —2B **64**
Pinehurst Pk. *W Mr* —1D **18**

Pinehurst Rd. *W Mr* —6C **10**
Pinelands Ct. *Bourn* —6C **42**
Pine Mnr. Rd. *Ashy H* —2H **11**
Pine Pk. Mans. *Poole* —3C **58**
Pine Rd. *Bourn* —4H **41**
Pine Rd. *Cor M* —2F **21**
Pinesprings Dri. *Broad* —3E **37**
Pines, The. *Poole* —5C **58**
Pinetops Clo. *Penn* —2D **52**
Pine Tree Glen. *Bourn* —4E **59**
Pine Tree Wlk. *Poole* —5F **37**
Pine Va. Cres. *Bourn* —2G **41**
Pine Vw. Clo. *Poole* —1C **54**
Pine Vw. Clo. *Ver* —2B **6**
Pine Vw. Rd. *Ver* —2B **6**
Pine Wlk. *Ver* —4F **7**
Pinewood Av. *Bourn* —6F **25**
Pinewood Clo. *Bourn* —6F **25**
Pinewood Clo. *Poole* —6A **36**
Pinewood Clo. *Walk* —3A **48**
Pinewood Gdns. *Fern* —2B **18**
Pinewood Rd. *Brnk P* —6D **58**
Pinewood Rd. *Fern* —1A **18**
Pinewood Rd. *Highc* —4H **47**
Pinewood Rd. *Hord* —2C **50**
Pinewood Rd. *St I* —3B **12**
Pinewood Rd. *Uptn* —6A **36**
Pipers Ash. *Ring* —3E **9**
Pipers Dri. *Christ* —6C **46**
Pippin Clo. *Christ* —3C **44**
Pippin Clo. *L'ton* —3G **53**
Pitmore La. *Sway & Penn* —1G **33**
Pittmore Rd. *Burt* —3G **45**
Pitts Pl. *New M* —3B **50**
Pitwines Clo. *Poole* —5A **56** (4D **4**)
Plantaganet Cres. *Bourn* —6H **23**
Plantation. *Evtn* —5A **52**
Plantation Ct. *L'ton* —1F **53**
Plantation Ct. *Poole* —4A **38**
Plantation Dri. *Walk* —3A **48**
Plantation Rd. *Poole* —4A **38**
Plant Pk. Rd. *Ring* —4E **13**
Plassey Cres. *Bourn* —6E **25**
Platoff Rd. *L'ton* —5G **53**
Playfields Dri. *Poole* —1A **58**
Pleasance Way. *New M* —2F **49**
Plecy Clo. *W Parl* —6B **18**
Plemont Clo. *Poole* —4A **40**
Pless Rd. *Mil S* —2A **66**
Plover Dri. *Mil S* —3F **67**
Plumer Rd. *Poole* —4G **37**
Poles La. *L'ton* —4G **53**
Policemans La. *Poole* —6A **36**
Pomona Clo. *Fern* —3B **18**
Pompey's La. *Fern* —5G **17**
(in two parts)
Pond Clo. *New M* —2G **49**
Ponsonby Rd. *Poole* —3H **57**
Pony Dri. *Uptn* —6D **36**
Poole Commerce Cen. *Poole*
—2B **58**
Poole Hill. *Bourn* —4F **59**
Poole La. *Bourn* —1B **40**
Poole La. Roundabout. *Bourn*
—1A **40**
Poole Rd. *Bourn* —3D **58**
Poole Rd. *Brnk* —3B **58**
Poole Rd. *Uptn & Poole* —6C **36**
Poole Rd. *Wim* —5E **15**
Popes Rd. *Poole* —1B **56**
Poplar Clo. *Brans* —3E **29**
Poplar Clo. *Highc* —5B **48**
Poplar Clo. *Poole* —5A **4**
Poplar Clo. *Wim* —4F **15**
Poplar Cres. *Ring* —4D **8**
Poplar La. *Brans* —2E **29**
Poplar Rd. *New M* —1B **50**
Poplar Way. *Ring* —4D **8**
Poppy Clo. *Christ* —5D **46**
Portarlington Clo. *Bourn* —5F **59**
Portarlington Rd. *Bourn* —4E **59**
Portchester Ct. *Bourn* —2B **60**
Portchester Pl. *Bourn* —2B **60**
Portchester Rd. *Bourn* —1A **60**

Portelet Clo. *Poole* —4H **39**
Porter Rd. *Poole* —6H **37**
Porters La. *Wim* —3C **16**
Portesham Gdns. *Bourn* —1B **42**
Portesham Way. *Poole* —2C **38**
Portfield Clo. *Christ* —5E **45**
Portfield Rd. *Christ* —6D **44**
Portland Pl. *Bourn* —3H **59** (1H **5**)
Portland Rd. *Bourn* —4A **42**
Portman Cres. *Bourn* —3H **61**
Portman Rd. *Bourn* —2F **61**
Portman Ter. *Bourn* —3H **61**
Portmore Clo. *Broad* —5A **22**
Portswood Dri. *Bourn* —1A **42**
Port Vw. Cvn. Pk. *Hurn* —1H **27**
Post Office La. *Poole* —3C **4**
Post Office La. *St I* —2C **12**
Post Office Rd. *Bourn*
—4H **59** (3G **5**)
Potterne Way. *T Leg* —5E **7**
Potters Way. *Poole* —5G **57**
Pottery Rd. *Poole* —5E **57**
Poulner Mobile Home Pk. *Ring*
—1E **9**
Poulner Pk. *Ring* —2E **9**
Pound Clo. *Poole* —2D **56**
Pound Clo. *Ring* —3C **8**
Pound La. *Christ* —1F **63**
Pound La. *Poole* —2C **56**
Pound Rd. *Penn* —3D **52**
Powell Rd. *Poole* —4F **57**
Powerscourt Rd. *Bart S* —6D **48**
Powis Clo. *New M* —2H **49**
Powlett Rd. *L'ton* —2G **53**
Preston Clo. *Uptn* —6C **36**
Preston La. *Burt* —3H **45**
Preston Rd. *Poole* —1A **56**
Preston Way. *Christ* —5F **47**
Prestwood Clo. *Bart S* —4F **49**
Priestlands La. *Penn* —2E **53**
Priestlands Pl. *L'ton* —2F **53**
Priestlands Rd. *Penn* —2E **53**
Priestley Rd. *Bourn* —4D **40**
Primrose Gdns. *Poole* —4F **37**
Primrose Way. *Christ* —4D **46**
Primrose Way. *Cor M* —4E **21**
Prince of Wales Rd. *Bourn*
—3D **58**
Prince's Ct. *Fern* —3B **18**
Princes Cres. *Lyn* —3H **71**
Princes Pl. *New M* —1A **50**
Princes Rd. *Fern* —4B **18**
Princess Av. *Christ* —1F **63**
Princess Rd. *Poole & Bourn*
(in two parts) —3C **58**
Pringles Clo. *Fern* —4C **18**
Pringles Dri. *Fern* —4C **18**
Priors Clo. *Christ* —6E **47**
Priors Rd. *Poole* —5F **37**
Priors Wlk. *Wim* —4D **14**
Priory Gdns. *W Mr* —1E **19**
Priory Ind. Pk. *Christ* —6D **46**
Priory Quay. *Christ* —2G **63**
Priory Rd. *Bourn* —5G **59** (5F **5**)
Priory Rd. *W Mr* —1E **19**
Priory Vw. Pl. *Bourn* —2A **42**
Priory Vw. Rd. *Bourn* —2A **42**
Priory Vw. Rd. *Burt* —2G **45**
Privet Rd. *Bourn* —5G **41**
Promenade. *Christ* —2D **64**
Promenade. *H'wthy* —6F **55**
Promenade. *Poole* —5H **69**
(in two parts)
Promenade. *Poole* —6C **56**
(Labrador Dri)
Promenade. *Poole* —3H **55** (1A **4**)
(Sterte Av. W.)
Prosperous St. *Poole*
—6A **56** (5B **4**)
Prunus Clo. *Fern* —2H **17**
Prunus Dri. *Fern* —2H **17**
Puddletown Cres. *Poole* —3D **38**
Pullman Ct. *W Mr* —5B **10**
Pullman Way. *Ring* —5C **8**
Purbeck Av. *Poole* —6E **55**

Purbeck Clo. *Poole* —6B **36**
Purbeck Dri. *Ver* —4D **6**
Purbeck Gdns. *Poole* —2D **56**
Purbeck Heights. *Poole* —2F **57**
Purbeck Rd. *Bart S* —6D **48**
Purbeck Rd. *Bourn* —4G **59** (4E **5**)
Purchase Rd. *Poole* —6D **40**
Purewell. *Christ* —1H **63**
Purewell Clo. *Christ* —1A **64**
Purewell Ct. *Christ* —6A **46**
Purewell Cross. *Christ* —1A **64**
Purewell Cross Rd. *Christ* —6G **45**
Purewell M. *Christ* —1H **63**
Pussex La. *Hurn* —3G **27**
Pye Clo. *Cor M* —4D **20**
Pye La. *Wim* —5D **14**
Pyrford Gdns. *L'ton* —3G **53**
Pyrford M. *L'ton* —3G **53**

Quaker Ct. *Ring* —5B **8**
Quarry Clo. *Wim* —2B **16**
Quarry Dri. *Wim* —2B **16**
Quarry Rd. *Wim* —2B **16**
Quay Hill. *L'ton* —1H **53**
Quayle Dri. *Bourn* —5B **24**
Quay Point. *Poole* —6A **56** (5B **4**)
Quay Rd. *Christ* —1F **63**
Quay Rd. *L'ton* —1H **53**
Quay St. *L'ton* —1H **53**
Quay, The. *Christ* —2G **63**
Quay, The. *Poole* —6H **55** (5A **4**)
Queen Anne Dri. *Wim* —3B **22**
Queen Elizabeth Av. *L'ton* —1F **53**
Queen Elizabeth Ct. *Wim* —5D **14**
Queen Katherine Rd. *L'ton* —2H **53**
Queen Mary Av. *Bourn* —3H **41**
Queens Av. *Christ* —2F **63**
Queensbury Mans. *Bourn* —4A **60**
Queens Clo. *W Mr* —6B **10**
Queens Ct. *Bourn* —5B **42**
Queen's Ct. Bourn —3F 59
(off Wharfdale Rd.)
Queens Ct. *New M* —2B **50**
Queens Gdns. *Bourn* —3F **59**
Queens Gro. *New M* —1A **50**
Queensland Rd. *Bourn* —2G **61**
Queensmount. *Bourn* —6C **42**
Queen's Pde. *Lyn* —3F **71**
Queen's Pk. Av. *Bourn* —5B **42**
Queens Pk. Gdns. *Bourn* —6C **42**
Queens Pk. Rd. *Bourn* —6D **42**
Queens Pk. S. Dri. *Bourn* —6D **42**
Queens Pk. W. Dri. *Bourn* —6C **42**
Queens Rd. *Bourn* —4F **59**
Queen's Rd. *Christ* —1A **64**
Queen's Rd. *Cor M* —6D **20**
Queens Rd. *Fern* —2B **18**
Queens Rd. *Lyn* —3G **71**
Queens Rd. *Poole* —3H **57**
Queen St. *L'ton* —2F **53**
Queensway. *New M* —2E **49**
Queens Way. *Ring* —4D **8**
Queenswood Av. *Bourn* —4E **43**
Queenswood Dri. *Fern* —2B **18**
Quince La. *Wim* —4G **15**
Quintin Clo. *Christ* —5H **47**
Quomp. *Ring* —4C **8**

Racecourse Vw. *Lyn* —2F **71**
Radipole Rd. *Poole* —3D **38**
Raglan Gdns. *Bourn* —3C **40**
Railway Ter. *Hint* —3G **47**
Raleigh Clo. *Christ* —2B **64**
Raleigh Clo. *New M* —2F **49**
Raleigh Clo. *Ring* —3E **9**
Raleigh Rd. *Poole* —3A **40**
Ralph Jessop Ct. *Poole* —6A **40**
Ralph Rd. *Cor M* —4D **20**
Ramley Rd. *Penn* —1C **52**
Rampart, The. *L'ton* —6F **35**
Ramsey Ct. *Christ* —1D **62**
Randalls Hill. *Lyt Mi* —4A **36**
Randolph Rd. *Bourn* —3E **61**

Randolph Rd. *Poole* —2G **57**
Ranelagh Rd. *Highc* —6H **47**
Ravenscourt Rd. *Bourn* —2A **62**
Ravenscourt Rd. *L'ton* —2F **53**
Ravensdale Clo. *Poole* —1G **57**
Ravenshall. *Bourn* —5F **59**
Ravens Way. *Mil S* —3D **66**
Ravenswood Pk. Cvn. Site. *Ring*
—6H **9**
Raven Way. *Christ* —2C **64**
Ravine Rd. *Bourn* —3H **61**
Ravine Rd. *Poole* —1B **70**
Raymond Clo. *Ver* —3F **7**
Raynards Ct. *Poole* —4D **56**
Rayners Dri. *Poole* —2H **57**
Rebbeck Rd. *Bourn* —1G **61**
Recreation Rd. *Poole* —1H **57**
Rectory Av. *Cor M* —2D **20**
Rectory Rd. *Poole* —1A **56**
Redan Clo. *Highc* —6H **47**
Redbreast Rd. *Bourn* —2A **42**
Redbreast Rd. N. *Bourn* —2A **42**
Redcliffe Clo. *Burt* —3G **45**
Redcotts La. *Wim* —4D **14**
(in two parts)
Redcotts Rd. *Wim* —4D **14**
Redhill Av. *Bourn* —3G **41**
Redhill Clo. *Bourn* —2G **41**
Redhill Ct. *Bourn* —1H **41**
Redhill Cres. *Bourn* —2H **41**
Redhill Dri. *Bourn* —3G **41**
Redhill Pk. Homes. *Bourn* —6H **25**
Redhill Roundabout. *Bourn*
—1H **41**
Redhoave Rd. *Poole* —3C **38**
Redhorn Clo. *Poole* —3C **54**
Redlands. *Poole* —2B **58**
Red La. *Cor M* —3A **20**
Redmans Vw. *Ver* —3C **6**
Red Oaks Clo. *Fern* —2H **17**
Red Roofs. *Fern* —6C **18**
Redshank Clo. *Poole* —4F **37**
Redvers Clo. *L'ton* —3G **53**
Redvers Rd. *Christ* —6A **46**
Redwood Clo. *L'ton* —6E **35**
Redwood Clo. *Ring* —4D **8**
Redwood Dri. *Fern* —1A **18**
Redwood Rd. *Poole* —5A **36**
Regency Cres. *Christ* —5D **44**
Regency Pl. *Ring* —3C **8**
Regent Dri. *Bourn* —5F **43**
Regent Way. *Christ* —1F **63**
Reid St. *Christ* —6E **45**
Rempstone Rd. *Wim* —2B **22**
Renault Dri. *Broad* —4G **37**
Renouf Clo. *Penn* —2E **53**
Restharrow. *Bourn* —3A **60**
Retreat Rd. *Wim* —5F **15**
Rhinefield Clo. *Broc* —2D **72**
Rhinefield Rd. *Broc* —2A **72**
Rhinefield Rd. *New M* —1E **31**
Rhiners Clo. *Sway* —1F **33**
Ribble Clo. *Broad* —3G **37**
Ricardo Cres. *Christ* —1C **64**
Rice Gdns. *Poole* —3D **54**
Rice Ter. *Poole* —3D **54**
Richard Clo. *Poole* —5B **36**
Richmond Ct. *Bourn* —6C **42**
Richmond Ct. *Mil S* —3C **66**
Richmond Ct. *New M* —2G **49**
Richmond Gdns. *Bourn*
—4H **59** (3G **5**)
Richmond Hill. *Bourn*
—4H **59** (4G **5**)
Richmond Hill Dri. *Bourn*
—4H **59** (3G **5**)
Richmond Ho. *Bourn*
—4H **59** (3G **5**)
Richmond Pk. Av. *Bourn* —6B **42**
Richmond Pk. Clo. *Bourn* —1D **60**
Richmond Pk. Cres. *Bourn*
—6C **42**
Richmond Pk. Rd. *Bourn* —6B **42**
Richmond Rd. *Poole* —2G **57**
Richmond Rd. *Wim* —5F **15**

Richmond Wood Rd. *Bourn* —6B **42**
Ridgefield Gdns. *Christ* —5F **47**
Ridgemount Gdns. *Poole* —4E **55**
Ridgeway. *Broad* —1H **37**
Ridgeway. *Cor M* —3D **20**
Ridge Way. *W Parl* —3G **25**
Ridgeway La. *L'ton* —3F **53**
Ridley Rd. *Bourn* —5H **41**
Ridout Clo. *Bourn* —4D **40**
Riggs Gdns. *Bourn* —3B **40**
Rigler Rd. *Poole* —6G **55**
Rimbury Way. *Christ* —5E **45**
Ringbury. *L'ton* —5F **35**
Ringwood. *W Mr & St L* —1E **19**
Ringwood Rd. *Bourn & Fern* —5B **24**
Ringwood Rd. *Brans & Walk* —2C **28**
Ringwood Rd. *Poole* —5F **39** (BH12 & BH11)
Ringwood Rd. *Poole* —3D **56** (BH14 & BH12)
Ringwood Rd. *T Leg* —2A **10**
Ringwood Rd. *Ver* —2D **6**
Ringwood Rd. Retail Pk. *Bourn* —2A **40**
Ringwood Rd. Service Rd. *Ashy H* —4B **12**
Ringwood Trad. Est. *Ring* —5C **8** (in two parts)
Ripon Rd. *Bourn* —5A **42**
Rise, The. *Broc* —3E **73**
Ritchie Pl. *W Mr* —3B **10**
Ritchie Rd. *Bourn* —1D **40**
River Clo. *Wim* —3E **15**
River Ct. *Hurn* —3G **27**
Riverdale La. *Christ* —1E **63**
River Gdns. *Mil S* —3E **67**
Riverlea Rd. *Christ* —1E **63**
Rivermead Gdns. *Christ* —3C **44**
Riversdale Rd. *Bourn* —3E **63**
Riverside. *Bourn* —1H **41**
Riverside. *Ring* —5B **8**
Riverside Av. *Bourn* —3H **43**
Riverside Bus. Pk. *L'ton* —1H **53**
Riverside La. *Bourn* —2D **62**
Riverside Pk. *Christ* —2E **63**
Riverside Pk. Ind. Est. *Wim* —5F **15**
Riverside Rd. *Bourn* —2D **62**
Riverside Rd. *W Mr* —5A **10**
Rivers Reach. *L'ton* —2H **53**
River Way. *Christ* —4B **44**
Riviera. *Bourn* —4B **60**
Riviera Ct. *Bourn* —4F **59**
Riviera Ct. *Poole* —2B **70**
R. L. Stevenson Av. *Bourn* —4D **58**
Roberts Clo. *Evtn* —4A **52**
Robertshaw Ho. *Lyn* —2F **71**
Roberts La. *Poole* —6F **37**
Roberts Rd. *Bourn* —1G **61**
Roberts Rd. *Poole* —4H **37**
Robin Cres. *New M* —6D **30**
Robin Gro. *New M* —3F **49**
Robins Way. *Christ* —2D **64**
Robinswood Dri. *Fern* —1B **18**
Robsall Clo. *Poole* —6A **40**
Rochester Rd. *Bourn* —1D **40**
Rockbourne Gdns. *New M* —5D **48**
Rockford Clo. *Bourn* —4D **62**
Rockley Cvn. Pk. *Poole* —4B **54**
Rockley Rd. *Poole* —5E **55**
Rodbourne Clo. *Evtn* —5H **51**
Rodney Clo. *Poole* —5C **40**
Rodney Ct. *Poole* —6A **56** (5C **4**)
Rodney Dri. *Christ* —1B **64**
Rodway. *Wim* —5E **15**
Rodwell Clo. *Bourn* —5E **25**
Roebuck Clo. *New M* —2H **49**
Roeshot Cres. *Christ* —4F **47**
Roeshot Hill. *Christ* —4E **47**
Roi-Mar Home Pk. *Bourn* —1D **42**
Rolls Dri. *Bourn* —3F **63**
Roman Heights. *Cor M* —3E **21**

Roman Rd. *Broad & Cor M* (in two parts) —6E **21**
Roman Rd. *Poole* —5E **37**
Romney Clo. *Bourn* —2G **41**
Romney Rd. *Bourn* —1G **41**
Romsey Rd. *Lyn* —2F **71**
Rookcliff. *Mil S* —3C **66**
Rookcliff Way. *Mil S* —3C **66**
Rookes La. *L'ton* —3F **53**
Rook Hill Rd. *Christ* —1D **64**
Roosevelt Cres. *Bourn* —5D **24**
Rope Hill. *Bold* —2E **35**
Ropers La. *Poole* —6D **36**
Ropley Rd. *Bourn* —6A **44**
Rosamund Av. *Wim* —2C **22**
Roscrea Clo. *Bourn* —3F **63**
Roscrea Dri. *Bourn* —3F **63**
Rosebery Clo. *Ver* —4G **7**
Rosebery Rd. *Bourn* —2G **61**
Rosebud Av. *Bourn* —3A **42**
Rosecrae Clo. *New M* —1F **49**
Rose Cres. *Poole* —1D **56**
Rosedale Clo. *Christ* —1A **64**
Rose Gdns. *Bourn* —3H **41**
Rosehill Clo. *Brans* —2D **28**
Rosehill Dri. *Brans* —2C **28**
Rosemary Gdns. *Poole* —6F **39**
Rosemary Rd. *Poole* —6F **39**
Rosemount Rd. *Bourn* —5D **58**
Rosewood Gdns. *New M* —1F **49**
Roslin Rd. *Bourn* —6G **41**
Roslin Rd. S. *Bourn* —6F **41** (in two parts)
Ross Gdns. *Bourn* —6G **23**
Ross Glades. *Bourn* —1G **59**
Rossiters Quay. *Christ* —1G **63**
Rossley Clo. *Christ* —3G **47**
Rossmore Pde. *Poole* —5F **39**
Rossmore Rd. *Poole* —5F **39**
Ross Rd. *Ring* —1E **9**
Rotary Clo. *Wim* —2H **15**
Rothbury Pk. *New M* —3H **49**
Rotherfield Rd. *Bourn* —4H **61**
Rotherfield Rd. *Highc* —4A **48**
Rothesay Dri. *Highc* —6G **47**
Rothesay Rd. *Bourn* —1E **59**
Rotterdam Dri. *Christ* —6H **45**
Roumelia La. *Bourn* —3E **61**
Roundhaye Rd. *Bourn* —6B **24**
Roundways. *Bourn* —2A **40**
Rowan Clo. *Christ* —5F **47**
Rowan Clo. *St L* —3H **11**
Rowan Clo. *Sway* —2F **33**
Rowan Dri. *Christ* —5F **47**
Rowan Dri. *Poole* —4E **37**
Rowan Dri. *Ver* —5F **7**
Rowans Pk. *L'ton* —2F **53**
Rowbarrow Clo. *Poole* —3C **38**
Rowena Rd. *Bourn* —2D **62**
Rowland Av. *Poole* —2C **56**
Rowlands Hill. *Wim* —4E **15**
Rownhams Rd. *Bourn* —2C **42**
Royal Arc. *Bourn* —3E **61**
Royal Clo. *Christ* —5D **44**
Royal Oak Rd. *Bourn* —6E **25**
Royden La. *Bold* —1F **35**
Royster Clo. *Poole* —4A **38**
Royston Dri. *Wim* —4F **15**
Royston Pl. *Bart S* —5H **49**
Rozelle Rd. *Poole* —3G **57**
Rozel Mnr. *Poole* —5D **58**
Ruben Dri. *Poole* —5D **54**
Rubens Clo. *New M* —2H **49**
Rufford Gdns. *Bourn* —2C **62**
Rufus Ct. *Lyn* —3G **71**
Rugby Rd. *Poole* —4G **37**
Runnymede Av. *Bourn* —5H **23**
Runton Rd. *Poole* —2B **58**
Runway, The. *Christ* —6D **46**
Rushall La. *Cor M* —1A **36**
Rushcombe Way. *Cor M* —5D **20**
Rushford Warren. *Christ* —2B **64**
Rushmere Rd. *Bourn* —6A **44**
Rushton Cres. *Bourn* —1H **59**
Ruskin Av. *Bourn* —2B **42**

Russel Ct. *New M* —2G **49**
Russell Cotes Rd. *Bourn* —5A **60**
Russell Dri. *Christ* —1H **63**
Russell Gdns. *Poole* —3C **54**
Russell Gdns. *St I* —2D **12**
Russel Rd. *Bourn* —5E **25**
Russet Clo. *Fern* —3B **18**
Russett Clo. *L'ton* —3H **53**
Rutland Mnr. *Poole* —3C **58**
Rutland Rd. *Bourn* —5B **42**
Rutland Rd. *Christ* —4D **44**
Ryall Rd. *Poole* —4B **38**
Ryan Clo. *Fern* —2A **18**
Ryan Gdns. *Bourn* —5D **24**
Ryan Gdns. *Fern* —2A **18**
Rydal Clo. *Christ* —1B **44**
Ryecroft Av. *Bourn* —6A **24**

Saddle Clo. *Wim* —3C **16**
Saffron Dri. *Christ* —5D **46**
Saffron Way. *Bourn* —2H **39**
St Albans Av. *Bourn* —6B **42**
St Albans Cres. *Bourn* —6B **42**
St Albans Rd. *Bourn* —6B **42**
St Aldhelms. *Poole* —3B **58**
St Aldhelm's Clo. *Poole* —4B **58**
St Aldhelm's Rd. *Poole* —3B **58**
St Andrews. *Christ* —1E **63**
St Andrews Rd. *Broad* —6G **21**
St Anne's Av. *Bourn* —2C **62**
St Annes Gdns. *L'ton* —2F **53**
St Anne's Rd. *Poole* —6B **36**
St Ann's Ct. *Bourn* —2E **61**
St Anthony's Rd. *Bourn* —2H **59**
St Antony's. *Bourn* —5F **59**
St Aubyns Ct. *Poole* —5H **55** (4A **4**)
St Aubyns La. *Hang* —2G **9**
St Augustin's Rd. *Bourn* —2H **59**
St Brelades. *Poole* —6G **57**
St Brelades Av. *Poole* —3H **39**
St Catherines. *Wim* —5E **15**
St Catherine's Hill La. *Christ* —3D **44**
St Catherine's Pde. *Christ* —4D **44**
St Catherine's Path. *Bourn* —4C **62**
St Catherine's Rd. *Bourn* —4C **62**
St Catherine's Way. *Christ* —2B **44**
St Clair Rd. *Poole* —3A **70**
St Clements Gdns. *Bourn* —2D **60**
St Clements La. *Poole* —6H **55** (5A **4**)
St Clements Rd. *Bourn* —2D **60**
St Clements Rd. *Poole* —6E **39**
St David's Ct. *Bourn* —2E **61**
St David's Rd. *Poole* —5B **36**
St Denys. *New M* —4H **49**
St George's Almshouses. *Poole* —5A **4**
St George's Av. *Bourn* —5C **42**
St Georges Av. *Poole* —5F **39**
St George's Clo. *Bourn* —5C **42**
St Georges Clo. *Christ* —6F **47**
St George's Ct. *Bourn* —2E **61**
St Georges Dri. *Brans* —3D **28**
St Georges Dri. *Fern* —5A **18**
St Helier Rd. *Bourn* —4H **39**
St Ives End La. *St I* —3C **12**
St Ives Gdns. *Bourn* —2H **59**
St Ives Pk. *Ashy H* —2C **12**
St Ives Wood. *St I* —2D **12**
St James. *Bourn* —4E **61**
St James Clo. *Poole* —6H **55** (5A **4**)
St James Rd. *Fern* —3G **17**
St James Rd. *Sway* —1G **33**
St James Sq. *Bourn* —2G **61**
St John's Clo. *Wim* —5F **15**
St John's Ct. *Bourn* —2E **61** (off Palmerston M.)
St Johns Gdns. *Bourn* —4H **41**
St John's Hill. *Wim* —4F **15**
St Johns Rd. *Bourn* —3E **61**
St John's Rd. *Christ* —1D **62**

St Johns Rd. *New M* —4G **31**
St John's Rd. *Poole* —3B **56**
St Just Clo. *Fern* —6H **17**
St Ledger's Pl. *Bourn* —1D **60**
St Ledger's Rd. *Bourn* —1D **60**
St Leonards Farm Cvn. Pk. *Fern* —2E **19**
St Leonard's Rd. *Bourn* —1B **60**
St Leonards Way. *Ashy H* —2H **11**
St Luke's Rd. *Bourn* —6H **41**
St Margaret's Av. *Christ* —1E **63**
St Margarets Clo. *Wim* —4C **14**
St Margaret's Hill. *Wim* —3C **14**
St Margaret's Rd. *Bourn* —3D **40**
St Margaret's Rd. *Poole* —3B **56**
St Marks Rd. *Bourn* —2D **40**
St Marks Rd. *Penn* —2D **52**
St Martins Rd. *Uptn* —6A **36**
St Mary Gro. *Hord* —3F **51**
St Mary's Clo. *Brans* —3E **29**
St Mary's Ct. *Bourn* —4C **62**
St Mary's M. *Fern* —5B **18**
St Mary's Rd. *Bourn* —1D **60**
St Mary's Rd. *Fern* —4B **18**
St Mary's Rd. *Poole* —4B **56**
St Merrin's Clo. *Bourn* —1E **41**
St Michael's. Bourn —4F **59** (off Norwich Av.)
St Michaels Clo. *Poole* —4E **55**
St Michaels Clo. *Ver* —4D **6**
St Michaels Ct. Bourn —4F **59** (off Poole Rd.)
St Michael's La. *Bourn* —4G **59** (4E **5**)
St Michael's M. *Bourn* —4E **5**
St Michael's Pl. *Bourn* —4E **5**
St Michael's Rd. *Bourn* —4G **59** (4E **5**)
St Michael's Rd. *Ver* —4D **6**
St Michael's Roundabout. *Bourn* —4F **59**
St Osmunds Rd. *Poole* —3G **57**
St Paul's La. *Bourn* —3B **60**
St Paul's Pl. *Bourn* —3A **60**
St Paul's Rd. *Bourn* —3A **60**
St Peter's Ct. *Bourn* —4A **60** (3H **5**)
St Peter's Cres. *Bourn* —3H **5**
St Peter's Rd. *Bourn* —4H **59** (4H **5**)
St Peter's Rd. *Poole* —3E **57**
St Peter's Roundabout. *Bourn* —4A **60**
St Peter's Wlk. *Bourn* —4G **5**
St Saviours Clo. *Bourn* —6A **44**
Saints Clo. *T Leg* —2A **10**
St Stephen's Ct. *Bourn* —2F **5**
St Stephen's La. *Ver* —3E **7**
St Stephen's Rd. *Bourn* —3G **59** (2E **5**)
St Stephen's Way. *Bourn* —4H **59** (3G **5**)
St Swithun's Rd. *Bourn* —3B **60**
St Swithun's Rd. S. *Bourn* —3B **60**
St Swithun's Roundabout. *Bourn* —4B **60**
St Thomas Clo. *Bourn* —3F **41**
St Thomas Pk. *L'ton* —2F **53**
St Thomas St. *L'ton* —2F **53**
St Valerie Rd. *Bourn* —2H **59** (1H **5**)
St Winifred's Rd. *Bourn* —2H **59**
Salerno Pl. *Poole* —5D **54**
Salisbury Rd. *Bourn* —3E **61**
Salisbury Rd. *Burt & Christ* —1G **45**
Salisbury Rd. *Poole* —2G **57**
Salisbury Rd. *Ring & Blash* —3B **8**
Salterns Ct. *Poole* —1F **69**
Salterns Rd. *Poole* —4E **57**
Salterns Way. *Poole* —1F **69**
Salter Rd. *Poole* —6F **69**
Saltgrass La. *Key* —5G **67**
Saltings Rd. *Poole* —1B **54**

Samber Clo. *L'ton* —1E **53**
Samphire Clo. *L'ton* —6F **35**
Samples Way. *Poole* —5D **38**
Samson Rd. *Poole* —4D **54**
Sancreed Rd. *Poole* —6A **40**
Sandbanks Bus. Cen. *Poole*
   —6F **69**
Sandbanks Rd. *Poole* —4D **56**
Sandbourne Rd. *Bourn* —6E **59**
Sandbourne Rd. *Poole* —3B **56**
Sandecotes Rd. *Poole* —3G **57**
Sanderlings. *Hight* —5E **9**
Sandford Clo. *Bourn* —2C **42**
Sandford Way. *Broad* —3F **37**
Sandhills Cvn. Pk. *Christ* —2D **64**
Sandhills Clo. *Poole* —3B **38**
Sandmartin Clo. *Bart S* —6F **49**
Sandon Ct. *Bourn* —6C **42**
Sandown Rd. *Christ* —1A **64**
Sandpiper Clo. *Poole* —4F **37**
Sandpit La. *Poole* —4B **56**
Sandringham Clo. *Bourn* —1B **42**
Sandringham Ct. *Bourn*
  (BH2)   —5H **59** (5G **5**)
Sandringham Ct. *Bourn* —1C **60**
  (BH8)
Sandringham Gdns. *Bourn*
   —1B **42**
Sandringham Rd. *Poole* —4F **57**
Sandy Clo. *Wim* —1A **16**
Sandyhurst Clo. *Poole* —4A **38**
Sandy La. *Bourn* —2H **61**
Sandy La. *Christ* —3C **44**
Sandy La. *Lyn* —4F **71**
Sandy La. *St I* —3B **12**
Sandy La. *T Leg* —1A **10**
Sandy La. *Uptn & Poole* —1A **54**
Sandy La. *Ver* —3E **7**
Sandy La. *Wim* —1A **16**
Sandy Mead Rd. *Bourn* —4F **43**
Sandy Plot. *Burt* —4G **45**
Sandy Way. *Bourn* —2G **41**
  (in two parts)
San Remo Towers. *Bosc* —4E **61**
Saracen Clo. *Penn* —4E **53**
Sarah Clo. *Bourn* —5H **43**
Sarah Sands Clo. *Christ* —5H **45**
Sark Rd. *Poole* —5H **39**
Sarum Av. *W Mr* —3C **10**
  (in two parts)
Sarum Ct. *Poole* —3G **57**
Sarum St. *Poole* —6H **55** (5A **4**)
Sarum Wlk. *L'ton* —5F **35**
Saulfland Dri. *Christ* —5F **47**
Saulfland Pl. *Christ* —5F **47**
Saville Ct. *Wim* —6F **15**
Saxonbury Rd. *Bourn* —1C **62**
Saxon Cen., The. *Christ* —6F **45**
Saxonford Rd. *Christ* —6E **47**
Saxonhurst Clo. *Bourn* —6G **25**
Saxonhurst Gdns. *Bourn* —1G **41**
Saxonhurst Rd. *Bourn* —1F **41**
Saxon King Gdns. *Bourn* —3F **63**
Saxon Pl. *L'ton* —5F **35**
Saxon Sq. *Christ* —1F **63**
Scarf Rd. *Poole* —5D **38**
School Clo. *L'ton* —2E **53**
School Clo. *Ver* —2E **7**
School La. *Bourn* —6D **24**
School La. *L'ton* —1G **53**
School La. *Mil S* —1E **67**
School La. *Pill* —2H **35**
School La. *Poole* —2A **56**
School La. *Ring* —4C **8**
School La. *St I* —2C **12**
School La. *Wim* —4D **14**
Scott Clo. *Poole* —4B **40**
Scotter Rd. *Bourn* —1H **61**
Scott Rd. *Poole* —4B **40**
Scott's Grn. *Christ* —5B **46**
Scotts Hills La. *Christ* —6H **45**
  (in two parts)
Seabank Clo. *Uptn* —6A **36**
Seabourne Pl. *Bourn* —2H **61**
Seabourne Rd. *Bourn* —2G **61**

Seabreeze Way. *Mil S* —1A **66**
Seacliff Ct. *Bourn* —4B **62**
Seacombe Rd. *Poole* —6F **69**
Seacroft Av. *Bart S* —5E **49**
Seafield Clo. *Bart S* —6F **49**
Seafield Dri. *Bourn* —2C **62**
Seafield Rd. *Bart S* —5E **49**
Seafield Rd. *Bourn* —3B **62**
Seafield Rd. *Christ* —1E **65**
Seagull Rd. *Bourn* —4C **42**
Seamoor La. *Bourn* —4D **58**
Seamoor Rd. *Bourn* —4D **58**
Sea Pines. *Mil S* —3C **66**
Sea Rd. *Bart S* —5E **49**
Sea Rd. *Bosc* —4E **61**
Sea Rd. *Mil S* —3E **67**
Sea Rd. *South* —4D **62**
Seaton Clo. *Highc* —5B **48**
Seaton Clo. *L'ton* —6G **35**
Seaton Rd. *Highc* —5B **48**
Seatown Clo. *Poole* —4E **39**
Sea Vw. Rd. *New M* —6C **48**
Sea Vw. Rd. *Park* —2E **57**
Sea Vw. Rd. *Uptn* —6A **36**
Sea Vw. Rd. *Walk* —4C **48**
Sea Vixen Ind. Est. *Christ* —6C **46**
Seaward Av. *Bart S* —6E **49**
Seaward Av. *Bourn* —3H **61**
Seaward Path. *Poole* —1C **70**
Seaway. *New M* —5H **49**
Seaway Av. *Christ* —6E **47**
Seawinds. *Mil S* —2A **66**
Second Marine Av. *Bart S* —6G **49**
Sedgley Rd. *Bourn* —5G **41**
Seed Warehouse, The. *Poole*
   —5B **4**
Selby Clo. *Broad* —2G **37**
Seldown. *Poole* —4B **56**
Seldown Bri. *Poole* —6B **56** (4D **4**)
Seldown La. *Poole* —4B **56** (3D **4**)
Seldown Rd. *Poole* —4B **56**
Selfridge Av. *Bourn* —4F **63**
Selfridge Clo. *Bourn* —4F **63**
Seliot Clo. *Poole* —2B **56**
Selkirk Clo. *Wim* —2C **22**
Sellwood Way. *New M* —5D **48**
Selwood Cvn. Pk. *Bourn* —4E **25**
Selworthy Clo. *Poole* —5E **57**
Serpentine Rd. *Poole*
   —4A **56** (2C **4**)
Setley Gdns. *Bourn* —2E **43**
Set Thorns Rd. *Sway* —1G **33**
Sevenoaks Dri. *Bourn* —6G **43**
Severn Rd. *Fern* —3E **19**
Seymour Rd. *Ring* —2D **8**
Shackleton Sq. *Brans* —2D **28**
Shaftesbury Clo. *W Mr* —5D **10**
Shaftesbury Rd. *Bourn* —1C **60**
Shaftesbury Rd. *Poole*
   —4B **56** (1D **4**)
Shaftesbury Rd. *W Mr* —6D **10**
Shags Mdw. *Lyn* —3F **71**
Shakespeare Rd. *Bourn* —6B **44**
Shakespeare Rd. *Wim* —3E **15**
Shallows La. *Bold* —3F **35**
Shamrock Ct. *Wim* —5E **15**
Shapland Av. *Bourn* —6A **24**
Shapwick Rd. *Poole* —6G **55**
Shard Clo. *Ver* —3E **7**
Sharlands Clo. *Broad* —2H **37**
Sharp Rd. *Poole* —6C **40**
Sharvells Rd. *Mil S* —2C **66**
Shaves La. *New M* —6G **31**
Shawford Gdns. *Bourn* —3D **42**
Shawford Rd. *Bourn* —2D **42**
Shaw Rd. *Ring* —1E **9**
Shears Brook Clo. *Brans* —2D **28**
Shelbourne Clo. *Bourn* —1C **60**
Shelbourne Rd. *Bourn* —1B **60**
Sheldrake Gdns. *Hord* —2F **51**
Sheldrake Rd. *Christ* —2C **64**
Shelley Clo. *Ashy H* —2H **11**
Shelley Clo. *Bourn* —2E **61**
Shelley Clo. *Christ* —6E **47**
Shelley Ct. *Fern* —4B **18**

Shelley Gdns. *Bourn* —2E **61**
Shelley Hamlets. *Christ* —6F **47**
Shelley Hill. *Christ* —6F **47**
Shelley Ho. *New M* —3G **49**
Shelley Rd. *Bourn* —2E **61**
Shelley Rd. *Poole* —2H **57**
Shelley Rd. E. *Bourn* —2E **61**
Shelley Way. *Mil S* —2D **66**
Shelton Rd. *Bourn* —1A **62**
Shepherd Clo. *Highc* —4H **47**
Shepherds Way. *Bourn* —6G **43**
Sheppards Fld. *Wim* —3D **14**
Sherborn Cres. *Poole* —3E **39**
Sherborne Dri. *Fern* —5B **18**
Sherfield Clo. *Bourn* —3D **42**
Sheringham Rd. *Poole* —2B **58**
Sherrin Clo. *Poole* —2B **56**
Sherwood Av. *Fern* —6A **18**
Sherwood Av. *Poole* —5D **56**
Sherwood Clo. *Christ* —6D **44**
Sherwood Dri. *Ver* —3F **7**
Shillingstone Dri. *Bourn* —1B **42**
Shillingstone Gdns. *Poole* —6B **40**
Shillito Rd. *Poole* —2H **57**
Shingle Bank Dri. *Mil S* —3D **66**
Shipstal Clo. *Poole* —3C **54**
Shipwrights Wlk. *Key* —4G **67**
Shires Clo. *Ring* —6C **8**
Shires Copse. *Bourn* —4D **62**
Shires Mead. *Ver* —3E **7**
Shirley Clo. *Brans* —2D **28**
Shirley Clo. *W Mr* —5C **10**
Shirley Holms. *L'ton* —2A **34**
Shirley Rd. *Bourn* —4A **42**
Shirley Rd. *Park* —1F **57**
*Shirley Rd. *Poole* —6C **36***
  (off Douglas Clo.)
Shore Av. *Poole* —1C **54**
Shore Clo. *Mil S* —3D **66**
Shore Clo. *Poole* —1C **54**
Shorefield Cvn. Pk. *Mil S* —6E **51**
Shorefield Cres. *Mil S* —2C **66**
Shorefield Rd. *Down* —1A **66**
Shorefield Way. *Mil S* —2C **66**
Shore Gdns. *Poole* —1B **54**
Shore La. *Poole* —2B **54**
Shore Rd. *Poole* —3H **69**
Short Clo. *Poole* —5C **40**
Shorts Clo. *Burt* —4G **45**
Shottsford Rd. *Poole* —2A **56**
Shrubb's Av. *L'ton* —1G **53**
Shrubbs Hill. *Lyn* —3F **71**
Shrubbs Hill Gdns. *Lyn* —4F **71**
Sidney Gdns. *Bourn* —1C **42**
Sidney Smith Ct. *Poole* —3C **38**
Silchester Clo. *Bourn*
   —2H **59** (1G **5**)
Silverbirch Clo. *Poole* —3C **58**
Silver Bus. Pk. *Christ* —6B **46**
Silverdale. *Bart S* —5H **49**
Silverdale Clo. *Broad* —1E **37**
Silver Jubilee Ct. *Bourn* —3C **40**
Silver St. *Christ* —1F **63**
Silver St. *Hord* —1D **50**
Silver Way. *Highc* —5G **47**
Silverways. *Highc* —5G **47**
Silverwood Clo. *Wim* —1B **22**
Simmonds Clo. *Poole* —2B **56**
Singleton Dri. *Bourn* —3E **41**
Siskin Clo. *Fern* —2H **17**
Sixpenny Clo. *Poole* —6B **40**
Skinner St. *Poole* —6A **56** (5B **4**)
Skipton Clo. *Broad* —3G **37**
Sky End La. *Hord* —3E **51**
Slade Clo. *Hord* —2E **51**
Slades Farm Rd. *Bourn* —4E **41**
Slade's La. *Bourn* —5E **41**
Sleepbrook Clo. *Ver* —3C **6**
Sleight La. *Cor M* —2C **20**
Slepe Cres. *Poole* —5B **40**
Slinn Rd. *Christ* —6A **46**
Slip Way. *Poole* —5H **55** (3A **4**)
Slough La. *Poole* —1A **54**
Smithfield Pl. *Bourn* —4H **41**
Smithson Clo. *Poole* —5D **40**

Smithy La. *New M* —5F **31**
Smugglers La. *Furz & Wim*
   —1F **15**
Smugglers La. N. *Christ* —3F **47**
Smugglers La. S. *Christ* —5F **47**
Smugglers Vw. *New M* —6C **48**
Smugglers Wood Rd. *Christ*
   —4F **47**
Snail's La. *Blash* —1C **8**
Snowdon Rd. *Bourn* —3E **59**
Snowdrop Gdns. *Christ* —4D **46**
Soberton Rd. *Bourn* —6D **42**
Solent Av. *L'ton* —2H **53**
Solent Clo. *L'ton* —2H **53**
Solent Ct. *Mil S* —3B **66**
Solent Dri. *Bart S* —6G **49**
Solent Flats. *Mil S* —3E **67**
Solent Lodge. *New M* —4F **49**
Solent Pines. *Mil S* —3B **66**
Solent Rd. *Bourn* —4E **63**
Solent Rd. *New M* —6D **48**
Solent Rd. *Walk* —3B **48**
Solent Vw. *Bourn* —4E **63**
Solent Vw. Ct. *Penn* —3E **53**
Solent Way. *Mil S* —3F **67**
Solly Clo. *Poole* —6A **40**
Soloman Way. *Poole* —5D **54**
Somerby Rd. *Poole* —1B **56**
Somerford Av. *Christ* —5D **46**
Somerford Bus. Pk. *Christ* —6C **46**
Somerford Rd. *Christ* —1A **64**
Somerford Way. *Christ* —6A **46**
Somerley Rd. *Bourn* —6A **42**
Somerley Vw. *Ring* —3C **8**
Somerset Rd. *Bourn* —2F **61**
Somerset Rd. *Christ* —6C **44**
Somerton Clo. *New M* —2B **50**
Somerville Rd. *Bourn* —4F **59**
Somerville Rd. *Ring* —3E **9**
Sonning Way. *Bourn* —3B **42**
Soper's La. *Christ* —1E **63**
Sopers La. *Poole* —4G **37**
Sopley Clo. *New M* —5D **48**
Sopwith Clo. *Christ* —1D **64**
Sopwith Cres. *Wim* —2C **22**
Sorrel Gdns. *Broad* —3F **37**
Sorrell Ct. *Christ* —5D **46**
Sorrell Way. *Christ* —5D **46**
Southampton Rd. *Broc* —1D **34**
Southampton Rd. *Lyn* —3G **71**
Southampton Rd. *Ring* —4B **8**
South Av. *New M* —3H **49**
Southbourne Cliff Dri. *Bourn*
   —4D **62**
Southbourne Coast Rd. *Bourn*
   —4C **62**
Southbourne Gro. *Bourn* —3A **62**
Southbourne Overcliff Dri. *Bourn*
   —4A **62**
Southbourne Promenade. *Bourn*
   —4A **62**
Southbourne Rd. *Bourn* —1H **61**
Southbourne Rd. *L'ton* —2E **53**
Southbourne Sands. *Bourn*
   —4B **62**
Southbrook Clo. *Poole* —3E **39**
Southcliffe Rd. *Christ* —1D **64**
Southcliffe Rd. *New M* —6D **48**
S. Cliff Rd. *Bourn* —5H **59** (6G **5**)
Southcote Rd. *Bourn* —3B **60**
Southdown Way. *W Mr* —6D **10**
S. E. Sector. *Hurn* —3G **27**
Southern Av. *W Mr* —6E **11**
Southernhay Rd. *Ver* —3F **7**
Southern La. *New M* —5F **49**
Southern Oaks. *Bart S* —4F **49**
Southern Rd. *Bourn* —3A **62**
Southern Rd. *L'ton* —2F **53**
Southey Rd. *Christ* —5B **46**
Southfield. *Ring* —5C **8**
Southfield M. *Ring* —5C **8**
South Gro. *L'ton* —2H **53**
S. Haven Clo. *Poole* —4B **54**
Southill Av. *Poole* —1G **57**
Southill Gdns. *Bourn* —4A **42**

Southill Rd. *Bourn* —4A **42**
Southill Rd. *Poole* —1G **57**
S. Kinson Dri. *Bourn* —1C **40**
Southlands. *Penn* —3E **53**
Southlands Av. *Bourn* —3D **62**
Southlands Av. *Cor M* —5D **20**
Southlands Clo. *Cor M* —5D **20**
Southlands Ct. *Broad* —2G **37**
Southlawns Wlk. *Bart S* —4F **49**
Southlea Av. *Bourn* —2D **62**
South Pk. Rd. *Poole* —5C **40**
South Rd. *Bourn* —2E **61**
South Rd. *Cor M* —4D **20**
South Rd. *Poole* —5A **56** (4C **4**)
South St. *Penn* —3E **53**
S. Sway La. *Sway* —3G **33**
S. View Pl. *Bourn* —5G **59** (5E **5**)
S. View Rd. *Christ* —1E **63**
Southville Rd. *Bourn* —2H **61**
South Weirs. *Broc* —4C **72**
S. Western Cres. *Poole* —5F **57**
Southwick Pl. *Bourn* —6A **44**
Southwick Rd. *Bourn* —1A **62**
Southwood Av. *Bourn* —3A **62**
Southwood Av. *Walk* —4A **48**
Southwood Clo. *Fern* —3A **18**
Southwood Clo. *Walk* —4A **48**
Sovereign Bus. Pk. *Poole* —1H **55**
Sovereign Cen. *Bourn* —3E **61**
Sovereign Clo. *Bourn* —5F **43**
Sparkford Clo. *Bourn* —5H **43**
Spartina Dri. *L'ton* —5G **35**
Speedwell Dri. *Christ* —5D **46**
Spencer Ct. *New M* —3G **49**
Spencer Rd. *Bourn* —3C **60**
Spencer Rd. *New M* —2G **49**
Spencer Rd. *Poole* —1A **70**
Spetisbury Clo. *Bourn* —2B **42**
Spicer Ct. *Bourn* —4G **59** (4E **5**)
Spicer La. *Bourn* —6A **24**
 (in two parts)
Spinacre. *Bart S* —5H **49**
Spindle Clo. *Broad* —3F **37**
Spindlewood Clo. *Bart S* —4G **49**
Spinners Clo. *W Mr* —6C **10**
Spinney Clo. *St L* —3H **11**
Spinneys La. *Fern* —4B **18**
Spinney, The. *Ashy H* —1B **12**
Spinney Way. *New M* —5G **31**
Spittlefields. *Ring* —4D **8**
Springbank Rd. *Bourn* —5F **43**
Springbourne Ct. *Bourn* —2D **60**
Spring Clo. *Ver* —4D **6**
Springdale Av. *Broad* —6F **21**
Springdale Gro. *Cor M* —1D **36**
Springdale Rd. *Cor M & Broad*
 —1D **36**
Springfield Av. *Bourn* —3E **63**
Springfield Av. *Christ* —3B **44**
Springfield Clo. *L'ton* —2H **53**
Springfield Clo. *Ver* —4D **6**
Springfield Cres. *Poole* —3F **57**
Springfield Gdns. *New M* —3B **50**
Springfield Rd. *Poole* —2E **57**
Springfield Rd. *Ver* —4D **6**
Spring Gdns. *Poole* —2H **57**
Spring La. *New M* —3B **50**
Spring Rd. *Bourn* —2C **60**
Spring Rd. *L'ton* —2H **53**
Springvale Av. *Bourn* —5F **43**
Springwater Clo. *Bourn* —2C **40**
Springwater Rd. *Bourn* —2C **40**
Spruce Clo. *Poole* —4E **37**
Spur Clo. *Wim* —3C **16**
Spurgeon Rd. *Bourn* —1H **61**
Spur Hill Av. *Poole* —4H **57**
Spur Rd. *Poole* —4H **57**
Square Clo. *Wim* —6E **17**
Square, The. *Bourn*
 —4H **59** (4G **5**)
Square, The. *L'ton* —2D **52**
Square, The. *Wim* —4D **14**
Squirrels Clo. *Christ* —3B **44**
Squirrel Wlk. *Ver* —4D **6**
Stables, The. *Christ* —6D **44**

Stacey Clo. *Poole* —6G **39**
Stacey Gdns. *Bourn* —3F **43**
Stafford Rd. *Bourn* —4A **60**
Stag Bus. Pk. *Ring* —6C **8**
Stag Clo. *New M* —1E **49**
Stagswood. *Ver* —3B **6**
Stalbridge Dri. *Fern* —5B **18**
Stalbridge Rd. *Poole* —6G **37**
Stalham Rd. *Poole* —1B **58**
Stallards La. *Ring* —4B **8**
Stamford Rd. *Bourn* —2A **62**
Stanfield Clo. *Poole* —6H **39**
 (in two parts)
Stanfield Rd. *Bourn* —5G **41**
Stanfield Rd. *Fern* —3A **18**
Stanfield Rd. *Poole* —6H **39**
Stanford Hill. *L'ton* —2F **53**
Stanford Ri. *Sway* —1F **33**
Stanford Rd. *L'ton* —2F **53**
Stanley Clo. *Ver* —4E **7**
Stanley Grn. Cres. *Poole* —2A **56**
Stanley Grn. Ind. Est. *Poole*
 —2H **55**
Stanley Grn. Rd. *Poole* —2A **56**
Stanley Pearce Ho. *Poole* —4A **38**
Stanley Rd. *Bourn* —2C **60**
Stanley Rd. *Highc* —5A **48**
Stanley Rd. *L'ton* —3H **53**
Stanley Rd. *Poole* —6B **56** (5C **4**)
Stannington Clo. *New M* —3H **49**
Stanpit. *Christ* —1A **64**
Stanton Rd. *Bourn* —3E **41**
Stapehill Cres. *Wim* —4C **16**
Stapehill Rd. *Wim* —4E **17**
Staple Clo. La. *Poole* —1A **56**
 (in three parts)
Staplecross La. *Christ* —5H **45**
Stapleford Av. *Fern* —3D **18**
Star La. *Ring* —4B **8**
Starlight Farm Clo. *Ver* —2E **7**
Station App. *Broad* —1G **37**
Station App. *Broc* —3F **73**
Station App. *New M* —2G **49**
Station Rd. *Christ* —6E **45**
Station Rd. *H'wthy* —6G **55**
Station Rd. *Hint* —2G **47**
Station Rd. *New M* —2G **49**
Station Rd. *Park* —3F **57**
Station Rd. *Sway* —1F **33**
Station Rd. *Ver* —2B **6**
Station Rd. *W Mr* —3B **10**
Station Rd. *Wim* —6F **15**
Station St. *L'ton* —1H **53**
Station Ter. *Wim* —5F **15**
Staunton. *Bourn* —5H **5**
Stedman Rd. *Bourn* —2H **61**
Steepdene. *Poole* —4F **57**
Steeple Clo. *Poole* —2B **38**
Steepleton Rd. *Broad* —3A **38**
Stella Ct. *Christ* —6B **48**
Stem La. *New M* —2E **49**
Stem La. Ind. Est. *New M* —2E **49**
Stem La. Trad. Est. *New M*
 —2E **49**
Stenhurst Rd. *Poole* —1C **56**
Stephen Langton Dri. *Bourn*
 —6H **23**
Stephen's Wlk. Ring —4B **8**
 (off Lyne's La.)
Stepnell Reach. *Poole* —2C **54**
Sterte Av. *Poole* —3H **55**
Sterte Av. W. *Poole* —3H **55**
Sterte Clo. *Poole* —3H **55**
Sterte Ct. *Poole* —3H **55** (1A **4**)
Sterte Esplanade. *Poole*
 —3A **56** (1B **4**)
Sterte Ind. Est. *Poole* —3H **55**
Sterte Rd. *Poole* —5A **56** (1B **4**)
Stevenson Cres. *Poole* —4H **57**
Stevenson Rd. *Bourn* —4E **63**
Stevensons Clo. *Wim* —5E **15**
Stewart Clo. *Bourn* —2C **60**
Stewart M. *Bourn* —2C **60**
Stewart Rd. *Bourn* —1A **60**
Stewarts Way. *Fern* —2C **18**

Stibbs Way. *Brans* —1E **29**
Stillmore Rd. *Bourn* —2H **39**
Stinsford Clo. *Bourn* —1B **42**
Stinsford Rd. *Poole* —4B **38**
Stirling Clo. *New M* —2H **49**
Stirling Ct. *New M* —2H **49**
Stirling Rd. *Bourn* —6G **41**
Stirling Way. *Christ* —1D **64**
Stirrup Clo. *Uptn* —6D **36**
Stirrup Clo. *Wim* —3C **16**
Stoborough Dri. *Broad* —3F **37**
Stockbridge Clo. *Poole* —3F **39**
Stocks Farm Rd. *W Parl* —2H **25**
Stokes Av. *Poole* —3A **56**
Stokewood Rd. *Bourn* —1H **59**
Stonechat Clo. *Fern* —1H **17**
Stonechat Ct. *Christ* —6B **46**
Stonecrop Clo. *Broad* —3F **37**
Stone Gdns. *Bourn* —3G **43**
Stone La. *Wim* —3C **14**
Stone La. Ind. Est. *Wim* —3C **14**
Stoneleigh. *Poole* —1B **70**
Stoneleigh Av. *Hord* —1D **50**
Stony La. *Burt & Christ* —2F **45**
Stony La. S. *Christ* —1G **63**
Stopples La. *Hord* —1D **50**
Story La. *Broad* —1H **37**
Stourbank Rd. *Christ* —1E **63**
Stourcliffe Av. *Bourn* —3A **62**
Stour Clo. *Wim* —5D **16**
Stour Ct. Poole —3C **58**
 (off Poole Rd.)
Stourcroft Dri. *Christ* —3B **44**
Stourfield Rd. *Bourn* —3H **61**
Stourpaine Rd. *Poole* —3B **38**
Stour Pk. *Bourn* —5G **25**
Stour Rd. *Bourn* —1C **60**
Stour Rd. *Christ* —2D **62**
Stourvale Av. *Christ* —5B **44**
Stourvale Pl. *Bourn* —2H **61**
Stourvale Rd. *Bourn* —2H **61**
Stour Vw. Gdns. *Cor M* —2E **21**
Stour Wlk. *Bourn* —1D **42**
Stour Wlk. *Wim* —6F **15**
Stour Way. *Christ* —3B **44**
Stourwood Av. *Bourn* —4A **62**
Stourwood Rd. *Bourn* —3B **62**
Stouts La. *Brans* —2D **28**
Strand St. *Poole* —6H **55** (5A **4**)
Stratfield Pl. *New M* —2E **49**
Stratford Pl. *L'ton* —6F **35**
Strathmore Dri. *Ver* —3E **7**
Strathmore Rd. *Bourn* —1A **42**
Stratton Rd. *Bourn* —1C **42**
Strete Mt. *Christ* —6A **46**
Stretton Ct. *Poole* —3F **57**
Strides La. *Ring* —4B **8**
Strode Gdns. *St I* —2D **12**
Stroud Clo. *Wim* —3A **16**
Strouden Av. *Bourn* —4B **42**
Strouden Rd. *Bourn* —4A **42**
Stroud Gdns. *Christ* —1A **64**
Stroud La. *Christ* —1A **64**
Stroud Pk. Av. *Christ* —1A **64**
Struan Clo. *Ashy H* —1B **12**
Struan Ct. *Ashy H* —1C **12**
Struan Dri. *Ashy H* —1C **12**
Struan Gdns. *Ashy H* —1B **12**
Stuart Clo. *Poole* —6B **36**
Stuart Rd. *Highc* —5B **48**
Stubbings Mdw Cvn. Pk. *Ring*
 —4A **8**
Studland Dri. *Mil S* —2C **66**
Studland Rd. *Bourn* —6E **59**
Studley Clo. *Highc* —5C **48**
Studley Ct. *New M* —5D **48**
Sturminster Rd. *Bourn* —1B **42**
Suffolk Av. *Christ* —3D **44**
Suffolk Clo. *Wim* —3C **16**
Suffolk Rd. *Bourn* —4F **59**
 (in two parts)
Suffolk Rd. S. *Bourn* —3F **59**
Summercroft Way. *W Mr* —4C **10**
Summerfield Clo. *Burt* —3G **45**
Summerfield Clo. *Wim* —5A **16**

Summerfields. *Bourn* —6F **43**
Summer Fields. *Ver* —5D **6**
Summerhill. *Poole* —6F **69**
Summers Av. *Bourn* —5D **24**
Summer's La. *Burt* —4H **45**
Summertrees Ct. *New M* —1B **50**
Sunbury Clo. *Bourn* —5C **24**
Sunbury Ct. *Bourn* —3F **5**
Sunderland Dri. *Christ* —6D **46**
Sundew Clo. *Christ* —4E **47**
Sundew Clo. *New M* —1B **50**
Sundew Rd. *Broad* —3E **37**
Sunningdale. *Christ* —1D **62**
Sunningdale. *Poole* —4C **56**
Sunningdale Cres. *Bourn* —1E **41**
Sunningdale Gdns. *Broad* —6G **21**
Sunnybank Dri. *Wim* —3B **16**
Sunnybank Rd. *Wim* —3B **16**
Sunnybank Way. *Wim* —3B **16**
Sunnyfield Rd. *Bart S* —5G **49**
Sunny Hill Ct. *Poole* —2H **57**
Sunnyhill Rd. *Bourn* —2H **61**
Sunny Hill Rd. *Poole* —2H **57**
Sunnylands Av. *Bourn* —3D **62**
Sunnymoor Rd. *Bourn* —4C **40**
Sunnyside Pk. Cvn. Site. *St I*
 —2E **13**
Sunnyside Rd. *Poole* —6H **39**
Sunridge Clo. *Poole* —1C **58**
Sunset Lodge. *Poole* —5C **58**
Surrey Clo. *Christ* —3D **44**
Surrey Gdns. *Bourn* —3E **59**
Surrey Lodge. *Bourn* —3F **59**
Surrey Rd. *Poole & Bourn* —2C **58**
Surrey Rd. S. *Bourn* —3E **59**
Sussex Clo. *Bourn* —6C **26**
Sutherland Av. *Broad* —6E **21**
Sutton Clo. *Poole* —3F **39**
Sutton Pl. *Broc* —3F **73**
Sutton Rd. *Bourn* —4B **42**
Swallow Clo. *Poole* —5F **37**
Swallow Dri. *Mil S* —3E **67**
Swallow Way. *Wim* —1A **16**
Swan Mead. *Hight* —5E **9**
Swanmore Clo. *Bourn* —6H **43**
Swanmore Rd. *Bourn* —1H **61**
Swansbury Dri. *Bourn* —3H **43**
Sway Gdns. *Bourn* —3D **42**
Sway Rd. *Broc* —6E **73**
Sway Rd. *New M* —5G **31**
Sway Rd. *Penn* —6A **34**
Sweep, The. *Ring* —4B **8**
Swift Clo. *Poole* —5F **37**
Swordfish Dri. *Christ* —6D **46**
Sycamore Clo. *Christ* —5B **44**
Sycamore Clo. *Mil S* —2C **66**
Sycamore Clo. *Poole* —4F **37**
Sycamore Ct. *Ring* —1E **9**
Sycamore Rd. *Hord* —1D **50**
Sydling Clo. *Poole* —3F **39**
Sydney Rd. *Broad* —2G **37**
Sydney Rd. *Christ* —4C **44**
Sylmor Gdns. *Bourn* —3A **42**
Sylvan Clo. *Hord* —3F **51**
Sylvan Clo. *St L* —3H **11**
Sylvan Rd. *Poole* —1F **57**
Symes Rd. *Poole* —3E **55**

Tadden Wlk. *Broad* —3F **37**
Tait Clo. *Poole* —6C **38**
Talbot Av. *Bourn* —5F **41**
Talbot Ct. *Bourn* —4H **41**
Talbot Dri. *Christ* —3H **47**
Talbot Dri. *Poole* —5D **40**
Talbot Hill Rd. *Bourn* —5F **41**
Talbot Meadows. *Poole* —5D **40**
Talbot M. *Bourn* —4D **40**
Talbot Ri. *Bourn* —3E **41**
Talbot Rd. *Bourn* —5F **41**
Talbot Roundabout. *Bourn* —6F **41**
Tamar Clo. *Fern* —4E **19**
Tamworth Rd. *Bourn* —2F **61**
Tanglewood Ct. *New M* —2H **49**
Tanglewood Lodge. *Poole* —5F **37**

Tangmere Clo. *Christ* —1D **64**
Tangmere Pl. *Poole* —6C **38**
Tan Howse Clo. *Bourn* —5H **43**
Tapper Ct. *Wim* —5G **15**
Tarn Dri. *Poole* —4F **37**
Tarrant Clo. *Poole* —3C **38**
Tarrant Rd. *Bourn* —2B **42**
Tasman Clo. *Christ* —5D **44**
Tatnam Cres. *Poole* —3B **56**
Tatnam Rd. *Poole* —3A **56**
Tattenham Rd. *Broc* —4E **73**
Taverner Clo. *Poole* —5B **56**
Taylor Dri. *Bourn* —1D **42**
Taylor's Bldgs. *Poole*
—6A **56** (5B **4**)
Teak Ho., The. *Poole* —1D **70**
Teasel Way. *W Mr* —6C **10**
Tedder Clo. *Bourn* —2D **40**
Tedder Gdns. *Bourn* —2D **40**
Tedder Rd. *Bourn* —2D **40**
Telford Rd. *Fern I* —1G **17**
Templar Clo. *Bourn* —4B **40**
Temple M. *Bourn* —1D **60**
Tennyson Rd. *Bourn* —3H **41**
Tennyson Rd. *Poole* —4E **57**
Tennyson Rd. *Wim* —3E **15**
Tensing Rd. *Christ* —5A **46**
Terbourba Cotts. *Sway* —2F **33**
Terence Av. *Poole* —4A **38**
Terence Rd. *Cor M* —6C **20**
Tern Ct. *Bourn* —1B **62**
Terrace Rd. *Bourn* —4G **59** (4F **5**)
Terrington Av. *Christ* —4G **47**
Thames All. *Poole* —5A **4**
Thames Clo. *Fern* —3E **19**
Thames M. *Poole* —6H **55** (5A **4**)
Thames St. *Poole* —6H **55** (5A **4**)
Thatched Cottage Pk. *Lyn* —2H **71**
Thatchers La. *Brans* —1B **28**
Theobald Rd. Hurn —3G 27
(off Brackley Clo.)
Thetchers Clo. *New M* —6H **31**
Thetford Rd. *Poole* —2B **58**
Thistlebarrow Rd. *Bourn* —1E **61**
Thomas Lockyer Clo. *Ver* —4E **7**
Thoresby Ct. *New M* —2E **49**
Thornbury Rd. *Bourn* —3E **63**
Thorncombe Clo. *Bourn* —1B **42**
Thorncombe Clo. *Poole* —4C **38**
Thorne Clo. *Ver* —3C **6**
Thorne Way. *T Leg* —1F **11**
Thornfield Dri. *Highc* —4H **47**
Thornham Rd. *New M* —2B **50**
Thornley Rd. *Bourn* —1F **41**
Thorn Rd. *Poole* —2B **38**
Thornton Clo. *Cor M* —6C **20**
Three Acre Clo. *New M* —5E **49**
Three Acre Dri. *Bart S* —5F **49**
Three Cross Rd. *W Moor* —1C **10**
Three Lions Clo. *Wim* —4D **14**
Throop Clo. *Bourn* —4G **43**
Throop Rd. *Bourn* —6D **26**
Throopside Av. *Bourn* —1D **42**
Thrush Rd. *Poole* —4G **39**
Thursby Rd. *Highc* —3H **47**
Thwaite Rd. *Poole* —2D **58**
Tidemill Clo. *Christ* —5E **45**
Tiffany Clo. *Hord* —1D **50**
Tilburg Rd. *Christ* —6H **45**
Tilebarn La. *Broc* —6E **73**
Timothy Clo. *Bourn* —6F **25**
Tincleton Gdns. *Bourn* —1B **42**
Tins, The. *L'ton* —1G **53**
Tin Yd. La. *Bock* —1H **45**
Tiptoe Rd. *New M* —2G **31**
Tithe Barn. *L'ton* —6G **35**
Todber Clo. *Bourn* —2H **39**
Tollard Clo. *Poole* —5A **40**
Tollard Ct. *Bourn* —6F **5**
Tollerford Rd. *Poole* —2B **38**
Tolpuddle Gdns. *Bourn* —1B **42**
Tolstoi Rd. *Poole* —1E **57**
Tonge Rd. *Bourn* —5D **24**
Top La. *Ring* —4C **8**
Torbay Rd. *Poole* —4G **57**

Totland Ct. *Mil S* —3C **66**
Totmel Rd. *Poole* —3E **39**
Tourney Rd. *Bourn* —5H **23**
Towans, The. *Poole* —5G **69**
Tower Ct. *Bourn* —5G **59** (6E **5**)
Tower La. *Wim* —3F **15**
Tower Pk. *Poole* —4F **39**
Tower Rd. *Bourn* —2E **61**
Tower Rd. *Poole* —5D **58**
Tower Rd. W. *Poole* —6C **58**
Towers Farm. *Cor M* —4D **20**
Towers Way. *Cor M* —4D **20**
Towngate Bri. *Poole*
—5A **56** (3B **4**)
Towngate Ho. *Poole* —2D **4**
Towngate Shop. Cen. *Poole*
—3C **4**
Townsend Clo. *Bourn* —5D **24**
Townsville Rd. *Bourn* —3B **42**
Tozer Clo. *Bourn* —3B **40**
Trafalgar Ct. *Christ* —2B **64**
Trafalgar Pl. *L'ton* —1H **53**
Trafalgar Rd. *Bourn* —6H **41**
Tranmere Clo. *L'ton* —3H **53**
Treebys Clo. *Burt* —4H **45**
Tree Hamlets. *Poole* —2C **54**
Treeside. *Christ* —3E **47**
Trefoil Way. *Christ* —5E **47**
Tregonwell Rd. *Bourn*
—4G **59** (4F **5**)
Trentham Av. *Bourn* —5H **43**
Trentham Clo. *Bourn* —5H **43**
Trent Way. *Fern* —3E **19**
Tresillian Clo. *Walk* —3B **48**
Tresillian Way. *Walk* —3B **48**
Trevone. *New M* —2H **49**
Triangle, The. *Bourn*
—4G **59** (4E **5**)
Triangle, The. *New M* —5C **48**
Triangle, The. *Poole* —6B **36**
Tricketts La. *Fern* —3D **18**
Trigon Rd. *Poole* —6B **38**
Tringham Ho. *Bourn* —5H **43**
Trinidad Cres. *Poole* —5G **39**
Trinidad Ho. *Poole* —5G **39**
Trinity Ind. Est. *Wim* —6G **15**
Trinity M. Bourn —4A 60
(off Lorne Pk.)
Trinity Rd. *Bourn* —3A **60**
Troak Clo. *Christ* —5A **46**
Troon Rd. *Broad* —6G **21**
Trotters La. *Wim* —3B **16**
Truman Rd. *Bourn* —5D **24**
Trumpeters Ct. *Wim* —4D **14**
Truscott Av. *Bourn* —6A **42**
Tuckers La. *Poole* —5F **55**
Tuck's Clo. *Brans* —2C **28**
Tuckton Clo. *Bourn* —3B **62**
Tuckton Rd. *Bourn* —3B **62**
Tudor Ct. *Poole* —1C **56**
Tudor Rd. *Broad* —1H **37**
Turbary Clo. *Poole* —5H **39**
Turbary Ct. *Fern* —3D **18**
Turbary Ct. *Poole* —5C **36**
Turbary Pk. Av. *Bourn* —2B **40**
Turbary Rd. *Fern* —2D **18**
Turbary Rd. *Poole* —6H **39**
Turbury Retail Pk. *Bourn* —2A **40**
Turks La. *Poole* —6E **57**
Turlin Rd. *Poole* —3C **54**
Turnberry Clo. *Christ* —1D **62**
Turners Farm Cres. *Hord* —3E **51**
Turnworth Clo. *Broad* —2A **38**
Tweedale Rd. *Bourn* —2C **42**
Tweed La. *Bold* —2F **35**
Twemlow Av. *Poole* —5D **56**
Twin Oaks Clo. *Broad* —2G **37**
Twyford Clo. *Bourn* —3D **42**
Twyford Way. *Poole* —3E **39**
Twynham Av. *Christ* —6E **45**
Twynham Rd. *Bourn* —4C **62**
Tylers Clo. *L'ton* —6F **35**
Tyndale Cres. *Bourn* —1C **42**
Tyneham Av. *Poole* —5G **39**
Tyrrell Gdns. *Bourn* —3G **43**

Tyrrells Ct. *Brans* —2D **28**
Tytherley Grn. *Bourn* —3D **42**

Uddens Dri. *Wim* —1D **16**
Uddens Trad. Est. *Wim* —3E **17**
Ugsdell Clo. *New M* —2G **49**
Ullswater Rd. *Wim* —1A **22**
Undercliff Dri. *Bourn*
—5A **60** (6H **5**)
Undercliff Rd. *Bourn* —4E **61**
Undershore. *L'ton* —4H **35**
Undershore Rd. *L'ton* —1H **53**
Underwood Clo. *Poole* —4H **37**
University Roundabout. *Bourn*
—5E **41**
Uplands Av. *Bart S* —5G **49**
Uplands Clo. *W Mr* —1E **19**
Uplands Rd. *Bourn* —4B **42**
Uplands Rd. *W Mr* —5D **10**
Uplyme Clo. *Poole* —3E **39**
Up. Common Rd. *Penn* —1B **52**
Up. Golf Links Rd. *Broad* —5H **21**
Up. Gordon Rd. *Highc* —4A **48**
Up. Hinton Rd. *Bourn*
—4H **59** (4H **5**)
Up. Norwich Rd. *Bourn*
—4F **59** (4E **5**)
Upper Rd. *Poole* —6F **39**
Up. Terrace Rd. *Bourn*
—4G **59** (4F **5**)
Uppleby Rd. *Poole* —2G **57**
(in two parts)
Upton Clo. *Poole* —6B **36**
Upton Ct. *Uptn* —6C **36**
Upton Cross Mobile Homes. *Poole*
—6C **36**
Upton Heath Est. *Poole* —6D **36**
Upton Rd. *Poole* —6E **37**
Upton Way. *Broad* —2E **37**
Upwey Av. *Poole* —4E **55**
Utrecht Ct. *Christ* —6H **45**

Vaggs La. *Hord* —4B **32**
Vale Clo. *Poole* —3A **58**
Vale Lodge. *Bourn* —2D **60**
Valencia Clo. *Christ* —1B **44**
Vale Rd. *Bourn* —3C **60**
Vale Rd. *Poole* —3A **58**
Valette Rd. *Bourn* —1A **42**
Valeview. *Sway* —4D **32**
Valiant Way. *Christ* —6D **46**
Valley Clo. *Christ* —2C **44**
Valley Rd. *Bourn* —2F **43**
Valley Vw. *Poole* —6D **40**
Vallis Clo. *Poole* —6B **56** (5D **4**)
Vanguard Rd. *Bourn* —4E **43**
Vanguard Rd. *Poole*
—5A **56** (3C **4**)
Vecta Clo. *Christ* —1E **65**
Vectis Rd. *Bart S* —6D **48**
Velvet Lawn Rd. *New M* —1F **49**
Venator Pl. *Wim* —3E **15**
Venning Av. *Bourn* —6A **24**
Ventry Clo. *Poole* —3B **58**
Ventura Cen., The. *Poole* —1D **54**
Ventura Pl. *Poole* —1D **54**
Verity Cres. *Poole* —4D **38**
Vernalls Clo. *Bourn* —6F **25**
Vernalls Gdns. *Bourn* —5F **25**
Verne Rd. *Ver* —4E **7**
Verney Clo. *Bourn* —2D **40**
Verney Rd. *Bourn* —2C **40**
Verno La. *Christ* —4E **47**
Verona Av. *Bourn* —2B **62**
Verulam Pl. *Bourn* —4H **59** (3H **5**)
Verulam Rd. *Poole* —3D **56**
Verwood Cres. *Bourn* —3E **63**
Verwood Ind. Est. *Ver* —3E **7**
Verwood Mnr. Ct. *Ver* —3D **6**
Verwood Rd. *T Leg* —2A **10** (6E **7**)
Vetch Clo. *Christ* —5D **46**
Vicarage Gdns. *Hord* —2E **51**
(in two parts)

Vicarage La. *Hord* —2E **51**
Vicarage Rd. *Bourn* —3G **41**
Vicarage Rd. *Poole* —2A **56**
Vicarage Rd. *Ver* —3D **6**
Vicarage Way. *Burt* —3H **45**
Vickers Clo. *Bourn* —3H **43**
Vickery Way. *Christ* —5H **45**
Victoria Av. *Bourn* —4G **41**
Victoria Clo. *Cor M* —1D **36**
Victoria Cres. *Poole* —1H **57**
Victoria Gdns. *Fern* —3B **18**
Victoria Gdns. *Ring* —5C **8**
Victoria Ho. *Fern* —4B **18**
Victoria Pk. Rd. *Bourn* —4G **41**
Victoria Pl. *Bourn* —2C **60**
Victoria Pl. *L'ton* —3G **53**
Victoria Pl. *Wim* —4D **14**
Victoria Rd. *Bourn* —2C **60**
Victoria Rd. *Christ* —2A **64**
Victoria Rd. *Fern* —3B **18**
Victoria Rd. *Mil S* —3B **66**
Victoria Rd. *Poole* —2G **57**
Victoria Rd. *Wim* —4D **14**
Victory Clo. *T Leg* —1F **11**
View Point Ct. *Poole* —1E **57**
Viewside Clo. *Cor M* —6C **20**
Viking Clo. *Bourn* —3E **63**
Viking Way. *Bourn* —3E **63**
Viking Way. *Christ* —2C **64**
Village Hall La. *T Leg* —1A **10**
Villette Clo. *Christ* —4E **45**
Vince Clo. *Bourn* —6D **24**
Vincent Clo. *New M* —3G **49**
Vincent Rd. *New M* —2F **49**
Vine Clo. *Bourn* —6G **43**
Vine Farm Clo. *Poole* —5E **41**
Vine Farm Rd. *Poole* —5D **40**
Vinegar Hill. *Mil S* —2D **66**
Vine Hill. *Wim* —4A **14**
Vineries Clo. *Wim* —3H **15**
Vineries, The. *Wim* —4H **15**
Vinery, The. *New M* —2H **49**
Vinery Wlk. *New M* —2H **49**
Viney Rd. *L'ton* —4G **53**
Vinneys Clo. *Burt* —3G **45**
Violet Farm Clo. *Cor M* —3D **20**
Violet La. *New M* —1G **49**
Virginia Clo. *Poole* —6G **39**
Viscount Clo. *Bourn* —5G **23**
Viscount Ct. *Bourn* —6H **23**
Viscount Dri. *Christ* —6D **46**
Viscount Wlk. *Bourn* —6G **23**
Vitre Gdns. *L'ton* —3G **53**
Vixen Wlk. *New M* —5H **31**
Voyager Ho. *Poole* —2D **4**
Vulcan Way. *Christ* —6D **46**

Wagtail Dri. *New M* —3F **49**
Wainsford Clo. *Penn* —2D **52**
(in two parts)
Wainsford Rd. *Evtn & Penn*
—3A **52**
Wakefield Av. *Bourn* —6G **25**
Wakely Gdns. *Bourn* —6C **24**
Wakely Rd. *Bourn* —6D **24**
Walcheren Pl. *Poole* —4C **54**
Walcott Av. *Christ* —4D **44**
Walditch Gdns. *Poole* —3C **38**
Waldren Clo. *Poole* —5B **56**
Walford Clo. *Wim* —3E **15**
Walford Gdns. *Wim* —3D **14**
Walhampton Hill. *L'ton* —6H **35**
Walkford La. *New M* —3D **48**
Walkford Rd. *Walk* —4B **48**
Walkford Way. *Walk* —4B **48**
Walkwood Av. *Bourn* —5H **43**
Wallace Rd. *Broad* —2G **37**
Walliscott Rd. *Bourn* —4C **40**
Wallisdown Heights. *Bourn*
—4B **40**
Wallisdown Rd. *Poole & Bourn*
—3H **39**
Wallisdown Roundabout. *Poole*
—4C **40**

Wallis Rd. *Bourn* —4D **40**
Walnut Clo. *New M* —2F **49**
Walpole Rd. *Bourn* —2D **60**
Walsford Rd. *Bourn* —2E **59**
Walsingham Dene. *Bourn* —5F **43**
Waltham Rd. *Bourn* —6H **43**
Walton Rd. *Bourn* —3E **41**
Walton Rd. *Poole* —1E **57**
Wanstead Clo. *Ring* —2D **8**
Warbler Clo. *Poole* —5B **36**
Warborne La. *P'mre* —2H **35**
Warburton Rd. *Poole* —5C **38**
Wareham Ct. *Bourn* —1H **61**
Wareham Ct. *Poole* —5E **55**
Wareham Rd. *Cor M* —2A **36**
Warland Way. *Cor M* —4E **21**
Warmwell Clo. *Bourn* —2B **42**
Warmwell Clo. *Poole* —3D **38**
Warnford Rd. *Bourn* —6H **43**
Warren Av. *Christ* —2B **64**
Warren Clo. *Ring* —2F **13**
Warren Dri. *Ring* —2F **13**
Warren Edge Clo. *Bourn* —4D **62**
Warren Edge Rd. *Bourn* —4D **62**
Warren La. *Ring* —2F **13**
Warren Pk. *Mil S* —1A **66**
Warren Rd. *Bourn* —5D **58**
Warren Rd. *Poole* —3H **57**
Warren Wlk. *Fern* —2H **17**
Warwick Av. *New M* —2H **49**
Warwick Ct. *Bourn* —6B **42**
Warwick Pl. *Bourn* —2G **61**
Warwick Rd. *Bourn* —2G **61**
Warwick Rd. *Poole* —4G **57**
Warwicks La. *Ver* —1A **6**
Washington Av. *Bourn* —1D **60**
Watcombe Rd. *Bourn* —3B **62**
Waterditch Rd. *Brans* —6D **28**
Waterford Clo. *L'ton* —2H **53**
Waterford Clo. *Poole* —5E **57**
Waterford Gdns. *Highc* —6A **48**
Waterford La. *L'ton* —2H **53**
Waterford Pl. *Highc* —6A **48**
Waterford Rd. *Highc* —5B **48**
Waterford Rd. *New M* —2A **50**
Water La. *Bourn* —6B **44**
Waterloo Rd. *Bourn* —6H **41**
Waterloo Rd. *Cor M* —5B **20**
Waterloo Rd. *L'ton* —1H **53**
Waterloo Rd. *Poole* —6H **37**
Waterloo Way. *Ring* —5C **8**
Watermead. *Christ* —2E **63**
Watermill Rd. *Christ* —5E **45**
Waters Edge. *Poole* —3H **69**
Waters Grn. *Broc* —2F **73**
Waters Grn. Ct. *Broc* —2F **73**
Watership Dri. *Ring* —5F **9**
Waterside. *Christ* —3B **64**
Waterside Clo. *Ring* —2D **8**
Waterston Clo. *Poole* —4B **38**
Water Tower Rd. *Broad* —1A **38**
Watery La. *Christ* —4C **46**
Watery La. *Poole* —6A **36**
Watkin Rd. *Bourn* —3F **61**
Watton Clo. *Bourn* —3G **43**
Wavell Av. *Poole* —4G **37**
Wavell Rd. *Bourn* —1D **40**
Wavendon Av. *Bart S* —5E **49**
Waverley Cres. *Poole* —2B **56**
Waverley Ho. *New M* —3H **49**
Waverley Rd. *New M* —3H **49**
Wayground Rd. *Cor M* —2E **21**
Wayman Rd. *Cor M* —5E **21**
Wayne Rd. *Poole* —1F **57**
Wayside Clo. *Mil S* —2D **66**
Wayside Rd. *Bourn* —3C **62**
Wayside Rd. *St L* —6A **12**
Waytown Clo. *Poole* —4B **38**
Weavers Clo. *W Mr* —6C **10**
Webbs Clo. *Ashy H* —1H **11**
Webbs Way. *Ashy H* —1A **12**
Webbs Way. *Bourn* —4B **40**
Webster Rd. *Bourn* —2A **42**
Wedgwood Dri. *Poole* —5E **57**
Wedgwood Gdns. *Brans* —2E **29**

Weldon Av. *Bourn* —6A **24**
Welland Rd. *Wim* —5F **15**
Wellands Rd. *Lyn* —3F **71**
Well Clo. *New M* —3F **49**
Wellesley Av. *Christ* —6D **46**
Wellington Av. *Christ* —6E **47**
Wellington Ct. *Bourn* —4F **59**
Wellington Ct. *New M* —2G **49**
Wellington Rd. *Bourn* —1A **60**
Wellington Rd. *Poole* —4G **57**
Well La. *Poole* —3A **56**
Wendover Clo. *Bart S* —4F **49**
Wendy Cres. *Fern* —6D **18**
Wentwood Gdns. *New M* —3B **50**
Wentworth Av. *Bourn* —3G **61**
Wentworth Clo. *Bourn* —4G **61**
Wentworth Dri. *Broad* —6G **21**
Wentworth Dri. *Christ* —1D **62**
Wescott Way. *Bourn* —1A **40**
Wesley Clo. *Bourn* —2C **60**
Wesley Rd. *Poole* —2G **57**
Wesley Rd. *Wim* —4F **15**
Wessex Av. *New M* —3G **49**
Wessex Clo. *Christ* —6E **47**
Wessex Est. *Ring* —3E **9**
Wessex Rd. *Poole* —4E **57**
Wessex Rd. *Ring* —3D **8**
Wessex Trade Cen. *Poole* —5F **39**
Wessex Way. *Bourn* —3D **58**
West Av. *T Leg* —2A **10**
Westbeams Rd. *Sway* —1F **33**
W. Borough. *Wim* —3D **14**
Westbourne Arc. *Bourn* —4D **58**
Westbourne Clo. *Bourn* —4E **59**
Westbourne Pk. Rd. *Bourn*
—5D **58**
Westbury Clo. *Bart S* —5G **49**
Westbury Clo. *Brans* —4C **28**
Westbury Clo. *Christ* —4F **47**
Westbury Ct. *Poole* —3F **57**
Westbury Rd. *Ring* —4D **8**
W. Butts St. *Poole* —5H **55** (3A **4**)
Westby Rd. *Bourn* —3E **61**
W. Cliff Cotts. *Bourn* —5E **5**
Westcliffe Bldgs. *Bart S* —6E **49**
W. Cliff Gdns. *Bourn*
—5G **59** (6E **5**)
W. Cliff M. *Bourn* —5G **59** (5F **5**)
W. Cliff Promenade. *Bourn* —5F **59**
(in two parts)
W. Cliff Rd. *Bourn* —4D **58**
W. Cliff Zig-Zag. *Bourn* —6E **5**
West Clo. *Bourn* —3E **63**
West Clo. *Penn* —3D **52**
West Clo. *Ver* —2B **6**
Westcroft Pde. *New M* —3G **49**
Westcroft Pk. *Broad* —1A **38**
Westdown Rd. *Bourn* —6C **24**
Westerham. *Poole* —4C **58**
Westerham Rd. *Bourn* —4D **58**
Western Av. *Bart S* —5D **48**
Western Av. *Bourn* —6F **25**
Western Av. *Poole* —4A **58**
Western Clo. *Bourn* —6F **25**
Westerngate. *Poole* —4D **58**
Western Rd. *L'ton* —1F **53**
Western Rd. *Poole* —1B **70**
Westfield. *Wim* —4D **14**
Westfield Clo. *Wim* —4D **14**
Westfield Gdns. *Christ* —4D **46**
Westfield Rd. *Bourn* —3C **62**
Westfield Rd. *L'ton* —3H **53**
Westgate Pk. *Bourn* —4D **58**
Westham Clo. *Poole* —2C **38**
West Hayes. *L'ton* —2H **53**
Westheath Rd. *Broad* —1H **37**
W. Hill Pl. *Bourn* —4G **59** (4E **5**)
W. Hill Rd. *Bourn* —4F **59**
W. Howe Clo. *Bourn* —1C **40**
W. Howe Ind. Est. *Bourn* —2A **40**
Westlands. *Brans* —3C **28**
West La. *Evtn* —4A **52**
W. Mansion. *Bourn* —4E **59**
Westminster Ct. *New M* —6F **49**
Westminster Rd. *Mil S* —3A **66**

Westminster Rd. *Poole* —6D **58**
Westminster Rd. E. *Poole*
—6D **58**
W. Moors Rd. *Fern* —3B **10**
W. Moors Rd. *T Leg* —2A **10**
W. Moors Rd. *W Mr & Fern*
—1C **18**
Westmoreland Ct. *Hord* —2D **50**
Weston Dri. *Bourn* —4B **60**
Weston Rd. *Wim* —2H **15**
Westons La. *Poole* —5A **56** (4B **4**)
W. Overcliff Dri. *Bourn* —5E **59**
Westover La. *Ring* —1F **13**
Westover Rd. *Bourn*
—4H **59** (4H **5**)
Westover Rd. *Mil S* —3D **66**
W. Quay Rd. Poole —6H **55** (5A **4**)
West Rd. *Bourn* —2G **61**
West Rd. *Brans* —2C **28**
West Rd. *Mil S* —2A **66**
West Row. *Wim* —5D **14**
W. Station Ter. Bourn —4F **59**
(off Queens Rd.)
West St. *Poole* —6H **55**
West St. *Ring* —4A **8**
West St. *Wim* —4D **14**
W. Undercliff Promenade. *Bourn*
—6E **59** (6E **5**)
Westview Rd. *Christ* —1A **64**
W. View Rd. *Poole* —3A **56** (1B **4**)
West Way. *Bourn* —3B **42**
West Way. *Broad* —3E **37**
West Way. *Penn* —3E **53**
W. Way Clo. *Bourn* —4B **42**
Westwood Av. *Fern* —3A **18**
Westwood Rd. *Lyn* —2F **71**
Westwoods Pk. *New M* —6D **30**
Wetherby Clo. *Broad* —3G **37**
Weyman's Av. *Bourn* —5E **25**
Weyman's Dri. *Bourn* —5E **25**
Weymouth Rd. *Poole* —2G **57**
Wharf Clo. *Poole* —1A **58**
Wharfdale Rd. *Bourn* —3E **59**
Wharfdale Rd. *Poole* —1H **57**
Wharncliffe Gdns. *Highc* —6A **48**
Wharncliffe Rd. *Bourn* —3D **60**
Wharncliffe Rd. *Highc* —6H **47**
Whatleigh Clo. *Poole*
—6A **56** (5C **4**)
Wheaton Grange. *Bourn* —3F **59**
Wheaton Rd. *Bourn* —2G **61**
Wheatplot Pk. Homes. *Bourn*
—6H **25**
Wheeler's La. *Bourn* —5G **23**
(in two parts)
Whincroft Clo. *Fern* —2C **18**
Whincroft Dri. *Fern* —2C **18**
Whitaker Cres. *Penn* —2E **53**
Whitby Av. *Broad* —3F **37**
Whitby Clo. *Christ* —1B **44**
Whitby Ct. *Mil S* —3B **66**
Whitby Cres. *Broad* —3F **37**
Whitby Rd. *Mil S* —3B **66**
Whitchurch Av. *Broad* —2A **38**
White Barn Cres. *Hord* —2E **51**
Whitebeam Way. *Ver* —4F **7**
Whitecliff Cres. *Poole* —5E **57**
Whitecliff Rd. *Poole* —5D **56**
White Clo. *Poole* —6E **39**
Whitecross Clo. *Poole* —2C **38**
White Farm Clo. *Bourn* —5F **41**
Whitefield Lodge. *New M* —2G **49**
Whitefield Rd. *New M* —2G **49**
Whitefield Rd. *Poole* —5E **57**
Whitehall. *Christ* —2F **63**
Whitehart Fields. *Ring* —3E **9**
Whitehayes Clo. *Burt* —3H **45**
Whitehayes Rd. *Burt* —3G **45**
White Horse Dri. *Poole* —2A **56**
White Horses. *Bart S* —6E **49**
Whitehouse Rd. *Wim* —1B **22**
White Knights. *Bart S* —6F **49**
Whitelegg Way. *Bourn* —6G **25**
White Lion Ct. *Ring* —4B **8**
Whitemoor Rd. *Broc* —2C **72**

Whiteways. *Wim* —3G **15**
Whitfield Pk. *Ring* —2D **12**
Whitley Way. *New M* —6H **31**
Whitsbury Clo. *Bourn* —3D **42**
Whittingham Ct. *Bourn* —2H **61**
Whittle Rd. *Fern I* —2F **17**
Whittles Way. *Poole*
—5H **55** (3A **4**)
Wick Clo. *New M* —3E **49**
Wick Dri. *New M* —3E **49**
Wicket Rd. *Bourn* —6E **25**
Wickfield Av. *Christ* —1F **63**
Wickfield Clo. *Christ* —1F **63**
Wickham Ct. *Fern* —3C **18**
Wickham Dri. *Cor M* —1D **36**
Wickham Rd. *Bourn* —2G **61**
Wick La. *Bourn* —2D **62**
Wick La. *Christ* —2F **63**
Wicklea Rd. *Bourn* —3F **63**
Wickmeads Rd. *Bourn* —2E **63**
Wick 1 Ind. Est. *New M* —3E **49**
Wick 2 Ind. Est. *New M* —3E **49**
Widbury Rd. *Penn* —3E **53**
Widden Clo. *Sway* —1F **33**
Widdicombe Av. *Poole* —5A **58**
Wide La. Clo. *Broc* —3E **73**
Widget Clo. *Bourn* —3D **40**
Widworthy Dri. *Broad* —6F **21**
Wight Wlk. *W Parl* —1G **25**
Wilderton Rd. *Poole* —4B **58**
Wilderton Rd. W. *Poole* —3C **58**
Wildfell Clo. *Christ* —4E **45**
Wildown Gdns. *Bourn* —4D **62**
Wildown Rd. *Bourn* —4E **63**
Wilfred Rd. *Bourn* —3F **61**
Wilkinson Dri. *Bourn* —3G **43**
Wilkins Way. *Poole* —5H **55** (4A **4**)
Willett Rd. *Ashtn* —1F **21**
William Clo. *Walk* —3A **48**
William Ct. *Christ* —6B **48**
William Rd. *Bourn* —6F **43**
William Rd. *L'ton* —6G **35**
Williams Ind. Pk. *New M* —3E **49**
Willis Way. *Poole* —1H **55**
Willow Clo. *Bourn* —2D **58**
Willow Clo. *Poole* —2D **54**
Willow Clo. *St L* —3H **11**
Willowdene Clo. *New M* —2A **50**
Willow Dri. *Christ* —2E **63**
Willow Dri. *Ring* —6C **8**
Willow Dri. *Wim* —3C **16**
Willow Mead. *Bourn* —1D **42**
Willow Pk. *Poole* —4D **56**
Willows, The. *New M* —5H **49**
Willow Tree Ho. *Penn* —3E **53**
Willow Tree Ri. *Bourn* —2D **40**
Willow Wlk. *Bart S* —6H **49**
Willow Way. *Christ* —2E **63**
Willow Way. *Fern* —1B **18**
Wills Clo. *Cor M* —1D **36**
Wills Rd. *Poole* —3B **58**
Willwood Clo. *Poole* —2B **38**
Wilmur Cres. *Poole* —1C **56**
Wilson Rd. *Bourn* —1D **60**
Wilson Rd. *Poole* —3G **57**
Wilton Clo. *Christ* —4B **44**
Wilton Gdns. *New M* —2F **49**
Wilton Rd. *Bourn* —2F **61**
Wiltshire Gdns. *Brans* —3B **28**
Wiltshire Rd. *Brans* —3B **28**
Wilverley Av. *Bourn* —3F **43**
Wilverley Clo. *Penn* —3D **52**
Wilverley Rd. *Broc* —3E **73**
Wilverley Rd. *Christ* —6C **46**
Wilverley Rd. *New M* —1F **31**
Wimborne Ho. *Bourn* —1H **59**
Wimborne Minster By-Pass. *Wim*
—6B **14**
Wimborne Rd. *Bourn* —1H **41**
(BH10 & BH9)
Wimborne Rd. *Bourn* —5B **24**
(BH11 & BH10)
Wimborne Rd. *Bourn*
(BH2)　　　　—3H **59** (2H **5**)
Wimborne Rd. *Cor M* —3D **20**